AFTER THE TALL TIMBER

RENATA ADLER
AFTER THE TALL TIMBER
COLLECTED NONFICTION

PREFACE BY MICHAEL WOLFF

NEW YORK REVIEW BOOKS

New York

THIS IS A NEW YORK REVIEW BOOK
PUBLISHED BY THE NEW YORK REVIEW OF BOOKS
435 Hudson Street, New York, NY 10014
www.nyrb.com

Adler, Renata.
 [Works. Selections]
 After the Tall Timber: Collected nonfiction / by Renata Adler ; preface by Michael Wolff.
    pages cm
 ISBN 978-1-59017-879-9 (hardback)
 I. Title.
 PS3551.D63A6 2015
 818'.54—dc23

                        2014038528

ISBN 978-1-59017-879-9
Available as an electronic book; ISBN 978-1-59017-880-5

Printed in the United States of America on acid-free paper.
1 0 9 8 7 6 5 4 3 2 1

FOR
STEPHEN

CONTENTS

PREFACE

RENATA ADLER has become something of a cult figure for a new generation of literary-minded young women since the 2013 re-release of her novels, *Speedboat* (1976) and *Pitch Dark* (1983). Those books represent an early point, and in many ways a high point, in the portrayal of a modern sort of angst—vulnerable women adrift in both the psychological and actual world. Adler herself can often seem like an iconic figure of fragility and lostness with her long bouts of literary absence and silence.

Here, however, in this collection of her most significant journalism, she is a diametrically opposite figure: a fierce and aggressive writer, known and feared and sometimes shunned for turning her stone-cold and contrarian judgments on her own professional class. I do not think it is an exaggeration to say that her writing is some of the most brutal ever directed at journalism itself.

Shortly before the publication of *Gone*, her broadside against *The New Yorker* and what the magazine became after it was sold in 1985 by its original owners, I was at a cocktail party on Manhattan's West Side at the home of a *New York Times* cultural supremo attended by a set of publishing myrmidons of frightening standing and lockstep opinions. Following the whispered name "Renata," I literally intruded on a clucking circle of these reproachful men planning their counterattacks against her: something must be done.

The writer Harold Brodkey, her friend and colleague at *The New Yorker*, once said to me, in the 1970s when she was having her famous and glamorous moment, that in his view, Renata could not decide whether to live an "interior writer's life" or "an exterior activist's life." At the time, I thought his comment was about her work in Washington in 1974 with the House Judiciary Committee's impeachment inquiry staff, where she had become a sort of history's ghostwriter—recruited to make inarticulate politicians sound like men worthy of impeaching a president—and then her decision, at the peak of her fame, to enroll at Yale Law School. Should she seek real worldly power or continue as a mere writer on the sidelines? (It is quite extraordinary to consider that real power might have been within her grasp.)

In fact, I think I misunderstood what Brodkey was saying. What she was wrestling with was not career suitability, but her divided nature: on the one hand, muddled fear and vulnerability, and on the other, clearheaded outrage and scorn.

These feelings are not, of course, mutually exclusive.

A person's vulnerability and fears do not mean that he or she cannot also summon a particular courage. Perhaps such fear compels a person to redouble his or her efforts and boldness. Adler, who, among her friends, is well known for not being able to navigate a few blocks or keep her possessions about her, nevertheless, during a particular period of twentieth-century turmoil showed up for the civil rights movement in Selma, Alabama, the genocidal conflict between Nigeria and Biafra, and the American descent into Vietnam.

It is this contradictory nature, I believe, that has made her such a conundrum: she seems so appealing and uncertain (ever in need of protection) and then changes her clothes and goes to war. Not to mention the fact that she has often gone to war with her own colleagues, making her not just a confusing figure but an anathema as well.

At some point, perhaps quite unaware, she crossed over from a career as a cosseted insider to a what-ever-are-we-going-to-do-with-her outsider.

She was born in Milan in 1938 to parents fleeing Nazi Germany. She grew up in Connecticut and went to Bryn Mawr, then to graduate school at Harvard and the Sorbonne. In 1963 she joined *The New Yorker* as a staff writer.

For the next twenty years or so, she was a leading light in a particular brilliant period of American writing. She was an "it" girl, complete with the iconic look and memorable pictures by Richard Avedon, provocative and fashionable. (I recall my parents, culture vultures in suburban New Jersey, discussing her with great awe.) *The New Yorker* then was the equivalent of something similar to HBO now—you wouldn't have missed it, or her.

In 1968, she became the *New York Times* film critic (the first woman in the job when being the first women was a miraculous transformation) at a moment when writing about film was, arguably, more influential than making films—and when *The New York Times* was the first and last critical word. In the early 1970s, she went to Washington where she became the Watergate committee's writer—at the epicenter of the most momentous public event of the era. Then came *Speedboat*, followed by Yale Law School, then *Pitch Dark*; then came her book *Reckless Disregard,* about the big twin libel lawsuits of the early 1980s, Westmoreland suing CBS, Sharon suing *Time;* and then, practically speaking, nothing.

Writer's careers, even ones that have reached a great height, are fragile things, and they can go wrong for many reasons and as the result of many choices: money, drugs, Hollywood, among others.

But Adler's career goes wrong, or at least astray, or far from the light, primarily for not being able to keep her silence. Adler is a good demonstration of the boundaries of art, that even serious writing is harshly proscribed, that the literary life has hard rules, that politics must be carefully played, that renegades—and, no doubt, especially women renegades—who go past an undrawn line are cast out.

She surely managed to cross many of the mightiest and most thin-skinned cultural institutions and arbiters. She offended *The New York Times*: first, writing excessively scathing film reviews for the paper; and then, a worse sin, quitting the *Times* after a year and returning to *The New Yorker.* Even now, with the *Times* having lost considerable power and clout, it is difficult to pursue a serious career in letters with its institutional disapproval shadowing you. And it has, literally for decades, pursued an odd, sour, spurned lover's vendetta against Adler (compounded and renewed by Adler's reflexive counterattacks on the paper), which she dissects in the introduction to *Canaries in the Mineshaft: Essays on Politics and Media* (2001), included here.

There is, of course, her famous—or infamous—review of Pauline Kael's book *When the Lights Go Down*. It's hard to remember what a cultural despot Kael, then the *New Yorker*'s film critic, was when Adler wrote her review in 1980. Kael was bully, drama queen, suck-up, disciplinarian, hysteric, and—taking jobs and inducements from the people she promoted—a bit corrupt, too. Still, opprobrium yet attaches to Adler for her sweeping emperor's-new-clothes leveling of Kael; and it certainly earned her no points with *The New Yorker*, their mutual employer. But the rightness of Adler's view of Kael as nasty, self-promoting gasbag only become more obvious as Kael's reputation disappeared after she lost her *New Yorker* post and power. She was unreadable, said Adler; and indeed, Kael is unread now.

Adler's cheerfully absurd recollections of the editing process at *The New York Times*, which serves as an introduction to the collection of movie reviews she wrote during her year, at the age of thirty, as the *Times*'s chief film critic, is perhaps the best exegesis of the leveling and zero-sum game that editors so often play, and another thwack on the *Times*'s nose.

Then, there is her Watergate view. She is one of the few—perhaps, the only—more-or-less liberal party to the proceedings to argue, against the orthodoxy of pretty much the entirety of liberal media, that, all in all, it was a fairly weak case against Richard Nixon (and that the real reasons for his resignation were hidden from view).

Oh yes, and you should hear her on Bob Woodward and Deep Throat. I don't know anyone else who has pointed out that Mark Felt—identified upon his death, years later, by Woodward as Deep Throat—was widely briefing, dishing to, and confiding in almost everybody involved in the investigation. He became, in other words, the happenstance face for what every professional journalist of a certain age knows to be—though, given Woodward's reach, few will say so—a convenient composite.

It is extremely difficult to explain how Bob Woodward's career could have progressed after Adler, on more than one occasion, took him apart. But then again that is the point about Woodward and Adler's critique of him, he—quite unlike Adler herself—has always existed in a compact with the power centers that he covers.

If there is anyone who has violated the clubbiness of the literary and journalistic world more than Adler I cannot think of whom.

Among the reasons, I believe, that she seems so fierce, impolite, unexpected, even outré, is that she has no politics—or no official politics. In her introduction, included here, to *Toward a Radical Middle: Fourteen Pieces of Reporting and Criticism* (1970), she offers perhaps one of the last defenses of centrism as a definition of reasonability and intellectual honesty. The irony of course is that it is centrism itself that has become a contrarian, radical and disturbing.

As she presciently described long ago, television talking heads (before they were called talking heads) are spokespeople whose positions can always be predicted; Adler's cannot because they are not based on membership in a particular club or linked to a commercial persona (or, now, a brand), unlike the myriad pundits whose worth is based on the consistency of their views. What is to be made of the usefulness or intellectual integrity of journalists and commentators whose positions are always known? They might as well never write at all—saving time for everyone. And yet, of course, the market accommodates them, whereas unanticipated views are met with hostility and confusion.

Adler is trying to write about people's motivations, about their inherent conflicts, about not what they say they believe in or stand for, but the largely happenstance circumstances that got them to their chance moment in the sun. All people and all events have another story. Nothing is as it represents itself to be. That is bound to be an unsettling and unpopular analysis.

Her politics, to the extent that she has any proscribed position, has to do with language. She unpacks to startling effect what people are actually saying. She is one of the few writers who hold people accountable for the words they use. In doing so, meaning, or assumed

meaning, often falls quickly away, and laziness, buffoonery, ignorance, and worlds without the most basic logic are revealed.

Her own prose, on the other hand, is quite unlike any journalism
being written today. It exists in service to itself, as its own standard,
as its own force, and not in support of political or commercial positions. It is a depressing realization that writing like this is really no
longer practiced, that journalism is not a writer's game anymore,
that the language of most journalism is as dead and meaningless as
the language of politics and of pop culture, from where so much of
it comes.

Adler is often writing about a writer's position in the larger world.
Hers is a meditation on the power that journalists accrue, often
falsely, as a product of media rather than language. A successful
journalist graduates from being a writer or a reporter into being a
politician or adroit entrepreneur—a fundamentally different business than pushing sentences.

Adler herself is an example of another kind of writer, a writer's
writer, if you will. One without institutional protection, or even
self-saving restraint. The ability to write with financial and emotional support—the sine qua non of being able to write—is predi-
cated on a successful relationship with a media power, a devil's deal
almost every writer gladly makes.

It is possible perhaps for an indomitable fighter to go it alone, to
face down the cultural bishops of the moment. But Adler, except in
her prose, is as indomitable as a mouse.

Fortunately, her writing speaks for itself.

—Michael Wolff

AFTER THE TALL TIMBER

TOWARD A RADICAL MIDDLE
INTRODUCTION

IN MAY, 1969, as I was watching *Another World*, Lee Randolph died. I had bought my television set more than two years before, after going to California to do a piece about the Sunset Strip. Buying the set had nothing to do with the piece at all, or any piece. But on assignment, in the sunny upper rooms of the Chateau Marmont in Los Angeles, I had had a case of laryngitis so extreme that I couldn't speak, even whisper on the telephone, and when I was not following the flower children of the Strip about, I stayed in my room watching daytime television—the soap operas, and when they were not on, the quiz programs. I became seriously preoccupied by them. The NBC peacock, with the announcement "the following program is brought to you in living color," was frustrating, even reproachful on a hotel room's black and white. When I got home, I bought a color set, my first TV, a Zenith Space Command with remote control, which I could operate from my bed.

For two and a half years—until now, in fact—I watched *Another World, The Doctors, Love of Life, Search for Tomorrow, Days of Our Lives*, and later *Hidden Faces* (I have never cared for *Secret Storm* or *Edge of Night*) whenever I could, and nearly always when I thought I should be doing other things. They had their tired stretches. I missed some crucial episodes. But when Lee Randolph died, a suicide who had lingered on for weeks, I watched her face being covered by a sheet, and I was ridden by the event for weeks. I suppose the script for Lee had run out, or that the actress had found another part. But it was not at all like losing a character in fiction of any other kind— not just an event in a two or ten hour imaginative experience, and then in memory. The soap operas ran along beside life five days out of seven. I saw the characters in them more often than my friends, knew their relationships, the towns. It had a continuity stronger even than the news, where stories and characters submerge and reappear—or don't—depending on where the limelight is. I know of no more constant, undisjunct narrative than the soap operas. Perhaps they are what personal life was like, before the violent, flash discontinuities of media news and personal air travel came along.

I had thought of my soap hours as a total waste of time, not a joke, not camp, not for a piece, not critically, a serious waste of time. But when the loss of Lee became such an important thing, I found that those two-and-a-half-year, open-ended narrative experiences define a lot of what I am and what I think, what I would like to write, what I think America, particularly a certain age and voice group, is, and what I think the American radical and intellectual communities are not. I guess I am part of an age group that, through being skipped, through never having had a generational voice, was forced into the broadest possible America. Even now (and we are in our thirties), we have no journals we publish, no exile we share, no brawls, no anecdotes, no war, no solidarity, no mark. In college, under Eisenhower, we were known for nothing, or for our apathy. A center of action seemed to have broken down in us. Lacking precisely the generational tie (through the media, mainly, kids now know about other kids) and just after the family unit began to dissolve, we knew what there was of our alienation privately, and not yet as a claim or a group experience. We now have vertical ties, loves, friendships, loyalties to people older, younger, other than ourselves. We are unnoticed even as we spread clear across what people call, without taking account of us, the generation gap.

I think that is our special note—we cut across. Across ages, idioms, stresses, cultural values, memories. At a moment of polarization, and other clichés that drain the language of meaning, the continuity of the American story seems to rest just now in us. The first age group to experience in its youth a murderous overvalue on precocity (which leads now to an idiot generational impasse), we held back. We grew up separately, without a rhetoric, drawing our ideas from age and cultural groups already formed, as we were not. The idiom of *Another World* is no more foreign to us than *The Green Hornet*, Joseph Conrad, *The New York Review of Books*, bourbon no more or less our own than marijuana is. Unaware of each other until now, we are in it all. Some of us have dropped a generation back, to lead a student movement that belies everything we are. Others have taken their positions quietly, in society as it was before we came and as, in the years of its most annihilating smugness, it nearly killed us off. But most of us, I think, were formed and remain one by one— formed by books and by the media, but, through the accident of our span of history, formed alone. And now I think we are a force.

In a way, in culture and in politics, we are the last custodians of language—because of the books we read and because history, in our time, has rung so many changes on the meaning of terms and we, having never generationally perpetrated anything, have no commitment to any distortion of them. Lacking slogans, we still have the private ear for distinctions, for words. I happen to know no one who regularly watches *Another World* (although millions of Americans clearly do), or who would watch it—except to do a piece on materialism, escapism, pop culture or something. But that is the point. I know of no one whose cultural and political experience I completely share. And yet there are elements of my soap hours that seem common to a particular, still unaccounted-for sort of activist in early middle years: on the set, a sense of the human condition and the rhythm of life, with endless recapitulations for those who have not been watching, going forward; in ourselves, the bouts of muteness, watching and inertia, the sense of work one ought to do in what is going on, the patience with continuity, even the nostalgia for a kind of corniness. And always a characteristic quality of attention, at a certain humorous remove from our own experience. Lacking an idiom entirely our own, we cannot adopt any single voice without a note of irony. (I can't write about the soap operas, or anything that does not make specific, human claims for action on my part, with perfect seriousness.) A suspicion of glibness or fluency has made the generation immediately after us value the rhetorical and inarticulate. Not us. We all seem to view the world still in words, as writers, arguers, archivists—even, perhaps even especially, those who do not write. In strange times, we have kept our language, energies and heads. (It is no surprise that the disturbances at San Francisco State dissolved under police called in by one—albeit aging and not very profound—semanticist.) And we are here.

I think the historical bridge and the moral limits of our experience—mine anyway—were defined in World War II, which most of us still remember as The War. Totalitarianism, freedom, genocide, courage, passion, gentleness, a community of decent men, most of my conceptions of idealism, the monstrous and the public world date from that war, in which we were too young to have a part. And the bland repressions and unacknowledged disillusion of the succeeding years. Everyone looked alike or tried to, every sort of maverick was cut off and lost. Art was the province of ladies' painting and lecture clubs; intelligence was subsumed in the grand idea of American know how. The schools were levellers for the general mediocrity; unions, parodying their origins and aims, were becoming entrenched forces for corruption and reaction. Odd cliffs were papered over. When, on his birthday in 1956, Adam Clayton Powell announced his support for Dwight David Eisenhower for president, the Republican candidate sent a birthday present to the people of Harlem— white trucks full of black cupcakes—and the present was graciously received. The dream everywhere was going flat. Teachers, who had begun in the Depression when, on the basis of their regular salaries, they could afford maids and were considered rich, were now poorer, embittered and threatened by any sort of difference. In small towns, in a travesty of the New Deal dream of education, teachers had risen above their own class to the extent that their brothers and their colleagues' brothers—contractors and factory workers—were no longer good enough for them. They seldom married. They subscribed to the Book of the Month Club and *Reader's Digest* and shared the general passion for the ordinary. Our rebellions then, in the years when the sum of hope was to be adjusted and popular, when boys still broke themselves at team sports on a military model, which would never be of use to them again (when, in fact, people still spoke of the Army for anybody as making a man of him), were separate and one by one, and threw us back, unknowing, on the past. Some of us cut school and invented juvenile delinquency, others read.

What I am trying to say is that if there is any age group that should loathe what is called the System in its bones that group is us. We had it, in spite of Korea, at its height—the years when society was going, to its own satisfaction, so extremely well; when telephones, neon signs, subways, Western Union worked, as they haven't since; and when, through and after Senator Joseph McCarthy, the spirit of the redneck, the junior college and the drum majorette had spread so deep into the land. I think the first post-war jolt the System had in its complacency, in our time, was not social or humanitarian, but technological: in 1957, when Sputnik went up. After that, there began to be a little room for change and mavericks, who, when there is not a desperate community lie at the heart of things, are the rule. But in the interim, before the general boredom had begun to lift, we, one by one, had made some beginnings, some progress on all the public and private fronts that now exist—frontiers that polarization, paradoxically, obscures and language has to be hard won and individual to approach at all.

Accessible, almost by generational default, to all the idioms of America, we also went overseas. We were the first non-military age group to travel internationally on an almost national scale. We knew, since we had been at the mercy of institutions so utterly, what institutions were like at home, and what American tourists were like, and were treated like, abroad. But there is a particular totalitarian lie at the heart of political cliché too, and the simplicities of "imperialism," "genocide," "materialism," "police brutality," "military-industrial complex," "racism," tossed about as though they were interchangeable, and as though they applied equally to anything with which one is out of temper, are not for us. Neither are the simplicities of anti-Communism, free world, "violence," and "radicalism" itself. We observed in The War the literal extreme of violence that men have done so far. Since then, bombs dropping on villages, cops beating kids on the head, kids throwing bottles at cops, the violence to the spirit of the McCarthy years, the violation of human dignity in exclusion and poverty—there is a degree of violence in them all, but a difference of degree, an extent of metaphor, and we still distinguish among literalisms, metaphors, questions of degree. Or radicalism. A radicalism that draws its terms from the System's violence in Vietnam, then claims to be driven to revolutionary violence of its own, and, as an act of revolution, turns upon the liberal universities has an inauthentic ring, a ring of sublimation, theater. If revolutionary outrage over Vietnam had had a substantive thrust of Guevara courage on the line, there would have been American brigades fighting for Hanoi—a disaster for the country, surely, but a disaster in authentic terms. (The white revolutionary movement certainly left the American South, where the physical risk was high, fast enough.) There is an authentic radicalism in this country now, but it does not abuse the metaphor of revolution. It is not the radicalism of rhetoric, theater, mannerism, psychodrama, air. And it is not paralyzed in its own unconsummated moral impulses by viewing every human problem at a single level of atrocity.

I think what has muddled terms, what has emptied vocabularies into rhetorics and made generations out of what are only persons after all, is, in the end, a major implication of The War. Ours was the first age group to experience the end of the Just War as a romantic possibility. There are no justifications for group violence in this country any more—no outlets for aggressive physical courage, irrational fervors, the fraternity of the barricades and the decent human war. And there aren't likely to be any. Technology has made the stakes too high. We knew that separately, saw the last great romantic group fight to the death, and knew we could never have one of our own. That sounds like a blessing, and perhaps historically it is, but it puts a tremendous strain on any generation of young. From now on, it is all patient effort, unsimple victories. In this, the Vietnam War was a hiatus in moral terms. The System lifted the vocabulary of the just war, in the name of the free world, to Vietnam, and found it did not work. Radicalism lifted essentially the same vocabulary and turned it, in the name of revolution, against the System, where it does not work either. The very fact that radicalism leans so comfortably, half-consciously, upon the System and its laws, goes on almost risk-free, beside *Another World*, confirms that the System's thrust is still, on an unprecedented scale, democratic and benign. No famous or privileged white revolutionaries have gone to jail for long just yet. But obscure and black radicals have, in numbers—which raises questions, I think, not so much of politics as of fame, privilege and the inauthentic revolutionary.

What these pieces, looking back, are about, if anything, is true radicalism as opposed to what I would call the mere mentality of the apocalypse. The apocalyptic vision has never been true to the America we know. By some accident of our size, our mix, our resources and the perfectibility of our laws, brinks vanish here and become frontiers, immense real tensions are resolved in a paradigm of the modern world, material resources make it possible to pose moral and social questions which have never been approached on such a scale before. I think that is where we are—we who have lived from The War till now—not too old or tired to give the whole thing up, not too young to remember a time when things were worse. And, through the accident of our span of years, not too simple in the quality of our experience to know that things get better (The War's end) and worse (the succeeding years) and better again (the great movement of non-violence sweeping out of the South to move the country briefly forward a bit) and, of course, worse. But when a term like violence undergoes, in less than thirty years, a declension from Auschwitz to the Democratic convention in Chicago, from A-bombing even to napalm, the System has improved. Terribly and with stumbling, but improved. And there are characters in these pieces—mocked for their tokenism when they succeeded, claimed as radical martyrs when they failed or died—who burned themselves out over an inch of that improvement. Which is how the human condition, in its historical continuity, or real radicalism, in its social framework, works at all.

But with the closing of The War option, with the loss of final and romantic victories, there is a tendency, particularly among intellectuals and the young, and oddly accelerated by an obscene confluence of psychoanalysis and the media, to think in terms of final solutions anyway. To use the vocabulary of total violence, with less and less consciousness of its ingredient of metaphor, to cultivate scorched earth madness as a form of consciousness (of courage, even), to call history mad, and to dismiss every growing, improving human enterprise as a form of tokenism, an irrelevance in which one has no obligation to take part. The System drew back from its apocalypse in Vietnam—always draws backs from brinks so far—restrained, in spite of everything, the full force of its technology. But the scorched earth psychology remains, particularly on the Left. I happened to encounter that psychology, long before Vietnam, first in the arts, when I was reviewing books. The professional alienist in fiction, the group polemicist in criticism, the unearned nihilist and overeasy breakthrough artist in mixed media, the blown mind vanguardist in the audience. Then (except for a few reviews of what I considered genuine, private innovators: "Conversations," "Instruments") I found I was doing a lot of overeasy polemic of my own, and I gave it up—except for one last piece on the breakthrough artists: "Selling an Enraged Bread Pudding."

Reporting was better, but somehow the apocalyptic sensibility had moved into politics too, into every part of life. Its earmarks were clenched teeth, personal agonies, rhetoric, the single plane of atrocity view of Western man, above all, a psychoanalytic concept of moral responsibility—based, not on conscience, which is exercised in substantive action, but on guilt, which is appeased in confession, sublimation, symbolic purge. Confessions were everywhere. The guilt became retroactive, vicarious, unappeasable: a country, incurably genocidal, and founded on a genocide; white Western man, blood insatiable, leaving nothing but war, exploitation and pollution in his wake. No matter that none of us (and few of our isolated, refugee fathers either) were here a hundred years ago to kill an Indian, that countless nations—India, for one—were founded by invasions that exterminated aborigines, that there have always been wars, within the limits of available technology, wherever man is (notably tribal slaughters in Africa, and in Vietnam ever since the Annamites), that Western powers have been the first to try to come to terms with an international responsibility for social, medical meliorism and military restraint. (With, of course, grotesque lapses. The question is whose mistakes there is time to be patient with.) Guilt, atrocity, the luxurious mystique of the everybody else, which liberates from responsibility for one's own time and place. There was a special radical infatuation with religions of the Orient, notably Hinduism and Zen—which produced, as it happens, some of the most repellent, anti-humanist, repressive and belligerent social systems in man's history. A let-them-starve-on-earth-Nirvana sensibility caught on among a Third-World-infatuated contingent of radicals.

There was nothing to show for the apocalyptic sensibility on any front—not in art, not in politics, not in mind expansion (a ghastly misnomer), not even in the apocalyptic-pornographic view of sex—no breakthroughs, only gesture, celebrity quietism, rage, symptom, backlash. Not Rimbaud and Baudelaire, child mutations of John Dewey and Freud. Symptoms do have their real effects on the status quo (even *Another World* has its impact on the world out here), but the effects were mindless, random, dumb, a non-negotiable demand to dismantle the human experiment and begin again. A view of evil as banal was distorted into a view of banality as evil, and of all meliorism as boring and banal. Intellectual cartwheels, bad art, spite politics (I gave up reporting that after "Radicalism in Debacle" at the Palmer House), and a happy collusion, by default, with the worst elements of the System: pure huckster fashion and the redneck Right. (It is not unthinkable that, except for the broader evolution of America, we should all be called one day before an investigating committee composed of Strom Thurmond, Tom Hayden and some suitable representative of pop art and café society.) And fame: the cry of alienation made good fellows and good copy. The gesture and rhetoric of revolution were well suited to that natural creator of discontinuous, lunatic constituencies, the media.

I think radicalism's flirtation with the media, its overvalue on personal image, personal sensibility, pure air, was nurtured by the spirit of the Kennedys. Their beauty, promise, absolute lack of delivery, and their power—a power which found its major application, in the end, only in controlling the image that the country was to have of them. I don't mean anything about the sincerity of the men themselves; I mean what they came to represent. The notion that you can love glamour and be concerned with grit, that you can promise in prose and never quite deliver in fact, that as long as power is wrested into the right hands (one's own) good will follow in time, the gap between image and substance, impulse and legislation—the country was simultaneously overstimulated and corrupted by these princelings of the air. Working for Senator Joseph McCarthy, silent in the censure vote, wiretapping, Mayor Daley, segregationist judges in the South, the logic of the Bay of Pigs and Vietnam (if Cuban exiles couldn't do it, American counterinsurgents could: win an easy, a "little war"), losing cufflinks simultaneously to blacks with hopes and white auto workers armed against the possibility that a black should ever live in peace beside them—none of it fit. It generated unreason and violence. All these disparities could be considered part of a personal process of education, or seem to be reconciled on some higher symbolic plane, but they were not true to the country, to the real balance and struggle of huge forces that is here. President Johnson, I think, delivered substantively on all that promise: the social legislation and, alas, the war. But Kennedyism, cut off en route, stayed in the air, style, media power, personal packaging. Suddenly there were too many stars, too many artists, too many who thought the world well lost for their own image and sensibilities. The new enemy was boredom, in the sense of lack of drama. The new currency was fame. With special implications for the intellectuals. Ours has not been a great thirty years for intellectuals. We saw, and survived, anti-intellectualism in this country, but we also saw a generation of intellectuals—Stalinist at the time of Stalin, quiescent in the McCarthy years, mesmerized by the power and beauty of the Kennedys, nerveless in the face of the radical redneck young—always weak, always somehow lifeless and wavering in the face of force and violence. But through it all, we saw something infinitely fragile and viable in the System, in its accommodations with radicals, rednecks, soldiers, blacks, thinkers, visionaries, lunatics, the ordinary, getting better.

I guess a radical middle, in age and in politics, acts out of a consciousness of how much has been gained, how far there is to go, and what there is to lose. It is content to be obscure—to measure and implement accommodations with the System: how many blacks and former poor in jobs, unions, polling booths, public office, neighborhoods, even in soap operas, how many soldiers withdrawn, how many arms unmade, how many material, aesthetic and technological advances applied to ameliorating the human condition, how to divorce liberalism from arrogance and violence. Not many advances, but some. Enough to stay aboard and to maintain distinctions on every side: to get the unpolarized student to his class without having him clubbed or teargassed by a cop—who is not too good at making distinctions either.

We have lived after all through two sunny periods of lies, and seen some of the truth in both of them: the Eisenhower lie that the noble American experiment was complete, that all was well, that there was no need to move; and the Kennedy era lie that with glamour, image and the instantaneous application of power you can gratify immediately, totally, those human concerns that are, in reality, met by inches, by years of work and suffering. I believe that the generation gap is in part an almost meteorological collision of those airs, the two lies of those years. Some have moved and see no reason why anyone else should rock the boat: others, impatient with the slowness of motion, see no reason to move at all until the coming of the Word. We are between. Our heroes, I suppose, mine anyway, are both famous and obscure: Martin Luther King, Bob Moses, Charles Evers, Alvin Poussaint of the Medical Committee on Human Rights, John Doar, others. Our thinkers—Hannah Arendt, Richard Rovere, Bayard Rustin, Harold Rosenberg, Daniel P. Moynihan, others—write from an awareness of precedent, of what has already been said and done and what can still be said and done, without mixing artistic and political metaphor. (Everything that has been said has, after all, been said many times.) In this collection, even in the dated or term-paper influenced pieces, there ought to be a sense of tendency, despite a suspicion of groups, of that emergent "we." We are not in the world for therapy. We are non-violent. Our values are corny ones, reason, decency, prosperity, human dignity, contact, the finest, broadest possible America. Some of us have despaired and, in the only indisputably sincere expression of the apocalyptic vision, immolated themselves. But somewhere there is a reconciliation of that auto worker and that black, not on a symbolic plane, but because history is irreversible and there is a real common interest in the rich, mixed quality of life. And three of us have just come back (substantively and yet with drama), from the way to perhaps other populations, outer limits, from the moon.

July 1969

THE MARCH FOR NON-VIOLENCE
FROM SELMA

THE THIRTY thousand people who at one point or another took part in this week's march from the Brown Chapel African Methodist Episcopal Church in Selma, Alabama, to the statehouse in Montgomery were giving highly dramatic expression to a principle that could be articulated only in the vaguest terms. They were a varied lot: local blacks, Northern clergymen, members of labor unions, delegates from state and city governments, entertainers, mothers pushing baby carriages, members of civil-rights groups more or less at odds with one another, isolated, shaggy marchers with an air of simple vagrancy, doctors, lawyers, teachers, children, college students, and a preponderance of what one marcher described as "ordinary, garden-variety civilians from just about everywhere." They were insulated in front by soldiers and television camera crews, overhead and underfoot by helicopters and Army demolition teams, at the sides and rear by more members of the press and military, and over all by agents of the FBI. Most of them were aware that protection along a route of more than fifty miles of hostile country could not be absolute (on the night before the march, a student who had come here from Boston University was slashed across the cheek with a razor blade), yet few of the thirty-two hundred marchers who set out on Sunday morning seemed to have a strong consciousness of risk. They did not have a sharply defined sense of purpose, either. President Johnson's speech about voting rights and Judge Johnson's granting of permission for the march to take place had made the march itself ceremonial—almost redundant. The immediate aims of the

---

Originally titled "Letter from Selma"

abortive earlier marches had been realized: the national conscience had been aroused and federal intervention had been secured. In a sense, the government of Alabama was now in rebellion, and the marchers, with the sanction and protection of the federal government, were demonstrating against a rebellious state. It was unclear what such a demonstration could hope to achieve. Few segregationists could be converted by it, the national commitment to civil rights would hardly be increased by it, there was certainly an element of danger in it, and for the local citizenry it might have a long and ugly aftermath. The marchers, who had five days and four nights in which to talk, tended for the most part to avoid discussions of principle, apparently in the hope that their good will, their sense of solidarity, and the sheer pageantry of the occasion would resolve matters at some symbolic level and yield a clear statement of practical purpose before the march came to an end.

From this point of view, the first few hours of Sunday morning in Selma were far from satisfying. Broad Street, the town's main thoroughfare, was deserted and indifferent. At the black First Baptist Church, on the corner of Sylvan Street and Jefferson Davis Avenue, denim-clad veterans of earlier marches stood wearily aloof from recruits, who ate watery scrambled eggs, drank watery coffee, and simply milled about. On Sylvan Street itself, an unpaved red sand road dividing identical rows of brick houses known as the George Washington Carver Development, crowds were gathering, some facing the entrance to the Brown Chapel Church, others on the steps of the church facing out. Inside the church, more people were milling, while a few tried to sleep on benches or on the floor. For several hours, nothing happened. The church service that was to begin the march was scheduled to take place at ten o'clock, but veterans advised newcomers—in the first of several bitter, self-mocking jokes that became current on the Selma-Montgomery road—that this was CPT, Colored People Time, and the service actually began more than an hour behind schedule.

In a field behind the housing development, the Reverend Andrew Young, executive director of Dr. Martin Luther King's Southern

Christian Leadership Conference (SCLC), which sponsored the march, was giving marshals and night security guards last-minute instructions in the tactics of non-violence. "Keep women and children in the middle," he said. "If there's a shot, stand up and make the others kneel down. Don't be lagging around, or you're going to get hurt. Don't rely on the troopers, either. If you're beaten on, crouch and put your hands over the back of your head. Don't put up your arm to ward off a blow. If you fall, fall right down and look dead. Get to know the people in your unit, so you can tell if somebody's missing or if there's somebody there who shouldn't be there. And listen! If you can't be nonviolent, let me know now." A young man in the standard denim overalls of the Student Nonviolent Coordinating Committee (SNCC) murmured, "Man, you've got it all so *structured*. There seems to be a certain anxiety here about *structure*." Everyone laughed, a bit nervously, and the marshals went to the front of the church.

The crowd there was growing, still arrayed in two lines, one facing in, the other facing out. There were National Guardsmen and local policemen, on foot and in jeeps and cars, along the sides of Sylvan Street and around its corners, at Jefferson Davis and Alabama Avenues. The marchers themselves appeared to have dressed for all kinds of weather and occasions—in denims, cassocks, tweed coats, ponchos, boots, sneakers, Shetland sweaters, silk dresses, college sweat shirts, sports shirts, khaki slacks, fur-collared coats, pea jackets, and trenchcoats. As they waited, they sang innumerable, increasingly dispirited choruses of "We Shall Overcome," "Ain't Gonna Let Nobody Turn Me 'Round," and other songs of the movement. There was a moment of excitement when Dr. King and other speakers assembled on the steps, but a succession of long, rhetorical, and, to a certain extent (when press helicopters buzzed too low or when the microphone went dead), inaudible speeches put a damper on that too. An enthusiastic lady, of a sort that often afflicts banquets and church suppers, sang several hymns of many stanzas, with little melody and much vibrato. Exhaust fumes from a television truck parked to the right of the steps began to choke some of the

marchers, and they walked away, coughing. Speakers praised one another extravagantly in monotonous political-convention cadences
("the man who …"). An irreverent, irritated voice with a Bronx accent shouted, "Would you mind please talking a little louder." Several members of the crowd sat down in the street, and the march
assumed the first of its many moods—that of tedium.

Then Dr. King began to speak, and suddenly, for no apparent reason, several Army jeeps drove straight through the center of the
crowd. ("Didn't realize we were interrupting," said one of the drivers, smiling. He had a DD, for Dixie Division, emblem on his uniform.) The startled crowd, divided in half for a moment, became
aware of its size. Dr. King's speech came to an end, and there was a
last, unified, and loud rendition of "We Shall Overcome." Then the
marshals quickly arranged the crowd in columns, six abreast—
women and children in the middle—and the procession set out
down Sylvan Street. It was about one o'clock. On Alabama Avenue,
the marchers turned right, passing lines of silent white citizens on
the sidewalks. On Broad Street, which is also U.S. Route 80 to
Montgomery, they turned left, and as segregationist loudspeakers
along the way blared "Bye, Bye, Blackbird" and the white onlookers
began to jeer, the marchers approached and crossed the Edmund
Pettus Bridge. And the march entered another mood—jubilation.

The day was sunny and cool. The flat road, an amalgam of asphalt
and the local sand, looked pink. The people in the line linked arms,
and the procession was long enough to permit the marchers to sing
five different civil-rights songs simultaneously without confusion;
the vanguard could not hear what the rear guard was singing. Occasionally, various leaders of the movement broke out of the line to
join interviewers from the television networks, which took turns using a camera truck that preceded the line of march. For the first few
miles, the highway was flanked by billboards ("Keep Selma Beautiful, Cover It with Dodge"), smaller signs (Rotary, Kiwanis, Lions,
Citizens Council), diners, and gas stations. Little clusters of white
onlookers appeared at various points along the road, some shouting
threats and insults, others silently waving Confederate flags, and

still others taking pictures of the marchers, presumably as a warning that their faces would not be forgotten when the march was over. The procession filled the two left lanes of the four-lane highway, but in the two right lanes traffic was proceeding almost normally. A black Volkswagen passed the marchers several times; on its doors and fenders were signs, lettered in whitewash: "MARTIN LUTHER KINK," "WALK, COON," "COONESVILLE, U.S.A.," AND "RENT YOUR PRIEST SUIT HERE." Several small children at the roadside waved toy rifles and popguns and chanted "Nigger lover!" "White nigger!" "Half-breed!" and other epithets. A man in front of a road-side diner thumbed his nose for the entire twenty minutes it took the procession to pass him, and a well-dressed matron briefly stopped her Chrysler, got out, stuck out her tongue, climbed in again, slammed the door, and drove off.

Several times, the march came to an abrupt halt, and in the middle ranks and the rear guard there were murmurs of alarm. Then it became clear that these were only rest stops, and the marchers relaxed and resumed their singing. Rented trucks, driven by ministers of the San Francisco Theological Seminary, carried portable toilets up and down the line. When press photographers attempted to take pictures of civil-rights leaders entering the men's rooms, the Reverend Mr. Young shouted, "Can't a man even go to the john in peace?" The photographers moved away. Three tired marchers rode a short distance on the water truck, and James Forman, the executive secretary of SNCC, who was being interviewed in French for Canadian television, broke off his interview to mutter as the truck passed, "Hey, man, you cats could walk." The marchers got down from the truck at once. Forman resumed his interview. "I think he's having trouble with his French," said one of the marchers. "He just said that no Negro in America is allowed to vote." "His French is all right," said another. "But he may be less concerned with the immediate truth than with stirring up the kind of chaos that makes things change."

By sunset of the first day, the caravan was more than seven miles from Selma, and most of the marchers returned by a special train to town, where some of them left for their home communities and others were put up for the night in the black development on Sylvan Street. Two hundred and eighty blacks, representing Alabama counties (a hundred and forty-eight from Dallas County, eighty-nine from Perry, twenty-three from Marengo, and twenty from Wilcox), and twenty whites, from all over the country, who had been chosen to make the entire journey to Montgomery (the court permitted no more than three hundred marchers on the twenty-mile stretch of Route 80 midway between Selma and Montgomery, where it is only a two-lane highway) turned off Route 80 onto a tarred road leading to the David Hall farm—their campsite for the night. Four large tents had already been pitched in a field. As the marchers lined up for supper (three tons of spaghetti), which was served to them on paper plates, from brand-new garbage pails, night fell. Groups of National Guardsmen who surrounded the farm lighted campfires. "It looks like Camelot," said one of the younger whites.

Camelot soon became very cold and damp. By nine o'clock, most of the marchers had retired to the tents, but within an hour they had to be roused and sorted out. One tent was for men, another for women, the third for the marchers' own night security patrol, and the fourth for the press. When everyone had been assigned to his or her proper tent, it developed that there was a shortage of blankets, winter clothes, and sleeping bags. A shivering group huddled around an incinerator, the campsite's only source of heat. A few marchers made their way to the loft of a barn beside the Hall farmhouse, to profit from the heat given off by the animals in the stalls below. Five guinea hens perched in a tree outside the barn. The march's security patrol wandered about with walkie-talkies; they had labelled their outposts Able, Baker, Charlie, and Dog, using the Army's old system, to set them apart from Alpha, Bravo, Charlie, and Delta, the outposts of the National Guard along the perimeter of the field. The night grew colder, damper, and darker, and the group around the incinerator fire grew uneasy.

There was talk of the march ahead through Lowndes County, where swamps and the woods behind them might easily shelter a sniper in a tree or a canoe. Several marchers claimed to have spotted members of the American Nazi Party along the line of march. Someone mentioned the Ku Klux Klan "counter-demonstration" that had taken place in Montgomery that afternoon.

"And the snakes," a man said.

"What snakes?" said a Northern voice.

"Copperheads and cottonmouth. It takes the heat to bring them out, but a trooper told me somebody's caught five baskets full and is letting them go where we camp tomorrow night."

"How'd the trooper hear about it?"

"Spies."

"Well, I suppose there might be spies right here in camp."

"There might. And bombs and mines. They cleared a few this afternoon. Man, this isn't any Boy Scout jamboree. It's something else."

By the time dawn came, the campers were a thoroughly chilled and bleary-eyed group. The oatmeal served at breakfast gave rise to a certain amount of mirth ("Tastes like fermented library paste," said one of the clergymen), and the news that the National Guardsmen had burned thirteen fence posts, two shovel handles, and an outhouse belonging to a neighboring church in order to keep warm during the night cheered everyone considerably. At a press conference held by Jack Rosenthal, the young Director of Public Information of the Justice Department, the rumors about snakes, bombs, and mines were checked out, and it was learned that none of them were true. A reporter waved several racist leaflets that had been dropped from an airplane and asked whether anything was being done to prevent such planes from dropping bombs. "What do you want us to do?" Rosenthal replied. "Use anti-aircraft guns?"

The procession set out promptly at 8 A.M. The distance to the next campsite—Rosa Steele's farm—was seventeen miles. Again the day was sunny, and as the air grew warmer some of the more sunburned members of the group donned berets or Stetsons or tied scarves or handkerchiefs around their heads. To the white onlookers who clustered beside the road, the three hundred marchers must have seemed a faintly piratical band. At the head of the line were Dr. and Mrs.

King, wearing green caps with earmuffs and reading newspapers as they walked. Not far behind them was a pale-green wagon (known to the marchers as the Green Dragon) with Mississippi license plates, in which rode doctors wearing armbands of the MCHR (the Medical Committee for Human Rights). Farther back were some of the younger civil-rights leaders: Hosea Williams, SCLC director of the march and veteran of the bitter struggle for public accommodations in Savannah, Georgia; the Reverend James Bevel, formerly of SNCC, now SCLC project director for Alabama (Mr. Bevel was wearing the many-colored yarmulke that has become almost his trademark—"a link," he says, "to our Old Testament heritage"); John Lewis, chairman of SNCC; and the Reverend Andrew Young.

Behind the leaders, some of the main personae of the march had begun to emerge, among them Joe Young, a blind greenhouse worker from Atlanta, Georgia, and Jim Letherer, a one-legged settlement-house worker from Saginaw, Michigan. ("Left! Left! Left!" the segregationist onlookers chanted as Mr. Letherer moved along on crutches.) Chuck Fager, a young worker for SCLC, wearing denims and a black yarmulke, was waving and shouting, "Come march with us! Why don't you come along and march with us?" ("It sets up a dialogue," he explained. "The last time I was in jail, a sheriff pulled me aside and asked me where the hell I was from. Any sort of talk like that sets up a dialogue.") Sister Mary Leoline, a nun from Christ the King parish in Kansas City, Kansas, was talking to John Bart Gerald, a young novelist from New York. "This is a great time to be alive," she said. A few members of the night security guard had somehow acquired cameras, and they were now photographing by-standers who were photographing marchers; it appeared that a sort of reciprocal Most Wanted list was being compiled. From time to time, the marchers were still singing ("Oh-h-h, Wallace, segregation's bound to fall"), and the chief of the Justice Department's Civil Rights Division, Assistant Attorney General John Doar, tall, tanned, and coatless, was striding back and forth along the line of march to see that all was going well.

Around two o'clock, as the middle ranks of marchers passed an intersection just outside Lowndes County, a female bystander apparently could stand it no longer. "They're carrying the flag upside down!" she screamed to the nearest trooper. "Isn't there a law against that? Can't you arrest them? Look at them so-called white men with church collars that they bought for fifty cents! And them de*virgin*ated nuns! I'm a Catholic myself, but it turns my stomach to see them. They said there was thousands yesterday, but there wasn't near a thousand. Them niggers and them girls! I've watched the whole thing three times, and there isn't a intelligent-looking one in the bunch. I feel sorry for the black folks. If they want to vote, why don't they just go out and register? Oh, honey, look! There goes a big one. Go home, scum! Go home, scum!" The procession began to sing a not very hearty version of "A Great Camp Meeting in the Promised Land."

Not all the bystanders along the road were white. At the boundary of Lowndes County (with a population of fifteen thousand, eighty per cent of them blacks, not one of whom had been registered to vote by March 1, 1965), John Maxwell, a black worker in a Lowndes County cotton-gin mill (at a salary of six dollars for a twelve-hour day), appeared at an intersection.

"Why don't you register to vote?" a reporter from the *Harvard Crimson* asked Mr. Maxwell.

"They'd put us off the place if I tried," Mr. Maxwell said.

In the town of Trickem, at the Nolan Elementary School— a small white shack on brick stilts, which had asbestos shingles, a corrugated-iron roof, six broken windows, and a broken wood floor patched with automobile license plates—a group of old people and barefoot children rushed out to embrace Dr. King. They had been waiting four hours.

"Will you march with us?" Dr. King asked an old man with a cane.

"I'll walk one step, anyway," said the man. "Because I know for every one step I'll take you'll take two."

The marchers broke into a chant. "*What* do you *want?*" they shouted encouragingly to the blacks at the roadside. The blacks smiled, but they did not give the expected response—"*Freedom!*" The marchers had to supply that themselves.

Late in the afternoon, as Route 80 passed through the swamps of Lowndes County, the marchers looked anxiously at the woods, covered with Spanish moss, which began a few yards back from the road. They reached Rosa Steele's farm at sunset. Many of them seemed dismayed to find that the campsite lay right beside the highway. Fresh rumors began to circulate: a young man had been seen putting a bomb under a roadside bridge; twenty white men, with pistols and shotguns, had been seen prowling through a neighboring field; testing security, a representative of the Pentagon had managed to penetrate the security lines without being asked to show his pass. Mr. Rosenthal again put these fears to rest. "The field has been combed by Army demolition teams," he said. "If anyone from the Pentagon had made it through unchecked, you can bet there would have been one hell of a fuss. And as for the man under the bridge, it was a little boy who got off his bicycle to relieve himself. The troopers found out these things. It's nice to know that they are this aware."

As darkness fell, Dr. King held a press conference. A black woman lifted up her three-year-old son so that he might catch a glimpse of Dr. King. She soon grew tired and had to put him down. "I'll take him," said a white man standing beside her, and he lifted the boy onto his shoulders. The boy did not glance at Dr. King; he was too busy gazing down at the white man's blond hair.

Again the night was cold and damp. At the entrance to the field, there was so much mud that boards and reeds had been scattered to provide traction for cars. Most of the marchers went to sleep in their four tents soon after supper, but at Steele's Service Station, across the highway, a crowd of blacks from the neighborhood had gathered. Some of them were dancing to music from a jukebox, and a few of the more energetic marchers, white and black, joined them.

"This is getting to be too much like a holiday," said a veteran of one of the earlier marches. "It doesn't tell the truth of what happened."

At about ten o'clock, the last of the marchers crossed the highway back to camp. Shortly afterward, a fleet of cars drove up to the service station and a group of white boys got out. Two of the boys were from Georgia, two were from Texas, one was from Tennessee, one was from Oklahoma, one was from Monroeville, Alabama, and one was from Selma. The Reverend Arthur E. Matott, a white minister from Perth Amboy, New Jersey, who was a member of the night patrol, saw them and walked across the highway to where they were standing. "Can I help you fellows?" Mr. Matott asked.

"We're just curious," the boy from Monroeville said. "Came out to see what it was like."

"How long are you planning to stay?" said Mr. Matott.

"Until we get ready to leave," the boy said.

A black member of the night patrol quietly joined Mr. Matott.

"I cut classes," said the boy from Tennessee. "Sort of impulsive. You hear all these stories. I wondered why you were marching."

"Well, you might say we're marching to get to know each other and to ease a little of the hate around here," Mr. Matott said.

"You don't need to march for that," said one the boys from Texas. "You're making it worse. The hate was being lessened and lessened by itself throughout the years."

"Was it?" asked the black member of the guard.

"It was," the Texas boy said.

"We never had much trouble in Nashville," said the boy from Tennessee. "Where you have no conflict, it's hard to conceive..."

"Why don't you-all go and liberate the Indian reservations, or something?" said the boy from Monroeville. "The Negroes around here are happy."

"I don't think they are," said Mr. Matott.

"I've lived in the South all my life, and I know that they are," the boy from Georgia said.

"I'm not happy," said the black guard.

"Well, just wait awhile," said the boy from Monroeville.

An attractive blond girl in a black turtleneck sweater, denim pants, and boots now crossed the highway from the camp. "Do you know where I can get a ride to Jackson?" she asked the black guard.

"This is Casey Hayden, from SNCC. She's the granddaughter of a Texas sheriff," said the minister, introducing her to the group.

A battered car drove up, and three more white boys emerged.

"I don't mean to bug you," the black whispered to the girl, "but did you realize we're surrounded?"

"You fellows from Selma?" Miss Hayden asked, turning to the three most recent arrivals.

"Yeah," said one, who was wearing a green zippered jacket, a black shirt, and black pants, and had a crew cut.

"What do you want?" Miss Hayden asked.

"I don't know," the boy answered.

"That's an honest answer," Miss Hayden said.

"It is," the boy said.

"What do you do?" Miss Hayden asked.

"Well, Miss, I actually *work* for a living, and I can tell you it's going to be hard on all of them when this is over," the boy said. "A lot of people in town are letting their maids go."

"Well, I don't suppose I'd want to have a maid anyway," Miss Hayden said amiably. "I guess I can do most things myself."

"That's not all, though," said another boy. "It's awfully bad down the road. Nothing's happened so far, but you can't ever tell. Selma's a peace-loving place, but that Lowndes County is something else."

"I guess some of these people feel they haven't got that much to lose," Miss Hayden said.

"I know," said the boy.

"Do you understand what they're marching about?" Miss Hayden asked.

"Yeah—fighting for freedom, something like that. That's the idea, along that line. It don't mean nothing," the boy said.

"And to make money," the third young man said. "The men are getting fifteen dollars a day for marching, and the girls are really making it big."

"Is that so?" said Miss Hayden?

"Yeah. Girl came into the Selma hospital this morning, fifteen hundred dollars in her wallet. She'd slept with forty-one."

"Forty-one what?" Miss Hayden asked.

"Niggers," the young man said.

"And what did she go to the hospital for?" Miss Hayden asked.

"Well, actually, Ma'am, she bled to death," the young man said.

"Where did you hear that?" Miss Hayden asked.

"In town," the young man said. "There's not much you can do, more than keep track of everything. It's a big mess."

"Well," Miss Hayden said, "I think it's going to get better."

"Hard to say," said one of the boys as they drifted back to their cars.

At midnight in the camp, Charles Mauldin, aged seventeen, the head of the Dallas County Student Union and a student at Selma's Hudson High School, which is black, was awakened in the security tent by several guards, who ushered in a rather frightened-looking black boy.

"What's going on?" asked Charles.

The boy replied that he was trying to found a black student movement in Lowndes County.

"That's fine," said Charles.

"The principal's dead set against it," the boy said.

"Then stay underground until you've got everybody organized," Charles said. "Then if he throws one out he'll have to throw you all out."

"You with SNCC or SCLC, or what?" the boy asked.

"I'm not with anything," Charles said. "I'm with them all. I used to just go to dances in Selma on Saturday nights and not belong to anything. Then I met John Love, who was SNCC project director down here, and I felt how he just sees himself in every Negro. Then I joined the movement."

"What about your folks?" the boy asked.

"My father's a truck driver, and at first they were against it, but now they don't push me and they don't hold me back," Charles said.

"Who've you had personal run-ins with?" the boy asked.

"I haven't had personal run-ins with anybody," Charles said. "I've been in jail three times, but never more than a few hours. They needed room to put other people in. Last week, I got let out, so I just had to march and get beaten on. In January, we had a march of little kids—we called it the Tots' March—but we were afraid they might get frightened, so we joined them, and some of us got put in jail. Nothing personal about it."

"Some of us think that for the march we might be better off staying in school," the boy said.

"Well, I think if you stay in school you're saying that you're satisfied," Charles said. "We had a hundred of our teachers marching partway with us. At first, I was against the march, but then I realized that although we're probably going to get the voting bill, we still don't have a lot of other things. It's dramatic, and it's an experience, so I came. I thought of a lot of terrible things that could happen, because we're committed to nonviolence, and I'm responsible for the kids from the Selma school. But then I thought, If they killed everyone on this march, it would be nothing compared to the number of people they've killed in the last three hundred years."

"You really believe in non-violence?" the boy asked Charles.

"I do," Charles said. "I used to think of it as just a tactic, but now I believe in it all the way. Now I'd just like to be tested."

"Weren't you tested enough when you were beaten on?" the boy asked.

"No, I mean an individual test, by myself," Charles said. "It's easy to talk about non-violence, but in a lot of cases you've got to be tested, and re-inspire yourself."

By 2 A.M., hardly anyone in the camp was awake except the late-shift night security patrol and a group of radio operators in a trailer truck, which served as a base for the walkie-talkies around the campsite and in the church back in Selma. The operators kept in constant touch with Selma, where prospective marchers were still arriving by the busload. Inside the trailer were Norman Talbot, a middle-aged black man from Selma who had borrowed the trailer from his uncle and was serving as its driver ("I used to work in a junk yard, until they fired me for joining the movement. I've got a five-year-old daughter, but after that I made it my business to come out in a big way"); Pete Muilenberg, a nineteen-year-old white student on leave of absence from Dartmouth to work for COFO, the Congress of Federated Organizations, in Mississippi; and Mike

Kenney, a twenty-nine-year-old white student who had quit graduate school at Iowa State to work for SNCC.

"SNCC isn't officially involved in this march," Mr. Kenney said to a marcher who visited him in the trailer early that morning. "Although individual SNCC workers can take part if they like. They say Martin Luther King and SNCC struck a bargain: SNCC wouldn't boycott this march if SCLC would take part in a demonstration in Washington to challenge the Mississippi members of Congress. We didn't want to bring in all these outsiders, and we wanted to keep marching on that Tuesday when King turned back. Man, there are cats in Selma now from up North saying, 'Which demonstration are you going to? Which one is the best?' As though it were a college prom, or something. I tell them they ought to have sense enough to be scared. 'What do you think you're down here for? For publicity, to show how many of you there are, and to get a few heads bashed in. Nobody needs you to lead them. SCLC has got plenty of leaders.' People need SNCC, though, for the technicians. Some of us took a two-day course in short-wave-radio repair from one of our guys, Marty Schiff, so we could set up their radios for them. Then, a lot of SNCC cats have come over here from Mississippi, where the romance has worn off a bit and it's time for our experts to take over—running schools, pairing off communities with communities up North, filing legal depositions against the Mississippi congressmen and against the worst of the police.

"We're called agitators from out of state. Well, take away the connotations and agitation is what we do, but we're not outsiders. Nobody who crosses a state line is an outsider. It's the same with racial lines. I don't give a damn about the Negro race, but I don't give a damn about the white race, either. I'm interested in breaking the fetters of thought. What this march is going to do is help the Alabama Negro to break his patterns of thought. It's also going to change the marchers when they go back home. The students who went back from the Mississippi project became dynamos. It's easier to join the movement than to get out. You have this commitment. There will be SNCC workers staying behind to keep things going in

Selma. We were here, working, a year and a half before SCLC came in. Man, there's a cartoon in our Jackson office showing the SNCC power structure, and it's just one big snarl. Some of us are in favor of more central organization, but most of us believe in the mystique of the local people. We're not running the COFO project in Mississippi next summer, because of the black-white tensions in SNCC. Some of the white cats feel they're being forced out, because of the racism. But I can understand it. The white invasion put the Negro cats in a predicament. Not even their movement was their own anymore. I'm staying with it, though. Every SNCC meeting is a traumatic experience for all of us, but even the turmoil is too real, too important, for me to get out now. It's what you might call the dramatic-results mentality. Some of the leaders may be evolving some pretty far-out political philosophy, but it's the workers who get things done—black-white tensions, left-right tensions, and all."

Later that morning, Tuesday, it began to rain, and the rain continued through most of the day. When the first drops fell, whites at the roadside cheered (a Southern adage says that "a nigger won't stay out in the rain"), but it soon became apparent that, even over hilly country, the procession was going at a more spirited pace than ever. Jim Letherer, on his crutches, appeared to be flagging. John Doar walked beside him for a while, joking and imperceptibly slowing his pace. Then Mr. Doar said, "Jim, come to the car a minute. I want to show you something back down the road." Jim disappeared from the march. In twenty minutes, he was walking again.

Back in Selma, thousands of out-of-towners had arrived and had been quietly absorbed into the black ghetto. On the outskirts of town, a sign had appeared showing a photograph of Martin Luther King at the Highlander Folk School and captioned "Martin Luther King at Communist School." Lying soggily upon the sidewalks were leaflets reading "An unemployed agitator ceases to agitate. Operation Ban. Selective hiring, firing, buying, selling." The Selma Avenue Church of Christ, whose congregation is white, displayed a sign reading "When You Pray, Be Not As Hypocrites Are, Standing in the Street. Matt: 6:5," and the Brown Chapel Church displayed a sign reading "Forward Ever, Backward Never. Visitors Welcome." Inside the church and its parsonage, things were bustling. There were notes tacked everywhere: "If you don't have official business here, please leave," "All those who wish to take hot baths, contact Mrs. Lilly," "Don't sleep here anymore. This is an office," "Please, the person who is trying to find me to return my suit coat and trench-coat, not having left it in my Rambler..."

"Everyone here in town is getting antsy," Melody Heaps, a white girl who had come in from Chicago, said to a reporter. "We're not allowed to march until Thursday, and there's nothing to do. On the other hand, we're giving the Selma Negroes a chance to take it easy. They know what they're doing, and we don't, so they can order us around a little."

"You know what just happened?" said a white clergyman from Ontario. "Some of those white segs splashed mud all over us. It was so funny and childish we just howled."

A little later, two clergymen picked up their luggage and left the church for the home of Mrs. Georgia Roberts, where, they had been told, they were to spend the night.

"I guess I can put you up," Mrs. Roberts said when they arrived. "Last night, I put up fourteen. I worked as a cook at the Selma Country Club for thirteen years, before they fired me for joining the movement. I've been friendly to all the other guests, so I guess you'll find me friendly, too. I never thought I'd see the day when we'd dare to march against the white government in the Black Belt of Alabama."

At the Tuesday-night campsite, a farm owned by the A. G. Gastons, a Birmingham black family who had become millionaires in various businesses, the ground was so wet that the marchers could walk through the clay-like mud only by moving their feet as though they were skating. A black family living in the middle of the property had received several intimidating phone calls during the day, and as a consequence, they barred their house to marchers. They held a party in their little front garden to watch the goings on.

The marchers had by then been joined by Mrs. Ann Cheatham,

an English housewife from Ealing, who had flown across the Atlantic just to take part in the last two days of marching. "It seems to me an outrage," she said. "I saw it on the telly—people being battered on the head. I came to show that the English are in sympathy. I can see there are a lot of odd bods on this march, but there were a lot in the marches on Aldermaston and Washington. This appalling business of barring white facilities to Negro children! People say it's not my business, but I would deny that. It's everybody's business."

In the early evening, a clergyman became violently ill, and doctors blamed the marchers' water supply. The marchers had all along complained that the water tasted of kerosene, and, upon investigation, it turned out the water was in fact polluted, having come from a truck that was ordinarily used for draining septic tanks. (Fortunately, no other marchers seemed to suffer from the contamination.) Later, the singer Odetta appeared at the campsite, and found all the marchers, including another singer, Pete Seeger, fast asleep.

Wednesday, the fourth and last full day of marching, was sunny again, and the marchers set out in good spirits. In the morning, a minister who had rashly dropped out at a gas station to make a telephone call was punched by the owner, and a freelance newspaper photographer was struck on the ear by a passerby. (Although he required three stitches, he was heartened by the fact that a Montgomery policeman had come, with a flying tackle, to his rescue.) There seemed, however, to be fewer segregationists by the side of the road than usual—perhaps because the Montgomery *Advertiser* had been running a two-page advertisement, prepared by the City Commissioner's Committee on Community Affairs, imploring citizens to be moderate and ignore the march. The coverage of the march in the Southern press had consistently amused the marchers. "Civil Righters Led by Communists" had been the headline in the Birmingham weekly *Independent;* the Selma *Times-Journal,* whose coverage of the march was relatively accurate, had editorialized about President Johnson, under the heading "A Modern Mussolini Speaks, 'We Shall Overcome,'" "No man in any generation...has ever held so much power in the palm of his hand, and that includes Caesar, Alexander, Genghis Khan, Napoleon, and Franklin D. Roosevelt"; and the Wednesday *Advertiser's* sole front-page item concerning the march was a one-column, twenty-one-line account, lower right, of the Alabama legislature's resolution condemning the demonstrators for being "sexually promiscuous." ("It is well known that the white Southern segregationist is obsessed with fornication," said John Lewis, chairman of SNCC. "And that is why there are so many shades of Negro.") At 9 A.M., Ray Robin announced over radio station WHHY, in Montgomery, that "there is now evidence that women are returning to their homes from the march as expectant unwed mothers." Several marchers commented, ironically, on the advanced state of medical science in Alabama.

By noon, most of the marchers were sunburned or just plain weather-burned. Two blacks scrawled the word "Vote" in sunburn cream on their foreheads and were photographed planting an American flag, Iwo Jima fashion, by the side of the road. Flags of all sorts, including state flags and church flags, had materialized in the hands of marchers. One of the few segregationists watching the procession stopped his jeering for a moment when he saw the American flag, and raised his hand in a salute. The singing had abated somewhat, and the marchers had become conversational.

"This area's a study in social psychopathology," said Henry Schwarzschild, executive secretary of LCDC (the Lawyers Constitutional Defense Committee). "In a way, they're asking for a show of force like this, to make them face reality."

"And there's the ignorance," said another civil-rights lawyer. "A relatively friendly sheriff in Sunflower County, Mississippi, warned me, confidentially, that my client was a 'blue-gum nigger.' 'Their mouths are filled with poison,' he said. 'Don't let him bite you.'"

"And what did you say?" asked a college student marching beside him.

"What could I say?" the lawyer replied. "I said I'd try to be careful."

"The way I see this march," said a young man from SNCC, "is as a march from the religious to the secular—from the chapel to the statehouse. For too long now, the Southern Negro's only refuge has been the church. That's why he prefers these SCLC ministers to the SNCC cats. But we're going to change all that."

"I'm worried, though, about the Maoists," said the student.

"What do you mean by that, exactly?" asked another marcher.

"A Maoist. You know. From the Mau Mau."

In the early afternoon, Dr. King and his wife, who had dropped out for a day in order for him to go to Cleveland to receive an award, rejoined the procession. The singing began again. Marching behind Dr. King was his friend the Reverend Morris H. Tynes, of Chicago, who teased Dr. King continuously. "Moses, can you let your people rest for a minute?" Mr. Tynes said. "Can you just let the homiletic smoke from your cigarette drift out of your mouth and engulf the multitude and let them rest?" Dr. King smiled. Some of the other marchers, who had tended to speak of him half in joking, half in reverent tones (most of them referred to him conversationally as "De Lawd"), laughed out loud.

A Volkswagen bus full of marchers from Chicago ran out of gas just short of the procession. "Now, we all believe in nonviolence," one of the passengers said to the driver, "but if you don't get this thing moving pretty soon . . ."

"Are you members of some sort of group?" asked a reporter, looking inside the bus.

"No," said the driver. "We're just individuals."

At last, on the outskirts of Montgomery, the marchers reached their fourth campsite—the Catholic City of St. Jude, consisting of a church, a hospital, and a school built in a style that might be called Contemporary Romanesque. The four tents were pitched by the time they arrived, and they marched onto the grounds singing "We *Have* Overcome." They also added two new verses to the song—"All the way from Selma" and "Our feet are soaked." Inside the gates of St. Jude's, they were greeted by a crowd of Montgomery blacks singing the national anthem.

"*What* do you *want?*" the marchers chanted.

This time, the response from the onlookers was immediate and loud: "*Freedom!*"

"*When* do you *want* it?"

"*Now!*"

"How *much* of it?"

"*All* of it!"

On its fourth night, the march began to look first like a football rally, then like a carnival and a hootenanny, and finally like something dangerously close to a hysterical mob. Perhaps because of a new feeling of confidence, the security check at the main gate had been practically abandoned. Thousands of marchers poured in from Selma and Montgomery, some of them carrying luggage, and no one had time to examine its contents. The campsite was cold and almost completely dark, and a bomb or a rifle shot would have left everyone helpless. Word got out that doctors on the march had treated several cases of strep throat, two of pneumonia, one of advanced pulmonary tuberculosis, and one of epilepsy, and because of the number and variety of sick and handicapped who had made the march a macabre new joke began to go the rounds: "What has five hundred and ninety-nine legs, five hundred and ninety-eight eyes, an indeterminate number of germs, and walks singing? The march from Selma."

An entertainment had been scheduled for nine o'clock that night, but it was several hours late getting started, and in the meantime the crowd of thousands churned about in the mud and chanted. A number of people climbed into trees near the platform where the entertainment was to take place. On the outskirts of St. Jude's, in a section normally set aside as a playground, a few children spun the handpowered carrousel, or climbed over the jungle gym in the dark. In the wires of the telephone poles around the field, the skeletons of old kites were just visible in the dim lights from the windows of St. Jude's Hospital.

A minister, who had been seeking for several hours to clear the platform, wept with chagrin. "Betcha old Sheriff Clark and his troopers could clear it!" someone shouted. In the darkness, there

were repeated cries for doctors, and a soldier stood on top of the radio trailer and beamed a flashlight into the crowd, trying to find the
sources of the cries. Thousands crowded around the platform, and
several of them were pressed against it and fell. Several others, mostly
members of the special group of three hundred marchers, fainted
from exhaustion. A number of entertainers, each of whom had been
given a dime to use for a phone call in case of an emergency, and all
of whom had been instructed to stand in groups of not fewer than
six, appeared on the platform. Among them were Shelley Winters,
Sammy Davis, Jr., Tony Perkins, Tony Bennett, and Nina Simone. A
number of girls in the crowd collapsed and, because there was no
other lighted space, had to be carried onstage, where Miss Winters
did her best to minister to them. Before long, twenty people, none of
them seriously ill or seriously injured, were carried off to the hospital
on stretchers. A large group started an agitated march within the
campsite.

"I'm tired," said a white college student. "If only I could walk
someplace and get a cab!"

"Man, that's not cool," said a black. "There are a lot of hostile
people outside that gate."

"Inside it, too, for all I know," said the student. "See any white
sheets?"

Finally, the entertainment got under way, and the situation improved. Tony Perkins and a few others spoke with well-considered
brevity. The crowd clapped along with the singers as they sang folk
songs and songs of the movement, and it laughed at the comedians,
including Dick Gregory, Nipsey Russell, Mike Nichols, and Elaine
May. ("I can't afford to call up the National Guard," said Mike Nichols, impersonating Governor Wallace. "Why not?" said Elaine May,
impersonating a telegraph operator. "It only costs a dime.")

At 2 A.M., the entertainment and speeches were over, and the
performers left for a Montgomery hotel, which was surrounded for
the remainder of the night by shouting segregationists. Most of the
crowd drifted off the field and headed for Montgomery, and the
tents were left at last to the marchers. Suddenly security tightened

up. At one point, the Reverend Andrew Young himself was asked for his credentials. The hours before dawn passed without incident.

On Thursday morning, the march expanded, pulled itself together, and turned at once serious and gay. It finally seemed that the whole nation was marching to Montgomery. Signs from every conceivable place and representing every conceivable religious denomination, philosophical viewpoint, labor union, and walk of life assembled at St. Jude's and lined up in orderly fashion. A Magic Marker pen passed from hand to hand, and new signs went up: "The Peace Corps Knows Integration Works," "So Does Canada," "American Indians" (carried by Fran Poafpybitty, a Comanche from Indiahoma, Oklahoma), "Freedom" in Greek letters (carried by a black girl), "Out of Vietnam into Selma" in Korean (carried by a white girl), "The Awe and Wonder of Human Dignity We Want to Maintain" (on a sandwich board worn by a succession of people), and, on two sticks tied together, with a blue silk scarf above it, a sign reading simply "Boston." A young white man in a gray flannel suit hurried back and forth among the platoons of marchers; on his attaché case was written "D. J. Bittner, Night Security."

Near the tents, Ivanhoe Donaldson and Frank Surocco (the first a black project director for SNCC in Atlanta, the second a white boy, also from SNCC) were distributing orange plastic jackets to the original three hundred marchers. The jackets, of the sort worn by construction workers, had been bought for eighty-nine cents apiece in Atlanta, and jackets like them had been worn throughout the march by the marshals, but for the marchers the orange jacket had become a singular status symbol. There was some dispute about who was entitled to wear one. There was also a dispute about the order of march. Some thought that the entertainers should go first, some that the leaders should. Roy Wilkins, of the NAACP, demurred on behalf of the leaders. Odetta said, "Man, don't let the morale crumble. The original three hundred deserve to be first." The Reverend Andrew Young was served with a summons in an action by the City of Selma and the Selma Bus Lines protesting the operation of buses in competition with the Selma company.

Finally, after another session of virtually inaudible speeches, the parade was ready to go. "Make way for the originals!" the marshals shouted, forming a cordon to hold back the other marchers and the press. Behind the three hundred came Martin Luther King, Ralph Bunche, A. Philip Randolph, the Reverend Ralph Abernathy, the Reverend Fred L. Shuttlesworth, Charles G. Gomillion, the Reverend F. D. Reese, and other civil-rights leaders; behind them came the grandfather of Jimmie Lee Jackson, the black boy who had been shot in nearby Perry County, and the Reverend Orloff Miller, a friend of the Reverend James Reeb's, who had been beaten with Reeb on the night of Reeb's murder; and behind them came a crowd of what turned out to be more than thirty thousand people. "We're not just down here for show," said Mr. Miller. "A lot of our people are staying here to help. But the show itself is important. When civil rights drops out of the headlines, the country forgets."

Stationed, like an advance man, hundreds of yards out in front of the procession as it made its way through the black section of Montgomery and, ultimately, past a hundred and four intersections was Charles Mauldin, dressed in his Hudson High sweat shirt and blue jeans and an orange jacket, and waving a little American flag and a megaphone. One pocket of his denims was split, and the fatigue in his gentle, intelligent face made him seem considerably younger than his seventeen years. "Come and march with us!" he shouted to black bystanders. "You can't make your witness standing on the corner. Come and march with us. We're going downtown. There's nothing to be afraid of. Come and march with us!"

"Tell 'em, baby," said Frank Surocco, who was a few yards back of Charles.

"Is everything safe up ahead?" asked the voice of Ivanhoe Donaldson through a walkie-talkie.

"We watching 'em, baby," said Surocco.

"Come and march with us!" said Charles Mauldin, to black and white bystanders alike.

In midtown Montgomery, at the Jefferson Davis Hotel, black maids were looking out of the windows and the white clientele was standing on the hotel marquee. Farther along, at the Whitley Hotel, black porters were looking out of windows on one side of the building and white customers were looking out of windows on the other. Troopers watched from the roof of the Brown Printing Company. The windows of the Montgomery Citizens Council were empty. Outside the Citizens Council building, a man stood waving a Confederate flag.

"What's your name?" a reporter asked.

"None of your goddam business," said the man.

At the intersection of Montgomery Street and Dexter Avenue (the avenue leading to the capitol), Charles Mauldin turned and looked around. "They're still coming out of St. Jude's," a reporter told him. And when the vanguard of the march reached the capitol steps, they were *still* coming out of St. Jude's. "You're only likely to see three great parades in a lifetime," said John Doar to a student who walked beside him, "and this is one of them." A brown dog had joined the crowd for the march up Dexter Avenue. On the sidewalk in front of the capitol, reporters stood on the press tables to look back. Charles and the rest of the orange-jacketed three hundred stood below. Behind them, the procession was gradually drawing together and to a halt. Ahead, a few green-clad, helmeted officers of the Alabama Game and Fish Service and some state officials blocked the capitol steps, at the top of which, covering the bronze that marks the spot where Jefferson Davis was inaugurated President of the Confederacy, was a plywood shield constructed at the order of Governor Wallace—"to keep that s.o.b. King from desecrating the Cradle of the Confederacy," according to a spokesman for the Governor. Martin Luther King had managed to draw a larger crowd than the leader of the Confederacy a hundred years before.

Onto a raised platform—erected by the marchers for the occasion—in a plaza between the crowd and the steps climbed a group of entertainers that included, at one point or another, Joan Baez; the Chad Mitchell Trio; Peter, Paul, and Mary; and Harry Belafonte. As Alabamians peered from the statehouse windows, black and white performers put their arms around each other's shoulders and began to sing. Although the songs were familiar and the front rank of the three hundred mouthed a few of the words, none of the crowd really sang along. Everybody simply cheered and applauded at the end of each number. Then Len Chandler, a young black folk singer who had marched most of the way, appeared on the platform. He was dressed peculiarly, as he had been on the road—in a yellow helmet, a flaglike blue cape with white stars on it, and denims—and the crowd at once joined him in singing:

"You've got to move when the spirit say move,
Move when the spirit say move.
When the spirit say move, you've got to move, oh, Lord.
You got to move when the spirit say move."

In the subsequent verses, Mr. Chandler changed "move" to "walk," "march," "vote," "picket," "cool it," and "love," and the crowd kept singing. Joan Baez, wearing a purple velvet dress and a large bronze crucifix, even broke into a rather reverent Frug.

After an invocation by a rabbi and speeches by the Reverend Ralph Abernathy, the crowd turned away from the Confederate and Alabama state flags flying from the capitol, faced its own American flags, and sang the national anthem. At its close, the Reverend Theodore Gill, president of the San Francisco Theological Seminary, looked before and behind him and said a simple prayer: "Forgive us our trespasses." One marcher applauded, and was immediately hushed. Then there was the succession of speeches, most of them eloquent, some of them pacific ("Friends of freedom," said Whitney Young, of the Urban League), others militant ("Fellow Freedom Fighters," said John Lewis, of SNCC), and nearly all of them filled with taunts of Governor Wallace as the list of grievances, intimidations, and brutalities committed by the state piled up.

"This march has become a rescue operation," Charles Mauldin said quietly to a friend as the speeches continued. "Most of those Negroes along the way have joined us, and although this Wallace-baiting sounds like a little boy whose big brother has come home, standing outside a bully's window to jeer, these Negroes are never going to be so afraid of the bully again. When the bill goes through, they're going to vote, and the white men down here are going to think twice before they try to stop them. Big brothers have come down from the North and everywhere, and they've shown that they're ready and willing to come down again. I don't think they're going to have to."

"It's good that even a few of the civil-rights *talkers* have joined us," said another marcher. "When those people feel they have to climb on the bandwagon, you know you're on the way to victory."

As one speaker followed another, as Ralph Bunche, who had marched for two full days, and A. Philip Randolph spoke, the civil-rights leaders saluted one another and gave signs of patching up their differences. (Mr. Abernathy, second-in-command of SCLC, slipped once and said, "Now here's James Peck, for James Farmer, to tell us whether CORE is with us." Peck ignored the implications of the "whether" and spoke as eloquently as the rest.) The crowd applauded politely throughout but gave no sign of real enthusiasm. SCLC and SNCC leaders seemed to be equally popular, but the NAACP and the Urban League, more active in other states than in Alabama, seemed to require a little help from Mr. Abernathy ("Now let's give a big hand to . . .") to get their applause. Some of the marchers crawled forward under the press tables and went to sleep. A Japanese reporter, who had been taking notes in his own language, seized one of the marchers as he crawled under a table, "What do you think of all this?" the reporter asked. "I think it's good," the marcher said. Some fell asleep in their places on Dexter Avenue. (Perhaps remembering the mob scenes of the night before, the crowd left its members ample breathing space in front of the capitol.) A scuffle broke out between marchers and white bystanders in front of Klein's Jewelry Store, but no one was seriously hurt. It rained a little, and Charles Mauldin said, "Wallace is seeing the clouds."

Albert Turner, of Marion, where Jimmie Lee Jackson was murdered, said from the platform, "I look worse than anybody else on this stage. That's because I marched fifty miles." Then he read the black voting statistics from Perry County. When he said, "We are not satisfied," the crowd gave him a rousing cheer. He looked down at his orange jacket and smiled. Mrs. Amelia Boynton spoke; during the previous demonstrations, she had been kicked and beaten, and jailed, for what some members of the press have come to call "resisting assault." She read the petition, mentioning the "psychotic climate" of the State of Alabama, that a delegation of marchers was seeking to present to Governor Wallace, and she was roundly applauded. Near the end of the ceremony, Rosa Parks, the "Mother of the Movement," who had set off Dr. King's first demonstration when she was jailed for refusing to yield her seat to a white man on a bus in Montgomery, received the most enthusiastic cheers of all. "Tell it! Tell! Tell!" some of the marchers shouted. "Speak! Speak!" Finally, after an extravagant introduction by Mr. Abernathy, who referred to Dr. King as "conceived by God" ("This personality cult is getting out of hand," said a college student, and, to judge by the apathetic reception of Mr. Abernathy's words, the crowd agreed), Dr. King himself spoke. There were some enthusiastic yells of "Speak! Speak!" and "Yessir! Yessir!" from the older members of the audience when Dr. King's speech began, but at first the younger members were subdued. Gradually, the whole crowd began to be stirred. By the time he reached his refrains—"Let us march on the ballot boxes.... We're on the move now.... How long? Not long"—and the final ringing "Glory, glory, hallelujah!" the crowd was with him entirely.

The director of the march, Hosea Williams, of SCLC, said some concluding words, remarking that there should be no lingering in Montgomery that night and exhorting the crowd to leave quietly and with dignity. There was a last rendition of "We Shall Overcome." Within ten minutes, Dexter Avenue was cleared of all but the press and the troopers.

A few hours later, the delegation and its petition were turned away by Governor Wallace. At the airport, where there had been some difficulty during the preceding days (an uncanny number of suitcases belonging to marchers were mislaid by the airlines), new flights had been scheduled to get the marchers out of Montgomery. Still, many marchers had to wait at the airport all night long. They rested on the floor, and on the lawn outside, and as often as the police cleared them away they reappeared and fell asleep again. Word came that Mrs. Viola Liuzzo had been shot. Some of the marchers went back to Selma at once. Others boarded planes for home. At the Montgomery airport exit was a permanent official sign reading "Glad You Could Come. Hurry Back."

The New Yorker
April 10, 1965

FLY TRANS-LOVE AIRWAYS

ON A LITTLE patch of land just outside the city limits of Los Angeles, on that portion of Sunset Boulevard which is called Sunset Strip, there is a large billboard that advertises a casino in Las Vegas. Set on top of the billboard, dressed in red boots, long red gloves, and black-and-white striped panties attached across the midriff to a red bikini top, is an immense, pink plaster chorus girl. One of her arms is bent, hand slightly forward and upraised, at the elbow. Her other arm extends, fingers outstretched, behind. One of her knees is raised. The other leg is the one she stands and slowly, continuously rotates on. Diagonally southwest across the street from the girl, much nearer the ground, on a little pedestal, another figure in red gloves, striped panties, and red top rotates in a similar pose. It is Bullwinkle the Moose. Somewhere west of the girl and east of the moose, the jurisdiction of the Los Angeles Police Department ends and the Los Angeles County Sheriff's territory begins. Since the Strip was for a good part of its history a center of gambling and prostitution, it has always remained part of the "county island" of West Hollywood, and resisted incorporation into the City of Los Angeles. For tax reasons, and perhaps because of rumors that the gambling, at least, will be allowed to return, it resists incorporation now. Very near this border outpost, on a recent Saturday night, a small band of Dickensian characters—two tall, pale women with thin, reddish hair; one short, stout, bustling brunette; and four men, rather unsteady on their feet—set up a portable loud-speaker system on the sidewalk and began to preach. Several boys and girls who had been sitting quietly on two of the benches that line the Strip at bus stops, and several others, who had been leaning against the white picket fence that surrounds a small pink-and-yellow café called Pandora's Box—closed, like several other rock-'n'-roll and cherry-Coke establishments, by the police, on account of some recent disturbances—gathered around to watch. One of them wore a kind of harlequin cap with many floppy, green earlike appendages, from each of which there hung a silver bell. Another wore blue jeans, a suede jacket, an undershirt, a mauve tie, and a top hat. Two wore gray Confederate jackets. Several wore wooly vests over shirts with leather laces at the collar—open to reveal striped turtleneck jerseys underneath. Nearly all wore slacks cut quite low at the hips, and one wore a lumberjacket. Although the night was quite cold, three were barefoot, and one had on apparently homemade red-and-black slippers turned up at the toes. The rest wore boots. All of them stood in a loose but attentive cluster a bit to one side of the preaching band.

"My happiest moment," a man who was missing a front tooth was saying, with a practiced homiletic quaver, into the microphone, "was when I saw myself a sinner. I traded in my sins for Jesus, and, believe me, I got the best of the deal." The teen-agers drifted a short way off, and the speaker raised his voice. "I know you young people," he said. "You talk dirty and your minds are dirty. You don't want no one to have a claim on you. You don't want to be obligated. But you're obligated, sinners, because there is a God above."

"How do you know?" asked the boy in the top hat.

"Because I love God," the man said hoarsely; and as he continued to preach, one of the tall, pale women went about nudging the teen-agers and offering them inspirational tracts—among them a green one entitled "7 Communists Go Singing Into Heaven."

A Los Angeles patrol car, containing two helmeted policemen staring straight ahead, cruised by.

"Why don't they ask these hypocrites to move along?" a barefoot girl in a shaggy sweater, slacks, and yachting cap said, in a bitter voice. "They're blocking the sidewalk. They're trying to incite us to riot. They're obviously winos. How come The Man never hassles anyone but the longhairs?"

"I want to listen to this," said a short, plump girl beside her. "I haven't had such a treat in years." Suddenly, she slung her large leather purse over her shoulder, pulled a few strands of hair over one eye, and, raising the other eyebrow, began to walk slowly and suggestively back and forth in front of the speaker, who turned sideways.

"This bearded sinner tells me he is Jewish," the speaker said, pointing to a young man wearing black slacks and a black shirt, with a pair of what appeared to be calipers hung on a string around his neck. "Well, I want to tell you about the greatest Jew that ever walked the earth...."

"Yodel, Billy," the barefoot girl in the yachting cap said to the young man in black. He began to yodel. The gap-toothed man continued to preach. The tall, pale woman continued to distribute pamphlets. The short, plump girl continued to walk back and forth. A bus pulled up in front of the benches, and a gray-haired, stolid-looking couple, evidently tourists, got laboriously out.

"O Lord, O Lord, O Lord, here they are, Henry, will you look at them," the lady said, smoothing down the skirt of her dress and looking directly at the girl in the yachting cap. "I'm glad I raised mine right."

"What are you looking at, you old bag?" the short, plump girl asked, standing still for a moment.

The couple began to walk away.

"It's Sonny and Cher," the boy in the top hat said as they passed him. "I'd know them anywhere."

The gap-toothed man had leaned away from his microphone and was now addressing the group in a rather intimate tone about "your dirty, filthy sins and your unclean habits."

The boy in the lumberjacket, who had been looking for some time at the girl in the yachting cap, suddenly walked over and took her hand. He led her wordlessly to a point directly in front of the man who was speaking, and kissed her. When, after several minutes, they looked up, the gap-toothed man (although he watched them with apparent fascination) was still preaching, so they kissed again and remained in each other's arms until the sound of a guitar farther down the street—in front of a café called the Fifth Estate—caused the teen-age group to disperse and drift toward the music.

"Before you go to bed this very night..." the speaker was saying, as the young longhairs walked away. And several of them tried—with such phrases as "turn on," "freak out," and "take the pill"—to complete his sentence for him.

What seems to have brought the Strip to its present impasse—it is practically deserted but for these little evangelical bands of elderly squares and young longhairs, bent on mutual conversion—was an economic battle with, and over, teen-agers; and what apparently drew the teen-agers to the Strip in the first place was a musical development. In the late fifties and early sixties, by all accounts, the Strip was dull. The old, expensive restaurants, left over from the golden days of Hollywood, were in a steep decline. Near the middle of the Strip, there was (and still is) an attractive stretch of clothing and antique shops called Sunset Plaza, but the rest was lined (and is) with hot-dog stands, car-rental agencies, and billboards—changed with the rapidity of flash cards—advertising casinos, airlines, films, and mortuaries.

Then, in 1963, a southern California surf-rock group, the Beach Boys, acquired a national reputation, and, beginning in 1964, the Los Angeles area—with Sonny and Cher, the Byrds, the Mamas and the Papas, the Lovin' Spoonful, and such indigenous and locally popular groups as Love, the Seeds, Iron Butterfly, and Buffalo Springfield—became a center for all kinds of rock. Phil Spector, the record producer, set up offices on the Strip; a huge teen dance hall called the Hullabaloo opened down the boulevard; and a number of night clubs on the Strip went rock. This drew—in addition to the teen-age clientele—some established, serious longhairs from the two-car bohemia in the canyons above the boulevard, more serious longhairs from the less affluent bohemias of Venice and Long Beach, and some motorcycle groups. The motorcycle groups were soon dispersed; a hint from a Sunset Plaza merchants' association caused red no-parking lines to be painted all along the curb where the motorcyclists were accustomed to park, and a hot-dog stand called the Plush Pup put up a sign announcing that complaints from neighbors had made it impossible for the place to welcome guests on motorcycles. The serious longhairs were soon made uncomfortable, too; some of their favorite haunts, like the Trip and the Action, were closed for various reasons, and the Strip itself became a very difficult place for the marijuana, drug, or LSD users among them to make a connection.

The serious longhairs returned—temporarily, at least—to their beaches and canyons; the teen-agers, however, remained awhile. The notorious sprawl of Los Angeles—where, for example, it may take a maid two and a half hours to make her way by bus from Watts to Beverly Hills—leaves the city at night diffused and lifeless. The Strip became a kind of Main Street where the young (who drove or hitched a ride from the surrounding area) could spend their time. They soon came in such numbers that they brought traffic nearly to a halt. Restaurant proprietors on the Strip, who saw their business dwindling even further, took steps. All last summer, invoking an old city-and-county curfew law that prohibits people under eighteen from lingering on the street after 10 P.M., the sheriff's men were stopping people with long hair or wearing unusual clothes to demand identification (draft cards, driver's licenses), as proof of age. In addition, a number of ad-hoc ordinances were put into effect. Twenty-one is the legal drinking age in California, but people eighteen and over had for years been welcome to dance at rock establishments with liquor licenses, where the minors got Cokes, while drinks were served to their elders; under a new ordinance, no one under twenty-one was permitted to dance in a place where liquor was served.

The Whisky a Go Go, once an important center for West Coast rock and one of the few places on the Strip to survive this legal maneuver, tried several solutions, in series. First, it continued serving liquor and put minors on benches in the balcony, but the young customers, who wanted to dance, went elsewhere. Then it stopped serving liquor and raised its admission price from two dollars to three; the minors came back, but the attractive liquor profits were lost. A few weeks ago, the Whisky enlarged its stage to occupy the entire dance floor, which means that there is no room to dance while a live performance is on. It also raised the price of admission to three-fifty, started serving liquor again, and required guests between eighteen and twenty-one to have their hands marked with an ultraviolet stamp, so that they would be easily identifiable as below drinking and dancing age. At the same time, the Whisky's entertainment went *Motown*—a change that the teen-agers, for complicated reasons of their own, associate with the return of the Mafia and Las Vegas interests to the Strip. (Young longhairs are almost unanimous in their conviction that they were cleared off the Strip to make room for more serious, less conspicuous forms of vice than lingering after curfew.) In any case, the Whisky's action could only make teen-agers feel less welcome there. Throughout the spring and summer, licenses permitting minors to be served anything at all were revoked at one place after another; several of these places reluctantly went adult and topless—a change that seemed to cause the authorities no distress. Gradually, the campaign worked. Few but the hardiest or most lost teen-agers cared to risk the "hassle" that awaited them on the Strip.

Then, just before Halloween, two high-school students mimeographed a hundred leaflets announcing a "demonstration" for the evening of November 12, 1966, in front of Pandora's Box, to protest "Police Mistreatment of Youth," and Al Mitchell, a former seaman in the merchant marine who runs the Fifth Estate, gave them the money to print a few thousand more. Mitchell, a moderate-looking man in his middle forties, had shot a film about the striking grape pickers of California, and he was preparing *Blue Fascism*, a documentary about the Los Angeles Police Department, at the time the leaflets were put out. On November 12, a crowd of thousands— high-school students, dropouts, New Left university students, parolees from a nearby reform school, serious longhairs, squares, runaways, sympathizers, passersby, and the merely curious—gathered in front of Pandora's Box, and Mitchell got more footage than he had anticipated. The crowd, through its sheer size, stopped traffic for a considerable period, and a few of its members caused a total of a hundred and fifty-eight dollars' worth of damage to a bus and a liquor store. (In a demonstration some weeks before, several UCLA football fans—disappointed that USC rather than their own team had been invited to the Rose Bowl—stopped every single car on the San Diego Freeway, ostensibly to see whether there were any USC students inside; the UCLA fans probably caused more damage, and certainly caused less outrage, than the crowd outside Pandora's Box.)

The Los Angeles police began to attack the crowd with billy clubs from the eastern side, driving them westward along the Strip. The sheriff's men, standing across the county line, saw what they thought was a hostile crowd of longhairs advancing on them and took action. Several people were hurt, others arrested. Later that night, when a group of teen-agers were gathered in Pandora's Box listening to a shy and talented group called the World War III, the police surrounded the building and ordered the management to close in seven minutes. A police bus pulled up and policemen pounded on the walls of Pandora's Box and ordered the occupants out—to arrest them for loitering after 10 P.M. William Tilden, a soft-spoken man in his thirties, who has managed Pandora's Box for seven years, let the teen-agers telephone their homes for permission to stay overnight. They finally left when the police were called off, about three in the morning. In the following weeks, Tilden was arrested on a felony charge—alleged assault on two police officers—for which he has yet to stand trial, Pandora's Box was closed and condemned, and a highway project that was to have demolished the place in 1969 was accelerated.

Since a teen-age establishment under suspension of license may legally open on holidays, Tilden opened his place on New Year's Eve. There was not room enough inside to dance, but the World War III played for several hours to a colorful, quiet audience. Tilden himself stood rather sadly outside, replying to a question posed by several young longhairs—whether he might open the place one day as a private club. He did not know; it depended on the outcome of his trial. There was an elegiac air to the occasion, and something incongruous: like a scene from *A Midsummer Night's Dream* taking place in a bomb shelter. On other evenings, there had been some demonstrations with which Al Mitchell was not involved, and two (on November 26th and on December 10th) with which he was. (He had asked Tilden to join him, but Tilden declined.) By this time, however, Mitchell had founded RAMCOM (the Rights of Assembly and Movement Committee), and he had been joined by an organization called CAFF (Community Action for Facts and Freedom), which included, among others, Lance Reventlow and the managers of the Beach Boys and the Byrds; by various unaffiliated parents, clergymen, and concerned adults in the community at large; and, indirectly, by the Provos, an anonymous anarchical group (whose original branch was formed in Holland), who complicated matters delightfully by singing Christmas carols on the Strip before Christmas, and on several occasions after. In mid-December, RAMCOM and CAFF negotiated a truce with the police—a truce that despite RAMCOM posters reading "Police Capitulate," has so far consisted only of a ban on demonstrations from the teen-age side.

All this profusion of issues and organizations seems to have bred a special California variety of cause-dilettante—hobby-activists who spend their leisure hours no longer even picketing but simply milling about on behalf of something until the police arrive and hit someone. The Strip demonstrations brought together yet again, under the general heading of Protest, those familiar adult co-demonstators— New Radicals, Zen mystics, aesthetic avant-gardists, and drug proselytizers—already so strangely easy in each other's company. They also brought police, wielding clubs on behalf of specific economic interests. The teen-agers (whom the police harassed, and on whose account the demonstrations were held) saw two life styles not so much in conflict as freezing each other into attitudes: on the one hand, the constellation that is longhair, bohemia, the New Left, individualism, sexual freedom, the East, drugs, the arts; on the other, arms, uniforms, conformity, the Right, convention, Red-baiting, authority, the System.

Some middle-hairs who were previously uncommitted made their choice—and thereby made more acute a division that had already existed between them. At Palisades High School, in a high-income suburb of Los Angeles, members of the football team shaved their heads by way of counter-protest to the incursions of the long-hairs. The longhairs, meanwhile, withdrew from the competitive life of what they refer to as the Yahoos—sports, grades, class elections, popularity contests—to devote themselves to music, poetry, and contemplation. It is not unlikely that a prosperous, more automated economy will make it possible for this split to persist into adult life: the Yahoos, on an essentially military model, occupying jobs; the longhairs, on an artistic model, devising ways of spending leisure time. At the moment, however, there is a growing fringe of waifs, vaguely committed to a moral drift that emerged for them from the confrontations on the Strip and from the general climate of events. The drift is Love; and the word, as it is now used among the teen-agers of California (and as it appears in the lyrics of their songs), embodies dreams of sexual liberation, sweetness, peace on earth, equality—and, strangely, drugs.

The way the drugs came into Love seems to be this: As the waifs abandoned the social mystique of their elders (work, repression, the power struggle), they looked for new magic and new mysteries. And the prophets of chemical insight, who claimed the same devotion to Love and the same lack of interest in the power struggle as the waifs, were only too glad to supply them. Allen Ginsberg, in an article entitled "Renaissance or Die," which appeared in the *Los Angeles Free Press* (a local New Left newspaper) last December, urged that "everybody who hears my voice, directly or indirectly, try the chemical LSD at least once, every man, woman, and child American in good health over the age of fourteen," and Richard Alpert (the former psychedelic teammate of Timothy Leary), in an article in *Oracle* (a newspaper of the hallucinogenic set), promised, "In about seven or eight years the psychedelic population of the United States will be able to vote anybody into office they want to, right? Through purely legal channels, right?" The new waifs, who, like many others in an age of ambiguities, are drawn to any expression of certainty or confidence, any semblance of vitality or inner happiness, have, under pressure and on the strength of such promises, gradually dropped out, in the Leary sense, to the point where they are economically unfit, devoutly bent on powerlessness, and where they can be used. They are used by the Left and the drug cultists to swell their ranks. They are used by politicians of the Right to attack the Left. And they are used by their more conventional peers just to brighten the landscape and slow down the race a little. The waifs drift about the centers of longhair activism, proselytizing for LSD and Methedrine (with arguments only slightly more extreme than the ones liberals use on behalf of fluoridation), and there is a strong possibility that although they speak of ruling the world with Love, they will simply vanish, like the children of the Children's Crusade, leaving just a trace of color and gentleness in their wake.

The Fifth Estate, a white stucco structure, managed by Mitchell and, until three weeks ago, owned by a publishing house that puts out *Teen, Hot Rod*, and *Guns and Ammo* magazines (and whose head, Robert E. Petersen, was, until recently, a city commissioner appointed by Mayor Samuel Yorty), used to be entered through a patio enclosed on two sides by one white and one yellow wall. The white wall, which faces the sidewalk, has been painted with black letters that spell out "WELCOME TO LOS ANGELES: CITY OF BLUE FASCISM." The yellow wall has become little more than a tilted arch over an immense hole and a complicated pile of debris. One Monday morning in January, a motorist veered from the westbound lane of the Strip, crossed the eastbound lane, and drove through the yellow wall, across the patio, through a large picture window, and into a room at the Fifth Estate in which films used to be shown. Since the accident happened at 4:30 A.M., no films were being shown at the time. Police who investigated claim that the driver had fallen asleep at the wheel. But a boy who was sitting in the room on a folding chair when the car drove in believes the man was merely drunk.

The Fifth Estate serves coffee, hot chocolate, Cokes, and sandwiches, but its customers do not normally eat or drink much. They play cards or chess at large, round tables, or they talk. Some of them, who earn their keep by looking after the place, sleep there. (The coffeehouse is, in any case, open until 6 A.M.) Because the Fifth Estate has no entertainment license, no one is permitted to sing or to play the guitar inside, and among writings and sketches covering the walls there is a warning to this effect. (The sheriff's men, equipped with glaring flashlights, run frequent checks in search of addicts and runaways, and to see that no one inside is playing or singing.) What playing or singing there is occurs outside, in the alleyway or near the painted wall in front.

On the patio of the Fifth Estate, on a recent Thursday night (Al Mitchell, the manager, was in a back room discussing with a young lawyer from the American Civil Liberties Union the possibility of deluging the Los Angeles Police Department with lawsuits, not in any hope of winning them but for nuisance value), a few young longhairs were gathered, more or less waiting around. One of the curious things about the young longhairs on the Strip these days is the special air with which they wait around: they seem already to inhabit some sort of leisure-time frontier, where all social problems have been solved and there remain no injustices but the ones in nature, where there is nothing to do but to wait in some small café for the coming of the Word. On this occasion, the waiting young longhairs (who will be presented here under fictional first names to protect their privacy) were Zak, a twenty-two-year-old, with sideburns, from Chicago; Marie, eighteen, Zak's girl, who lives more or less with her parents in Los Angeles; Dot, another eighteen-year-old girl (wearing a dress made of white lace over burgundy satin, pale burgundy tights, and black ballet slippers, and, around her neck, a string of Indian bells), who lives with the family of another girl, "because my mother and I don't get along"; and Len, a seventeen-year-old waiter and boarder at the Fifth Estate, who had left his home in New Jersey early in October with a friend (who got homesick and hitch-hiked back after a week). There was also another longhair, obviously much older than the rest, whose vest was covered with buttons reading "Jesus Pleases," "Come to Middle Earth," and "At Least George Murphy Could Dance," among other things, and who was reading a copy of the *Free Press*.

Len, who said he planned to return home "as soon as they don't need my help out here anymore," expressed sorrow that he had forgotten to write to his eleven-year-old sister on her birthday.

"I never know what to write home," Zak said, scuffing one of his boots on the stones. "What am I going to write? Hello, I'm here, you're there, hello? What else is there to say? It's always a hassle."

Dot said she would be returning to her own house for a few days, to babysit with her younger brother and sister while her parents went on a holiday to Las Vegas. (The frequency with which California teen-agers are asked to care for their younger siblings, or their friends' siblings, creates a thriving nomad-baby-sitter economy.) She asked Zak and Marie whether they would pick her up the following evening—to go first to the studio of a sculptor named Vito, and later on (from 2 to 6 A.M.) to a rock session called the After Hours at the Hullabaloo.

Zak said he couldn't afford it. He had invested all his money in applying for a license to open a coffeehouse—which, since the name "The Trip" was already taken, he hoped to call The Travel Agency. His application had made no progress at all, and he was waiting for Al Mitchell, who had promised to let him call his coffeehouse, for a time, the Fifth Estate Annex. Marie said she would hitch a ride to Dot's place, without Zak, and she and Dot could hitch a ride to Vito's place together.

A young man, fairly conventionally dressed and coiffed, crossed the patio toward the group. "Has the Man been here tonight?" he asked, speaking low and rapidly.

"No," Zak said.

The young man immediately removed his jacket and tie, and

brushed what proved to be an astonishing amount of hair forward from behind his ears. "Out there, I have to think of my job," he said, and slouched against a wall to wait around with the rest.

The *Free Press* recently opened a bookstore on Fairfax Avenue, which intersects Sunset Boulevard a few yards from the eastern end of the Strip. The store is right across the street from Canter's Restaurant, a large delicatessen, inside and in front of which, for some months now, the longhairs—old and young, and of every persuasion—have been gathering at two every morning. The reaction of the restaurant's manager to the types who now frequent his place is less than hospitable; he comments, as they pass to their tables, "What a sight!" and "Why don't they wash?" and he stands, vigilant, at the cash register to block the entrance of anyone who is not wearing shoes. (A policeman outside tries to keep the crowd there from blocking the sidewalk and from engaging in traffic in marijuana or drugs.) The *Free Press* bookstore, called the Kazoo, is open from ten in the morning until 2 A.M. In addition to a very wide and good selection of paperbacks, it sells many books and pamphlets about the assassination of President Kennedy, innumerable little magazines and obscure works (including a six-page poem, "The Love Book," by Lenore Kandel, which was recently confiscated on grounds of obscenity in San Francisco), many works on drugs and hallucinogens, and some works on religions of the East (including one called *Practical Mysticism*). There is also a counter at which the shop sells objets d'art, buttons ("Ronald Reagan for Fuehrer," "Be Creative, Invent a Sexual Perversion," "Visit Your Mother Today. Maybe She Hasn't Had Any Problems Lately"), posters of movie stars, psychedelic (systematically distorted and ballooning) posters for rock groups, pastel cigarette papers, and holders, called "roach clips," for conserving the last drag on marijuana butts.

At 1 A.M. on the Friday when Marie and Dot were to hitch a ride to Vito's, John Hammond, a bearded clerk at the Kazoo, was consoling a teen-age girl who had walked into the store in tears. "A little LSD therapy is okay, but nothing with needles," he was saying. "You want to open yourself up, not close yourself down. Find the easiest way to go, and if it's functional, that's beautiful." Some of the other clerks were knocking down walls to make room for a bookshelf, and Mrs. Art Kunkin, wife of the editor and publisher of the *Free Press*, was talking with two young entrepreneurs who were earning part of their way through college by distributing—to order—posters, bumper stickers, decals for sweat shirts, flutes, and buttons. It turned out they could supply, in particular, some highly coveted Lenny Bruce posters, and Mrs. Kunkin asked whether they could deliver a few dozen right away. She sighed as they went out the door. "It's always nice to have a brush with the ultimate success," she said.

That same morning, farther up Fairfax Avenue, in front of a coffeehouse called the Blue Grotto, whose customers generally sit about in semi-darkness in a kind of gentle half sleep, the police arrested two young longhairs on suspicion of armed robbery.

At eleven-thirty that Friday night, when Dot (still wearing the dress of white lace over burgundy satin and the string of Indian bells, but now with white net stockings and black buckled shoes) and Marie (wearing a pale-green dress, white net stockings, and brown buckled shoes) entered the home and sculpture school of Vito Paulekas—a storefront and three floors, known to all simply as Vito's place—the entryway was dark, but the pale bare feet of a young man slouched on a chair against the wall were visible. Vito called to the girls from the top of a flight of stairs to go down and see the sculptures in the basement. They went down. The sculpture class for the evening was over, but several people were still at work on red clay nudes, supported by dowels and wire armatures. The basement walls were covered with signs, among them a thinly lettered one reading, "Dear President Johnson. Being spring, I would prefer more flowers."

A woman in a canvas shirt, burlap slacks, and boots, who was modelling a large bust of a man, asked Dot to come over and look. "What does he look like to you?" she asked. "I mean, what sort of person?"

"He looks like a groovy guy," Dot said.

"I mean, what sort of impression does he make? Does he attract you physically?" the woman asked.

Before Dot could answer, a tall, slender girl in a polo shirt and blue jeans—looking about sixteen, and wearing a scalloped horn from an old phonograph on her head—drew Dot away to look at a small erotic sculpture, on a shelf full of small erotic sculptures, all of which (like the lettering on the psychedelic posters at the Kazoo) were distorted, like reflections in a hall of mirrors. "I just made this new one tonight," she said. "What do you think of it? It's Vito and Sue. Isn't it groovy?" (Sue is Vito's wife.)

Dot said that the little sculpture was groovy, and the girl led the way upstairs. It turned out that her name was Meg, that her parents brought her to stay at Vito's house every weekend, and that she was twelve.

The second floor of Vito's house is a kind of lair, with Oriental decor, Oriental music piped in from below, and walls hung with tapestries, bits of colored glass, feather dusters, beads, dolls, a dart board, a bamboo screen, a violin, and an armadillo shell. Between two sofas set against opposite walls is a coffee table supported by cinder blocks. On the table that night were a copy of *Time*, several delicately painted tongue depressors, some assorted photographs, a piece of velvet, a branch of pussy willow, a copy of *Playboy*, a copy of *Torrid Cinema* (with an article about Vito in it), a half-completed pair of red-and-black leather sandals turned up at the toes, and a pot of glue. The young man whose bare feet had been visible in the entryway had followed Dot, Marie, and Meg up the stairs. He immediately picked up the pot of glue and began to sniff.

"Hey, that's for the sandals," Meg said. "You know nobody gets high in Vito's house."

The boy put the gluepot down.

Vito, a man in his early fifties, with a sandy mustache and pale-blue eyes, entered the room and said hello to everyone. He was wearing velvet slacks and a pale embroidered cape. Sue, who was pregnant, followed him in. She was wearing a short dress, tights, and a crocheted poncho, and on her fingers she had eight rings. Vito announced that they were both going to take a nap in preparation for the After Hours at the Hullabaloo. Meg suddenly became very tense, and raced out of the room. "What shall I wear?" she shouted several times to Sue from an adjoining room. "Same thing we wear to the freakouts?" When she reappeared, she had drawn fine interlacing green lines around her eyes and across the bridge of her nose. She was wearing a poncho, completely open at the sides, apparently made out of a fluffy white bedspread, and a pair of slacks, which the poncho did not quite reach, made of the same material, bell-bottomed, and cut low at the hips. Vito and Sue retired for their nap, requesting Meg to wake them at 1 A.M.

Meg sat down next to Dot and Marie, and explained that Vito had arranged for them all to dance at the Hullabaloo as performers, because of a complicated licensing regulation. "They're wiping out the dancing, so everybody's getting zonked out, right?" she said. "As soon as everybody's on one thing, they make it illegal. Some of those kids they arrest on the Strip, you know, they call up the parents and say, 'We've got your kid on suspicion of narcotics.' 'Suspicion of narcotics.' They just don't like the kids and the dancing. They could arrest you on suspicion of being a Martian. They could arrest you for using the wrong deodorant."

"People don't think," Dot said. "It was dead on the Strip without the kids there."

"They're going to be locked in their own houses sooner or later without us, and they don't even know it," Meg said. "But a whole lot of people are strange. I'm not even sure they're well—are you ready for that? Everybody should dance, and love, and go about their business, right? But those poor cops, those poor screwed-up cops, they don't have the words to yell, so they just scream, you know—they just came down the Strip screaming. They're frightened, right?"

"Nobody had guns," Marie said, referring to the night of November 12th.

"They didn't have guns," Meg said. "They were afraid they'd use them, they were that screwed up."

"They were afraid if they brought guns, the guns would get broken," Marie said. "We would have broken them."

"Man, if you have this hostility, you learn to take it out in loving ways," Meg said. "If you love somebody, you really groove with them, right? I'm writing things down in a book for myself, because my parents—well, they're very beautiful for their own thing, but they just don't know."

"My parents just can't stand it," Marie said. "They can't stand my bare feet. They can't stand to see me sleep all day. They say, 'You ought to find a job. You ought to be self-supporting.' I say, 'Why? All I do is sleep here once in a while. Why can't I have a free life?' My mother worries about the people I hang out with. I can't explain—people aren't what they look like or what they wear. . . .'"

"You're judged by the people you run with, right?" Meg said. "I'm adopted, and my parents really love me. And that's too bad, because my real mother was probably some unwed mother that I could have grooved with." She picked up the pussy willow and waved it thoughtfully. "Sometimes I'm so messed up you don't even know," she said. "I'm not even sure if I'm really here."

"I worry about that, too," Marie said. "Sometimes I think I'm dead and I'm hallucinating the whole thing."

Three girls, all dressed in dark-blue skirts and jackets, with dark-blue hats, and with lace handkerchiefs in their jacket pockets, came up the staircase, looked around, and silently went down the stairs again.

Meg, whose slacks were splitting slightly at the seams, took them off, went to get a needle and some thread, and sat down to sew.

"Have you ever had the idea you might be in somebody else's dream?" Dot asked.

"Well, if you're hallucinating the whole thing, you can change it, right?" Meg said, biting off the thread. "It's like when you're having a bad trip—you see what's real, or what you think is real, and you get upset. You've got to say to yourself, 'You're on a drug, it's only a drug.' Sometimes it takes awhile to change it. But can you imagine how creative your mind must be if you're dreaming the whole thing?"

The conversation stayed on metaphysics for another hour, during which the girls in the dark suits appeared twice more and the boy with bare feet never uttered a word. At one point, Dot and Meg began to reminisce about how they had become acquainted—in a juvenile home, where Meg had been sent as a "habitual runaway," and Dot for the vaguer offense of what she described as being "in danger of leading an idle and desolate life." They spoke of a ghost story the Mexican inmates used to tell—about "La Harona," a woman who, crazed by syphilis, killed her children.

"They said if you shouted 'La Harona!' five times, she would come to you," Meg said, "and a lot of kids in my unit wanted to test it."

"I was so terrified I cried all night," Dot said. "They said she comes through mirrors." Both girls still seemed terrified at this thought.

"Wouldn't it be funny if you could look at yourself without looking in a mirror?" Meg said. Then she began talking about a boy friend who had first brought her to Vito's. "I was completely freaked out at the time," she said. "Pete just brought me here, and I grooved on the place. He used to wear two belts and wild flowers. Now he plays in a jazz group and wears a suit, but I still love him. The chick he married loves me, too, but I think two's company."

One of the three girls in blue suits now appeared at the top of the stairs again, wearing gold-rimmed glasses and carrying a piece of the red clay. She began to dance by herself.

Dot and Meg spoke of their last day at the juvenile home. They had sculpted a large eye together in an art class, and they had asked for permission to take it with them when they left.

"But the teacher at juvey said, 'You have to finish it,'" Meg said. "And, of course, we told her it was finished. But she said, 'No, that isn't finished, you have to paint it.'" "So we didn't get to take it," Dot said.

By this time, Vito and Sue were getting up from their nap, and a crowd gradually assembled at the top of the stairs. A fourth girl in dark blue now joined the three others. An Oriental boy in a paisley shirt and suede pants appeared, and then a girl in a scarlet pants suit, and one in a purple pants suit (both wore matching derbies and ties), and a man in what looked like a matador outfit, a man with chaps and a ten-gallon hat, a girl in a piece of silk bordered and tufted with fur, a girl in a fringed deerslayer jacket and orange bell-bottom trousers, a bearded man in a kind of bishop's mantle, and several others in puff hats or floppy hats or with red bows tied all over their hair. The entire group departed in four carloads for Sunset Boulevard, to dance onstage in the After Hours at the Hullabaloo.

At 2 A.M. on Saturday, January 14th, the Hullabaloo, which holds about two thousand people, and which lies directly across the boulevard from the Hollywood Palladium (where, earlier that evening, Lawrence Welk had played for the National Smooth Dancer's Association Ball), was so full that the longhairs waiting outside occupied the entire block, not in any sort of line but extending radially over the area. A parking lot beside the Hullabaloo was full of cars, nearly all with their radios on, so a kind of concert of Donovan, the Beach Boys, Sonny and Cher, and Buffalo Springfield ("Fly translove airways / Getcha there on time.... Gotta keep those a'lovin' vibrations a'happenin' with her.... The beat goes on.... Paranoia strikes deep / Into your life it will creep") was rising from the asphalt. Vito led his group in among the cars and around to the back of the building, where, after being questioned only briefly at the entrance, he smuggled them as "performers" up a ramp, and onto the back of the stage. Since the hours before morning had been Friday the thirteenth, thirteen groups were scheduled to play: the Sound Machine, the Mandala, the Peanut Butter Conspiracy, the Smokestack Lightning, the Factory, the Electric Prune, the Yellow Payges, the Sons of Adam, the Coloring Book, the Wild Ones, Iron Butterfly, the Seeds, and Love. The stage floor was a rotating platform divided in two by a backdrop curtain, so that while one group was playing the next could be warming up. (This arrangement created a sound backstage not unlike the one intentionally produced by some of the groups in the course of their normal engagements. Love, for example, often plays with someone else's record of another song as background music.) The area backstage was full of people in costumes of one sort or another—denims, satins, burlaps, suedes, and one tutu. A lonely troubadour wearing knickers and a ruffled shirt walked around throughout the performances strumming a guitar. No one seemed to know him, and he was not a member of any group.

When the Sound Machine started to play, with a beat so deeply resonant that many members of the audience began to cough, Vito sent some of his group onstage. These included Meg, Dot, the barefoot boy, Vito's pregnant wife, and six others, and from the reaction of the audience—a polite but unsurprised attentiveness—it was obvious that they had seen the group before. Meg raised her arms and began to run quite gracefully about the stage, Dot began to bend at the waist and straighten up with regularity, as though she were keening, Sue began to wave her arms about in the air, pivot, and droop from side to side, and the barefoot boy began to sway quietly in place. The others frugged or improvised. The members of Vito's troupe who had remained backstage soon grew restless, and Vito kept promising them that they could go on at any moment. But the girl in the tutu could bear it no longer; she ran out onstage. A few seconds later, Meg's pants began to split again, and some of the audience started to laugh—though not unkindly—and applaud. Meg, looking rather frantic about the eyes, arrived backstage.

"Fix your pants, baby," Vito said quite calmly, producing what he called a "fraternity button," designed by him. "Just relax." Meg took the button, pinned her pants, and returned onstage.

By 5 A.M., six groups had played, and the Monkees, the Miracles, and the Mamas and the Papas had joined the audience. Vito's group had been taken offstage earlier when it was announced that all further dancing would be done by two union dancers, in red spangles, on the balconies of the dance hall. Within moments, however, the two union dancers had been supplemented by a dancer in a silver costume and silver boots, who materialized onstage, and since no one seemed to know whether she was union or not, Vito took this as a cue to send his group back onstage, where they remained. The size of the audience had not diminished in the slightest, nor had the volume of the radio concert in the parking lot. At five, there was a pause, and both the audience and Vito's group seemed tense; everyone was quite sure that it was Love's turn to play. By five-twenty, when there was still no sign of Love, the management was trying to divert the crowd with jukebox music. The audience, however, appeared quite accustomed to delays of this sort; the pause seemed to bear out their expectation that Love would be the next group to go on.

It was. A record was cut off abruptly, the front curtain rose, a group of four whites and three blacks was revealed, and the lead singer, dressed in a black stocking cap and brown pants and vest, leaned slightly sideways, yawned briefly, and began to sing. The group, with what seemed a kind of driving, electronic desperation, played a song called "My Flash on You." When the song was over, the audience cheered a kind of desperation cheer, as one might cheer an acquittal verdict for a defendant against whom the case looked bad. The group played two more numbers, and then, in the middle of a song called "She Comes in Colors," the lead singer walked off. He did not return for several minutes, but the group played on. Then, when he did return, he ignored the microphone and sat down abruptly on a crate amid the electronic equipment. Several times, as the group still played, he seemed on the point of rising but sat down again. Finally, he rose, walked carefully forward, and, grasping the microphone, leaned forward a few moments, with teeth bared, and began to sing. He sang a long time, then stopped and let the group play several minutes more. Suddenly, in a calm speaking voice, he wished the audience a Merry Christmas and reminded them that Halloween might soon return. The front curtain dropped. The audience cheered again.

There was another extended pause, and then the Seeds appeared. They were greeted with an affection almost as obvious and ardent as the reception given Love. Shortly after the Seeds had finished, the Peanut Butter Conspiracy began to play. And shortly after that (since the Hullabaloo is permitted to stay open only until 6 A.M.) the police, by unplugging the Conspiracy's electronic equipment and rounding up Vito's obviously exhausted but still enthusiastic dancers, induced the audience to leave. Only eight groups out of the

scheduled thirteen had played, but the After Hours at the Hullabaloo was over.

In the early hours of the morning, posters had appeared at the
Fifth Estate and the Kazoo and outside the Hullabaloo and Pandora's Box announcing "A Gathering of All Tribes, a Human Be-In,"
for noon on Saturday, in Los Angeles' Griffith Park—in sympathy
with a similar event, with Allen Ginsberg, Timothy Leary, and Dick
Gregory, to be held at the same hour in San Francisco. By 1:30 P.M.
on Saturday, the park, which is in the canyons above Sunset Boulevard, had the air of a small-town picnic ground, with, instead of
friendly interlocking groups from the Lions, Kiwanis, and Rotary,
friendly interlocking groups from the drug, New Left, and teen-rock
establishments. The Sound Machine was playing once again. Someone was distributing olive branches. Someone else was selling *Oracle*. Someone else was selling colored paper flowers. A fourth person
was giving paper flowers away. Several people had brought their children, their dogs, and, in paper bags, their lunch. One young man
was lying barefoot on the grass (it was a sunny day) with an Army
helmet, painted gold, over his face; he kept running his fingers softly
across the top of a lunchbox at his side. A St. Bernard with a paper
flower in its collar was licking the young man's toes. Several transistor radios were playing softly. Vito and Meg were there, and so were
Marie and Dot, the bearded clerk from the Kazoo and the girl he
had consoled, and the boy who had not written to his eleven-year-
old sister in New Jersey. A photographer for a fashion-trade publication was unobtrusively taking pictures. There were no police around
at all.

The New Yorker
February 25, 1967

LETTER FROM THE SIX-DAY WAR

IN THE years since 1948, when Israel fought its war of independence against Egypt, Jordan, Syria, Lebanon, and Iraq, the Israeli government had to prepare for, among other undesirable contingencies, what the defense establishment referred to as Mikre Hakol (the Eventuality of Everybody)—a concerted attack upon Israel by all the Arab countries along its uneven, militarily and geographically unsound frontier. Until two weeks ago, the possibility of Mikre Hakol seemed quite remote. Then, by an incredible series of overlapping miscalculations by almost everyone involved in the Middle East, Israel was brought to the brink of annihilation, the United Nations—which, in a sense, had been born as a peacekeeping force in Palestine in 1949— was about to dissolve as even a useful forum over the same question in 1967, and the Soviet Union and United States narrowly missed a nuclear confrontation. The rapidity with which Israel won the war (for such a small country there could be, in fact, no such thing as winning slowly) seems to have bailed out the great powers and the UN (although a statement by French Foreign Minister Couve de Murville, on June 7th, to the effect that France had foreseen the satisfactory outcome of events was greeted with hoots in the French Assembly, and British Foreign Minister George Brown found it necessary to remark, on the same day, in Parliament, "I deplore this tendency to giggle whenever the United Nations' authority is mentioned").

The war for Israel was a costly one, brought on in part by the refusal of the Western nations, in a kind of displaced intellectual racism, to take any statements—including racist threats—made by the

Originally titled "Letter from Israel"

Arab nations seriously. Israel won, at great risk and with great sacrifice, alone. This time, it would not, for the sake of the good will of its friends (whose good faith had been tested and found wanting in events at the Gulf of Aqaba), subject itself to the same risks and sacrifices again. The victory would, with tact and statesmanship, lead to that cooperative revival of the Middle East which had always been one of the dreams of Zionism. Israel has much to offer the Arab states; and for Israel itself peace would mean an end to the strain of maintaining a constant posture of defense, of being forced to trade at a distance of thousands of miles instead of with its immediate and natural neighbors, and of being economically dependent on help from Jews in the Diaspora. But it is impossible to negotiate with someone who does not know where his own self-interest lies, and the radical regimes of Cairo and Damascus would have to negotiate reasonably, recognizing at last the existence of the Israeli state, or go.

It is also impossible to inhabit a geographical absurdity. The Gaza Strip, which leads like a boarding ramp into Israel along the southwest coast; the wedge of Jordan that protrudes into Israel from Jenin to the Dead Sea (and that made possible the shelling of Tel Aviv on Israel's west coast from a point well beyond its eastern border); the division of Jerusalem, which leaves its civilian population virtually indefensible; and the Syrian positions above Galilee, which made impossible any accommodation over water rights (and which made the shelling of Israeli settlements, farmers, and fishermen such a common occurrence that for nineteen years northern Israelis have referred to mortar fire as "Syrian rainfall")—in all these cases the boundaries would have to be redrawn. The Israelis would have to contribute to, and the Arab nations cooperate in, a resettlement of Arab refugees. But a simple (and, as recent events have proved, meaningless) guarantee by the United Nations would not do this time. All parties would have to work out the conditions under which they could live together and return from a twenty-year siege to their domestic concerns.

To this end, Israel did not settle for a simple military victory, as it had in the campaigns of 1948 and 1956. It persisted to the point of virtual annihilation of the Arab professional armies. The victory could bring—by force or by reason—stability in the Middle East. It could even, by preempting the news and capturing the popular imagination for a while, take some of the pressure off conflicts in other areas, notably Vietnam. The West, without risking a soldier—without even, in fact, honoring one of its firmest commitments—had shared in a resounding victory over a Russian-supported totalitarian regime. The balance of power, or even the idea of the balance of power, and the relationship of the great powers to the small had been altered in ways that have yet to be fully explored; the United States might have some new room, and Russia some new incentives, to negotiate. (The fact that the Russians should have been supporting the Arab countries at all was one of the historical ironies of the situation. The Arabs had originally opposed the establishment of a Jewish state in Palestine not out of anti-Jewish fanaticism but out of the Arab chieftains' reasoned fear of what effect the sight of prospering Socialist cooperatives might have on their feudal sheikhdoms and caliphates. Russia, expecting an ally, had been one of the first nations to recognize the State of Israel. Now the prospering immigrants found themselves viewed as colonialists, and the Arab regimes were using the arms of Moscow and some of the rhetoric of revolution.)

All this, of course, has been altered by the outcome of the Eventuality of Everybody. The speed and thoroughness with which this outcome was achieved make it seem in retrospect like a foregone conclusion. It was not. Even the fact that war should come, with anyone, in any form at all, at least so soon, did not seem, in the days preceding June 5th, anything like a certainty.

Thursday, June 1st: An American Jew of German descent who now makes his home in New York arrived at Lod Airport, in Tel Aviv, and got into a battered old taxi, which was already carrying a few passengers, for the ride to Jerusalem. His daughter was spending her junior year abroad at the Hebrew University, and he was going to try to persuade her to come home. He thought he recognized a pattern to events, and he was afraid. He had been merely depressed by previous violations of international guarantees to Israel—free passage through the Suez Canal, for example, or free access to the Old City of Jerusalem—but the blockade of the Strait of Tiran had made it impossible for him to sleep. While the great powers temporized and rationalized, he felt that a little country's territory and morale were being worn away. It reminded him exactly, he said, of the dismemberment of Czechoslovakia. Foreseeing, as he thought, its inevitable consequences, he wanted his daughter home. The taxi picked up several passengers along the road (which was nearly deserted but still lined with the carapaces of armored cars destroyed in 1948), and on the outskirts of Jerusalem the worried gentleman got out.

The city itself resembled, on that Thursday before the war, a sunny sparsely populated colony for the infirm. Even the taxi driver wore a leather glove concealing an artificial hand, and most of the pedestrians (there were few cars) were either old or lame or very young and scruffy and truant-looking. The King David Hotel was nearly empty, except for some journalists and a few indomitable tourists. Zvi Avrame, the large, middle-aged manager of the King David, engaged his guests in merry conversation, and new arrivals at the reception desk were offered rooms overlooking the Old City ("There you have the view") or overlooking the YMCA on the Israeli side ("There it is more safe."). The entrance to the YMCA—the scene of bitter fighting in 1948—was concealed by sandbags, but aside from these, and from the strange emptiness of the streets, Jerusalem had made no obvious preparations for a state of war. From some windows, the sound of radios tuned to Kol Yisroel, the Voice of Israel, drifted over the city. Since the early stages of mobilization, Kol Yisroel had been broadcasting only Israeli songs, Hebrew news, and (recognizing that few Israelis over twenty-five speak the national language perfectly) two news programs each day in French, Rumanian, Yiddish, English, Hungarian, Russian, and Ladino. On Thursday, June 1st, Kol Yisroel announced in eight languages that the Mapai Party of Premier Levi Eshkol had at last formed an emergency Cabinet with the Gahal Party and with Ben Gurion's Rafi Party (although BiGi himself, as the Israelis call him, had remained aloof), and that the Rafi Party's General Moshe Dayan had been appointed Minister of Defense.

Friday, June 2nd, in Tel Aviv was listless and stiflingly dull. The city was uncrowded, but it seemed as though everyone might merely be taking a siesta. In fact, quite a number of people were off at the beaches and swimming pools. Several international journalists, having exhausted their color stories about a proud, encircled people unafraid in the face of overwhelming odds, or the economic impossibility of maintaining a civilian army on perpetual alert, were preparing to go home. It began to seem that even the appointment of Dayan had been only a bit of stage business in the little off-Hot Line theatrical productions to which the small nations seemed now to be reduced. It appeared that Nasser's production had all the angels, and that even *lack* of initiative had passed out of the hands of Israel to London, Paris, and Washington. The oppressive sense that nothing at all was going to happen created the feeling that access to the world's attention was being closed along with passage through the Gulf of Aqaba. Israel seemed about to drop out of the news.

At the Chaim Weizmann Institute, in Rehovoth, on Friday night, however, people seemed both more active and less sanguine than in Tel Aviv. The Orthodox rabbis in Jerusalem had announced that for the Army the obligations of the Sabbath were temporarily suspended, and some of the inhabitants of Rehovoth felt that war might begin the following morning. (The rabbis had earlier suspended their campaign against autopsies, and this sort of concession had led some people to expect war on every Sabbath since the beginning of the crisis.) The Weizmann Institute—whose cornerstone was laid to the sound of distant gunfire in 1946—has become over the years a kind of dream haven for pure science, an intellectual aerie amid green lawns, orange groves, and bougainvillea between Jerusalem and Tel Aviv. Agricultural research at the Institute had contributed vitally to Israel's unprecedented programs for reclamation of the soil. Theoretical research in nuclear physics and chemistry had succeeded so well that scientists were turning their attention to newer fields, like high-energy physics and research with RNA. One of the country's crowning and yet most characteristic achievements, the Institute had for weeks been on an emergency footing. (For one thing, a prevailing myth among the Arab nations that an atomic bomb was housed there made it a prime target for enemy bombing.) Of forty-three men at work on constructing a new building for the Institute, forty had been called up into the Army. Those members of the scientific staff who had not been called up as soldiers or military advisers, or put to work on special scientific projects related to mobilization, were busy taping windows or wrapping up sensitive or explosive instruments against the threat of attack. The children of the community were taking first-aid courses. Research biologists who had taken medical degrees but never actually treated patients were setting up emergency clinics. Sandbags and supports for basement ceilings were being put up in all the buildings of the Institute. In addition to their other work, scientists with walkie-talkies strapped to their waists took part in patrolling the Institute's grounds at night.

War, of course, did not break out on Saturday morning. Instead, wives and children took advantage of the Sabbath to join their men for picnics at the front. In effect, the front in a country of Israel's size was everywhere. But border kibbutzim like Nir Yitzhak and Shalom Karem, at the edge of the Negev and the Gaza Strip, were particularly full of families reclining with picnic baskets under the trees near the webby, shapeless tents in which the soldiers had been living for two weeks. The station wagons parked by the side of the road, and the tanned, rangy aspect of the men, made it look as though there had been an unlikely suburban commute from Scarsdale to the land of Owen Wister. The men—masons from Beersheba, bank tellers from Haifa, curtain manufacturers from Tel Aviv—were all dressed in highly personal variations on the Army uniform. In an army where no officer may order his men to charge, but only to follow him, there is a great deal of informality. "Tell my mother I am beautiful in my uniform," a soldier helping the civilians of Nir Yitzhak to harvest peaches said to a visitor from home. But, without any actual battle eagerness, the general attitude seemed to be "What are they waiting for?" and "Let's get it over with."

On Saturday afternoon, in Tel Aviv, Moshe Dayan held a press conference in which he apologized for having nothing to announce. He answered every question urbanely, with a crooked smile, looking confident and slightly sinister. He remarked that he would be "glad and surprised" if a diplomatic solution to the blockade could be found, and, in answer to a question about disposing of Egypt once and for all, he said, "I don't think in war there is any such thing as 'once and for all.' I don't think 'once and for all' can be applied to war." Although Dayan had been able to infuse with all the drama of his person an interview that contained no news at all, the fact remained that there was no news and no clear way out, and that patience was wearing thin.

That evening at Rehovoth, some friends gathered for coffee in the living room of David Samuel, grandson of the first British High Commissioner for Palestine, and himself a professor of nuclear chemistry at the Institute. Three friends—Amos de Shalit, Michael Feldman, and Gideon Yekutieli—were professors there as well. One, Peter Hansen, was a young English research chemist, doing post-doctoral work at the Institute, who had chosen, for the duration of the crisis, against his embassy's advice, to stay. Hansen said he had read in a column by an English correspondent that if Dayan had not been appointed he would have been brought to power by a military coup. Everyone laughed. "How can they say a military coup?" said Mrs. Yekutieli. "When an entire country has been called into the Army, a military coup would be an election." There was a discussion of the restlessness of several men who had not been called up: a frogman, a paratrooper, and a middle-aged pilot. (The pilot subsequently offered his services as a crop duster.) Mrs. Samuel said that she thought an insufficiently hearty welcome was being accorded the volunteers who were coming into Israel from other countries to fight, to give blood, or to work. She felt there should at least be a poster to greet them at the airport. "It could be a tourist poster also," someone suggested. "'See Israel While It Still Exists.'"

On Sunday, June 4th, a number of soldiers—a tenth of the Army, according to some estimates—were given a day's leave, and several of the North African soldiers (sometimes referred to euphemistically as the Southern French) took advantage of their leave to return for a day to their families in the port of Elath. Elath seemed confident that war would not break out there. In the first place, people said, the port was now too strongly fortified, and, in the second, at the first sign of trouble the soldiers would blow up the neighboring port of Aqaba, Jordan's only outlet to the sea. In tents all along the beach, near the empty resort hotels, was the remnant of an international collection of waifs and strays with long hair and guitars whom one now finds in so many unlikely places, and who had long been making Elath a beatnik nomad's rendezvous. When they needed money, they presented themselves in the morning at a café called Leon's, where they were recruited to dig trenches or to work for a day in King Solomon's Mines. At night, they gathered in a discothèque called the Half Past Midnight (where there were also several African students who had been stranded in Elath when their passage home through the Gulf had been postponed by the blockade). Asked why the nomads had not taken the advice of their various embassies and left the port, a long-haired guitar player from Stuttgart looked up cheerfully and said, "*Was? Wenn es grad lustig wird?*" (Soldiers emplaning on a civilian flight from Elath to Tel Aviv were asked to check their guns in the cargo section.)

On Sunday night, at Rehovoth, the professors' wives were just completing their course in how to render assistance at the Kaplan Hospital if war should break out. The cement walls of the still uncompleted building in which they met were lined with stretchers and sawhorses to put the stretchers on. The women were issued forms, in duplicate, on which they could check off a doctor's diagnosis, and thereby save him the time of writing things down himself. The lecturer, normally a gynecologist, warned the women that even to a seasoned medical man a casualty of war looks different from any other sort of patient. After the first four hours, he assured them, they would get used to it. He reviewed the forms with them, the ways of ascertaining the wounded man's identity (the pockets of civilian casualties, who did not, of course, have dog tags, would have to be searched), and he went down the checklist for gravity of wounds—mild, medium, serious, mortal. There were several questions about the word "mortal." The doctor had used the wrong word in Hebrew—one meaning "mortal" in the sense of "human being." The matter was soon cleared up. One of the women crouched on the floor with her hands locked behind her head to show the position her daughter in kindergarten had been taught to adopt in case of bombing. "'This is how the bunny sits,' she told me," the woman said. "'See the bunny ears?'"

Late Sunday night, the Army informed the civilian guard at Rehovoth that they might let up on the security watch.

On Monday, June 5th: at 8 A.M. the air-raid sirens went off all over Israel, and everyone knew that the country was at war. In one of the bomb shelters at the Institute, five languages were being spoken, with absolute calm, by scientists, children, visitors, and maids. A few minutes later, the all clear sounded, and everyone went to work, as though it were an ordinary day. General Dayan's voice came over the radio, speaking to the troops and announcing that tank battles were taking place at that moment in the Negev. *"Attaque à l'aube,"* one of the scientists said as he walked to his laboratory. "That's good for us. It means that we've got the rising sun in the east behind us. In the Negev, the sun is pretty blinding."

At 10 A.M. Monday, in his office, Meyer Weisgal, the president of the Weizmann Institute, an important Zionist, a good friend of the late Chaim Weizmann, and one of the greatest fund-raisers of all time, was dictating—to his wife, Shirley—some telegrams to Americans, appealing for funds for war relief. Guns could be heard in the distance, planes were screaming overhead, and sirens, which the Weisgals ignored, went off from time to time. "Send them full-rate, Mrs. Weisgal," said Yaki, their chauffeur and handyman. "We're going to win this war." When Mr. Weisgal had finished dictating, the telegrams were taken into the next room for his secretary to type. As guns, planes, and sirens continued to sound (by this time, it was becoming nearly impossible to distinguish the alert from the all clear, so that half of Israel was undoubtedly going down into the shelters while the other half was coming out of them), Mr. Weisgal told a joke. A Jew, he said was walking down the street, crying bitterly. A friend approached and asked him what was the matter.

"You see," said the Jew, "I am an optimist."

"An optimist?" said the friend. "Then why are you crying?"

"So," said the Jew. "You think in these times it's so easy to be an optimist?"

Someone turned on the radio, where the code names of units designated for full mobilization were being read out: Alternating Current, Pleasant Shaving, Peace and Greetings, Electric Broiler, Bitter Rice, Silver Lining, Wedding March, Gates of Salvation. There were twenty-three in all, and buses were lining the main street of Rehovoth to pick up the men called to duty.

There were more thundering sounds, and Mrs. Weisgal said, "When I think of the casualties. When I think of the mothers." The siren went off again.

"Don't listen," Mr. Weisgal said, and instructed her to read him a letter that had arrived that morning. The letter, written five days before, was about the situation in Israel. "'. . . I was afflicted by a sense of absolute despair,'" Mrs. Weisgal read aloud, "'which has since left me.'" Everyone laughed.

Toward eleven o'clock, a man with a helmet, a briefcase, and a civil-defense armband came in. "The news is good," he said.

"What do you mean?" Mrs. Weisgal asked.

"I can't say," he said, and left.

Toward afternoon, the sirens became fewer. In a taxi gathering hitchhikers on the route to Tel Aviv, someone, apparently American, said, "There is always the Sixth Fleet, in case something happens."

"My impression is that something has happened," an Israeli replied mildly.

A passenger suddenly announced in Yiddish that he had four sons at the front—he was not at liberty to reveal which front—and that since he himself had been a member of the Palmach, the commando unit of the pre-independence Army of Israel, he had written them that he hoped they would not give him cause to be ashamed of them. Three of them had been born after the war of 1948. *"Aber zie machen gut,"* he said firmly. *"Unzere kinder machen gut."*

Tel Aviv, on the first afternoon of the war, was not much changed, except that all windows had been taped in accordance with instructions delivered over Kol Yisroel. Word had come that several kibbutzim along the Gaza Strip were being shelled, that Ein Gev, near the Syrian frontier, was under fire, that Haifa and Jerusalem were being attacked, and that for some reason the resort of Nethanya and the Arab village of Safad were being bombed. People seemed most worried about the civilian population of Jerusalem. An English translation of Dayan's speech to the troops was broadcast, announcing that the Arabs were being supported from Kuwait to Algeria. "I need not tell you," he added, in brief remarks to the civilian population, "that we are a small people but a courageous one . . ."

On Tuesday morning at five, in Tel Aviv, there was an air-raid alarm (it turned out to have been a mistake); there had been none during the night. Bus service to Jerusalem was almost normal, except that, on account of Israeli Army emplacements, buses had to make a detour of several kilometers through En Karem. On one bus, Kol Yisroel was audible, and, looking over into Jordan from the highway, one could see smoke rising from a town on Jordan's wedge into Israel and verify the report that Israeli troops were taking Latrun. Because Jerusalem had been shelled throughout the night (the Egyptian general, who, under the terms of the Hussein-Nasser pact, had been put in charge of Jordan's Army, had often in the past expressed his belief in the shelling of civilians, since it diverted troops to their defense), and was still being shelled by day, most of the population of the city was in shelters. Israeli troops were attacking gun emplacements in the Old City, taking care to observe the order to preserve the monuments of all faiths, if possible. The King David Hotel had incurred minor damage—a tree down, a few broken windows, some slight injuries to members of the staff, but Zvi Avrame, who had been called up, was now wearing a uniform and seemed enormously gratified.

In the streets outside, a few helmeted civilians and some restless little boys kept telling one another to walk close to the walls and to run across streets leading toward Jordan. From several directions, there was the sound of machine-gun and mortar fire. In the early afternoon, three journalists walked into the government press office and were received with cheers. Accredited to Jordan, they had been stationed in the Old City, unable to file copy, for several days. When the Israeli troops came, they had simply walked across into the New City to file their copy there. Then they walked back again. It was announced that General Dayan had had tea on Mount Scopus that morning.

Sometime in the course of Tuesday, an Army official called a meeting of intellectuals in an office in Tel Aviv. He had invited delegates from Rehovoth, from Technion, from the Academy, and from the Hebrew University in Jerusalem. (Because of the peculiar configuration of the shelling at that hour, the professors from Jerusalem were unable to attend.) He wanted to ask their advice on a number of questions, and to brief them on the progress of the war. The war was succeeding so far beyond the most optimistic expectations that there were problems that must be faced at once. The entire Egyptian Army had been mobilized at the front when the war began, but Israel had spent the tense waiting period retraining reserves and repairing machinery, and the Egyptian Air Force had been destroyed in the first hours of Monday morning. Apparently misled by the true reports over Kol Yisroel that many Israeli border settlements had been attacked, and by the false reports from the Voice of Thunder in Cairo that Beersheba had been taken and that Tel Aviv was in flames, King Hussein of Jordan—to the surprise and special regret of Israel—had entered the war by noon, and in the afternoon the Jordanian Air Force was destroyed as well. The Syrians, originally the country most rabidly committed to the immediate extermination of Israel, were apparently enraged by the reconciliation between Nasser and Hussein, whom Damascus was still determined to overthrow. Syria had entered the war by degrees throughout the day, and by nightfall the Syrian Air Force was destroyed.

Fighting was going well on the ground on all fronts, and the problem was where to stop. Hussein, it seemed, was powerless to forbid the shelling of Jerusalem by Jordanian troops under Egyptian command, so it would be necessary for the Israelis to take the Old City. (The Rockefeller Institute, containing the Dead Sea Scrolls, the Army spokesman announced, smiling ironically at the particular stir of interest that this aroused in his scholarly audience, had already been captured.) It was clear that Jerusalem could not be divided again. Would it be a good idea to announce plans to internationalize the Old City before it was completely in Israeli hands? There was another problem, he went on: captured Egyptian documents, which had been translated only the night before, revealed that Nasser was far more seriously committed to the destruction of Israelis as Jews, and far more taken with the old Nazi programs, than had been supposed; plans, on the Nazi model, had been drawn up for the time after Israel's defeat. The question was whether to release these documents. What Israel wanted from this war, after all, was a lasting peace with its Arab neighbors. The two primary obstacles to this peace were the problems of Jerusalem and the Arab refugees. These problems could be solved. What purpose would be served in humiliating an already defeated Arab people by revealing the plans its leader may have had for destroying civilians? The question was discussed, inconclusively, for some time.

Finally, the spokesman raised a question that had been puzzling the administration: What had happened to Egypt's missiles? Were the ones shown so often on parade merely dummies? He mentioned the other possibilities: mechanical failure, fear of a mythical superweapon at Rehovoth, or pressure from Moscow to avoid what would have been purely futile destruction of cities. This led him to another matter: the Russians were not famous for their loyalty to losers, and the Arabs had lost. Was there any point in approaching the Russians now—or, at least, the Rumanians, who had declared themselves in such moderate terms? Several professors of Russian descent expressed themselves emotionally on the prospect of a rapprochement with their native land, but the others seemed skeptical. Certain questions, the spokesman said, in concluding the discussion (several professors present had to return to their laboratories or their military units), would simply be resolved by events, but, he said, "We will settle for nothing but peace this time."

In the blacked-out living room of Professor David Samuel, on Tuesday, the second night of the war (which had ceased, after its first few hours of uncertainty, to seem, except at the front, anything like war in the movies), the members of the household were gathered: Professor Samuel; his wife, Rinna; Tally, a girl of eighteen, who had been studying for her baccalaureate examinations; Yoram, a boy of fifteen, who had been compulsively volunteering for every kind of service since the war broke out; and Naomi, a girl of three, who had slept on Monday night in the shelter, and who now went to bed making siren noises. Tally said that her English exam for the following morning had been cancelled—"obviously." And Yoram announced that not only had he been put in charge of any fractures that might occur if his school were bombed but he was being called out that night for courier duty. "Well, if you think I relish the idea . . ." his mother began, and then simply advised him to change his undershirt. At nine, Professor Samuel left on some errand about which no one asked, and which was to occupy him until morning.

Kol Yisroel reported, with the understatement that it was to display throughout the war, that fighting had now penetrated to the Egyptian side of the Sinai border. (In fact, Gaza had fallen, and soldiers were already beginning to find pairs and clusters of boots in the desert, which, they knew from the 1956 Sinai campaign, meant that the Egyptians were in barefoot rout.) The *Jerusalem Post* for the day, in mentioning the fact that casualties were beginning to come into Israeli hospitals, and that all of them were patient and brave, did not neglect to mention a soldier who, with one eye shot away and the other damaged, was as brave as the rest. He was a Jordanian legionnaire, the *Post* reported and he kept repeating the only Hebrew words he knew: "We are brothers. We are brothers."

Someone mentioned that a Hebrew idiom for Arabs is "cousins," or "sons of our uncle," and that although the connotation was slightly pejorative, it need not always be that way. Someone praised the bravery, in particular, of the Jordanian legionnaires.

"I really think the reason we fight better is because we have no hinterland," Yoram said. "We can't swim to America. We simply have nowhere else to go." He left through the blacked-out doorway and went into the moonlight, to begin his courier duty. "A perfect night for bombing," he said, looking into the clear sky. But there were no alarms at all that night.

On Wednesday morning, the casualties began pouring out of buses into the Kaplan Hospital, where the Rehovoth wives were waiting to work. Tally's class at school was called to help out, and Professor Samuel remarked as he drove her to the hospital, "I don't know what these girls are going to see there." The wounded were silent, and as each stretcher was brought in it was immediately surrounded by many volunteers of both sexes, solicitous of the comfort of the wounded man. It turned out that among those critically wounded on the previous day was the son of the gynecologist who had had difficulty with the word "mortal" three nights before. "For us, you know, the Army, it isn't an anonymous thing," someone remarked. "To us, everyone killed at the front is a tragedy."

By nightfall, Kol Yisroel reported that the Israelis had taken Sharm-el-Sheik, the shofar had long been blown at the Wailing Wall by the chief rabbi of the military, and Meyer Weisgal, sitting in his own darkened house with his wife and a group of friends, was contemplating the offers of help for the Institute he had received from patrons and scientists all over the world. Later still, Professor Samuel (doubtless like many other professors at the Institute, and like citizens all over Israel) put away a pistol, which had served him in former wars (he had been in four of them: in 1939, 1948, 1956, and 1967), and with which he had been prepared to defend his family—in that oasis of technology, in a nation of two and a half million—if the war had gone otherwise.

The New Yorker
June 17, 1967

THE BLACK POWER MARCH IN MISSISSIPPI

FOR THREE weeks in June, a civil-rights demonstration, under black leadership, and with local blacks in the overwhelming majority, passed successfully from the northern border of Mississippi to the state capital, crossing several counties whose most distinguished citizens had been blacks who died for civil rights. One of the triumphs of that demonstration—the James Meredith March Against Fear—was that none of the marchers were murdered. They were not, like the Selma marchers, protected by the federal government. They demanded protection from the state, and, with certain lapses along the way, they got it. For those weeks in June, Mississippians saw state troopers surrounding blacks not to oppress but to shield them, not to give them orders but to come to terms with their demands. With the support of federal law, and the authority of their own courage and intelligence, the black leaders required the government of Mississippi to deal with them—for the first time—as men. For this reason, if for no other, the march marked a turning point in the black's relationship to the white community, North and South.

From its beginnings, ever since Abolition, the civil-rights movement has been the child of Northern white liberalism. The Southern segregationist has regarded the black man as his child in a different sense. With the march, the movement proved that as long as the law prevents acts of violence against it from going unpunished, it can assume its own adult leadership—including responsibility for its own radical children. On this occasion, the children were the workers of SNCC (the Student Nonviolent Coordinating Committee),

---

Originally titled "Notes and Comment" in The Talk of the Town

and the worried parents were the workers of SCLC (the Southern
Christian Leadership Conference). Other members of the family
were the understanding older relative, CORE (the Congress of Racial
Equality); two rich, conservative older relatives, the NAACP (the
National Association for the Advancement of Colored People) and
the National Urban League; and two industrious cousins, MCHR
(the Medical Committee for Human Rights) and the Delta Ministry of the NCC (the National Council of Churches). The issues, but
for their repercussions outside the state of Mississippi, would not
have been issues at all. All branches of the movement were united in
trying to develop political assertiveness where the need is great—
among the black masses, too poor to afford the restaurants integrated by sit-ins, too ignorant to attend the colleges now open to
them, too heavily oppressed to vote. The leaders, by marching in a
state where they are hated by violent men, hoped to dramatize personal courage, and to inspire local blacks to take the physical and
economic risks that still accompany a black's registering to vote in
Mississippi. For every large minority, the vote is the key to political
power, and that SNCC's rallying cry of "Black Power!" should have
proved divisive—and even dangerous—is only the latest in a series
of ironies that have beset that organization from the beginning.

A campus offshoot of Dr. Martin Luther King's SCLC, SNCC
always comes to the national attention when it is on the brink of going out of existence. SNCC workers—young intellectuals who have
tried valiantly to "speak to the needs" of a poor black community—
drew the movement to the rural South, only to be outdone by better-
organized and better-financed civil rights groups and by the federal
government. SNCC leaders were subject to grinding pressures—
personal danger, responsibility for lives, internal dissension—which
seemed to wear them down. And it was SNCC leaders—whose
awareness of the complexity of moral and social issues had always,
characteristically, involved them in agonized conferences lasting several weeks—who came up with the simplistic "Black Power!" slogan.

To the marchers, the meaning of the chant was clear: it was a rallying cry for blacks to vote as a bloc, to take over communities in

which they constitute a majority, and to exercise some political le-
verage in communities in which they constitute a large minority.
The local black audience—full of affection for the young radicals
but all too conscious of what the power realities in Mississippi are—
virtually ignored the chant as bravado. White Southerners heard the
challenge to white supremacy and braced themselves. And Northern liberals, already bored or disaffected by tensions in the movement, heard only the overtones; a mob chanting anything, and
particularly a spondee followed by an unaccented syllable, seemed
distressingly reminiscent of prewar German rhetoric, and alienated
white sympathies—which the movement will need as long as the
need for a movement exists—still further. (What black extremists
in the Northern ghettos heard remains to be seen.) "Black Power!"
turned out to be, at best, an expression of political naïveté; at worst,
it could be misconstrued as a call to violence, which would bring on
retaliatory violence to oppress the blacks more heavily than ever, and
cause the country to cheat itself once again of the equal participation of its black minority.

Another irony, which almost obscured the purpose of the march,
was that violence should appear to be a major issue in the movement.
The only marcher who seriously advocated "violent revolution" was
a white college graduate, unemployed, wearing a baseball cap and a
few days' growth of beard. He became known to reporters as the
House Marxist, and he provoked from black marchers such comments as "I don't know what to say to you," "The first thing you
whites want to do when you come to the movement is make policy,"
"Everyone has a right to his opinion until he hurts someone else,"
and "We gonna have a non-violent march no matter who here." The
House Marxist joined the march at Batesville and left it at Grenada—muttering that the march itself was "only a tool of the power
structure in Washington."

It is true that the marchers were often kept awake for much of the
night by discussions of the black's right to bear arms in his own defense. But the issue was always just that—self-defense—and discussions of it were largely academic. Even SCLC workers have tacitly

acknowledged that the strategy of non-violence, so effective in integrating lunch counters, is simply pointless when it comes to facing armed night riders on a Southern highway. Black communities have for years afforded their civil-rights workers what protection they could, and not even the Mississippi government has made an issue of it. The march's ideologues—mostly Northern pacifists and hipsters, who kept insisting that the argument lay "between a Selma and a Watts"—brought the question unnecessarily into the open and managed to produce what eventually became a split in the movement. (The mere fact that Medgar Evers, James Chaney, Andrew Goodman, and Michael Schwerner, among so many, are dead while Byron de La Beckwith, Sheriff Lawrence Rainey, and Deputy Sheriff Cecil Price, among so many others, are still alive should be testimony enough to the movement's commitment to non-violence. There have been no white-supremacist martyrs yet.) Marchers who, giving way under the strain, exchanged threats and insults with bystanders were quickly surrounded by other marchers and roundly scolded; but when a memorial service in Philadelphia, Mississippi, was engulfed by a white mob armed with hoes and axe handles, the marchers fought back with their fists, and no one—not even the vocal pacifists—protested.

Perhaps the reason for the disproportionate emphasis on divisive issues during the march was that civil-rights news—like news of any unified, protracted struggle against injustice—becomes boring. One march, except to the marchers, is very like another. Tents, hot days, worried nights, songs, rallies, heroes, villains, even tear gas and clubbings—the props are becoming stereotyped. Radicals and moderate observers alike long for a breakthrough into something fresh. The institution of the civil-rights march, however, is likely to occupy a long moment in American history, and the country might as well become familiar with the cast.

THE DRONES: In every march, there seem to be a number of white participants from out of the state who come with only the fuzziest comprehension of the issues but with a strong conviction that civil rights is a good thing to walk for. The last to be informed of events and decisions—after the police, the press, the nation as a whole—the drones trudge wearily along. They become objects of hostility when black marchers—forgetting that the only whites within scorning distance are likely to be friendly whites—mistake who their enemies are. In the March Against Fear, the drones turned out to be the only continuous marchers. Leaders dropped out repeatedly—Martin Luther King to attend to affairs in Chicago, Floyd McKissick for a speaking engagement in New York, Stokely Carmichael for a television appearance in Washington—and most of the local blacks could march only part of the way. But the drones stuck it out. Some were thrust into action, and reacted in various ways to dangers of which they had not been fully aware. A mustachioed anthropologist from a Northern university, for example, volunteered for a voter-registration task force in Charleston, Mississippi. When the white population proved hostile, he simply drove back to the march, leaving the rest of the task force to fend for itself. After two more incidents of this kind, he was punched in the jaw by another marcher, and wisely went home. Two drones from the North arrived in a station wagon, bringing their three-year-old son with them. The child, whom they left alone for naps in their car by the side of the road, became covered with mosquito bites, and was twice found wandering by himself, screaming in terror at the sight of a large, barking dog. On the night of the tent-pitching in Canton, Mississippi, the child was rendered unconscious by tear gas, but his parents were preoccupied with what they thought was the need to precipitate another episode. "We've got to pitch those tents again," they insisted, on the second night in Canton. "By backing down, we're only deceiving the local people." (The drones were the last to learn it was the local blacks who decided that they had proved their point and that another act of civil disobedience would be unnecessarily dangerous.)

THE PRESS: Reporters have become, despite their neutrality as observers, an integral part of the movement, as they cover one of the last of the just wars. Some of the time, the television networks alone had more than a hundred men accompanying the march, with planes and helicopters overhead, couriers cruising along the line of march in cars, a press truck, and walkie-talkies adding to the din of the already crowded airwaves. (The night security guard, the Deacons for Defense and Justice, and even passing Klansmen were all equipped with citizens'-band radios. The police and the FBI, of course, had radios of their own.) At times when the marchers were silent, the only sounds along the route were disembodied voices on the radio.

The press was jeered by roadside segregationists, threatened by troopers during the tear-gassing in Canton, harassed by a water moccasin planted aboard the press truck in Yalobusha County, and attacked outright by the mob in Philadelphia, but all this did not make the civil-rights workers any the less unhappy with what they came to regard as their unfavorable reviews. Marchers accused the reporters of exaggerating dissension in the movement (when there was a brief argument aboard the press truck, marchers gleefully cried, "Dissension in the press! A split! A split!" Reporters responded with cries of "Press Power!"), and even of generating some dissension by distorted reporting of events.

As far as the wire services were concerned, the marchers had a point. The Associated Press, in particular, made almost daily errors in its coverage—errors that seemed to reflect a less than sympathetic view. The AP quoted Stokely Carmichael's cry, in the face of the tear gas, "Now is the time to separate the men from the mice!" as "Now is the time to separate the men from the whites!"—implying racism in what had been only a call for courage. It repeatedly identified Willie Ricks, a demagogue affiliated with SNCC, as an aide to Dr. King, of SCLC—implying that the organization most deeply committed to non-violence was severely compromised. The sort of story that AP was determined to listen for and report is suggested by a question that an AP correspondent asked some civil-rights workers who were arming themselves to repel a second attack on their headquarters in Philadelphia; he wondered whether the incident would "encourage Negroes in the promiscuous killing of whites." In a sense, of course, the AP's mistaken report of James

Meredith's death was what brought the civil-rights leaders and the press to Memphis in the first place; but there were signs each day that subscribers to the wire service, North and South, were getting a distorted version of what was going on in Mississippi. Other members of the press were more than competent. Their mere presence contributed substantially to the safety of the marchers, and they have proved to be an important factor in the pacification of the South.

THE WHITE SUPREMACISTS: Stock characters out of the Southern bestiary, they line the route of every march. Shouting epithets, waving flags, wielding hoses, throwing objects, or just gazing in malevolent silence, they congregate most often at gas stations and grocery stores—a grotesque parody of small-town America. In conversation, they invariably protest that "our niggers are happy," express earnest worry about "niggers raping our women," and show their only traces of real animation when they contemplate disposing of the problem. "I'd spray the whole bunch with sulfuric acid," said a Navy recruiter in Greenwood. "What I'd do," said a tourist from Arab, Alabama, sputtering over his grits, "I'd get me some dynamite, and run me a line to the side of the road..."

The more cultivated elements of the segregationist community have evolved their own schizophrenic logic. "Negroes have always been able to vote here," the Greenwood newspaper proudly editorialized, and added, "This county was one of the first in the country to receive federal registrars." "You better get out of here before you need an undertaker," a sheriff said to a voter-registration task force. Then he muttered to himself, "They just came in here, mouthin'."

But there are signs of progress, or at least of resignation. "We didn't want this to happen, but what the hell!" said Joseph Lee, the editor of the newspaper in Grenada—a town that had twice run out a team of COFO (Council of Federated Organizations) workers, but in which the marchers registered more than twelve hundred voters. "There are things we used to do that we don't know now why we did them. We didn't know why we did them then. There are still some people who hang back and look sore. And a man who's a little weak in the head can make as much trouble as a Rhodes Scholar. But these days I tell my own Negroes to get their fanny on over and register." The Grenada city manager, however, was reconciled in his own way. "Most of your Negroes registering are either very old or young," he said. "Your old ones—well, the vote isn't till 1967. And the young ones—a lot of them will be going to Vietnam. And some of them won't be coming back."

There are advances in law enforcement. Despite the fact that several marchers were kicked and beaten by troopers during the tear-gas episode (a medical worker suffered three broken ribs and a collapsed lung), the troopers were not—by the standards of Watts, for example—especially brutal; they exercised what might be termed self-restraint. The sheriff of Sunflower County, where the White Citizens Councils were born, is a graduate of the FBI school and, like many other local officials whom the Justice Department has quietly encouraged to attend federal schools, cooperates in seeing to it that federal law is observed. Charles Snodgrass, in charge of the march for the Mississippi Highway Patrol, won the marchers' respect for his integrity; and he worked closely with John Doar—an Assistant Attorney General so respected by blacks and whites alike that, in the words of one marcher, "He seems to be the only one left in the Justice Department who knows what's going on. Without John Doar, there'd be a lot more dead in Mississippi."

Even the most extreme elements are, almost unconsciously, changing. The mob in Philadelphia, shouting, surging forward, throwing eggs and Coke bottles, listened to every phrase spoken by Dr. King long enough to scream an ugly answer to it. (Sometimes they listened and screamed so carefully that Dr. King appeared to be leading them in a responsive reading.) And a waitress in Jackson readily conceded, "Your whites in Neshoba County, they're the meanest people in the state." (Then she added, as if overcome by her own liberalism, "They got Indian blood in them.") And there are some real liberals. "It takes about ten drinks for me to say what I really think," a lady in Jackson said. "Why, we've never done anything that's right for the Negro. All we did was starve him, and work him, and shoot him in the back. I don't see how they could run their counties any worse than the whites have been running them."

THE LOCAL BLACKS: Strong leadership is developing in the small communities, and the march left little registration teams everywhere in its wake. Canton alone already had Annie Devine, of the Mississippi Freedom Democratic Party, who, with mud still on her dress and with her eyes still red from the tear gas, rose to announce, simply, "We are not going to stay ignorant, and backward, and scared"; and young Flonzie Goodlow, of the NAACP, who, despite white intimidation and jealous opposition from misguided workers for SNCC in the past, brought so many blacks to vote that she could announce her own intention of running for registrar in 1967; and George Raymond, of CORE, who was a voice of gentle moderation throughout the march, and diverted the marchers at moments of crisis with singing. Then, there are the local non-leaders, like the delegation from Holmes County that came to offer the marchers lodging, and, upon learning that the march was skirting Holmes, acknowledged, "There are other places in badder shape. Whichever way they go, we're going to support it." And like Hura Montgomery, a black farmer in Louise, who permitted the marchers to pitch their tents on his land. "I was possibly hoping they wouldn't ask," he said, "but somebody had to let them in."

THE MARCH LEADERS: Robert Green, of SCLC, a tall young professor of psychology at Michigan State, was liaison man for the march. Addressing the local police with quiet authority, planting an American flag on the statue of Jefferson Davis in Grenada ("The South you led will never stand again. Mississippi must become part of the Union"), leaping over the cowcatcher to board a locomotive moving toward the line of march in Jackson (he commanded the engineer to stop, and persuaded the angry marchers to keep marching), reassuring a troubled white worker for the Urban League ("We need the conservative groups, too. We need to engage the problem at every level"), and reasoning quietly with the few advocates of arms among the marchers ("The whites will simply seal you off and crush you, as they did in Watts. Our only course is to confront them again and again with the force of non-violence. It's the glory of the movement"), Green played a part in the march which itself changed the face of Mississippi. The police respected his fearlessness and his dignity. The towns were so shaken by his treatment of the monument in Grenada that several other monuments along the route were guarded by six black trusties from the state penitentiary, to prevent a recurrence of the desecration. And the marchers were sufficiently impressed by his courage and intelligence to respond consistently to his leadership.

Floyd McKissick, the national director of CORE, was always called upon to lead the marchers on days when they had to start promptly and walk fast, and to make practical announcements concerning strategy and finances. McKissick, an attorney from Durham, North Carolina, marched for the most part with patience and good humor. When a lady from Charleston, Mississippi, a black woman, came to the campsite at Enid Dam in the night to wish him well, and to tell him that "there are [liberal] whites in Charleston who are just as scared as we are," he discussed with her for an hour the question of whether it was time for the movement to make contact with white liberals in Mississippi. It was McKissick who served the marchers their lunch on days when he led them, and who, after many nights disrupted by the arguments of ideologues, the buzzing of transistor radios, and the nervous jokes of the night security guard, announced that "anyone who disturbs the marchers' sleep tonight will be hauled out and sent home." It was McKissick who mediated between SNCC and SCLC. But on the night of the tear gas in Canton McKissick's patience simply broke. The contrast between police treatment of peaceful black trespassers on the grounds of an illegally segregated school and the reluctance of the police in Philadelphia to intervene against an armed white mob seemed to overwhelm the lawyer in him. He was almost incoherent with rage, and close to tears. "I'm tired of having to *negotiate* for our constitutional *rights*," he said. "Some people said we ought to confront President Johnson. I say the hell with it. When the tear gas came, I fell off that truck like a scrambled egg. You didn't want that school, but they made it yours. They don't call it *white* power. They just call it *power*. I'm committed to non-violence, but I say what we need is to get us some *black* power."

Stokely Carmichael, the young chairman of SNCC, argued most persuasively for black political power, and when, as he saw it, he was continuously misrepresented by the press, he became obdurate and began to make himself eminently misrepresentable. What he had in mind throughout the march was a Populist movement in the South: White SNCC workers would address themselves to the white poor, black SNCC workers would address themselves to the black poor, and since the blacks would outnumber the whites, the new Populists would naturally be under black leadership, and would present an encouraging example of black effectiveness to blacks throughout the country.

Tall, lean and intellectual, Carmichael spoke to the crowds at night, punctuating his words with a finger pointed at the ground, enunciating a phrase slowly and then repeating it rapidly, bending his knees to add emphasis to his soft, tense voice. It was Carmichael who said, "It is time to stop being ashamed of being black. It is time to stop trying to be white. When you see your daughter playing in the fields, with her nappy hair, and her wide nose, and her thick lips, tell her she is beautiful. *Tell your daughter she is beautiful.*" It was Carmichael who, wherever he went, picked up children and carried them, and who, when the marchers swarmed into a black lady's house for a drink of water, reprimanded them by saying, "None of you asked where that lady got the water. None of you bothered to find out that she has to carry that water in buckets a mile and a half. These are things we ought to be talking about." (Carmichael himself hauled water for the lady.)

It was also Carmichael who, having lived for six summers under the fear and strain that assail a SNCC worker in the South, became hysterical for several minutes after the tear-gas episode in Canton. "Don't make your stand here," said Carmichael, the militant, sobbing and wandering about in circles. "I just can't stand to see any more people get shot." The following evening, it was Carmichael who wanted the marchers to risk putting up the tents again in the schoolyard, and who, overruled by Dr. King and the local people, sulked. (When James Lawson, a member of SCLC, and a founder of SNCC, told him later that he had been wrong, he accepted the criticism and agreed.) Although on the night of the Philadelphia riot* Carmichael said, "This is SNCC's night, man. This is our suit," he never forced an issue, never exhorted the marchers to violence, never, in spite of his militancy, put people in unnecessary danger. And it was Carmichael, the militant, who, in the words of one reporter, "came all over shy" when fifteen thousand people, assembled in Tougaloo, sang "Happy Birthday" to him (twenty-five) and James Meredith (thirty-three); and the night itself seemed to break out in smiles. (As for Meredith, who had been such an enigma throughout his personal ordeal, he simply melted before this friendly, sentimental face of America. "This is the happiest birthday I've ever had," he said.) In later interviews, Carmichael (like Meredith) was as uncompromising in not urging non-violence—and in not urging violence, either—as he had ever been.

Dr. Martin Luther King, of SCLC, proved on the march that he is still *the* leader of the movement, and perhaps the most forceful voice of conscience in the country. People came from all over Mississippi to see him, and responded to the measured, rational cadences of his voice. Time after time, he averted a crisis among the marchers, and his aides—Hosea Williams, leading gentle hymns and silent night marches, and Andy Young, making soft, persuasive speeches— called forth the same extraordinary discipline with which he is able to inspire the movement. Turning to Sheriff Rainey, in Philadelphia, and saying, "I believe in my heart that the murderers are somewhere around me at this moment," and turning back to the marchers, under attack from a far larger crowd, to say, "I am not afraid of any man," Dr. King set an example of pure courage. Exhorting the

---

*In Philadelphia, Mississippi, a voter registration crew was attacked one morning with ax handles, hoes, tear gas, and rifle butts. Dr. Martin Luther King led a return march the following morning.

marchers in Canton to remain calm under the tear gas, or addressing a church full of blacks in Cleveland, Mississippi, so movingly
that a five-year-old girl began to sob and say over and over again, "I
want to go with him," Dr. King was a superb spiritual leader. Bringing a busload of juvenile-gang leaders from Chicago to Mississippi,
in the hope of diverting their energies to the non-violent cause of
civil rights, Dr. King proved himself again an incomparable strate-
gist and pedagogue. And a few phrases like "America, land of the
free and home of the brave. Land of free white men, and home of
brave Negroes" proved that Dr. King's rhetoric has not lost its cutting edge.

The march was led by complicated men with divergent ideologies, just as the movement is, and their differences are the same ones
that divide the nation at large. The response of the white community—alarm and hurt among liberals, and, among reactionaries,
alarm and threats to use the white man's undeniably superior
force—conceals a failure to hear what the movement is saying. For
too long, civil rights has been treated as though it were only the
blacks' struggle, with some benevolent white liberal support to help
it along; what the movement seeks now is not benevolence but a recognition of reality: the black man's rights are *law*—and for the white
community to resist or ignore the law implies the collapse of an entire legal and moral system. It has become intolerable to the black
man to win so slowly what is his by right, and it has become too
costly, in every possible sense, to go on denying him his just place in
this society.

The New Yorker
July 16, 1966

RADICALISM IN DEBACLE
THE PALMER HOUSE

THE NATIONAL New Politics Convention, which was held at the Palmer House in Chicago over the Labor Day weekend, began as a call from the National Conference for New Politics—an organization that has given financial support to radical candidates in various elections since early in 1966—for delegates from all radical and liberal groups opposed to the American involvement in Vietnam to unite on a course of political action for 1968. The convention presented, from the first, a travesty of radical politics at work. In the quality of its radical dissent, the no longer New Left—which had seemed in its youth somewhere midway between the plain frivolity of a college prank and the struggle of a generation out of apathy into social consciousness—now seemed a vulgar joke, contributing as much to serious national concern with the problems of war, racism, and poverty as a mean drunk to the workings of a fire brigade. Throughout the convention, delegates seemed constantly to emerge, wet-lipped and trembling, from some crowded elevator, some torrent of abuse, some marathon misrepresentation of fact, some pointless totalitarian maneuver, or some terminal sophistry to pronounce themselves "radicalized." Being "radicalized" had, among alumni of earlier New Left conventions, two possible meanings: voting against one's principles with an expression of Machiavellian deviousness, or discussing one's politics as a most interesting turn in one's personal psychology. Among novices, being "radicalized" meant having been persuaded of something by radicals.

One of the reasons for the complete disintegration of the New

---

Originally titled "Letter from Palmer House"

Politics was the convention's persistent debasement of language. The word "revolution," for example, was used for every nuance of dissent. There were the electoral revolutionaries, who meant to change American foreign policy simply by voting the present Administration out. And there were the moral revolutionaries, like Dr. Martin Luther King, who sought to bring about certain kinds of social change by the pressure of non-violent civil disobedience. Closer to violence were the therapeutic-activity revolutionaries, former members of SDS (Students for a Democratic Society), FSM (the Free Speech Movement), and Vietnam Summer, who seemed to find in ceaseless local organizing—around any issue or tactic demonstrably certain of failure—a kind of personal release, which effective social action might deny them; and the aesthetic-analogy revolutionaries, who discussed riots as though they were folk songs or pieces of local theater, subject to appraisal in literary terms ("authentic," "beautiful"). There were the historical, after-them-us syllogist revolutionaries, who applauded all riots as pre-revolutionary, an incitement to right-wing repression, which would, in turn, inevitably—presumably as it did in prewar Germany—bring on popular revolution and lasting peace; and the amphetamine revolutionaries, who seem to regard uncontrollable, permanent upheaval, on the model of the Red Guard, as both a prescription for restoring personal vitality and the most vigorous expression of participatory democracy at work. Finally, there were some local criminals, who, despite the determination of the "radicalized" to view them as revolutionaries, pursued their isolated acts of mugging in the elevators and vandalism in the halls, and who, as a closing touch, stole three hundred dollars from the only people present who had defied a genuinely oppressive power structure at great risk and in the name of genuine new politics—the delegation of the Mississippi Freedom Democratic Party.

It was obvious that the only way all these "revolutionaries" could find common ground—the only way Steve Newman, of the (Maoist) Progressive Labor Party, could agree in any detail with, say, Dr. Benjamin Spock, of the baby book—was by jettisoning meaning from vocabulary. Within a short time, such a phrase as "bringing down the system" was used equally for the program of a citizen who sought to speed along by legal means the natural evolution of his country—which, he would readily concede, was already the noblest social experiment, on the largest scale, in history—and for the program of an arsonist committed to the country's literal destruction. When words are used so cheaply, experience becomes surreal; acts are unhinged from consequences and all sense of personal responsibility is lost. At the Palmer House, the word "genocide" began to be tossed about as though it could apply to acts of simple rudeness, and eventually speaker after speaker—from Arthur Waskow, of Washington's Institute for Policy Studies, in plenary session, to the Reverend William Sloane Coffin, Jr., Chaplain of Yale University, at table—could argue that a list of thirteen proposals submitted, along with an ultimatum, to the convention by what was called the Black Caucus should be endorsed without modification of any kind, regardless of the substance of the individual proposals, in a spirit of interracial unity. That this implied a paternalistic white racism that would startle a South African plantation owner seemed not to enter the minds of these speakers—or of the convention at large, which endorsed the list and delegated to the Black Caucus all authority for amending the proposals in the future.

The list ranged from an accusation that blacks had been systematically excluded from "the decision-making process" of the convention (one of the convention's two chairmen, Julian Bond, the Georgia assemblyman, was black, as were its keynote speaker, Dr. Martin Luther King, nine of the twenty-five members of its Steering Committee, and six of the twenty-four members of its executive board; moreover, no actual "decision-making" had taken place before the adoption of the thirteen Black Caucus proposals), through a condemnation of "the imperialistic Zionist war" (the Black Caucus itself subsequently reversed this condemnation, so the convention found itself in the position of having both endorsed a proposal and pre-endorsed, carte blanche, so to speak, its reversal), to demands for the formation of "white civilizing committees" to deal with "the beast-like character" of "all white communities . . . as exemplified by George

Lincoln Rockwells and Lyndon Baines Johnsons," for "immediate reparation for the historic physical, sexual, mental, and economic exploitation of black people," and for support of all resolutions passed by the Black Power Conference in Newark. No white person could in good faith endorse the substance of all the proposals. Certainly many of the white people at the convention knew the statement about decision-making to be false, and many did not know what the resolutions of the Newark Black Power Conference were, since no official list was ever issued and it is not certain that any was ever drawn up.

From the moment the ultimatum was accepted, the convention became a charade. To disregard substance in favor of a spirit of unity was to justify McCarthy's empty lists of names on account of the spirit of patriotism in which he waved them about. But the real white-racist presumption lay in thinking that a specious endorsement of inane proposals was an act of support for blacks—or, for that matter, in thinking that most blacks could endorse the resolutions either. From the beginning of the convention, the "radicalized" whites had resolutely refused to deal with any competent or intelligent blacks—any rational blacks, as it turned out—as authentic blacks. Non-failed non-whites were simply regarded as sell-outs to the system, and ignored. The effect of this was to produce what can only be described as a new, young, guerrilla-talking Uncle Tom, to transact nitty-gritty politics with his radical white counterpart. The assembled revolutionaries (whose voting strength was determined on the basis of the number of "activists" they cared to claim at home) selected such blacks, on the model of H. Rap Brown, to speak for the romantic, rioting, "authentic" children of the ghetto (for "the ten thousand activists in Newark," as John F. Maher, Jr., of the Cambridge Vietnam Summer, put it, in a meeting, "who were willing to die to change their way of life"), for the Black Caucus, for all the other blacks at the convention, and for the nameless, faceless, personalityless black monolith that the American Black has now—in the white-radical racist imagination—become.

The tragedy is, of course, that no one speaks for the young rioters, since no leader has emerged from them yet; and Rap Brown seems merely to tag along rhetorically after them. The Black Caucus, which never consisted of more than fifty delegates, sometimes spoke for the majority of the black delegates to the convention and sometimes did not. Its composition changed often. It occasionally broke into groups or disbanded, and entry to it was often denied to some blacks by goons at the door. By choosing to empower the Black Caucus to speak for the entire convention, the convention simultaneously abdicated in its favor and denied it respect. A radicalism whose one worthy aim had been "to give people more of a voice in the decisions that affect their lives" relinquished its own voice at once, and celebrated the birth of the New Politics by voting itself totalitarian.

Two days of pre-convention sessions—called, in the prospectus, "the pre-convention"—had started off quite differently, as a gentle convocation of kooks. The main factions of plotters and counter-plotters, traditional at New Left reunions, had not yet arrived to present their strategies. (The Socialist Workers Party, together with other Trotskyists, favored the establishment of a third party; in default of a permanent party, they were willing to settle for a temporary national ticket, with their own candidates for President and Vice-President. The "non-electoral local organizers"—like the SDS and Vietnam Summer people who believe in organizing rent strikes, cooperatives, and demonstrations, rather than in the vote—came mainly for the purpose of blocking any national ticket and getting some money. The W. E. B. Du Bois Clubs and the Communist Party would have liked a national ticket, but in order to preserve unity and avoid alienating the non-electoral bloc they were willing to settle for local organizing and the option for a national ticket later on. Their position corresponded closely with the one taken by Mrs. Donna Allen, of the Women Strike for Peace. The California delegation—which was also known as the New Politics group, because its position corresponded most closely with the original position of the National Conference—favored leaving each state free to have a national ticket if it wanted one, and possibly maintaining the Conference as a nationwide hookup for the various national tickets of the states. The likely candidates for President and Vice-President in

California were, respectively, Simon Casady—co-chairman of the convention, and a former head of the California Democratic Council, deposed for his opposition to the war in Vietnam—and Robert Scheer, managing editor of *Ramparts* and a former candidate for Representative from California. In default of local options for locally chosen candidates, the California group was willing to settle for a national ticket chosen by the convention. Democratic Councilman Theodore Weiss, of Manhattan, together with other Democrats, favored working through the regular parties for candidates opposed to the war in Vietnam. In default of that, they were willing to settle for a national King-Spock ticket. A Chicagoan named Arthur Rubin was running for President himself; his platform consisted of an explanation of "the generally misunderstood film *Blow-Up*" and a map of the universe "available in a variety of versions." A group called the Student Mobilization Committee came to recruit demonstrators to immobilize the Pentagon on October 21st. And some young people came only to look for jobs with established radical organizations.)

Within hours after registration, on the Tuesday evening before Labor Day, other delegates, less firmly committed politically, were roaming the corridors of the Palmer House—a huge, ornate, labyrinthine hotel, with a basement arcade, a sub-basement arcade, gusty, arctic air-conditioning, and small, transient-looking rooms. The obvious intention of these delegates in coming early was to have truly sweeping reforms to offer for consideration when the convention began. Non-political guests at the hotel that Tuesday seemed to view the delegates with tolerant smiles, pointing them out in the lobby as "the student convention." (On Wednesday, the hotel closed the swimming pool "for repairs." By Thursday, the convention was being described bitterly as "those draft-card burners." Saturday morning, the lady clerks at the newsstand were worriedly insisting that *The New York Times* had not yet arrived: "I told you we shouldn't have opened early, Bea. Here's one of them just won't go away." But by Sunday—the day before the convention ended—things were fairly normal: players in a local bridge tournament regained their concentration, and Sandra Max and David Wasserman, two apparently apolitical Chicagoans, were married without incident in the Red Lacquer Ballroom, where a White Radical Caucus had met the night before.)

Wednesday morning, after a welcoming speech by Co-Chairman Simon Casady, a kindly, bewildered-looking gray-haired man, the preconvention delegates split into committees: one for Resolutions, one for Perspectives, and one for Structures. The Black Caucus, which has been a tradition of radical conventions since the early days of SNCC (the Student Nonviolent Coordinating Committee), was already in separate session. SNCC itself (sometimes referred to as the Non-Student Violent Disintegrating Committee) is now—except as a source of publicity measured in column inches detrimental to the cause of civil rights—to all intents and purposes, defunct. Somehow, it never quite recovered from the federal government's passage of the Civil Rights Act of 1964 and the white radicals' defection to the more fashionable causes of campus free speech and Vietnam protest. The Black Caucus, however, remains, as though to preserve in memory the idealistic, soul-searching band that SNCC once was.

The Structures Committee met on the third floor, in Private Dining Room 8—a tiny, dimly lit imitation-Romanesque chapel, featuring cloudy chandeliers, a false hearth, false timbers decorating the ceiling, old branching wall lamps, folding chairs, and a medieval bestiary, with false heraldic devices, painted on its walls. The committee spent the two days before the convention discussing whether it ought to present to the conference a proposal that the New Politics disband altogether and leave its delegates to their local organizing. (Many delegates, it turned out, had come to the convention committed to its dissolution.) The Perspectives Committee, which met in the Red Lacquer Ballroom, on the fourth floor, spent the preconvention days deciding whether to propose to the convention that it endorse a permanent third party, that it choose a third-party ticket only for 1968, that it endorse no ticket or party or nationwide hookup of tickets, that it disband for non-electoral local organizing, or that it endorse a platform set up by a Subcommittee on Perspectives, which concerned Mexican-American relations, the Dominican intervention, the Greek regime, strip-mining in Appalachia, the inequities of the income tax, and a number of other issues over which there was considerable indignation.

The Committee on Resolutions, which met in the Wabash Parlor, on the third floor, was by far the most thorough and animated. Under the dual chairmanship of Steven Jonas, a bearded young man from New York's Medical Committee to End the War in Vietnam, and Bertram Garskof, a bearded psychology professor from Michigan State University (and a member of the convention's Steering Committee), the Committee on Resolutions immediately split into four subcommittees to revise the American political and social system from top to bottom. The four subcommittees all met in the same room, but each sent a courier to each of the others every fifteen minutes, to make sure there was no duplication of effort. By Wednesday noon, Resolutions had abolished the capitalist system. By evening, it had revised policy in detail, solved the problems of the cities, deplored alimony, and endorsed sexual freedom for citizens under twenty-one. ("We'll pick up votes on that when the youth reaches voting age," someone said approvingly. Jonas, normally the kindest of chairmen, looked reproachful. "I was hoping we were above winning votes," he said. "I hoped we were working on principles.") By Thursday morning, it had legalized marijuana, pronounced heroin medically harmless, established more humane old-age homes, and resolved that "if police agencies would do their jobs, organized crime can be smashed." (Garskof proposed that all white police be removed at once from black communities. "But there are understanding white cops," someone protested. "Then let them work in Scarsdale," Garskof replied.)

By Thursday afternoon, so many resolutions had been passed that the committee established a subcommittee to improve the literary style of all its previous resolutions. Then, perhaps dissatisfied because there was so little left to do, Garskof deplored the lack of black representation on the Steering Committee. Since he was on the

Steering Committee himself and should have known better, it was odd that he should make such a complaint, but his beard—even in the context of new radicalism—was an eccentric one, running straight, dense, and furry back along the underside of his chin, never touching his jaws at all, and it is not unlikely that he was just trying to liven things up a little. Two resolutions were immediately passed: one expressing grief over the separatism of the Black Caucus, and the other deploring the lack of black representation on the Steering Committee. Martin Peretz, an instructor in government at Harvard and a member of the convention's executive board, objected. "You are trying to railroad chaos through this convention," he said, and he deplored the committee's "militant ignorance." (Later, Peretz said to Todd Gitlin, of Chicago's JOIN Community Union, that he resented the implication that the Steering Committee had been "coopted." "Don't let's get up tight about cooptation," Gitlin replied.)

In any case, more than half the Committee on Resolutions ultimately walked out, to form a Whites in Support of the Black Caucus Caucus, and what turned out to be the major preoccupation of the convention—attitudes toward the Black Caucus—was established. From then on, there was so much talk of caucuses of one sort or another—the White Radical Caucus, the White Revolutionary Caucus, the Radical Alternatives Caucus, the Poor People's Caucus, the Women Strike for Peace Caucus, the Mobilization Caucus, the Labor Caucus, the California Caucus, the Anti-King-Spock Caucus—that delegates seemed to be not so much discussing a New Politics as croaking mating calls to one another from adjoining lily pads. On Thursday evening, the Black Caucus itself consisted mainly of local Chicago teen-agers and Black Nationalists, who ordered (and charged to the convention) a lavish meal, and who advocated withdrawing from the New Politics Convention altogether, to join a Black People's Convention to be held on the other side of town. The Reverend Ralph Abernathy, of Dr. King's Southern Christian Leadership Conference, however, briefly entered the group with what he called "some of our folk," and persuaded the others to remain—for a while, at least—with the still nominally integrated New Politics Convention.

Thursday night, in Chicago's Coliseum, a large, ugly stone fortification on the South Side, the full convention met for the first time. Julian Bond, the convention's co-chairman, was introduced by the moderator, Ossie Davis, as "a black terror in tennis shoes." He spoke briefly and then left the Coliseum, and he took no further part in the convention. Dick Gregory delivered one of his less effective monologues, in an apparent attempt to unite the convention by offering an apologia for its more extreme elements ("Every Jew in America over thirty years old knows another Jew that hates niggers. Well, it's even, baby"). He remained with the convention another day and then left to march for open housing in Milwaukee. And Dr. King delivered his keynote speech, a long and, for him, rather flat peroration, in a tired voice. As he spoke, some local black teen-agers shouted threats and insults at him from the back of the room. Black members of the audience tried to quiet them down, but within moments a few self-styled members of SNCC were charging through the crowd whispering "Make way for Rap Brown." (This never failed to produce an awed "Where? Where?" from whatever white radicals were nearby.)

The Reverend Andrew Young, of the Southern Christian Leadership Conference (a member of the convention's executive board), turned to a white liberal lawyer with whom he had worked on many campaigns in the South. "These cats don't know the country has taken a swing to the right," he said. "I wish the violence and riots had political significance, but they don't."

"They just have political consequences," the lawyer said.

"Yeah. All bad," the Reverend Mr. Young said. He left the convention that evening.

Some teen-agers marked a cardboard box "Contributions for Our Black Brothers in Prison," and laughed loudly whenever whites dropped money in it. Two photographers who attempted to take pictures of these transactions were threatened ("You gonna lose that camera"), and it was only the quiet appearance of Dick Gregory, who caught two boys in a rather firm, friendly grip around the neck from behind, that dispersed the teen-agers. "Why, here's Brother Dick Gregory," they said, and they walked away, laughing and slapping each other's palms.

Dr. King left the convention the following morning.

At the convention's first official plenary session, on Friday morning, at the Palmer House, Gary Weissman, the chairman of the plenary (he had been an officer of the National Student Association but had abandoned it for the SDS), announced to the delegates, whom he addressed as "Brothers and Sisters," that "the purpose of this convention is to enable the delegates to do what they wish to do."

Arthur Waskow, of the Steering Committee, immediately introduced a motion for the democratization of the Steering Committee with "members of all regions and all caucuses, if they feel they are not represented."

Sidney Lens, of the Labor Caucus, said, "Brother Chairman, I would move that the proposal be amended to include on the Steering Committee fifty per cent of the black people, to represent the thousands and millions who for four hundred years..."

In one of the long speeches that ensued (there were references to "this convention, with all its beauty and power" and to "this Chicago palace, with the country looking on"), someone referred to Appalachia as being in "the South," and a delegate rose to denounce this symptom of insensitivity to the problems of Appalachia. Someone proposed an amendment to Lens' proposal, and he accepted it. The chairman pronounced this acceptance out of order. Lens disagreed. "Brother Chairman," he said, "I've been thirty years a labor bureaucrat, and if I don't know that I don't know anything."

Many delegates questioned whether the plenary should continue to meet unless the Black Caucus joined it.

Paul Booth, a former national secretary of SDS, rose and threatened, if the discussion went on much longer without a consensus, to move to table whatever motion was on the floor.

A Mrs. Warfield, a black woman from Rochester, rose to suggest that she lead a delegation to the Black Caucus, wherever it was currently being held, to express understanding of whatever its demands might currently be.

Someone denounced this proposal as out of order, but the chairman disagreed. "This body is free to be as parliamentary as it likes," he said.

"Perhaps we could use the old Steering Committee as adviser to the new Steering Committee," a delegate proposed, referring to the motion for more black representation on the Steering Committee.

"What is the criterion for being black?" someone asked. Since one of the delegates in the Black Caucus was Miss Grace Suzuki, this was not an altogether unreasonable question.

"It won't hurt the convention to send a delegation," Mrs. Warfield said, rather impatiently. "I'll be standing here, if anyone wants to approach me."

"I'll tell you who's black," another speaker began. "If you were with us in Detroit, if you were with us in Newark, and Watts, and Cincinnati…"

Mrs. Warfield began to lead her delegation—ten or eleven whites and four blacks—out of the room.

The motion was put to a vote. "What will mean an aye vote and what will mean a no vote?" someone shouted. There was no answer.

The motion passed.

Someone proposed that the plenary adjourn until the Black Caucus had given its response to Mrs. Warfield, but the Chair ruled him out of order and shut off his microphone.

A delegate from Indiana rose to deplore the enlargement of the Steering Committee.

"You are debating a motion that has already passed—is that correct?" the chairman asked.

"That is correct," the delegate replied.

Mrs. Warfield's delegation never found the Black Caucus—or, rather, Mrs. Warfield left her delegation behind while she sought out all rooms that happened to have blacks in them. "Don't discuss among yourselves," she said as she left. "There will only be so much confusion." The members of the delegation stayed on a staircase, adjuring one another not to talk, for fear of government agencies and the press. Mrs. Warfield returned to them briefly, to announce that she would continue her search. "Go back to the convention floor," she said. "Remember who you are—the committee to bring a black structure into this convention." Barry Jones, a black who had actually participated in the Black Caucus, kept repeating that the caucus had disbanded earlier in the day. The whites ignored him. "Darling, not in the presence of the press," a white woman said. Mr. Jones gave up.

Friday afternoon, in what had been described in the convention program as "a panel discussion of perspectives," a number of people delivered speeches. In the middle of a discourse by Manhattan Councilman Weiss, who argued, not altogether tastefully, that the regular Democratic Party might still give dissidents "a couple of shots at Lyndon Johnson—speaking figuratively, of course," Floyd McKissick, of CORE, preceded by five blacks in a flying wedge, walked down an empty aisle to the platform. By the time Weiss had finished speaking, all the chairs on the platform were occupied, and he unceremoniously climbed off. McKissick, standing between two impassive, bearded, gum-chewing blacks in fezzes and khaki jackets (one of whom performed a sort of ballet with his hands while McKissick was speaking), began his speech.

In the two years since the Mississippi March and the advent of the Black Power slogan, McKissick has tried to remain in touch with radicals and liberals alike, keeping his public utterances wild and his private influence moderate. It is a strange course to take, and the effort has told on him. His rhetoric veers back and forth from center to extreme. His head bobs and his voice climbs octaves. He blinks continuously. In describing the destruction wrought by Molotov cocktails, his words to the white man were "Hell, man. You made this problem. You clean it up." He spoke of "the twin brothers, capitalism and racism," and he referred to all blacks who had risen to positions of national influence not as "blacks" but, contemptuously, as "Negroes." Then he remarked that no good could come to the black people from the New Politics Convention (he subsequently withdrew CORE from the Conference entirely), and invited all whites to attend the Black People's Convention that night instead. (Later, apparently under pressure from members of the Black Caucus, he revoked the invitation.) Preceded by the flying wedge, he left.

Robert Scheer then made a speech urging that the convention address itself to "the vicious nightmare" (boredom, wife hatred, alienation) of life in white America. Like many radicals, he managed to refer to the unarguable proposition that material affluence has not brought complete happiness, and to make the reference itself sound like an alternative offer. He seemed to imply that a revolution of the prosperous was imminent. Regarded by many as the Bobby Kennedy of the New Left (since the New Left thinks it bitterly opposes the real Bobby Kennedy), he was given a standing ovation. Another white radical, Robert Cook, formerly of the Yale SDS, now of the New Haven AIM (American Independent Movement), argued that whites should support black riots by diverting police to other areas during the looting and sniping in the ghetto. He was applauded also.

That night, the White Revolutionary Caucus (which consisted mainly of pale, thin, bespectacled women and pale, torpid men, making plans for guerrilla warfare) barred blacks from its meeting; the White Radical Caucus (which consisted mainly of members of SDS, Vietnam Summer, and other local-project organizations) plotted to sway the convention from a national ticket, in order to use the Conference mainly as a servicing facility for the local organizers; and the Black Caucus—despite a last-minute plea from McKissick, who made a brief appearance there—voted to submit its thirteen proposals, along with an ultimatum stating that if they were not passed by noon of the following day the Black Caucus would leave the convention. All through the night, in an orgy of confession about their childhood feelings toward blacks, the whites on the Steering Committee considered the ultimatum. Ivanhoc Donaldson, a black member of SNCC, argued that since the blacks at the convention were the only radicals really "in motion," no real white radicals should balk at the letter of their demands. There was a great deal of soul-searching by whites. ("I have thirty years of working for civil rights," a white liberal said. "At least, nobody can take that away from me." Whereupon, with some dime-store analysis of his motives, they took it away from him.) Martin Peretz walked out. The Steering Committee voted to submit the ultimatum to a "special plenary," to be called the following morning, and by dawn most of its members were ready to pronounce themselves "radicalized."

Casady announced to a crowded Grand Ballroom on Saturday morning that a session's declaring itself a plenary did not make it so and that he could not participate in an extra-legal plenary. Then he too walked out. (His walkout, with Peretz's of the preceding night, initiated a kind of daily ritual; the few responsible whites at the convention often found themselves walking out, only to walk right back in, and out again.) The front center section of the plenary was roped off and reserved for members of the Black Caucus, creating the impression that if only someone had thought to rope off the back of the buses in Birmingham and shout "Black Power!" the civil-rights movement would never have been necessary. Gary Weissman, who again presided, let the gathering "formally, duly convene itself as a plenary," and thereafter granted what he called "the indulgence of the Chair" to all deviations from parliamentary procedure that were favorable to the ultimatum. A woman who pointed out that one of the resolutions endorsed "wars of liberation," though many at the convention were pacifists, was ruled out of order. Several members of the Steering Committee, in the first of what became a series of conspiratorial jags, spoke in favor of accepting the ultimatum. The white radicals argued that the thirteen proposals should be accepted, regardless of their content, which was pronounced "irrelevant." (White radicals were constantly consigning matters, and people, of substance to some limbo of irrelevance.) Sidney Lens, representing the Labor Caucus, favored "not proposing to split words or commas or periods." Everyone seemed determined to foster a black illusion that the only whites interested in political cooperation were those who would accept terms of complete capitulation. Robert Scheer, who got up to make a motion to go the "Zionist imperialism" resolution one better, was inadvertently shouted down. In a heated interchange with the chairman, Charles Samson, who at that point was spokesman for the Black Caucus, denied Scheer's right to speak at all. "All of a sudden this person pops up," Samson said, pointing at Scheer in absolute outrage, "and he wants to make an amendment." Several blacks who wished to speak against the adoption of the proposals were hustled from the room by enforcers from the Black Caucus, and threatened and silenced outside. One of the enforcers who ushered several blacks out was an African Nationalist from California who was rumored to be the United Nations Ambassador from Tanzania. The ultimatum was accepted, three to one, and the plenary closed after the chairman proposed, and declared adopted by acclamation, a resolution to send a congratulatory telegram to Ho Chi Minh on the occasion of the twenty-second anniversary of Vietnamese independence.

That afternoon, the White Radical Caucus was troubled. Its coup against a third ticket and in favor of local organizing had never got off the ground, and, as one member after another pointed out, the Israel resolution would scare off liberal money, and the bad press that the morning's developments would receive might scare off everyone else. No one mentioned the possibility that the resolutions might be substantively wrong—only the possibility that they might alienate support. Several members of the caucus proposed that the white local organizers withdraw from the convention and form an organization of their own. Todd Gitlin pointed out that "the convention might still rise from its ash," that, in any case, most members of the White Radical Caucus had voted for the resolutions, and that it might be worthwhile staying around to "neutralize" the convention. Eric Mann, a white organizer from Newark, and one of the few radicals present who never cast a disingenuous vote, suggested that the organizers remain at the convention to paralyze it by keeping the others from endorsing a national ticket and "from doing all the screwy things they want to do."

Saturday evening, the plenary voted down the proposal to form a permanent third party. Again, a delegate proposed that the plenary adjourn until the Black Caucus, which had again withdrawn into itself, was present, but his proposal was not accepted. The Black Caucus itself was in a state of shock. The advocates of withdrawal from the convention, who had rammed the thirteen proposals through the caucus in the first place, had been certain that the plenary would turn the proposals down, leaving the blacks with an excuse to move to the Black People's Convention on the other side of town. Now they walked out anyway, leaving the Black Caucus to the moderates. Claude Lightfoot, of the Communist Party (rated as moderate by the radical left), and several members of the Du Bois Clubs, also Communist, soon took over, to give the Black Caucus some direction.

The White Radical Caucus, meanwhile, was in session on another floor, still plotting whether to sway the convention from the idea of putting up even a temporary third ticket or to leave the convention. Theodore Steege, a white member of the Ann Arbor SDS, announced that the Black Caucus had come to a new conclusion: Since the white delegates had been willing to accept the Black Caucus ultimatum, the Black Caucus knew that it was not dealing with real radicals; it would therefore either withdraw from the convention or consider supporting a third-ticket proposal and withdrawing support from the local organizers. The only black present—who later turned out not to have been a participant in the convention at all—shouted from the back of the room that this information was false. His word was accepted. A delegate from the Third Ticket Caucus appeared before the White Radical Caucus to offer what came to be known as the California Compromise. The California people, mainly the staff of *Ramparts*, wanted to be free to put up a ticket of their own, and the proposed compromise was for all states to be free to put up local and national third tickets if they liked, but for the convention to go on record as mainly supporting non-electoral organizing. The White Radical Caucus adopted the California Compromise.

The delegates at Saturday night's plenary, however, did not understand the California Compromise. In fact, most of them had never heard of it. A little old woman got up to say that she never liked to make an important decision without "sleeping and pray-

ing," that she disapproved of all the "intrigue," and that she hoped
no vote would be taken before morning. She was applauded. A hip-
pie wearing a headband and a card reading "Free"—one of two hip-
pies who showed up at the convention—tried to speak and was
denied the microphone. Before the California Compromise could
be introduced, a vote was taken and the third ticket was defeated by
two votes. A black delegate appeared and announced that the Black
Caucus was once again being excluded from the decision-making
process and that it would announce the method of its participation
in the morning. A motion to postpone all decisions until then was
defeated. Delegates from the White Radical Caucus and the Third
Ticket Caucus agreed privately to reintroduce the California Compromise the following day.

Sunday afternoon, Rap Brown was scheduled to speak to the plenary, but, at the insistence of James Forman, who was once the executive secretary of SNCC and is now its international-affairs
director, he agreed to speak to the Black Caucus instead. Forman,
however, addressed the plenary session—originally announced as a
Black Liberation Panel—for several hours, in the course of which he
"passed" whatever resolutions he chose (although it was not a voting
plenary); denied the microphone to anyone else; declared himself
"dictator" at one point and then, when Peretz and some other whites
at last walked out, dismissed the whole thing, rather unconvinc-
ingly, as a joke; and made a proposal that both calumnied the genuine plight of the poor and may puzzle genuine revolutionaries in
other countries for years to come. As an act of revolution, he suggested a boycott of 1968 General Motors cars. He was given several
standing ovations, and by the end of his harangue most people present agreed with the amphetamine radicals that although he might
not have said anything either true or important, he had "really
turned them on." (Bertram Garskof declared himself honored, at
this point, to be part of "the white tail on the real movement.")

In the late afternoon, before the evening plenary, the Black Caucus made its new demands known: the plenary was to be regarded as
merely another committee of the convention, and the Black Caucus

was to be granted fifty per cent of the total convention vote. The White Radicals, who had been thinking of nothing but their conspiratorial compromise, were bewildered. Only one of them, in their caucus, spoke against the new demands. "I know it's all irrelevant and meaningless," David Simpson, of the University of Georgia SDS, said. "I'm just not going to vote for it, because it's such a sick thing. I just don't want to be part of such a sick thing."

In the California group, Simon Casady said to Warren Hinckle, executive editor of *Ramparts*, "I guess what they're asking is to let them hold our wallet, and we might as well let them."

"Especially since there's nothing in it," Hinckle said.

At the Third Party Caucus, rhetoric had lapsed into the style of another age. "We have preserved the unity of this convention," a delegate of the Socialist Workers Party was saying, "to present an alternative to the American people." "Hear! Hear!" the delegates replied.

At that evening's plenary, where the Black Caucus demand for half the convention's vote was introduced, Communist Party and Du Bois Club members rose one after another to endorse "our black brothers'" position. What had happened, it turned out, was that while the white radicals were planning their local-organizing coup, and then settling for the California Compromise, the Communist Party and the Du Bois Clubs had temporarily, for whatever it might be worth to them, taken over the Black Caucus, and, through it, the entire convention—an achievement roughly comparable to embezzling a sieveful of smog. By inducing the Black Caucus to make the demand at all, the Communists had turned blacks against whites: if the white radicals voted for it, they lost their power over any further decisions of the New Politics (including the power to paralyze a third ticket); if against, they lost black cooperation. "Radicalized," they voted for. ("Masochistic fascists," the Reverend James Bevel, a black veteran of innumerable civil-rights campaigns, called them later on.) In the plenary, any black who walked up to a microphone to speak—even *for* the new demand—was approached by two tall young members of the Black Caucus and persuaded to sit down again. The demand was accepted, and a pink card representing half the convention's votes was given to Carlos Russell, a poverty worker from Brooklyn, who was now the Black Caucus chairman.

From this moment on, the Black Caucus showed itself to be more intelligent, more sensible, and more independent than any other group at the convention, and than the convention as a whole. To begin with, after a unity speech by Russell, the Black Caucus adjourned the plenary. Then, as white petitioners from the White Radical Caucus, the Third Ticket Caucus, the newly formed Israel Caucus, and even the pre-convention Resolutions Committee and the Progressive Labor Party cooled their heels in an anteroom, and delegates from SANE and Women Strike for Peace (who had either abstained or voted for) wandered about in the ranks of the "radicalized," the Black Caucus—in a surge of good feeling—let any black in who cared to come. As a result, the Black Caucus may have had the first genuine discussion of the entire convention. When William Higgs, a white associate of the radical National Lawyers Guild, who was out in the corridor, cast about in his mind for the name of some black he might know inside the caucus, and finally succeeded in summoning one—a woman delegate from the Mississippi Freedom Democratic Party—he failed to persuade her that a national third ticket would really help her much in Mississippi. ("I see what you mean, Bill," she said when she came out into the hall, "but I can't help thinking I need all the energy I got for the local issues.") And Steve Newman, of the Progressive Labor Party, who now threw in his lot with the local organizers, and against the conservative, third-ticket-strategy Communists (since Maoists believe in revolution by non-electoral means), never got a chance to talk to anyone at all. By the time the plenary reconvened, at midnight, the Black Caucus had endorsed a proposal by the Communist Party's Claude Lightfoot: local organizing, with a third-ticket decision to be deferred. But, in another surge of fellow-feeling, the spokesman for the Black Caucus—having heard the White Radical Caucus's point of view through an intermediary, Ivanhoe Donaldson—phrased his proposal as though it were the California Compromise. No one protested. Everyone was baffled. And it passed.

Monday morning, Arthur Waskow, of the Institute for Policy Studies and of the Steering Committee, tried to dissuade a woman from the Women's Rights Caucus from introducing a proposal that women be granted fifty-one per cent of the vote at the plenary. "You're not thinking politically," he said. "It will sound like a joke. A parody. I think you're completely insensitive to the politics of this convention." The White Radical Caucus was in session once again. Eric Mann said he thought that they would have to reckon with the possibility that most of the money except the Communist Party money would now withdraw from the Conference but that there was no point in being too fussy about where money for local organizing was coming from. In the two half-black, half-white committees—one for organizing, one for the third ticket—that would be set up in that afternoon's plenary, he went on, Scheer's people could be counted on to see to it that the Communist Party did not run away with the third ticket. And the white half of the local organizers could be turned into a white SNCC.

Then the plotting began again, in the intimate, nearly inaudible voices that are part of the white-radical mystique: "people already in motion," "implement specific programs at the local level," "relate," "in that bag," "where they're at," "doing their thing," "power structure," "coalesce with," "crystal-clear," "relevant," "beautiful." It seemed that some awful rhetorical cycle was coming to a close. A radical movement born out of a corruption of the vocabulary of civil rights—preempting the terms that belonged to a truly oppressed minority and applying them to the situation of some bored children committed to choosing what intellectual morsels they liked from the buffet of life at a middle-class educational institution in California—now luxuriated in the cool political vocabulary, while the urban civil-rights movement, having nearly abandoned its access to the power structure, thrashed about in local paroxysms of self-destruction. Both had become so simplistically opposed to order of any kind that society may become simplistic and repressive in dealing with them. There just may be no romance in moving forward at the pace that keeping two ideas in one's head at the same time implies; at least, there have been no heroes of the radical center yet. But the New Politics, black and white, seems to have turned from a political or moral force into an incendiary spectacle, a sterile, mindless, violence-enamored form of play. In the final plenary, the Black Caucus, in addition to reversing its Israel resolution, managed to pass a few resolutions opposing Vietnam and the draft, and to appoint the two committees to recommend things for the New Politics—if there should be any—to do in the future.

The New Yorker
September 23, 1967

G. GORDON LIDDY IN AMERICA

"HIS EYES. They're so cold," one woman said to another, on the sidewalk outside a radio station in Portland, Oregon. "I've never seen such flat, cold eyes. He looks just like a reptile. A *reptile*."

When Frances Purcell Liddy heard, in Oxon Hill, Maryland, that Robert Conrad, an actor, might buy the screen rights to her husband's autobiography, *Will*, she was pleased. She had seen Conrad on television, in *A Man Called Sloan*, and noticed what she called a twinkle in his eyes. She thought photographs somehow never managed to convey the twinkle in the eyes of her husband, G. Gordon Liddy.

Liddy himself had overheard the comment of the lady in Oregon; he knew, as was evident from the lady's tone, that she intended to express intense admiration. At the same time, since the comment was accompanied and followed by a hopeful glance at him, he thought politeness obliged him to reply. "I didn't know what to say," he said, regretfully, some moments later. "I just didn't feel I could say thank you." So he said nothing.

Will, by G. Gordon Liddy, was published in late April by St. Martin's Press. *Time*, in its issue of April 21, 1980 (cover story, "Is Capitalism Working?"), had run excerpts from the book, under the heading "Exclusive: Watergate Sphinx Finally Talks." The excerpts contained five pieces of information which seemed to determine all subsequent coverage of the book, in reviews and by the press: that Liddy, as a small boy in the care of a German maid, had been impressed by prewar Nazi radio broadcasts and even, until his father explained to him what Naziism was, inspired by them; that, as a fearful and neurasthenic child, and later, as a man, in times of stress, he had tested his courage by subjecting himself to physical ordeals, most disturbingly the holding of flames to his arms and hands; that, being less tall and less good at mathematics than he would have liked, he hoped to, and in fact did, marry a tall blond woman who was good at math, a choice which, he wrote, was influenced by considerations of his "gene pool"; that he had apparently been prepared, as a civil servant, if ordered to and for reasons of "national security," to kill the columnist Jack Anderson; and that he had later been prepared, in prison and for reasons that seemed unclear even to him, to kill his fellow prisoner, former friend, and co-conspirator in the break-in at the Watergate, E. Howard Hunt.

Beginning on the Monday of the week in which that issue of *Time* appeared, the switchboard at St. Martin's Press was overwhelmed with local and long-distance requests for interviews. On Thursday, Liddy was scheduled to be interviewed on the morning news broadcasts of two networks—ABC's *Good Morning America* and NBC's *Today*. To talk with Liddy, ABC had invited "a member of our *Good Morning America* family," Jack Anderson; for *Today*, NBC had invited E. Howard Hunt. Liddy and Anderson, who had never met, agreed to appear together. Hunt had accepted NBC's invitation (a book of his own, a thriller, was about to be published); but both he and Liddy had, separately, insisted that they appear on separate segments of the program, that they not actually meet. *Today's* producers hoped, all the same, to bring about a confrontation on the air.

Within ABC, as it happened, there had already been an angry struggle over Liddy—between the network's entertainment and its news executives. The news branch claimed that he was news and that, as news, he belonged on an early-evening news broadcast. Entertainment claimed him for the mixed format of a morning show. News lost this dispute, but before it was resolved, in the late hours of Tuesday night, ABC news had filmed an interview with Liddy, which was virtually sneaked onto the air at 11:30 P.M., on Wednesday night's *Nightline*, several hours before Liddy's scheduled *Good Morning America* debut. Since this scoop marked a little insurrection, Liddy's name was not listed in newspaper advertisements for Wednesday's *Nightline*. News listed him instead for *20/20*, on Thursday, at 10:00 P.M. Viewers of ABC's night news programs thus had two consecutive surprises. On Wednesday night, an unannounced appearance by G. Gordon Liddy. On Thursday night, the following cryptic announcement:

> This final note. The interview with G. Gordon Liddy scheduled for tonight on *20/20* was broadcast last night on *Nightline*.

At 6:45 on Thursday morning, G. Gordon Liddy sat in the makeup room of the *Good Morning America* studios, on West Sixty-third Street in New York. He was dressed, as usual, in a dark suit and tie; and he was talking to the makeup people with a combination of formality, attentiveness, and good manners, which seemed always a little to disconcert people who met him for the first time. He had signed three copies of *Will* for members of the ABC crew. A newspaper reporter, one of several assigned to Liddy that first week, mentioned that a letter Liddy wrote in prison had recently been sold for $125. "In that case my wife is sitting on a fortune," Liddy said. Outside in the hall, Jack Anderson could be heard. "I don't have to shake hands with him, do I?" Anderson said; "I may have to restrain myself from punching him in the nose." Some moments later, when they were introduced, Liddy and Anderson shook hands. They entered the lighted set at the front of a darkened studio. They took armchairs across from each other, on either side of the anchorman, David Hartman, who sat on an ample sofa, among plants, yellow walls, bookshelves, lamps, a coffee table. "It's six fifty-four. Quiet, folks," a voice said to the people scattered in the dark behind the cameras. "Forty-five seconds, folks. Fifteen seconds. Quiet. Shh." A stillness. "Good morning," Hartman said to his viewers across the country. "It's seven o'clock." He introduced G. Gordon Liddy, "the best-known of the Watergate conspirators." He mentioned Liddy's book, "In it, he reveals that he had plans to kill Jack Anderson." Then he said, "Good morning, Jack. And good morning, Mr. Liddy." The program, and G. Gordon Liddy's eight-week tour of America, were under way.

"Perhaps more than any of the Watergate characters," *Time* had said, in an obviously bewildered introduction to its excerpts, "Liddy embodied the principles underlying the scandal that destroyed a President." It seemed clear, however, not just from the excerpts but from Liddy's conduct in all the years since Watergate, that whatever the "principles" underlying the scandal may have been, no Watergate character embodied them less. Ever since the first reports, in 1972, of the events that became known as Watergate—throughout the trials, the Ervin Committee hearings, the impeachment inquiry, the resignation of Richard Nixon from the presidency of the United States, the various prison terms, acquittals, memoirs, commutations—the conduct of G. Gordon Liddy, and his alone, had seemed in two respects remarkable. While other participants talked, in truths, or lies, or half-truths, Gordon Liddy kept his silence. And, in the midst of a political scandal never completely understood but obviously in important ways and on an unprecedented scale financial, Liddy shredded cash. The second fact was less widely remarked on than the first. Destruction of cash, from Natasha's burning of rubles in *The Brothers Karamazov* to American millionaires' lighting their cigars with dollars in the tabloids, has always been an imaginatively powerful idea. Amid bribes, hush money, "contributions" foreign and domestic, private and corporate, voluntary and extorted, open and secret, Liddy's first instinct, when the break-in was discovered, had been not to take or to hide dollars but to destroy them. And far from eliciting money for his silence—in a story that consisted so largely of paid silences alternating with testimony designed to exonerate a speaker, implicate others, get a lenient sentence—Liddy was

left, after fifty-two months in various prisons, with debts, for fines
and legal fees, of more than $300,000. People thought him crazy, or
sinister, or honorable, or even heroic; but Liddy was known primarily for his refusals, and in these he was alone.

Silence and, apparently, indifference to money. Apart from that,
in a country that was reading, and watching, tales of espionage, de-
tection, mysteries, thrillers, Liddy was known to have been at least
twice, on June 17, 1972, in Democratic headquarters at the Watergate; on September 3, 1971, at the office of Daniel Ellsberg's psychiatrist, a conspirator, a burglar, and a sort of secret agent. Before that,
he had been a lawyer, a candidate for Congress, a prosecutor in
Dutchess County, for five years an agent of the FBI. He seemed to
combine, then, in his person several characters in contemporary fiction: the criminal, the policeman, the district attorney, and the spy.
In the Ellsberg break-in, moreover, Liddy was a government employee, acting in his official capacity, on the authority of high officials of the government. In the Watergate burglary, he was a private
citizen, employed by politicians to act in knowing violation of existing law. Though the personnel and even the objectives of the two
events may have been similar, their implications were vastly different. Liddy somehow managed, with these two acts, to pose successively a Nuremberg or Eichmann question (When is a man obliged,
in conscience, to disobey what he believes to be a lawful governmental order?) and the key question of civil disobedience (When does a
man have the right, in conscience, to defy certain laws within a legal
system on whose basic protection he relies?). One is the problem of a
functionary, in a government's abuse of power; the other, almost on
the contrary, the problem of a rebel. Both acts occur within a system
which the actor regards as, on the whole, legitimate and benign.
Both questions were, of course, formulated most precisely and in the
greatest depth by Hannah Arendt. But never together—that is, as
the predicament of a single spirit. And never, certainly, for a man
like Liddy, who took, as Ms. Arendt pointed out a civil disobedient
is obliged to take, the legal consequences of his own acts (those years
in prison); who never did obey an order at variance with his con-

science; and who never, so far as is known or likely, did or caused physical harm to anyone at all. Finally, Liddy had, in his own way and almost incidentally, played out a drama of ex-radicals in the fifties, refusing not just to name names or to extricate himself at the expense of former associates but to invoke any constitutional protection for his reticence.

Throughout the years, and until the publication of *Will*, there was, inevitably, an impression that Liddy's silence must conceal some vital secret, some great fact or explanation to complete the story of events in which he played a part. "You have played a vitally important role in a major historical development," Stewart Alsop wrote to Liddy, in July 1973, "and it seems to me that by now you owe it to yourself, and indeed to history, to say more about that role." *Will* has many qualities, and contains several kinds of information: but one thing clear from it is that Liddy knew nothing quite so broad, even about Watergate. During most of the cover-up, he was in prison. Before that, if one can trust his account of what he knew, and, on the basis of evidence in and outside the book, it is almost impossible not to trust it, Liddy's own pieces of Watergate information, though not unimportant, were few. Liddy knew that he had told Richard Kleindienst, the Attorney General of the United States, in considerable detail about the Watergate break-in, within hours of its occurrence. Kleindienst rebuffed him, and did nothing to further the investigation until April 1973, when John Dean's testimony to federal prosecutors led to Kleindienst's resignation—along with H. R. Haldeman's, John Ehrlichman's, and Dean's. Liddy knew that Robert Mardian, former assistant attorney general for internal security, had taken charge, as early as June 20, 1972, of the initial phases of the cover-up. And he knew that Gordon Strachan, Haldeman's chief assistant at the White House, had known about the break-ins at the Watergate. None of these three men went to prison. The statute of limitations has, in any event, run out on all Watergate offenses, one reason for Liddy's having postponed till now the writing of his book. Kleindienst was never indicted for obstruction of justice. Mardian was indicted and convicted of conspiracy, but acquitted on appeal. Strachan, who like Kleindienst and Mardian persistently and indignantly proclaimed his innocence, was never convicted of anything and was particularly commended for his candor at the Ervin Committee hearings by the chairman, Sam Ervin.

From a strictly Watergate point of view, these may all have been facts of historic consequence—particularly the information about Strachan. There had always been a missing link (specifically, a missing memorandum in a numbered series of twenty memoranda) in the chain of evidence from Watergate to Strachan; as there had always been missing pieces (specifically, just what facts Liddy had told him) in the link to Kleindienst. The information about Mardian, whose indictment rested on quite other evidence, was entirely new. Liddy, of course, had details of many other kinds, but Liddy's allegations about the three men, if he had spoken at the time, would have led, directly and inescapably, to the President; and it is Strachan who would inevitably, by implicating Haldeman, have implicated the President, for having authorized the break-in after all. In that event, on the plane of the historical what-if, if Liddy had, at the time, told all he knew, it is almost certain that President Nixon, immediately after the 1972 election, would have taken responsibility for the break-in, explained it somehow, and gone on to serve out his constitutional term. It was, after all, the cover-up, prolonged, intricate, disintegrating over a period of more than twenty months, that became finally intolerable; it took more than two years of extraordinary events and processes before a mechanism for removal of the President was in place. Of that long disintegration of the cover-up, Liddy, who tries carefully to distinguish what he speculates about from what he knows as fact, has only an impression. A sweep of Jeb Magruder's hand toward a desk drawer which held Republicans' derogatory information about Democrats caused Liddy to believe that the purpose of the break-in was to find what derogatory information the Democrats had about Republicans. Liddy does not dwell at all upon these, his Watergate scoops, such as they are (three historic felonies at the highest level, one sweep of the hand). And in the

course of all his travels, no interviewer. Watergate reporter, or reviewer mentioned any but the last, the sweep. And few mentioned
that.

What they did all mention, and want to talk about, was Liddy as
a Nazi sympathizer; Liddy as a racist believer in genetics; Liddy as a
burner of his own hand; Liddy, and this with the greatest fascination, as a man prepared to kill. Also, increasingly and perhaps surprisingly, Liddy as a philosopher about the human condition and
Liddy as a commentator on American political affairs. He was
asked, everywhere, what he would do in President Carter's place
about foreign policy, what were his thoughts on the nature of good
and evil, how people ought to raise their children (the Liddys have
five, two daughters, three sons, between the ages of seventeen and
twenty-two), what is the relation between hope and death, free enterprise and regulation, military preparedness and the democratic
system, and so on. Some interviewers addressed him in the most re-
spectful terms, as a kind of statesman. Others seemed to bait him as
a dangerous fanatic. Others still to treat him as though there were
no distinction, as though statesman, fanatic, writer, presumptive
killer were all essentially the same.

"Tell me, Mr. Liddy," a distinctly hostile television interviewer
asked him, in Los Angeles, right after the failed helicopter rescue
mission to Iran, "if Richard Nixon were still President, would our
hostages still be in Teheran?" She spoke with an air of wariness and
triumph, as though she had risked the violence of a madman to pro-
voke an item of sensational news. "If Richard Nixon were still President," Liddy replied, amiably and without hesitation, "the *Shah*
would still be in Teheran."

All over the country, interviewers asked him who he thought had
really killed President Kennedy. "I'm not a believer in conspiracy
theories of history," he would say. "Such a conspiracy would have
had to be too large. So many people could never keep a secret." He
was often asked the identity of Woodward and Bernstein's informant, Deep Throat. Each time, he replied that he was virtually certain, just as any reader of *All the President's Men* would be certain,

that there was no single such person, that it was a literary device to cover a variety of sources. And then he would add that since he was in prison during most of the period covered by the book, he could know no more about the matter than anybody else.

Sometimes, in fact quite frequently, in the middle of Liddy's most reasoned and polite replies, there would emerge what Michael Denneny, Liddy's young editor at St. Martin's Press—a friend and student, as it happens, of Hannah Arendt and Harold Rosenberg at the University of Chicago; also, a founding editor of the gay magazine *Christopher Street*—would characterize as the imp. A passage in Liddy's book, for instance, describes a time in his childhood when, ashamed of having wept over a wounded squirrel, he decided to nerve himself for the army, in case that war should last long enough for him to join it, by helping to kill and pluck chickens in a neighbor's chicken coop. "How," an outraged and trembling lady asked him in San Francisco, "can you equate the killing of chickens with the taking of a human life?" "Well, madam," Liddy said, "you have to begin somewhere."

Dick Cavett, who devoted three successive programs to interviews with Liddy, seemed particularly mesmerized by the subject of killing. Exactly how, by what means, he asked within the first minute of the first program, had Liddy planned to kill Jack Anderson? With a knife, Liddy said, or by breaking his neck. Gasps. "Just like that," someone in the audience whispered. In returning constantly to that sort of question ("But aren't you glad you didn't kill John Dean?"), Cavett seemed almost unaware that, at least on the evidence of his autobiography, or of the public record, Liddy was not in fact a violent man. And that if he were, it would be remarkably imprudent to interview him in this way. Having referred, for instance, to "your almost unbearable appetite for violence," Cavett asked, "Can you see how people would be uneasy to have you out on the streets?" "You're so likeable," Liddy said, soothingly. "There's just no problem with you at all." Cavett said he meant other people. "If they're your friends," Liddy said, "then I'm sure they're likeable, too." Even Cavett laughed at this. "See me after class," he said. But

on occasions when the lady in Portland, and now, doubtless, the Cavett audience, and the lady in San Francisco as well, saw the reptile,
and Frances Liddy would detect the twinkle, Denneny and others
thought they saw the imp.

In 1978, Liddy had published a rather good, conventional thriller—
in no way related to Watergate, or even to politics. Its hero was of
complicated Italian background. His mistress was Chinese-Ameri-
can. Among other plot developments was an inspired alliance, for
good purposes, of the Mafia and the tongs. St. Martin's Press had
published that thriller, called *Out of Control*, and sent Liddy on a
book tour to promote it. Interviewers had inevitably wanted to discuss Watergate. Liddy had refused. With *Will*, which rapidly became, as *Out of Control* was not, a best-seller, there was of course
another book tour. There were, at the same time, two other tours: a
journalistic circuit, in which one reporter after another tried to find
in Liddy's book, and in his person, "news value" of some kind; and a
people's tour, in which various groups asked Liddy to address them,
and individuals, on the street or even in late-night phone calls (the
Liddys' number has never been unlisted), asked Liddy's views, or
told him theirs, on the basis of the kind of man they, in the years
since Watergate, had thought him to be. In the first week, the week
of the *Time* excerpts, the journalistic tour tended, not surprisingly,
to predominate. Soon afterward, it gave way to the other two.

"It's twenty-five after seven now," David Hartman said to his *Good
Morning America* audience. He still sat on a sofa between chairs occupied by G. Gordon Liddy and Jack Anderson. "In his autobiography, *Will*, G. Gordon Liddy said that he urged that Jack Anderson
be killed. Before the break, we were discussing that." *During* the
break, Liddy and Anderson had in fact been discussing other matters. Liddy had complimented Anderson for his black belt in karate.
Anderson had modestly pointed to his own increasing waistline.

Hartman had asked Anderson why he would appear on a program that would almost certainly sell copies of Liddy's book. Anderson had said, "This book must be read." Liddy had said, "I've certainly sold a lot of his columns in the past." "Mr. Liddy," Hartman continued, "what did Richard Nixon know?" Liddy said he had no idea and that he declined to speculate. "I want to ask you something else," Anderson said, dropping for almost the first time in the course of the broadcast the subject of killing, "I wrote at the time that you were an admirer of Adolf Hitler. Is that true?" "No," Liddy said, and began the story of the German maid in his childhood. More conversation. Commercials. "It's seven-thirty," Hartman said. "Most people wouldn't consider G. Gordon Liddy to be a very nice man...." Weather. Commercials. News. Commercials. Time. More weather report. "It's twenty minutes before eight right now," Hartman said. "This is the first time these two gentlemen have met." Anderson told a long anecdote about President Nixon's having embarrassed Henry Kissinger on the yacht *Sequoia*. "Well, what is your question?" Liddy asked. Anderson said that Nixon's "deep abiding resentment" of the press might have contributed to the notion of killing him, Jack Anderson. Liddy said that, although Nixon reciprocated the press' "deep abiding animosity" toward him, the whole matter had nothing to do with that but with the question of whether Anderson had in fact compromised a CIA source abroad.

"Mr. Liddy," Hartman suddenly said, "what in your opinion is the value of human life?" Liddy said, "The value of human life is sacred." Hartman asked whether Liddy's case had not been a matter of blind obedience. "I don't believe in blind obedience," Liddy said. "I do believe in reason, and you must be answerable to your conscience. Ultimately, it comes down to a matter of individual conscience." "How then," Hartman went on, undeterred and still referring to the idea of killing Jack Anderson, "are you different from those German soldiers who said they were just following orders?" "I wasn't following orders, was I?" Liddy said. "I proposed it."

Anderson left, to return to Washington. Commercials for two ABC soap operas, *One Life to Live* and *All My Children*. The program resumed. "You wanted to be a dangerous man," Hartman said. "No," Liddy said, "let me explain to you. When I was a little child . . ." Conversation about childhood fears. Hartman read aloud a passage from Liddy's book: "That sounds like someone who is really desperate." Liddy said, "I was." More conversation. "You really are not afraid to die," Hartman said. "No. I mean we're all gonna die," Liddy said. Talk about the episode of killing chickens. "You don't seem simply to be just willing to kill," Hartman said. "It's almost killing as a celebration." No, Liddy said. Talk about why Liddy had waited to write the book until after statutes of limitations had run out, even for associates he no longer liked or admired. Liddy said he had been taught that "One does not seek to extricate oneself at the expense of friends or associates, whether they are erstwhile or not." More talk. "Thank you, Mr. Liddy. It's four minutes, almost four minutes before eight. We'll be right back," Hartman said. Liddy went off, by NBC limousine, to the *Today* show.

Immediate mention, by *Today* host Tom Brokaw, of killing and G. Gordon Liddy. "Killing takes up a very small part of the actual book," Liddy said. Brokaw, who had not read it, continued. "This is a nation, Mr. Liddy, of laws, not of men," he said. "We do not respond to just what our superiors tell us, whether it's here at NBC or even in the government." ["I don't know about *him*," said one of the men looking at screens and flicking dials in the control room, "but here at NBC we do *exactly* what our superiors tell us."] Security for Liddy's appearance on the *Today* show had been so tight that no newspaper reporters were allowed in the studio; a few stood behind the men at the control-room dials.

"Do you have any contemporary heroes?" Brokaw asked. "Let me think a minute," Liddy said. "No. They're all dead." Who were they? "Leonidas, Catherine de Medici, Machiavelli, Caesar, MacArthur, Patton." Conversation. "We have E. Howard Hunt who is waiting offstage here," Brokaw said. "There's a certain tension in the air." ("If there's any flicker in his eyes, stay with him, stay with him," said the director in the control room. The camera was on Liddy. There was no flicker. The camera moved to Brokaw.) "A few minutes ago, we heard some bizarre Watergate stories from Gordon Liddy," Brokaw said, reading from a cue card, "and we'll be talking again with him in a moment. Coming up, our TV critic, Gene Shalit." Shalit appeared on the screen.

"There's a lot of press out in the corridors," he said. "A lot of newspaper reporters. I was interested in Liddy's heroes. The first one, I agree with. When he first said Leonidas, it didn't click. I thought he meant a ballet dancer at the Music Hall. Well, I don't have any heroes in public life. My heroes are in the arts." A brief meditation. "What does *heroes* mean anyway? Edwin Newman said a 'sung hero' was a sandwich in a Chinese restaurant. People are no longer larger than life." Some news, regarding Ezer Weizmann's resignation from the Israeli cabinet, and the acquisition, by Norton Simon and his wife, Jennifer Jones, of a single painting for $3.7 million. Some commercials. "It's eight-thirty, good morning," Brokaw said. Then he asked Liddy what he would say to people, "and I suspect I might be one of them," who thought Liddy's autobiography, his whole story perhaps, might be "a media hype." "Well, I did the fifty-two and a half months," Liddy said. "There's nothing manufactured about that." Brokaw asked whether Liddy thought Charles Colson's religious conversion, in the years after Watergate, had been genuine. "I can't look inside the man's head," Liddy replied. "I have no idea." Brokaw asked, "Would you ask your children to grow up to be like you?" "No," Liddy said. "I want them to grow up to be the way they want to be." More conversation. "Let him out. Get the other guy in," the man in the control room said. As E. Howard Hunt entered the studio to be interviewed, Liddy and two reporters went down in the elevator and out to the street.

On the sidewalk, at Rockefeller Plaza, a young black woman said, "Congratulations. I agree. It all depends on where you stand." Liddy and the reporters crossed Fifth Avenue and walked toward the Westbury to have breakfast. Liddy now said that, in spite of the guards and the tight security, just as he was entering the *Today* studio, a worried man, carrying a briefcase, had approached him. "He said, 'Mr. Liddy, I need your counsel,'" Liddy recalled. "I said, 'I'm sorry. I'm afraid I've been disbarred.'" It turned out that the man had a complicated theory that a popular White House physician who had resigned in a controversy over drug prescriptions, was in fact a Soviet agent. None of the NBC staff knew the man with the briefcase. A guard had finally spotted him and sent him away. "I mean, here's this guy with a theory that the President is the Mongolian candidate," Liddy said, "and *he's* the only one who gets through security."

A passerby waved, and Claire Crawford, a reporter for *People* magazine, which was planning a cover story on Liddy for its next issue, asked Liddy how strangers generally reacted to him. "Some people say, 'I'm proud of you,' and some say, 'I hope your dog dies,'" Liddy said. "Nobody seems to be neutral. Although a lot of people behave as though they know they've seen my face somewhere, but they can't quite place who I am." Ms. Crawford said she knew the syndrome well. She had once been working on a piece about Spiro Agnew, when he was Vice President and at the height of his popularity. A passerby had looked at him intently, puzzled, then brightened and approached. "I know you," he had said, enthusiastically. "You're Ed McMahon."

On Saturday morning, two days after Liddy's New York network interviews, I took a cab from Washington National Airport to the Liddys' house, in Oxon Hill, Maryland. The driver, who was black, said he was going to take the afternoon off to drive to a wedding in Philadelphia. He asked whether I might be going to a wedding in Oxon Hill. I said no. Then, seeing that he had on the seat beside him a copy of the *Washington Post*, opened to a feature story, in the Style section, on G. Gordon Liddy's book, I said I was going to the Liddys' house. He whistled, then paused. "Believe it or not, I was locked up with him," he said. "In the D.C. jail. I wanted to meet him, but I never got to." Another pause. "I admired him for two reasons. Number

one, he helped a lot of inmates. And number two, he didn't talk."
Then, the driver wrote down his name, address, and phone number,
in case his passenger, or Liddy himself, should ever want to call.

Oxon Hill is a quiet, well-kept suburban town where a lot of present and former military people live. The Liddys' house, on Ivanhoe
Road, is of wood and brick, with an ivy-covered chimney. A sign in
the yard advertised lawn mowing. There were two cats, both in the
last stages of pregnancy, and one dog, a hound of some sort, which
kept at a considerable distance from the house. The Liddys have four
cars, all old and with a lot of mileage on them: a Jeep; an improbably
worn and unkempt Cadillac; a Volvo, which their daughter Alexandra keeps at the College of New Rochelle, where she is a nursing
student; and a battered Ford. On this Saturday, *People* was paying
for Alexandra and the other two absent children, Jim, a senior at
Mercersberg Academy, and Tom, a junior at St. Albans, in Washington, to come home. Grace, who was taking a semester at the University of Maryland, and Raymond, a student at a local public school,
were already at home. Claire Crawford, the reporter, and a photographer from *People* were expected at noon.

Liddy was pale and rather haggard. For two days he had been unable to eat solid food, on account of a cracked and infected molar.
Frances Liddy was tidying up a room off the kitchen, which, piled
with magazines, books, and newspapers, serves as a combination
study and auxiliary living room. Raymond drove off in the Ford to
get mustard and mayonnaise for the sandwiches that his mother intended to serve at lunch. The household had gotten up relatively late
that morning. Liddy had been scheduled, early on the previous evening, to appear on a radio show, *Buchanan and Braden*—Patrick
Buchanan, the Republican columnist and former speechwriter for
President Nixon; Thomas Braden, the Democratic columnist and
friend of the Kennedys, more recently author of *Eight Is Enough*.
The two-hour radio program had been such a success—although
one woman had called in to say, "The thought of a man like you
working in the White House simply makes me want to *scream*"—
and Braden, Buchanan, and Liddy had found themselves in agree-

ment on so many issues, particularly the proper conduct of American foreign policy, that the interviewers had invited Liddy to appear on their television program later that night. They kept him so long on the TV show that their scheduled guest, former ambassador to Moscow Malcolm Toon, had complained and threatened to leave. After the program, Frances Liddy had stayed up in order to complete the family's tax returns, which were more than usually complicated this year, because of the book.

For the past ten years, Frances Liddy, who holds a master's degree in education, has been teaching in downtown Washington, at an elementary school which is almost completely black. "This time of year," she said, pausing to sit down and have a cigarette, "teachers are tired. Children don't sit still; they become hyperactive. Not just in urban schools. Everywhere. They don't read, nobody reads to them. They don't even play house anymore. There isn't the imagination. Except when they're watching television, they don't sit still." She was tired, too, she said, because the past few weeks, when the book and the *Time* excerpts were being edited, had been a strain. "Imagine if *Time* had leaked," she said, "and here we are, a family known for our silence." She laughed. She had read each chapter of the book, she said, as her husband wrote it. "I thought, Now people will know what I've gone through all these years." Then she added, "It's very strange to read it, and realize it's your whole life."

Raymond returned from his errand. His mother put out her cigarette, and started to make sandwiches on a sideboard between the kitchen and the auxiliary living room study. A cab drew up. Sandy, looking like any attractive, well-educated young woman returning from college, walked into the kitchen. "I need money," she said, meaning to pay for the taxi. "Everybody always does," her mother said. When the cab had been paid, Sandy began to help with the preparations for lunch. "I have to be back at school tonight," she said; also, "I'm starving." Frances expressed approval of her daughter's peach-colored suit, then remarked that she was not wearing panty hose. "It's summer, Mom, you don't have to wear them," Sandy said. "That's not my understanding," her mother said.

They both sat down, Frances to smoke another cigarette, Sandy to eat her sandwich. Sandy abruptly mentioned the *Time* excerpts. "I've never been so shocked in my life," she said. "I haven't read the book. I don't know what *else* is in there. We never even had time to sit down and discuss it as a family." Her mother said nothing. "Somebody actually walked up to me on campus and said, 'Are you as crazy as your father?'" Sandy said. Then, with her version of the Liddy twinkle, "I said, 'Yeah, and you better watch out.'"

Ms. Crawford and the photographer arrived, together with Pam Mason, an undergraduate at Dartmouth, who was spending the year in a "journalism internship" at *People*. The three went with Liddy and Raymond to the main, larger living room, where there was a piano. "We're still two children short," Frances said. Phrases drifted through the open door, reminiscences of the forties, "piano lessons," "recital," "largo," "'Master Liddy will now play 'Largo.'" Mother and daughter talked a while longer, in the living room/study. A limousine drove up, delivering Jim. "Why does he get a limousine," Sandy said, laughing, "and I get just a taxi?" She finished her sandwich. Jim walked in. "Go and say hello to your father," Frances Liddy said.

The phone rang. "Raymond," Frances said. "I think it's Mrs. Tower." Senator John Tower's wife was calling to inquire about Raymond's lawn mowing. While Liddy was still in prison, all the children took up various jobs. Sandy, for instance, earned her first year's college tuition by driving a city bus at night. Tom, at the same time, talked his way into St. Albans, Washington's finest private school, under a special program for minorities and foreign indigents. The front door banged. "Thomas has arrived," Frances said. "Tom has arrived?" Liddy's voice asked from the next room. "Tom has arrived, in his usual splendor. With his laundry bag. Don't you have a clean shirt? And, Tom, your *hair*. It's all right. Just go and get a clean shirt." "I have a laundry bag full of dirty shirts," Tom said. He had just come from the final rehearsal for the St. Albans production of *The Boys from Syracuse*, in which he played a starring role. He was wearing tattered army pants, a shirt, sneakers. "No. Go and take one of your father's shirts," his mother said. Mild protests. "Thomas, your mother says you're not wearing a clean shirt," Liddy said, amused, "and that your hair looks like a mare's nest. Go and take one of my shirts." "You know, you'll never get it back," Tom said, starting up the stairs. "I know I'll never get it back," his father said.

The *People* photographer began to wander around, looking for a place to set his tripod. "I don't know just what I want yet," he said. "Anything on this floor," Liddy said. "Evidently the second floor is off-limits." The reporter and Pam Mason were in the main living room, interviewing Liddy children. Was there anything they had found odd, as they were growing up, about their father? No. Anything eccentric? Again no. Raymond wandered into the kitchen, and poured himself something that appeared to be chocolate milk from a pitcher on the sideboard. "What's this?" he asked, before taking a sip. "It's poison," Frances Liddy said. "Your mother, of course, is trying to poison you." Raymond drank his chocolate milk.

Only one of the children, Grace, who was apparently in her room upstairs, had not joined the group talking with the reporter. "Do you think you could get Grace to come and sit with us?" her father asked. "Let's get Grace to come down and join us." One of the children started up the stairs. "Be diplomatic now," their mother said. Grace came down and sat with the others. There was laughter, anecdotes. In answer to a question, Liddy mentioned his pride in each of his children. "Of course, I was away during most of their formative years," he said. He went upstairs to get some medication for his tooth. Had their father never embarrassed them? the reporter resumed at once. No, he hadn't. Did the children have habits of which their parents disapproved? Drinking? Marijuana? No. The children, trying obviously to oblige, took up any line of conversation that did not reflect badly on their father or the family.

In the living room study, Frances Liddy had another cigarette, and spoke of her often-disappointed hope that one of the pregnant cats, a calico, would this time produce a calico male. Jim walked in, and began to explain the aloofness of the dog, Hounddog. The hound had strayed into the Liddy yard several years ago, "when Pop was in prison." "We already had two dogs," Jim said. "Hounddog was very shy, very scared. He stayed around because of the other dogs, I think. He would play with them just out of our reach. Finally, we could pet him, then we took the ticks off him. He didn't like it much. Whenever we would touch him, he was shaking and jumping. Pop would always ask about our progress with Hounddog. Then the other two dogs died." One was poisoned. The other was hit by a car. "So of the three dogs we had," Jim said, "the stray is left."

Liddy came in with the photographer, talking of cameras. "You know, a lot of situations I find I cannot use a flash," Liddy said. "I hate a flash," the photographer said; then, "I still don't know just what I want." Liddy asked whether anyone would like coffee. The photographer would. "Can you make me a cup?" Frances asked. Liddy made coffee and passed the cups around. "See, somebody loves me after all," Frances said. The photographer went back, with Liddy and Jim, to the room where the other children were still being interviewed.

"When he was away, the family just had to unify," Frances said. "Everybody learned to cook. Many days, after teaching school, I thought I would never survive. But the children would say, 'Now, Mother.' They were between nine and fourteen. I thought, Either he's going to be released, or he's not going to be released. We have to give it every chance. And I got them swimming. In swimming, there isn't any fussiness about male or female. Most coaches are good strong men kids can look up to. It's not like those other sports, ice hockey, the Little League, which are so competitive, where you have children straining muscles they should not; and where you have fathers, mothers and fathers, who haven't accomplished anything since seventh grade, living through their nine-year-olds. In swimming, you don't have that. It's a good clean sport. It took up a lot of their energy, it was good for their bodies, the environment was healthy. So I thought, I'd better get those boys in the water and keep them out of trouble. The older children made meals, when we came home at nine o'clock at night. Weekends, I would cook like mad. Some days I was so worn out I thought there was no way I could have driven them one more day. Then, they started to get old enough to drive. I thought, I've just got to work to get him out. Because one night it dawned on me, These children were going to be grown up and *gone* by the time he got out.

"So I worked to get him out. There were committees, George C. Higgins was a godsend, television appearances. I used to say, 'Did you watch me? Did you see your mother on television?' They need their privacy at that age. They had usually watched *Saturday Night Live*. But we kept the ties going. And they had to be kept. Gordon is very much a family man. He's always been so interested in his children. They all have their individuality. I encourage that, I guess, because I was an only child. To raise them as individuals. But we talk about everything. Now, we're both running to make up for the upset, because their lives of course were not normal in those years." She paused. "When he's an old man, they will come," she said. "Pretty soon, there'll already be another"—she hesitated—"facet to their view of him. And in five years, they'll see another facet. And when they're thirty, another." Pause. "You work on that, when you build a family. When he is an old man, they will come."

Everyone took a break, and adjourned to the sideboard for lunch. Jim, who would go to Fordham in the fall, and Tom, who had not decided on a college yet, questioned Pam Mason earnestly about Dartmouth. Sandy talked about what she called a major issue in medicine: tension between doctors and nurses. Nurses increasingly competent and well-trained, doctors, ever more diffident, frightened of malpractice suits, and unwilling to acknowledge the increased responsibility of nurses. She mentioned an old patient at the hospital where she works at night, and the efforts by nurses, over a period of weeks, to get doctors to pay attention to his bed sores. Finally, a young doctor had operated on the old man, without anesthetic, right there on the ward. "You'd think they would listen to the nurses sooner," she said, "or at least show some compassion until God took him away."

The photographer, meanwhile, had decided what he wanted. "Mr. Liddy," he said, "would you just hold your hand over a flame for me?" Liddy declined. In that case, would Liddy put on a ring with jagged edges, honed as a weapon when Liddy was in prison, and make a fist? "I just need one zinger picture," the photographer said. "It's unfortunate, but that's the way the magazine operates." In the end, Liddy put on the ring, but declined to make a threatening gesture. The photographer took some pictures of him, and of the whole family standing in the yard. "You got what you wanted," Liddy said as he was taking off the ring, "and I didn't get what I didn't want." The following week, *People* ran a piece several pages long. Lacking a photograph with a flame, however, it was not a cover story.

At 6 A.M. on Monday, a few people sat, with their early morning pallor, coughs, expressionless faces, in the lobby of the Waldorf-Astoria. Some were reading newspapers. A young woman was reading a paperback, *De Votre Inconscient*. All seemed waiting for diverse errands and appointments. A huge Seiko map high up on one wall flashed the time in various time zones of the world. Little black billboards with white plastic letters announced meetings scheduled to take place in the hotel that day: the National Association of Manufacturers, the New York City Central Labor Council, Descente America, Inc., Young & Rubicam, the Knights of Malta. At 6:15 A.M., two maintenance men, one black, one white, carried the hotel's large American flag to the Lexington Avenue entrance, where they unrolled and raised it. At 6:25, the Muzak went on; at 6:30, the lobby chandeliers, and the lights in the men's and ladies' rooms. At 6:45, a limousine rented by St. Martin's Press drew up at the Park Avenue entrance. Danny, the driver, and Mindy, a young publicity assistant at St. Martin's Press, met Liddy just inside the hotel door. Liddy was scheduled that day for eight radio and television interviews. In the course of the morning, Mindy and a reporter persuaded the St. Martin's publicity department to cancel two interviews. They took Liddy to a dentist. By that time, three interviews had already passed.

As the limousine set out along Park Avenue, Mindy gave Liddy an envelope containing money for expenses on his trip. "I haven't seen that kind of money since I was giving it to the Cubans," Liddy said. Mindy remarked how "refreshing" it was to have an author who carefully accounted for what he spent in cash. At the corner of Madison Avenue and Fifty-second Street, a car ran into the limousine and crumpled the front fender. Danny and the driver of the car got out. A little contretemps ensued. A police car arrived. Liddy recalled a night in early 1973, when a car had crashed into his jeep. The damage had not been serious. But the driver of the other car, a retired general, who was slightly drunk, had been outraged. "He kept saying, 'Citizen's arrest! I hold you in a citizen's arrest,'" Liddy recalled. "I said, 'No need for this citizen's arrest stuff. Let's wait for the State Police.' He said, 'Citizen's arrest! Do you realize you could get thirty days for this?' I said, 'It's okay. I've already got twenty-one years.' He said, 'My God, are you *him?*'"

"Mr. Liddy, we live under a rule of law in this country," Shelley Henrye began, on the Shelley Henrye radio show, and the interview took a not unfamiliar course. When the listener phone calls started coming in ("Did you know anything about the Kennedy assassination before it happened?"), they were not unfamiliar, either. At a console, separated by a glass panel from Liddy and Ms. Henrye, a young man was fielding calls. The whole switchboard remained lit up. "I'm sorry, I can't take your question," he said. "Good question. Please hang on and we'll get to you"; "I'm gonna take you first. Will you turn your radio down. Okay, gottcha"; "Uh-huh, so what's your question? Well, tell me, because it makes a difference"; "Good. There's a question he can answer in spades"; "I'm sorry. During the commercial break I asked him that question and he said he had nothing to say about it"; "All right. Be as brief as you can because we're running against the clock." Then, a caller who identified himself as Dick Tuck was on the air. Liddy greeted the man Democrats thought of as their merry prankster of the 1968 and 1972 campaigns, with real delight. He saluted him as a practitioner of "world-class dirty tricks," "when we were on the other side of the fence." Tuck laughed. "A prison fence?" he asked. Liddy laughed. "Not anymore," he said.

After Liddy's session at the dentist's, an interviewer at the UPI radio station said, in welcome, "I expected your eyes to be blue." He asked whether Liddy would like coffee or lunch. Liddy asked for yogurt, on account of his tooth. A little refrigerator, in the rather shabby office, turned out to contain five flavors of yogurt. The interviewer asked whether they might begin to tape at once. Liddy asked whether he might eat his yogurt while they talked. "Sure," the interviewer said. "This isn't NBC. This is UPI. Just don't slurp on the microphone." Then, they talked, of "morality or ethics, and the rule of reason," of "free will versus individual responsibility." "What's your highest value?" the interviewer asked. "Country, family," Liddy said, then more softly, "friends." When Liddy emerged from the radio station, the limousine stood empty at the curb. Danny, who had been sent to fill a prescription made out by the dentist, had apparently vanished. So had Mindy. When they came back, it turned out that Mindy had been making phone calls. Danny, in addition to filling the prescription, had bought a copy of Liddy's book.

On *News Center 4*, as Liddy appeared in the studio, Tom Snyder, the host, was interviewing Irving Schiff, the New Haven "tax refusenik," who, on what he says are constitutional and other grounds, has paid "not one dime in income taxes since 1973." "That's kind of a dangerous thing," Snyder said. Schiff reminded him that the American Revolution was provoked by "taxation without representation." He started to give five reasons not to pay income taxes. "One, it's patriotic. Two, it will improve your social life, talking about it. Three, if I were to pay my taxes the government would merely waste more money." He spoke of the "subterranean underground" of people who conduct their transactions in cash, to avoid records for tax purposes. He spoke of the fake "churches, trusts, and charitable clubs" being formed to avoid paying taxes for "the Disneyland on the Potomac." "People are dropping out in droves," he said. Next, Snyder interviewed the actress who played the heroine, Joanna Tate, on the soap opera *Search for Tomorrow*, which had run for twenty-seven years. "It's not everyday life," the actress said, of the program. "That would be boring." Commercials. An announcement that an interview with Liddy was coming up. "First, we're going to cook," a television chef said, and made an omelette. Commercials. Then, Tom Snyder said, by way of introduction, "Today, Gordon Liddy is not afraid of anything."

By late afternoon, Liddy had two New York interviews remaining, before he left for Chicago and the West: one, with Scott Kaufer and Paul Slansky of the *Soho News*; the other, with Judy Klemesrud of *The New York Times*. The *Soho News* reporters arrived at Liddy's room in the Waldorf. Slansky at once asked Liddy to review Richard Nixon's book, *The Third War*, for the *Soho News*. Liddy thanked him but said that, during the next few weeks, he would have no time "to do so in a scholarly and thoughtful way." "I've not read the *Time* excerpts," Slansky said, "I've just read the book." It became clear at once that these were by far the most competent interviewers Liddy had had so far. They asked him what questions he had been asked the most, and then asked no one else's questions. They asked him when he had decided to write the book. "After it was absolutely clear that nothing could be salvaged at all," Liddy replied, "and I realized that, for historians, my book would have to be a primary source." They asked him whether Maurice Stans, finance chairman of the Committee to Re-Elect the President, and certainly the biggest political fund-raiser in history, had known about the Watergate. And Liddy (in perhaps a strong instance of his credulity) said, "He didn't know. You see, he didn't need to know." They asked whether he liked the press to think him crazy, "just to keep them off the trail." He replied, "To a little extent, I'll have to admit I've exploited it a bit"; and added that a lot had "sprung from the anticipation of my caricature." In answer to a question, Liddy was saying, "People who like to kill are sick people," when, at the door, there was a loud, peremptory knock. There was a startled pause. A voice bellowed, "Room checking!" They asked him, about the Watergate scandal, "Is there anybody who could have been removed who would have stopped it?" He replied, "No. You'd have had to blow away a cast of thousands."

They asked him what he read, whether he helped his wife with "domestic chores," what he thought of a Nixon quote about him on the tape of June 23, 1972 ("just locker-room talk," he said, calmly), whether he cared about the pennant races, "Do you think people draw the wrong conclusion from your fascination with things German?" To the last question, Liddy gave quintessentially a writer's reply. "I think my book is my best shot," he said. Just before they left, Slansky and Kaufer asked him to record the following messages for their home answering tapes: "Hi. This is G. Gordon Liddy. Please leave your message when you hear the tone. Or I'll kill you"; "Hi. This is G. Gordon Liddy. Please leave your message when you hear the tone. Or I'll break your knees." Curiously enough, though Slansky and Kaufer leaked the contents of these answering tapes to *The New York Times* People column, which published an item about them, they did not use one word of their interview, which was also taped, in the *Soho News*, but ran a brief, friendly item, "Ten Reasons to Like G. Gordon Liddy," instead.

En route to the airport, Danny announced that he was "twenty percent through" Liddy's book. "It reads easily. It's written fluidly," he said. Mindy reported that she had heard a radio interview with former Vice President Agnew, in which he claimed, apropos of Liddy's book, that a high government official had warned him (Agnew) that he must resign from the vice presidency, that he faced "assassination" unless he resigned. Liddy asked whether Mindy had remembered to bring two copies of his book, which he wanted to inscribe to the two dentists who had worked on his teeth. She had. One of the dentists, she said, had called St. Martin's Press to find out how Liddy was, and the switchboard operator, thinking the call was from a crank, had said, "There's a dentist on the line." Liddy signed the books.

Traffic was slow, because, Danny said, it was Earth Day. Liddy mentioned an interview in which he had met Jan Teller, daughter of the scientist Edward Teller. Before Liddy went on the air, Ms. Teller had sewed on a button that had fallen off his jacket. "We had a heck of a good conversation," he said. He recalled an interview with National Public Radio. "A bit adversarial," he said. "Politely so, however." Danny turned on the car radio. "The Casper Citron Show with G. Gordon Liddy." Why, Citron asked, had Liddy waited until the statute of limitations had expired, even for people he did not like. "Otherwise, it's not a matter of principle," Liddy said. "It's a matter of vindictiveness." Why should anyone buy a book by a convicted felon? "Think of O'Henry, Villon, Daniel Defoe," Liddy said. "They all did time."

On Tuesday night, shortly after eight, Gordon Liddy stood outside the doors of O'Hare Airport in Chicago. At nine, he was scheduled to begin a two-hour interview with Dr. Milton Rosenberg, a professor of sociology at the University of Chicago, who happens also to run the city's most popular nightly talk show. Taxis, limousines, and private cars passed Liddy on the ramp. There was no sign of the limousine hired by St. Martin's Press. Liddy stood for some minutes beside his suitcase and his garment bag. Then he went inside, to see whether the chauffeur might somehow have missed him at the baggage claim. A tall dark man, carrying a suit jacket, with loosened tie and open shirt collar, walked up to Liddy, shook his hand, and, addressing him by name, offered him a ride into the city. Liddy thanked him, but explained that he was looking for a limousine that had been hired for him. The tall man offered his own driver and limousine. He was going to the Drake Hotel, he said. Liddy called the agency that should have sent his car. They said they had sent it. Liddy waited another ten minutes under the lights, in the dark outside O'Hare. He looked at his watch. The tall man and his limousine were still there. At his insistence, Liddy and I got into the backseat. The tall man sat, beside the uniformed chauffeur, in front.

"I gotta tell you, you're one of the few stand-up guys in the world, in the entire world," the man said, leaning his elbow over the front seat and further loosening his tie. "And you can use my limousine. I just happen to think that your conduct, okay? regardless of the circumstances, the sacrifices, whatever reasons possessed you, I respect you immensely. Immensely. I respect your family. Whatever you may think of the President, for better or for worse. Out of respect for the man, and on behalf of his office, you made the sacrifice. Not many in the entire world would do the same."

"I hope you're wrong," Liddy said. Then he muttered something about the exemplary conduct of prisoners of war, returning from Hanoi, and that "nobody makes a continuing fuss over them."

"I'm not talking about *groups*," the tall man said, firmly. "I take things on an individualistic basis. I've seen an awful lot. I've known so many miscreants. I'm chairman and chief executive of a company, okay? I have money, a lot of emoluments. But I've seen some terrible, terrible weak links." He paused and looked out of the window. "My business is jukeboxes, vending machines. Also hearing aids, bandages, crap like that. The worst part of business, the most tragic part of business, okay? you make your first mistake and guys start copping out on you. *And they were partners at the time.*" He looked out of the window again. "In any business you sometimes have to cut corners," he said. "In consultation with your partners. I heard that clown Hunt, forgive me for being subjective and personal, but I can tell you, *one man on my team like you . . .*"

Liddy took up the reference to Hunt. "I happen to have been surrounded by the spectacularly weak," he said.

"No," the man said, again firmly. "So many miscreants. Such terrible, terrible weak links. Now a classic example is Joel Dolkart, of Gulf & Western, who's indicted for stealing two million dollars. And then started to cop out on Charlie Bluhdorn. Who built a very fine conglomerate, I might add. And the miserable miscreant plea bargains. Now who pays for that?" Silence. "The shareholders. And this lousy bum walks the streets."

"In the FBI, we knew," Liddy said, taking up the reference to plea bargains, "if a fellow knows something, he'll tell you. If he doesn't, he'll make it up."

"Sometimes I think there's only two stand-up guys in Chicago.

That's Adolph," he turned to the driver, who was black, "and me. Tonight, I'm taking a judge, and his girlfriend, to dinner. An impecunious judge. You know what I'm talking about. So many miscreants. Such bad judgment retrospectively." He turned, and again leaned his elbow over the seat-back. "There was a man in our organization, okay? I refer to as our John Dean. He talked his stinking guts out. One day I looked at him in the office, I said, 'So help me God, you are our John Dean.'"

Liddy said nothing.

"Look, I mean, I started work, I was eleven, as mail boy for a bank. Then there was a man, the man was an absolute genius, an absolute financial genius. A friend. When I tell you he gave me checks for x, y, and z deal, 'your interest.' And I never even knew what x, y, and z deal was. One day, he said, 'I've made a tender offer. B. F. Goodrich. Two and a half million dollars for each of us. I was scared shitless, to be honest with you. The banker said, 'Will you tell that Jew bastard to get out of B. F. Goodrich, or we'll stop his line at the bank.' So we gracefully withdrew. But there was one half a million dollars, for each of us, in one day. In one afternoon. That's some story."

"It's the American way," Liddy said.

"I don't know if it's the American way or not." Another pause. "My son got married a week ago Saturday. Both sons are in law school. In Chicago. You know, the joy; my greatest aspiration as a young husband and father was the fear How am I going to educate my children. My greatest achievement was to educate my sons. As for my daughter, so far her grades are not good enough. We have this joke, I may have to build or buy a college for her education."

"They can't take what's in your head," Liddy said.

"That. And. Or. Experience." A long silence. "Especially in a community like that. I mean a prison. I think there's a time, when people should talk. But when all the other rats jump off the ship, and one man does not, that man has character. I don't say this because you're here, because we'll probably never see each other again. But for you to make the sacrifice you did, for *honor*'s sake. You're, in my opinion, the only good thing that came out of Watergate."

"I'm an educated man," Liddy said. "I was compensated for it."

The limousine stopped at the Drake Hotel. The man gave both Liddy and me his address and phone number, "as a courtesy." He told the driver to take Liddy directly to the radio station. "This is Adolph," he said, earnestly, in farewell. "You should get to know him."

Adolph set out into the nighttime traffic. "Are you taping tonight, or are you going on live?" he asked. Liddy said live. Adolph mentioned the failure of Liddy's own limousine to show up. "Here's our card," he said. "In case you need (chuckle) dependable service."

The radio station building was a two-story yellow-brick structure, in a remote, poorly lighted area of the city, among vacant asphalt lots. A guard just inside the entrance took Liddy's garment bag and suitcase and put them in a supermarket shopping cart. It was not clear to what use the supermarket cart was ordinarily put inside a radio station. A young woman appeared, the *Milt Rosenberg Show*'s producer, and led the way down a corridor to a small, dingy cafeteria. She brought Liddy some coffee, in a paper cup. They sat down at a table.

"You're the cool one," said a friendly, professorial voice from the doorway. Milt Rosenberg. "The last time you were here"—when Liddy had come to promote his thriller—"you never mentioned you were writing this book." "*You're* the cool one," Liddy replied, greeting Rosenberg with obvious pleasure. "The last time I was here, you never mentioned that you have a title. I didn't know you were Professor." They talked a while. Liddy kept addressing his host as "Dr. Rosenberg." "Let's strike a bargain," Rosenberg said. "You are Gordon. I am Milt."

Milt led the way upstairs, down a corridor of offices locked for the night, into the studio. An announcer was just doing the nine o'clock news: "George Bush and Edward Kennedy have slim leads in the Illinois primary." Liddy and Milt sat beside each other at a sort of conference table. They put on earphones. Rosenberg, in introducing Liddy and his book ("A book of multiple value, I think, of compelling value. Excellent autobiography"), turned to Liddy and said, "It reveals qualities in yourself that you may not be aware of." Liddy said that, as a young man unsure whether to become an operatic tenor or a lawyer, he had taken, as did so many of his generation, the Johnson O'Connor aptitude tests. They had suggested that his talents might lie in publishing or in something literary. "It appears, after all these years," he said, "that they were right and I was wrong."

Rosenberg spoke awhile: "My summary of your vita to date includes your years with the FBI, some of them spent just in our backyard. Gary, Indiana," and mentioned the plan to kill Jack Anderson. "But it did not get executed," he said. "*He* did not get executed," Liddy corrected, mildly. Rosenberg spoke of "values that are based on Machiavelli but suggest Nietzsche," of matters of "*Weltanschauung* versus *Uebersicht,*" of "Some values perhaps that are of a different modality from those that inform our way of life?" A moment's silence. "My turn?" Liddy asked. He spoke of his perception that the crisis in the country at the time of Watergate consisted not of "gentle little girls in bare feet carrying daisies" but of campus riots, burning cities, and so forth. "In that context, with that perception, always distinguishing between mere protesters and bomb throwers," he said, he had taken the actions that he took. A listener called in to ask how Liddy could possibly justify the break-in at the office of Ellsberg's psychiatrist. "We did not know what we had there in Dr. Ellsberg," Liddy said. Commercials. A jingle: "Crunchies. Delicious. They're everything they're cracked up to be," "Are you aware of anything I have asked you, Gordon," Rosenberg asked, while their microphones were turned off, "that might make you uncomfortable in any way?" Liddy said no, it was always stimulating to talk with Dr. Rosenberg.

"A document of our time," Rosenberg resumed, speaking of *Will,* when he and Liddy were back on the air. He mentioned Liddy's marriage and genetics. Liddy said that Charles Lindbergh had spoken of similar considerations in his marriage to Anne Morrow. (Anne Morrow Lindbergh had appeared that week, on *60 Minutes,* to promote her book about her husband.) They spoke of "Social Darwinism"; then, of spying for political purposes. "It's as American as apple pie," Liddy said. "It's right out of *The Last Hurrah*. It's the way the game is played." When the subject of Liddy's childhood interest in Naziism came up, Liddy mentioned that, before the war, the custom in all American public schools was to pledge allegiance to the flag with a straight-arm, palm-down salute. Rosenberg asked Liddy whether he thought his book was "the definitive history" of Watergate; and Liddy replied, "No. I'm probably disqualified from writing the history. I'm too close to it. Where do I get off doing that? I might be wrong. You see what I mean." Liddy made a distinction between the purposes of what he called Watergates I and II. "In the second break-in, the focus changed," he said, "from the spoken to the written word. We were sent to photograph all files." Rosenberg asked, given the uselessness of those files, whether Watergate resulted from "a Matterhorn complex. They had to break in because it's there." Liddy said no. Commercials. When the microphones were off, Liddy asked, "Going well?" Rosenberg replied, "How could it not?"

On the air, Rosenberg alluded to Machiavelli once again. "You might conclude that it's all right to be a good soldier of the Prince," he said, "but you'd better find a Prince who's ruthless enough, as yours was not." "I'd say that's a pretty good summary," Liddy said. Nearly an hour and a half had passed. The program was turned over entirely to phone calls from listeners: "I'm a practicing attorney. I've read only the review in *Time*. I'm a free thinker and a humanist. How many misguided souls like you are still at large in government?"; "I feel you were very seriously used. Knowing your nature to be blunt and brutal, I think you were being used, and I think it's sad." One man called to inquire what Liddy thought of "the Ehrlichman thesis," that McCord was a double agent, sent in to bring the Nixon administration down. Liddy replied that he did not think so, that he was not a subscriber to the conspiracy theory of history. Then, someone asked what he called the "nitty-gritty question," one that prompted considerable speculation in almost every book about Watergate: why the tape on the lock of the door to the Watergate complex had been placed horizontally (so that it was visible even on a shut door) instead of vertically. Liddy explained it very carefully. All maintenance men, he said, taped locks horizontally, for the simple reason that vertically placed tape would not hold. "But try it. Put it on vertically, and see if it holds. You'll find it pops right off." More questions, theories about CIA conspiracies, theories about the death, in an airplane crash, of Mrs. E. Howard Hunt. "Look, what you have here," Liddy said, "is the phenomenon of obsession with the details of enormously publicized events." And that was that. Rosenberg returned to matters of philosophy and statecraft.

Liddy said he thought that, as a result of the Vietnam War, Americans were permitting their foreign policy to be conducted both timidly and as though they inhabited a safe and benign world. "We can no longer afford the luxury of that illusion," he said. Rosenberg said, "You're left with a very dark vision of the future." Liddy asked him to imagine a bad neighborhood, and a man, looking like a wimp, with a fat wallet, walking toward a man with a machine gun. "Let's not be the guy who looks like a wimp," he said, becoming, for the first time in his trip, overtly hortatory. More talk. "You're a very interesting man," Rosenberg said, at the end of the program, "and a totally honest one." Outside, on the sidewalk, he said, "Come back again, and let's talk about prison conditions." Liddy said he would.

The next morning, Liddy left his hotel to shop for suspenders. On account of his tooth, he had by now not eaten solid food in nearly a week. He could not further tighten his belt. A woman walked up to him and said, perfectly amiably, "Death to the CIA." As he walked, with a newspaperman, outside the Commodities Exchange, a man, who identified himself as a commodities broker, shook Liddy's hand and said he admired him. "You're in a riskier business than mine ever was," Liddy said. Suddenly, in a corridor, a young man emerged from an office and greeted Liddy with considerable affection. It was Dwight Chapin, the former White House appointments secretary, who went to prison for a Watergate-related felony. He is now editor of something called *Success Magazine*, which is published by the biggest public contributor to the Nixon campaign, R. Clement Stone.

Stone had hoped to be ambassador to London. So had another large contributor, Russell Firestone. According to Ervin Committee records, Firestone had written to Chapin, after a meeting with President Nixon, "Thank you for permitting me to bask in the radiance of his presence." Neither man became ambassador to London.

Liddy's stay in Los Angeles coincided with a Southern California balloon race. Steve Harvey, a young reporter who had for several days been covering the balloon race for the *Los Angeles Times*, was assigned for a day to cover Gordon Liddy. "I do off-beat features," Harvey said, with a little shrug. At eight o'clock in the morning, Liddy and the young reporter set off from Liddy's hotel, L'Ermitage, by limousine for an interview on the Mikael Jackson radio show. "I thought you'd be out there with the balloons," Jackson said, when Liddy introduced him to Steve Harvey. "I had to interrupt the balloons," Harvey said. They entered the studio, a small gray room, with a dartboard whose target was a large photograph of Ayatollah Khomeini, and with various signs (a picture of a cymbal, for instance, captioned "status cymbal") and other *objets* strewn about. On Jackson's desk, beside his microphone, was a book, *How to Live With Your Teenager*. The news was coming through a speaker: "Secretary of State Cyrus Vance has resigned…with a 'heavy heart'… says he will support the President on other issues." A voice said, through the intercom, "I have that Vance resignation, if you want it on tape." "Thanks," Jackson said. "I've got it live." Then, he turned to Liddy. "Welcome back," he said. "Is it cold out there? Is it raining?" No. "So my forecast here is entirely wrong." A red light flashed, airtime.

"This is really gonna be a wildly busy morning," Jackson said, in English-accented (he was born in England), staccato American slang. "We'll have Dick Gregory calling in, from his fifteenth day of fasting in Teheran. Jack Nelson, calling in from Washington. Also, coming up, our food critic, Elma Dells." Then, his interview with Liddy: "You were dangerous, brave. To what end?"; "Are they all childish games?"; "Was it all worth it? Did it serve any purpose?"; "This is better written than the first book"; "How do you feel about Carter now?" During a break, Jackson sang along with a commercial for Gallo Salami. "Is it going all right?" Liddy asked. "A little tight," Jackson said. "We don't have the rapport we had last time."

On the air again, in reply to a question about Secretary Vance, Liddy was saying, "He's a lawyer." "Liar?" Jackson asked. "Lawyer," Liddy said. They discussed the failed mission in the Iranian desert. Liddy compared it to Dieppe, and other early failures of World War II. "What matters in life, sir?" Jackson asked, abruptly. "Doing one's very best," Liddy said, then recalled Winston Churchill's advice to a class at Eton, "Never give up. Never. Never. Never. Never." "I can see the mail now," Jackson said, drumming his fingers on the desk during another break. "How come you didn't attack G. Gordon Liddy?"

On the air, more conversation. Many listener phone calls. Several hostile callers, attempting to *spring* their angry remarks after some innocuous opening sentences, gave their views away with the sarcastic tone of the first syllable. "He's not much better than other people in government," one caller said, after a fairly long and abstract meditation. "He's nothing but a *pansy*." Liddy called this a "declarative statement," and asked, "What is your question?" "You could never have this on the BBC," Jackson said during the next commercial break.

In Liddy's hotel room, the interviewer for Los Angeles *NewsCenter 4* looked at Steve Harvey, and at me, with some suspicion. "You fancy yourself a hero," she said to Liddy. "But a lot of people went to jail because you remained silent. What would you say to them, Mr. Liddy?" "Who?" Liddy said, genuinely bewildered. The interviewer changed the subject. What did Liddy think of ABSCAM? He said that, as a lawyer, he sensed entrapment in it. "What would you say to the many people who regard themselves as being had by Richard Nixon?" the interviewer asked. "Who?" Liddy said again. "Many people regard you as a morally bankrupt man," she began again. Silence. "Do you see yourself as a morally bankrupt man?" "No," he said. "I do not." Whom did he support for President. Liddy declined to answer. "I might get myself into a position of a gratuitous endorsement, and that would be harmful to the candidate," he said. "Come now, Mr. Liddy, isn't that a cop-out?" she said. "When you're peddling your book, when you're doing a TV interview to sell your book, in effect don't you think it's a cop-out not to react?" "I have just reacted," Liddy said. "I understand that I have not reacted in the way you want me to. I'm sorry." "In all honesty, Mr. Liddy, why should anyone buy a book by a criminal?" Liddy gave his O'Henry, Villon, Defoe answer. The interviewer asked what he thought of "the world situation in the next few months." He said it looked grim. War? "Not in the next few months, but sooner rather than later." What kind of war? "War over natural resources in the Middle East." The interviewer asked the cameraman to stop the camera.

Liddy and the interviewer talked about military preparedness for a while. Liddy spoke of the bad neighborhood, the fat wallet, and the wimp. The interviewer at once asked that the camera be turned on again. "Mr. Liddy," she said then, "do you think Cy Vance is a wimp?" "No," he said. "I think Cyrus Vance did the honorable thing. When you disagree with a policy, you resign over it. A time came when he could not publicly support the President, he resigned." "Is it more fun writing a book than conducting spy missions?" she asked. "It's not fun at all," Liddy said. "Both are hard work." The interviewer asked, "Mr. Liddy, if Richard Nixon were still President, would the hostages still be in Teheran?" Liddy gave his "The *Shah* would still be in Teheran" reply. "Do you think the country's attitudes are changing more in line with the Liddy view of how things should be done?" "I hope so," he said. The interviewer gave up.

As she and the cameraman were leaving, the cameraman turned to Liddy. "I have to agree with you," he said. A friend of his, a reserve officer, had made a trip to inspect a military base, and had told the cameraman, "The equipment out there is all junk." "The skies are black," Liddy said, shaking his head, "with chickens coming home to roost." The interviewer later called both Steve Harvey and me, to ask what sort of pieces we were doing. ("We're keeping them honest,"

Harvey said to me.) *NewsCenter 4* that night simply reported that the book was out. Of the interview, there were just the lines about Nixon and the Shah.

At noon on the first Friday in May, Gordon and Frances Liddy were due on the playing fields of the St. Albans School in Washington, D.C., where this year's Track & Field Meet of the District of Columbia Special Olympics was being held. The Special Olympics, which have occurred annually all over the country since 1968, consist of sports events for retarded or otherwise damaged children. At 10 A.M., Eunice Kennedy Shriver, who was one of the most enthusiastic founders of the national program, had administered the Special Olympics Oath. A runner had lighted a special torch. Races and games had begun all over the field. Gordon Liddy was to be one of the honorary judges or, more precisely, awarders of ribbons. The events are so organized that as many children as possible will receive ribbons of some sort. The three top competitors in each of many simultaneous and successive events are encouraged to climb on pedestals in front of a reviewing stand, where an announcer calls out their names through a microphone. Judges, with handfuls of first-, second-, and third-prize ribbons, stand in front of the pedestals. The children naturally are of various heights and ages. Not all of them understand what the ribbons are for or that, given the height of the pedestals and the height of the judges, taller children must lean downward to have ribbons pinned on their T-shirts. Three judges, one of whom was an army colonel, were pinning ribbons somewhere on the clothing of a very rapid succession of winning children. Since the work of pinning and congratulating is a strenuous and not unathletic business, the adults worked in shifts. Liddy's shift was in the afternoon.

At one end of the field, at the finish line of one of the longer racetracks, Tom Liddy, wearing his army pants, sneakers, and a sports shirt, stood, with six other boys from St. Albans. Each was carrying a stopwatch and holding on to a section of an often-torn and re-knotted colored string, which served as the finishing tape. "Who's got the guy with the green pants and white shirt?" Tom asked, as children lined up in their lanes at the starting line for the beginning of one race. "I've got the tall guy in blue," one of his classmates said. "Let's do it by numbers," another boy said. They were each timing, and otherwise watching out for, a child in a single lane. The children had numbers pinned to the front of their shirts. A card, with name, age, and school, was pinned to the back. The timers decided to keep track by numbers. "Remember, if someone comes barrelin' down and doesn't want to stop at the finish line," one of the older boys said, "let 'em come. Sometimes they don't like to stop."

"ALL RIGHT! ALL RIGHT! ALL RIGHT!" Tom bellowed, in the hearty way of athletes on playing fields and basketball courts. Then, as the race began, "Way to go. Way to go. Way to *go*." An extraordinary number of people seemed to be cheering each child and then hugging each child as the races finished. It turned out that adults and St. Albans students in charge of the meet had been divided into timers, huggers, and runners. The runners accompanied each child, after every race, back to an area near the reviewing stand where there was the group from his own school. In every race at Tom's track, there were stragglers, children who walked all the way, or turned back, or simply stopped running. The seven boys at the finish line would cheer, beckon, wave, smile, and advance slightly toward those children, until the last child had reached the finishing tape, and been given his hug. "Congratulations. Boy! You really moved. You flew," the timers would say. "Is that all right? You pleased? Hey, c'mere, I've gotta get your name and everything." Timers would read the child's name on the back of his shirt and record the time. A hug. For the most part, the children hugged back, or slapped hands, or simply grinned. Some of the larger children came along the track with such force and speed that the seven holders of stopwatches would have to step back a bit, to avoid being bowled over. The finishing tape kept advancing toward small stragglers, retreating before large, pounding racers. "Watson, do you have a class?" a girl student asked one of the timers. He said he did. She took his place.

Gordon and Frances Liddy arrived at the reviewing stand. A student immediately introduced herself to him and set him to awarding ribbons. Frances walked around the field toward where Tom was. She had wanted to talk to him about his grades, but, seeing how busy he was (all the timers, huggers, and runners, by this time, looked as though they had taken part in an athletic marathon themselves), she decided to raise the matter by letter instead. "In first place, *Roulette Taylor*!" a girl student's voice shouted, with hoarse enthusiasm, over the loudspeaker; all the announcers' voices were starting to go. "It's very good for our kids, very important to them," a St. Albans mother said to me. "It exposes them to a serious, important part of reality." "I'm standing all by myself," a very little girl said, standing next to her. "I'm all by myself. I'm all alone." "Why, I'm all alone, too," the St. Albans mother said at once, and lifted her up to watch a race.

During a break, Eunice Shriver and Gordon Liddy had a brief conversation. A member of the student organizing committee told Frances that Tom would be in charge of the Special Olympics next year. Somebody was in a bulldog costume (Frances had for years been in charge of the washing of it), and she thought for a moment it was her son. "I almost hugged it," she said, "but then I saw the legs were too thin." The races began again. Tom was by now lifting up every child that came near him at the finish line. So was Ronald Brown, a black student and national champion in the 100 meters, who had been admitted to St. Albans under the same program as Tom Liddy. Music came over a loudspeaker. A white child, with a number on his T-shirt, stood in front of it, rapt in a kind of ritual dance. Only first-prize ribbons were left; most children in the final races got first-prize ribbons. "I've been sort of encouraging people along," a girl student said, happily, to the Liddys as they were leaving, "and I'm just *dead*."

After being stranded in Kansas City by an Ozark Airlines strike, Liddy arrived one night in St. Louis, at the Marriott Hotel. He had been looking forward to his stay there, he said, because of the hotel chain's "Rolls-Royce Silver Shadow ads." "Is this your first experience with Marriott?" he said they asked him at the desk. He said it was. "Everybody's saying 'Hi,' as in the ads," he said, in telling the story the next morning. "All I'm asking for is shelter, and everybody's saying 'Hi.' They call a boy named Charlie to the desk, and say, 'Mr. Liddy, this is Charlie.' Charlie says. 'Hi.' We take an elevator, and walk down a hall. Charlie throws open a door, and says, 'Mr. Liddy, your *room*!' Evidently, it isn't. There's a man in the bed. There's an airline captain's jacket hanging over a chair. Your first Marriott experience. Off Charlie runs. Only one elevator works, so there is a wait. I'm there, outside the room, standing on one foot and then the other. Alone with the baggage cart. Two women walk by. One says, 'I think that's Gordon Liddy.' The other says, 'I don't think he's got a room.' Charlie comes back. We go to another room, on another floor. He throws open the door. 'Mr. Liddy, your *room*!' A man sleeping in the bed. Another pilot's jacket. Even the rank is the same. You know, this is my first Marriott. It's after midnight. Finally, I get a room.

"When I'm in bed, I start to hear this little sirenlike whistle, in the air-conditioning. I think, I'll endure this because Bill Arript [of Marriott] was so good to Sally Harmony." (Ms. Harmony, who was Liddy's secretary at the time of Watergate, is unforgettable to viewers of the Ervin Committee hearings, for at least one line: Asked whether, when she was typing from photocopies with the outline of gloved fingers at their edges, she had not guessed that the work in progress was clandestine, Ms. Harmony replied, "I knew it was clandestine. But to me, Senator, clandestine does not mean illegal. And I can keep a secret." Later, Marriott gave Ms. Harmony a job.) "But I just can't sleep. So I call downstairs. Up comes this maintenance fellow. He checks. Then he says, 'It's the air conditioner. There's dirt in the cones. Sometimes, even when you turn them off, there will be this little whistle.' I said, 'I'm sure your analysis is correct. But can you fix it?' He said, 'Not before tomorrow.'"

At the airport in Minneapolis-St. Paul, there was again no limousine—or rather, there was a mysterious locked and empty limousine. No driver. Liddy took a cab to his hotel. On the flight to
Detroit, Republic Airlines lost Liddy's luggage. A day later, they
found it. An interviewer for the *Detroit Free Press* said to Liddy,
"You are remembered as a second-rate burglar. How would you prefer to be remembered?" Liddy said, "More favorably." When the interview was over, Liddy said, "I think that fellow believed we were
having a tough-guy contest in there."

Back in New York for a brief visit, which included three appearances
(a breakfast meeting of advertisers and businessmen, organized by
the Smith-Greenland Agency; an address at lunch to the Coast
Guard Officers Club on Governor's Island; and an afternoon taping
of the three interviews with Dick Cavett), Liddy stood on a sidewalk, waiting for a taxi. Finding none, he looked repeatedly at his
watch. An off-duty cab drew up. "I disagree with your views, but I
like you. Get in," the driver said. Liddy got in. The driver said he was
already late. He was going to pick up his wife, in Queens. Then, describing himself as "a moderate Jewish liberal," he began a long dis-
quisition about himself, his background, his politics, his wife,
Queens. At an intersection, he saw a man with a briefcase, trying to
hail a cab. "Where are you going? LaGuardia?" he shouted. The man
said, "LaGuardia Airport." "I'd like to help this other fellow out,"
the driver said, remarking that LaGuardia was near enough to
Queens. Then, having introduced Liddy to the passenger, he resumed his discourse, about politics, his wife, Queens, the quality of
city life, Mayor Koch. At a red light he turned, with an interroga-
tory inflection, to his new passenger for agreement. "Am I right? Or
am I right?" "Well," the man said, "I'm from *Ohio*."

During the cab ride Liddy told me that he and Frances had begun
a negotiation, which he hoped would be successful. They had put in
a bid for a house, on the Potomac, which had originally been built

for Alan Drury, author of, among other Washington novels, *Advise and Consent*. They expected to have an answer within the week.

At the businessmen's breakfast, Liddy stood for a moment in silence at the microphone. Then, rather loudly and startlingly, he said, "Boo!" His audience laughed, a bit uncertainly. Previous speakers at these breakfasts had included Harrison Salisbury, Arthur Ashe, Theodore Kheel, Mayor Koch, Pete Rozelle, Martha Graham, George Gallup, William Safire, Jack Valenti. ("We were going to have Princess Ashraf last month," a man told me, as he was putting on his name tag, "but the idea was shot down.") The Smith-Greenland Agency had somehow created the impression, within St. Martin's Press and also with Liddy, that audiences for these breakfasts were limited to members of the Fortune 500 (although actually the guests were mainly advertising people). After his "Boo!" and with a few other equivocal jokes and interjections, Liddy addressed what he had been led to believe were "movers and shakers" with a long, impassioned stem-winder about American politics, foreign policy, and morale. The Founding Fathers, he said, had been wise but tough men, and the world was still and would be a tough place, always. "It is that way, and it's been that way since the mind of man runneth not to the contrary." He was worried, he said, about the country's "post-Vietnam War abhorrence of battle." Not that he believed in battle, except when there was no other choice, but he believed in preparedness for it. He was concerned, he said, when a great democratic country chose to rely on an all-voluntary, and underpaid, professional army. Among peaceful nations with armed, trained citizenry, he mentioned Switzerland, then said, "I think Universal Military Training is the fairest way to go."

He approved, he said, of President Carter's "resolve" in undertaking the Iranian desert rescue mission. He was not of course qualified to appraise its planning. He recognized its difficulty. "A helicopter," he said, "was once defined as ten thousand nuts and bolts trying to fly off in the same direction." At the same time, he worried about the "mind-set" of contingency plans for failure. For this audience, though, no mention of the wimp, the bad neighborhood, the wallet. First, the Founding Fathers. Now, Liddy spoke of the conquistadores, who had no contingency plans for failure. "They burned their ships behind them," he said. "They didn't start their mission ready to say abort, abort, abort." He worried that the country, irresolute, was growing "weaker and weaker." Then, he ended on a ringing, hortatory note, and took questions—of which there were very many. Toward the end, a tall black man got to his feet, and asked, "How do you see your own future?" Liddy said, "Well, let's face it, I had my shot. And I missed." Then, he told of a famous admiral, a man so abrasive that he fell into disfavor and obscurity, until World War I broke out and his country needed him. A correspondent had asked the admiral how he could account for his recall to a post of great importance. "When the shells start to fly," the admiral replied, "they call on the sons of bitches." Liddy paused a bit wistfully.

The chairman of Smith-Greenland finally called the questions short, then made a few remarks about Liddy's "forceful personality." "As evidence," he said, rather oddly, "he has five wonderful children." Liddy said, "I was away during their formative years." Several people gathered around him when he had finished speaking. Several others milled about, muttering to one another that he was "crazy" or "insane."

Some of his remarks this time about where America stood, however, had been so unremittingly bleak that I asked him, when we had left the breakfast, why he usually seemed, by temperament, so sanguine. "I see these problems recognized as problems by serious people in a position to do something about them," he said. Then, he recalled that, after a lot of ineffectual bumbling, the country had pulled itself together for World War II. "Of course this time, the reaction time with missiles makes it unlike World War II. We have less time to protect ourselves from folly, and there is a steeper price. But I measure the price of failure against the great reward attendant to success." He mentioned that we have, after all, a constitutional democracy. "Some might favor having a President answerable to

Parliament," he said. "And the White House press corps is a poor substitute."

In the car, a shiny new Mercedes, which had picked Liddy up at the Waldorf for the drive to lunch on Governor's Island, the driver, a Coast Guard officer, described how eager and then how glad he had been to avoid service in Vietnam. "I didn't wanna stop a bullet," he said. "I didn't even wanna slow one down." On the drive downtown and during the fifteen-minute ferry ride, he and Liddy chatted amiably. The officer said his wife had just had a hysterectomy, but was feeling better. Liddy said he was glad she was feeling better. The ferry docked. "Guess you haven't been here since the Korean conflict," the officer said to Liddy. Then he took us on a quick tour of the island's Coast Guard installations: its golf course; its housing; its view of the Statue of Liberty; its nursery school (the Hooligan Haven Day Care Center); its lot for the repair of damaged or rusting buoys. He parked in front of the Governor's Island Officers Club. "Those who enter here," said a sign in the hallway, "shall buy a round of cheer. Those who do not pay with verve, we shall refuse to serve."

During drinks on the terrace, Liddy was introduced to a lot of Coast Guard officers, several of whom asked him to sign copies of his book, and most of whom seemed to be drinking a quantity of Bloody Marys. At lunch, after all visitors, including Coast Guardsmen from other installations, had been introduced, and had acknowledged the introduction by rising slightly in their chairs, Liddy gave another stem-winder. There were no black Coast Guardsmen in the room, and only one Coast Guard woman. Someone at my table remarked that, last year, at the Coast Guard Academy in Groton, "the homecoming queen was a cadet."

Again, there were a lot of questions, most of them decidedly unmilitaristic. An early questioner referred to "your rather Spartan discipline, the Prisoner of Zenda-type stuff." "Let me clear the record," Liddy interrupted. "I have never done time in Zenda. Though I seem to have done time everywhere else." "What level did you have reason to think approval or disapproval of your operations was bucked up to?" "At least to a level that had access to the Oval Office. But we had to leave the President in a position of plausible denial," Liddy said. One questioner mentioned the anomalous appointment of General Alexander Haig to succeed H. R. Haldeman as chief of the White House staff. "Did you ever have reason to think we were in danger of a military takeover?" he asked. Liddy thought a moment. "Never," he said. "Not the military, in their wildest fantasies, never. It's just not in the institutional memory of the military, in this country, to think that way."

Someone asked how, if Liddy had received an order to kill an American civilian, he could ever have reconciled it with his conscience. Liddy said he recognized that any reasonable man might have a moral doubt about any order to kill. "It's only, if you have these problems, get out of that line of work," he said. General Gerard, a retired reserve officer in his middle eighties, got to his feet. "I wonder if this would be correct," he said. "If someone, the President, were to call one of us and say, 'Your country needs you to do something, above or outside the Constitution, to save your country,' wouldn't we do likewise? If you were called in such a situation, would you just say, 'Forget it'?" Silence. Someone asked, "After they were caught, why didn't everyone just say, 'We did it,' and get it over with? Is that simplistic?" Liddy said that, in Washington, cover-up at the highest level was an unvarying custom and an institutional reflex. "It's all a cover-up, in Washington," he said. "I mean, that's what they do down there." The questions continued for three hours.

The next afternoon, Liddy taped his three interviews for the Dick Cavett Show. They began shortly after one o'clock. "Good evening," Cavett said, as usual, at the beginning of the first half hour. The audience, which was aghast at almost every instant of the interview, seemed to find nothing at all odd in being greeted with "Good evening," before two in the afternoon. They applauded dutifully, as studio audiences do applaud, when a sign reading "Applause" flashed.

At the beginning of both of the next two half hours, Cavett would say, "Good evening. Tonight we're continuing last night's interview with Gordon Liddy." The audience did not seem to find that peculiar, either. With something analogous, perhaps, to the press' incapacity from time to time to formulate an issue, the studio audience, while it must have been perfectly aware that three nights could hardly have passed, literally, in a single afternoon, seemed unable to discern what was literal in the rather grotesque conversation before them, and what was not. Or perhaps they did know, exactly, and the gasps themselves were not to be taken literally. Or perhaps, again, they had suspended their disbelief so far, that three nights did pass for them early one afternoon.

Later, in a cab on the way to Chelsea, I asked Liddy how negotiations were going for the purchase of the house on the Potomac. He said he had reason to hope that their offer would be accepted. He was not sure. Moreover, as a result of a cutback by the District of Columbia Board of Education, Frances Liddy had received notice that she had lost her teaching job. For the moment, apart from his book, the Liddys had no income. We were on our way to a tavern on Nineteenth Street for Liddy's first conversation with Eric Norden, a writer who wanted to do an interview with him for *Playboy*. Norden had told him that *Playboy* interviews were done with tape recorders. Liddy, not surprisingly, had bought a tape recorder of his own. At the tavern, the bartender greeted Liddy with particular affection. A zealous supporter of the IRA, he had done time with Liddy, for smuggling and unauthorized possession of firearms.

In July, Liddy was inducted, as an Honorary Member, into the Honor Legion of the Police Department of New York. "Composed of members of the police force of the City of New York, comprising all ranks, who, during the last sixty-eight years, have received departmental recognition...for deeds of valor performed at imminent risk of life, or who have been recommended for meritorious acts....It holds in one great bond of comradeship the honored men of the department, the bravest of the brave. It recognizes no rank. It is a force within a force, a tower of strength to combat evil, an inspiration from within, a beacon of hope for the weak, a haven for good.... Its tenets: self-respect, courage, loyalty, and devotion to duty." He had also become a member of the Association of Platform Speakers, which would book him for speeches all over the country, for a fee. The fees would be particularly welcome. Although Frances, as abruptly as she had been notified that she had lost her teaching job, had received notice that she was rehired, the Liddys had calculated that, with Sandy, Grace, and Jim at college, and Raymond and Tom in private schools, the cost of the children's education alone for next year would be $31,000. Liddy had completed his interviews with *Playboy*. And he had accepted an invitation to speak, on August 22, to the annual convention of the Association of Independent Truckers of America, in Colorado Springs.

Gordon and Frances Liddy arrived at Washington's Dulles Airport for their flight to Denver, just as the airborne mobile lounge for passengers was leaving the main building for the plane. Liddy told me that, last week, while Raymond was driving the Cadillac, which by now had 200,000 miles on it, "the steering went." "And," Liddy continued, "the fourth gear of the Volvo is no more." The bid on the Alan Drury house had been accepted. The Liddys were now trying to sell their house in Oxon Hill. Frances said that the reason they had been so nearly late for the flight, however, was that she had left at the last possible moment from her zoo course. Zoo course? As soon as she was reinstated as a teacher, she had enrolled, at the Washington Zoo, in a cram workshop for twelve teachers "in teaching children how to appreciate the zoo." She was pleased that zoos weren't just zoos anymore, but were actively breeding endangered species and educating children. "It's good for the kids, of course. And it's good for me, working with people who are so enthralled." She spoke of how glad she was to have been rehired, after "the shock of being rifted." Rifted? "Reduction in force," she said. "When you're suddenly rifted, after ten years, you go through a lot of feelings. You've got to be dedicated to have stayed with it that long. Special programs for the difficult kids are virtually nonexistent. So you have to make a choice. Either I'm going to go crazy, or I'll stay because I really like to teach. There are always one or two kids each year that you know you've helped, two out of twenty-five you really feel you save. About half of them are going to make it anyway. Only two or three are going to go down the drain. And you don't need to put those down a well. They just need special education programs. Now everybody wants to save birds and fishes. Much as I love birds and fishes, they are not our most important natural resource." I asked about her cats. There had not been a calico male, but the local veterinarian had a list of people wanting kittens from each litter. "It's fun to have births," Frances Liddy said. Jim, the Liddy's third child, had been born in Denver, nineteen years ago, when Liddy was with the Denver office of the FBI. Frances had not been back since. "In the FBI, you get restationed so often," she said, "but with seniority, you get a choice. And for a lot of agents, Denver is the office of preference. For their last years." The Liddys were going to stay on a few days, after the truckers convention, "to see Colorado people that we knew." "It says a lot about the kind of people they are," she said, "that we would be friends after those nineteen years."

At the Denver airport, we were met by a policeman, a policewoman, and Bill Scheffer, vice president of Overdrive—an organization which, in addition to sponsoring annual conventions, publishes a magazine, runs a pension fund, gives legal assistance, lobbies in Washington, and performs other services for the Association of Independent Truckers of America. The Independent Truckers, who own and drive their own trucks, are not only distinct from the Teamsters—the Teamsters have tried for years, through legislation and by other, often violent, means to put them out of business. In fact, a combination of political and business interests has made it highly unlikely that Independents, many of whom are husband-

and-wife teams, driving a single rig, will manage to survive. Like all drivers, they are particularly vulnerable to rising fuel costs. Like all truckers, they resent the "double nickel," the fifty-five-mile-an-hour speed limit, which of course costs them driving time—and, Scheffer claims, in spite of government pronouncements to the contrary, fuel. Owing to regulations by the Interstate Commerce Commission, however, and pressures by the Teamsters, and the response of politicians to those pressures, the Independents are subject to special rules, and special costs and taxes. They are obliged by law, for instance, to pay 27 percent of the proceeds from most interstate hauls to interstate carriers which are already licensed by the ICC. Independents are unable to obtain such licenses. The so-called trucking deregulation bill, The Motor Carriers Act of 1980, which had just passed Congress, was designed to eliminate such inequities and abuses. Under election-year pressure from the Teamsters, Scheffer said, as he drove the Liddys and me from Denver to Colorado Springs, the Trucking Deregulation Act had become "just a cosmetic piece of nothing."

Earlier this year, when the Independents succeeded for a time in a protest, a truck blockade of Washington, some Teamsters tried to break it. A few Independents shot at them that time. Scheffer, who had come to Colorado from Washington, where he testified before the Senate Subcommittee on Surface Transportation, said the Independents were planning another such boycott for October 20. "Congress only reacts to a crisis," he said. "So sometimes you have to create one." He mentioned that, in addition to Liddy, the speakers at this convention were Congressman Philip Crane, who had run for the Republican nomination for President, and who was one of five candidates said to have been considered by Ronald Reagan for his running mate, and Congressman John Rousselot of California, one of the most powerful and respected House conservatives.

Liddy inquired about the make of car we were in. Scheffer, with mild disgust, said it was "one of the most underpowered cars Ford ever made." Liddy looked at the rather many dials on the dashboard, which resembled an instrument panel in a cockpit. Scheffer pointed to one which read Miles to Destination. "I don't know how it can indicate that," he said, reflectively, "since it doesn't know what our destination is." Then, he told us what we might have guessed, that this was not his car. He drove very fast and well. He spoke of Overdrive's part in the three years of litigation which finally got rid of the kind of speed traps by which Justices of the Peace in small towns used to augment their incomes. "Three years," he said, "to get that overturned." Then he spoke of the present administration's Department of Transportation, and its head, Joan Claybrook, who was once an assistant to Ralph Nader. "Joan Claybrook is against everything on wheels," he said. "And Carter is probably the most anti-trucking President we've ever had." He mentioned a relatively minor matter, a new regulation by which the DOT was trying to force all truckers to change their rearview mirrors. "Such a goofy thing," he said, "but a huge financial burden for our industry." He pointed, silently but with obvious disapproval, to a state police car, blue lights flashing, and a trooper giving a summons for speeding to a driver at the side of an oncoming lane.

The highway we were on was broad and uncrowded, four lanes separated by a wide green divider. Scheffer slowed down, just perceptibly, and eased from the left lane into the right. He did not point or even seem to look this time at a police car lurking beside our own lane. "There are a lot of good radar detectors you can buy now, on the market," he said. Then, with considerable satisfaction, he described court cases and public exhibitions in which he (Scheffer was once an engineer and later trained by the army as a radar specialist) and other representatives of the Independent Truckers Association had demonstrated the ineffectiveness of police radar in detecting speeders. "A trooper was going on about how effective and reliable it is, blah, blah, blah. Then we gave our demonstration. They were embarrassed. The *L.A. Times* caught a picture of a trooper, furious, beating on his dashboard. They used our caption: State Trooper Makes a Minor Adjustment to His Radar," Scheffer said.

A car whizzed by us on the left. Scheffer said, "He's really going," Liddy mentioned that in some states, Pennsylvania for example, there are signs reading Keep Right Except to Pass. Scheffer nodded, approvingly. He returned to the subject of the Department of Transportation. "Diesel truck races are now becoming very popular," he said. "Sometimes, of course, you get so much torque that the right-front tires blow. Because of the heat and the weight. Now, Joan Claybrook has done everything in her power to stop those races." No one said anything. "Well, all right. But can you imagine, she came out to one of our conventions. And she brought us a Department of Transportation film called *Underride*. Its message was, You're all potential killers and murderers. I mean, can you imagine? These guys know their profession. They have families. She brings them this audiovisual aid for kids." He dismissed as government propaganda, too, the request that Americans, as an act of patriotic energy conservation, drive less this summer. "We have research proving," he said, "that you use less fuel on a camping trip in the car with your whole family of four than you would have used if you'd spent your entire vacation at home." Suddenly, he turned to Liddy and asked him what reaction there had been to him across the country. "Most people are favorable. Not all, of course," Liddy said. "But most Americans, let's face it, do not like a snitch."

Scheffer arrived in Colorado Springs, and pulled into the driveway of the Four Seasons Motel. Most of the parking lot was covered by a circus tent, which contained equipment of interest to truckers. The rest was covered with vans and rigs of every size. Scheffer pointed to a converted city bus, with signs reading Overdrive, Honk If You Want to Save the American Dream, Truckers for Free Enterprise, etc. Scheffer had told us that, when the association had inquired of the Four Seasons whether the truckers might hold this year's convention there, the motel's management had written, as managements in such situations customarily do, to the site of last year's convention, a motel in Nashville, to ask what sort of guests these independent truckers were. "They told us Nashville's recommendation said ours was the best convention they'd ever had," Scheffer said. From the minute we entered the lobby, it became clear why this might be true. The convention looked like the sweetest-natured, best-mannered, grave, friendly, strong, and yet highly varied large group of Americans I had ever seen. There were few blacks, and I saw no Asian or Spanish-Americans. Most of the men present had at one time been Teamsters, when the Independent Truckers Association was not yet strong enough to make it possible for them not to be. Most of the women, including the secretaries and copy editors of *Overdrive*, had at one time been, or still were, truckers. And the financial and regulatory difficulties which the Independents have faced in recent years made it remarkable that so wide a variety of owner-drivers should still have the time, the money, and the tenacity to attend a convention of this sort, or even to exist. They did not drink much—I never saw more than three people in the bar. So they could not have been desirable guests in that big-spender sense. But I remembered a hotel detective in New York, saying that, of all conventions, hotels most dread associations of psychologists or psychiatrists, who are forever hiring prostitutes, male or female, and refusing to pay in full, or having their wallets stolen, or getting hurt, or otherwise becoming involved with the police. The truckers, from one small, frail driver who was nearly ninety, to the many couples, with or without well-behaved but animated children, spent their money in the restaurant and coffee shop. Teenage sons and daughters, when they were not in the pool or at the Ping-Pong table, spent their change in a little gallery of pinball machines. And there was nothing of even Shriner-level mischief in anyone at all.

At the reception desk, Scheffer detached a walkie-talkie from his belt and, speaking into it, asked where Michael Parkhurst, president of Overdrive and the Independent Truckers Association, was. A voice said, "He's right here." Scheffer said, "But I don't know where 'here' is." There was a little static. Then, the voice said that Parkhurst would meet Scheffer and the Liddys in the Liddys' room. The Liddys' room turned out to be a duplex, with a bar on which there was Scotch, bourbon, gin, vodka, Seven-Up, Coca-Cola, a bouquet of flowers, and a bottle of champagne, on ice. There was also, rolled up, a large poster, with a red circle crossed by a diagonal red bar, which to drivers all over the world means No Entry, superimposed on a

picture of a peanut. The Liddys laughed. "We also have one of Khomeini," Scheffer said. Michael Parkhurst came in, a large, dark-
haired man in his late forties, who looked as though he might have
spent his adult years, as he has, in fact, spent them, giving the Teamster leadership their first serious opposition. He apologized at once
to Liddy. Congressman Crane, it seemed, had refused to speak at
tomorrow's barbecue if Liddy was going to speak there. "I guess he's
one of those who thinks once you've put nail polish on your nails, it
never comes off," he said. But that, in his view, was the congressman's problem. Liddy was scheduled to speak then, and could do so
if he liked. "I don't want to make it difficult for you," Liddy said.
"Whatever is easiest for you. I don't want to cause you any problem."
Then, as Parkhurst continued, rather dourly, to discuss Congressman Crane's objections, Liddy said, "I don't want to make *you* uncomfortable. I don't mind making *him* uncomfortable." In the end,
it was decided that Crane would speak, then leave if he liked when
Liddy spoke. Liddy asked how accurate the scheduling would be.
"We're always right on the money where time is concerned," Scheffer
said. Parkhurst said he had not checked the local bookstores, to see
whether they had copies of Liddy's book. "I didn't come out here, to
your convention, to sell my book," Liddy said.

It was 7:45 P.M. At eight, inside the motel's only ballroom, there
was to be an Ice Cream Parlor, sponsored by the Detroit Diesel
Company. Just outside the ballroom, the letters ITA (for Independent Truckers of America) were sculptured in ice. A couple were
photographing their baby in front of the letters. Behind them, about
two hundred truckers, of all ages, with many children, waited for
the doors to open. Many of the adults, and most of the children,
were holding the strings of pink balloons. Promptly at eight, the
doors did open. People filed in, served themselves with many flavors
of ice cream from two large tables, then sat down at small round tables with red-and-white checkered tablecloths. When the little tables were filled, people sat on the floor. Congressman Rousselot was
scheduled to speak at nine. The congressman's legs are severely crip-
pled. At the request of his administrative assistant, a desk had been

placed in front of the microphone at which the congressman would stand. Shortly before nine, the congressman looked around the ballroom. He asked that the desk be taken away. He removed his suit jacket and his tie. "These are my kind of people," he said, and hobbled to the microphone. He spoke for more than an hour. He mentioned a small businessman's proposal to HUD for the use of a piece of real estate. HUD had replied that he would require the approval of twenty-eight separate agencies. HUD had also pointed out that he had not, as required, traced the deed of his property (which was located several miles outside Baton Rouge) back beyond the year 1803. The businessman had replied in turn, "Gentlemen: I was unaware that any educated man did not know that 1803 was the date of the Louisiana Purchase." He then went on to trace title to the King of France, to the Indians, to Jesus, and to God, adding, "I hope you're satisfied." The congressman spoke of over-regulation by the federal government, of the country drifting toward "dictatorship by bureaucracy." He spoke of the federal food stamp program, which had been intended to be small, local, addressed to the rural poor, and which had burgeoned from 440,000 recipients in its first year to 22 million in fiscal 1979. He said he wanted to "get the federal government out of your pockets, and off your backs," and so forth. He said, "Thank you for what you do. For your posters and your bumper stickers. You do more good than you might think." He asked them to "educate," by which he meant lobby, or put pressure on, their congressmen. He mentioned that contractors had managed to "reeducate" Congress in the matter of common situs picketing, when the unions thought they had permanently "educated" it to the opposite effect.

When the questions came, their tone was earnest, often sad. Could he help reduce the excise tax on trucks and parts? He hadn't known there was such a tax, but "I'll vote for any tax cuts any time, at the federal level." A questioner said that, as an American, he had always thought and spoken in terms of inches, feet, yards, pounds. Now, on account of "the multinations and the scientific community," who wanted a uniform worldwide system for their own convenience, he was forced to undergo the cost of converting to the metric system. "Congressman," the trucker concluded, "are they going to take our language away from us next?" Rousselot replied that he understood that the conversion from pounds, feet, inches, etc., to the metric system was "voluntary." "How can it be voluntary," another trucker asked, "if it's on the road signs of the interstate?" The congressman said that, since he normally traveled by plane, he was not overly familiar with the interstate highway system. He would look into the matter. When the questions were over, he received a standing ovation. It was clear that the Independents were, as he had thought, "his kind of people." It was also clear that he had not known much about them before.

After the Ice Cream Parlor closed, the Liddys, Scheffer, and I, had hamburgers in the coffee shop, with Walda Abbott, a woman from Los Angeles, in her middle thirties, who is the attorney for the Association of Independent Truckers of America. "Walda," a man named Jack Hurlbutt said, from an adjoining table, "if there are a hundred thousand of us, how come we can't get every one of us in the country together, and get some of the deregulation that we want?" "It's because they're Independents, Jack," Ms. Abbott said. "It's just the nature of the beast." Ms. Abbott turned out to have lived for six years in Singapore, where she had worked on a publishing venture with an attorney I had met when he was still working for the civil rights movement in the South. I asked her how on earth she had happened to become the attorney for the ITA. She and Parkhurst and Scheffer, she said, had known one another when they were growing up in Pittsburgh. She had gone to law school. Scheffer had gone to engineering school, then became a Teamster. Parkhurst had become a Teamster, then founded the ITA. When she had come back from Singapore, where she had gone more or less for the sake of travel, Parkhurst and Scheffer had hired her. That was all. The nearly ninety-year-old trucker walked by. Liddy asked what routes he drove. Scheffer said he hauled fruits and vegetables from Florida to Hunts Point Market, in New York.

The Liddys and I knew Hunts Point, the New York equivalent, in the South Bronx, of Les Halles, though considerably rougher. Trucks of food arrive and depart all night long. Just outside the market, in winter, little bands of people warm themselves over fires in steel drums. There are often fights, inside the market and on its perimeter, in spite of policemen stationed at various checkpoints. Scheffer asked whether we had seen the "lumpers." We had not, did not even know what they were. Scheffer said that the regulations regarding lumpers were among the costly impositions that Independents, and only they, are required to bear. To load or unload his truck, an Independent is required to employ a lumper, forty dollars to load, forty dollars to unload. Moreover, under a tax regulation which Teamster and ICC-licensed carrier lobbyists had pushed through Congress, the IRS does not permit Independents to take a deduction for the use of lumpers. It falls not, as might have been expected, under the deduction for "ordinary and necessary business expenses" but under the "No Deduction for Casual Labor Rule." One night, several years ago, Scheffer, wanting to avoid the eighty-dollar expense, had unloaded and reloaded his own truck. As he drove through the Hunts Point exit, he was shot. He showed us the scar on his arm. No policeman had moved to help him. As we went off to our rooms, the Liddys asked where they might buy some Overdrive T-shirts, like the ones some teenagers were wearing in the hall. The next day, Liddy gave yet another, the best, of his stem-winders. He received a standing ovation far longer than Congressman Rousselot's. Congressman Crane received polite applause.

The last week in August, the Liddy's offer on the Alan Drury house was definitely accepted. In the first days of September, the issue of *Playboy* with the Liddy interview appeared. The interviewer, who had interviewed Liddy in sessions lasting part of each of three days, wrote that he had "spent the better part of ten days with him." Since Liddy had taped the conversations as the interviewer was taping them, and since he had asked to see the transcripts, the interviewer had sent him the transcripts, for his approval. Liddy had been surprised to find not only that his answers were changed, and that other answers, which he had never given, were attributed to him, but that even many of the *questions*, which both real and invented answers and even poorly edited sections of *Will* were set as replies to, had been made up as well. He had been told to make what corrections he liked. He edited out only things that he had not only never said but would never conceivably say, references to "my brutal captors" in the D.C. jail, for example, or sentences like "I have always lived on the razor's edge." He also corrected factual errors. West Cornwall, New Jersey, he pointed out, for example, is not and never was "on the Hudson River." He cut out a few passages from his book, which had been misquoted and used as his answers, in conversation, to questions that had never been put and with which they had nothing to do. The interviewer had thanked him for all these corrections, the one about the geographical location of West Cornwall, New Jersey, along with the rest.

In the issue of *Playboy* that appeared on the stands, not a single one of the corrections was made. Liddy still has his tapes. In one of his earliest radio interviews, he had said, concerning the notion of celebrity, "To some people, it doesn't matter whether you're Liza Minnelli or the Son of Sam." In another, he had said, to an interviewer whom he liked, and who had asked him whether, honestly, he had no remaining fear, "Maybe. The fear of boredom." But when, with the tapes in his possession, he read the issue of *Playboy*, he seemed, only for a moment but for the first time since I have known him, somewhat depressed, and a bit demoralized.

1980

BUT OHIO. WELL, I GUESS THAT'S ONE STATE WHERE THEY ELECT TO LOCK AND LOAD THE NATIONAL GUARD

AT SIX o'clock one recent Saturday morning, a Karmann Ghia and several other civilian vehicles were parked in the rain outside the Seventh Regiment Armory, at Park Avenue and Sixty-sixth Street. Inside, several uniformed young men were rushing about carrying duffel bags down the carpeted stairs and along wood-paneled corridors to the huge central arena of the armory, where several military vehicles were preparing to move out. A jeep carrying a 105-mm. recoilless rifle was being loaded onto a carrier, and men were climbing into other jeeps and trucks. The First Battalion of the 107th Infantry (New York National Guard) was preparing to join two battalions from the armory at Lexington Avenue and Twenty-fifth Street, one battalion from the armory at Thirty-fourth and Park, and units from armories in Brooklyn, Long Island, Flushing, and (for some organizational reason) Pennsylvania, to undergo—as the Forty-second (Rainbow) Division of the New York National Guard—their two weeks of summer training at Camp Drum. Camp Drum itself, which is in upstate New York, was regarded as too strenuous a trip for a single day, so after rest stops at a racetrack in Goshen and at Whitney Point, the convoy would bivouac just one night at the state fairgrounds in Syracuse. "Inherent in our organization," said Colonel Dominic Pellicio about the Guard convoy's capacity to bivouac, "is an ability to stay out and eat."

Kitchen trucks had set out for Syracuse an hour earlier. To avoid traveling on the Sabbath, an Orthodox Jewish chaplain had gone up the day before. Colonel Pellicio (commander of New York City's

---

Originally titled "A Reporter at Large"

Guard units, senior brigade commander during the March postal strike and in his civilian life a contractor) greeted some of his men (another chaplain, a law student, a resident in urology) and made a last-minute check of a long list of hospitals along the convoy's route. "You know, these men drive these vehicles maybe three, four times a year," he said. "In the rain it can be very dangerous." Then, after the first units of jeeps and trucks had left, he set out in his military sedan (complete with a siren, which he did not use) into the rain on Lexington Avenue, across Central Park at Sixty-fifth Street, and onto the West Side Highway toward a "marshaling point" in Teterboro, New Jersey. The reason the colonel had chosen Teterboro, which is not on the most direct route to upstate New York, was to avoid "the traffic density on the New York Thruway" and to "give my men some experience" on a new convoy route to Camp Drum.

There were Guardsmen posted to wave directions at many intersections and at all bridges and toll booths on the way to New Jersey Route 17. The first units arrived on schedule, at 0734 hours, at the marshaling area—a parking lot across from the Teterboro Airport. But by 0816 hours, the colonel learned, two vehicles were already lost (one broke down, one was hit by a station wagon), and more would be lost, with maintenance problems, along the way. Vehicles continued for three hours, desultorily, to arrive at the marshaling area. Meanwhile, the men smoked, caught some sleep in the trucks, or ate sandwiches from the first of their several box lunches. Most were armed with M-1 rifles, while "key" men carried pistols, and one (like Colonel Pellicio himself, an older man and a veteran of World War II) wore a bayonet in a camouflaged sheath at his waist. A lot of the younger men wore mustaches. Maneuvers at Camp Drum, the colonel said, would consist mainly in borrowing a hundred or two hundred tanks, using them, and, at the end of the two weeks, returning them to the regular army. Last summer, a Guardsman had knocked himself unconscious falling off a tank the first day. "But our main concern is the safety of the men in these vehicles," the colonel said. "Getting them up to camp is always the biggest problem." The weather was clearing a bit, and two civilians drove up safely enough, at 0927 hours, to the

Teterboro Airport. "Hey," one of them said as they passed the mar-shaling area. "Will you look at them weekend soldiers."

The National Guard is one of the oldest, most muddled and crisis-ridden lethal forces in our history. At present, it consists of 478,860 men (394,133 of them in the Army National Guard, 84,727 in the Air National Guard), 2,774 local armories, 68 Army Guard airfields, 90 Air Guard flying bases, an annual appropriation slightly in excess of one billion dollars (of which $972,364,000 is paid by the federal government, the rest by the states), several billion dollars' worth of more or less obsolete federal military equipment, one of the oldest, most effective lobbies (the National Guard Association, founded in 1879) in Washington, and long, not altogether tamper-proof waiting lists—one at every Guard armory in each of the fifty states, Puerto Rico, and the District of Columbia. What training Guardsmen ac-tually receive (six months of basic army training, a few drills each year, and two weeks of camp in each of six successive summers) is almost exclusively for war, but of the several hundred occasions on which Guardsmen have been called up since 1945, all but two have been local natural disasters or civil disturbances lasting about a week. National Guardsmen have otherwise remained at home and pursued their civilian careers. Since National Guardsmen are ac-countable, except in times of declared war or federalization for ex-treme emergency, not to the federal government but to the governors of their respective states, National Guard units are really State Guard units—a fragmented, fifty-two-part duplicate of the regular army reserve. They are also exempt from the draft.

The National Guard's history—like its present composition and purpose, if any—is a kind of swamp. Nearly every state Guard unit has its own historian. The only attempt at an exhaustive history of the whole National Guard, *The Minute Man in Peace and War*, by Major General Jim Dan Hill, of Wisconsin (published in 1964 by the Stackpole Company, Harrisburg, Pennsylvania), consists largely of obscure grievances against politicians and journalists, from Stephen Crane and Richard Harding Davis to "a young political-science teacher in a Midwestern college," whom the general cannot even bring himself to name, and irate defenses of the Guard against charges of draft-dodging, incompetence, redundancy, favoritism, strikebreaking, snobbery, unpreparedness, patronage, loafing, irresponsibility, boondoggle, cowardice, obsoleteness, and bungling— charges that have evidently been leveled against the Guard throughout its history. The general's style is everywhere idiosyncratically partisan ("The Guard must have seemed Heaven-sent for the role of a whipping boy riding into the desert astride a dejected scapegoat"). Although his research is probably the best there is, a sentence in his preface may explain a lot: Concerning the bibliographical notes with which each chapter ends, the general writes, "Without exception, they are far from all-inclusive."

The contemporary National Guard can trace its origins to the Organized Militia of the original thirteen colonies, who, in various units and capacities, defended their own homes, conducted raiding parties against the Indians, and fought the Revolutionary War in Washington's Continental Army. After the Revolution, to avert the threat to democracy inherent in any professional "standing army" (and with some doubt that the country contained enough paupers to fill such an army), Jefferson hoped that every citizen might be trained to be a soldier, civilian in peace, prepared to defend his country in war. Baron von Steuben, who had been Inspector General of the Revolutionary forces, argued that this was unrealistic, "It would be as sensible and consistent to say every Citizen should be a Sailor." Washington himself proposed a small, paid regular army to protect the country's frontiers and also a larger civilian organized militia in each of the several states. In the end, the Constitution embodied all three ideas: an unorganized Enrolled Militia, consisting of all male citizens eligible for military service only in time of war; a small Regular Army of professional soldiers, accountable first and only to the President as Commander-in-Chief; and a state Organized Militia of citizen-soldiers, "reserving to the States, respectively, the Appointment of Officers, and the Authority of training the Militia according to the Discipline prescribed by Congress." It is this clause in the Constitution (Article I, Section 8, Clause 16, commonly known as the Militia Clause) that leaves us, in a nuclear age, with a National Guard.

Since then, especially as the danger of Indians, state insurrections, or land invasions by way of Canada or Mexico becomes remote, there has been a continual dispute about what the Guard is meant to do—and it is possible that the Militia Clause, together with the later misnomer "National Guard," has somehow maintained throughout our history an uneven, crazy, dangerous collection of state military forces whose purpose is undefinable and which it is impossible either to train for some national purpose or to disband. The misnomer "National Guard" itself dates from a trip Lafayette made to America in 1824. In honor of his visit, a group of New York City peacetime volunteers—young men who had drilled and caroused together quite a bit, designed and bought their own uniforms, elected their own officers, compared horses, paraded, and called themselves the Seventh Regiment—renamed themselves the "National Guards," after the distinguished Paris corps commanded by Lafayette. In 1832, the regiment dropped the *s*. In 1862, the Volunteer Militia of all New York State adopted the name. The Massachusetts Volunteer Militia, who considered themselves the original citizen-soldiers of Lexington, resisted the change to the last, but in 1903 the National Guard became the federally recognized (and, for the first time, in part federally subsidized) collection of state militias which it is today.

The Guard's post-Revolutionary appearances in American history include participation or evasion of some sort in all the country's wars, including the Mexican, which all the New England states were reluctant to join, and the War of 1812, in which neither Massachusetts nor Connecticut cared to take part. The Guard had its greatest strength in those days, and until the time of the automobile, in the urban centers of the North and East—if only because these areas, being the nation's most densely populated, could most easily muster units to drill and parade. In 1860, the governor of New York State alone could summon more units of infantry, cavalry, and artillery than the entire regular army of the United States. Since most recruiting in the Civil War was done by the states, it could be argued that most of the Union soldiers (all but the United States Army Regulars) and *all* the Confederate troops (led by Colonel Jefferson Davis, of the First Mississippi Rifles, as Commander-in-Chief) were organized militia, and that the War Between the States was largely a war between what might now be called units of the National Guard. But North and South had recourse, in the Civil War, to the draft, and it is more characteristic of the Guard's subsequent anomalous role in our history that New York's Seventh Regiment (the one for which the whole Guard, after all, was named) spent most of the Civil War at home and distinguished itself mainly by suppressing the bloody Draft Riots of 1863.

The National Guard really enters modern history, in anything like its current form and spirit, in the 1870s and 1880s, as a strike-breaking force. Regiments of organized militia had turned out as early as 1794 to crush the Whiskey Rebellion. Southern states, years before the Civil War, had maintained large militias for fear of slave revolts. New York's Seventh Regiment had already killed twenty-two and wounded thirty-six in the Astor Place Riot of 1849 (over the relative merits of a proletarian production of *Macbeth* in the Bowery and a white-tie performance at the Opera House). Militias had been used to suppress industrial disorders in Missouri and Kansas, vigilante groups in California, striking miners in Colorado. But in 1877, with railroad strikes in Martinsburg, West Virginia, in Baltimore, Chicago, and St. Louis, and, more particularly, with the Pullman Strike and Haymarket Riot of 1886, the National Guard earned a reputation as a business-financed, elitist, repressively antilabor force; and throughout the Depression, until World War II, most unions still banned their members from taking any part in the Guard. It was in the 1880s that the grotesque, turreted redbrick armories were built for Guard cavalry. The Seventh Regiment built its own, the one at Park Avenue and Sixty-sixth, in 1880, and still owns it. Squadron A, an equally upper-class nineteenth-century unit, lost its armory, on Park Avenue and Ninety-fourth, a few years ago and regretfully disbanded, to become just the Squadron A Club, in rented, wood-paneled rooms at the Biltmore Hotel. Businessmen financed the Guard in those years, and wealthy young men joined it, to keep the immigrant laborers orderly, state by state.

A history of New York City's Squadron A, NYNG (New York National Guard), includes several journals kept by young Guardsmen of the time. There are proud references to Squadron A as "all millionaires" and as being as exclusive as "any club in New York." There are accounts of breaking a railroad strike in Buffalo in 1892, a trolley strike in Brooklyn in 1895, and a strike at the Croton Dam in 1900. The sort of enemy the Guardsmen thought they were protecting the state against is implied by references to encounters with Italian laborers as "the Italian Wars," cheerful allusions to Central European workers' abject fear of horses with men on them, and in a poem written for the unit as late as 1925:

> ...There's a garment strike on and it's got to be broke,
> So ye lawyers and bankers and salesmen so free,
> Turn out—you're Hussars of the NYNG...
> The strikers are gathered in Washington Square,
> Their war cry "Oi, oi Gewalt" pierces the air...

There are also candid accounts of "promiscuous shooting at phantoms" in the Croton Strike (on the way to which the unit's commander was thrown from his horse and broke his leg); pointless racing about, firing of blanks, and cries of "You're dead!" at the Guard Manassas Maneuvers, in 1904; mothers perennially sending caviar and foie gras to their sons on duty; a Guardsman who, in one pistol drill, accidentally blew a hole in the ceiling and, in the next, blew a hole through the floor of the armory; endless showy parades through New York to accompany such visitors as the Duke of Veragua, the Infanta Eulalia, and the Chinese Viceroy, Li Hung Chang;

constant explosions, during strike duty, of shells that had fallen from the belts of sleeping Guardsmen into their straw bedding; and accidents, fires, and equipment mix-ups on every maneuver of every kind through the years. In 1939, the year the squadron's history was published, Squadron A of the New York National Guard was arguing passionately that the imminent World War II, despite tanks and other machines, would prove the absolute indispensability of cavalrymen on real horses for the national defense.

In years when there were no wars and there was no strike duty, Guard units tended to languish in their armories, and, even in rural areas, to become social clubs, like the Kiwanis or Elks. They liked to march and to rise in rank, but their preparedness for the two world wars, when they did break out, was problematical. Had it not been for the strength of its lobby in Washington, the Guard might, on several occasions, have been abolished altogether. In *The National Guard in Politics*, a study of "one of the most successful pressure groups in a system noted for the advantages that it gives pressure groups," Martha Derthick, an associate professor of political science at Boston College, says that the major goals of the National Guard lobby in Washington have always been two: federal support of the Guard (regular army pay for Guard drills, federal military equipment, federal money for armories, federal recognition of Guard officers), along with freedom from federal control—that is, state appointment of officers, state control of units, state standards for training, and, in case of war, federal mobilization of state Guard units intact.

In order to gain these federal concessions and subsidies while maintaining states' rights (in the early 1900s, southern and midwestern states'-rights congressmen had become the main supporters of the Guard, the northeastern states having more or less lost interest in it), the National Guard had to argue that it was the nation's principal military reserve force. The National Defense Act of 1916 gave it that status. Guard divisions were renamed and officially

renumbered, divisions 26 to 75 inclusive, and sent off to World War
I—with mixed results. Some Guard units *were* preserved intact,
with their own state patronage-appointed officers. Many of those
officers soon had to be replaced for sheer incompetence. Some Guard
units were used as "depot divisions," just to supply replacements for
casualties among regular army division volunteers and draftees. Out
of leftover Guard units from several states, the army created the
symbolic, "overarching" interstate Forty-second (Rainbow) Division, in which Douglas MacArthur served as brigade commander in
France. The Rainbow has since become the division that left with
Colonel Pellicio for Camp Drum.

After World War I, the Guard, except for its lobby (led by a
Guard officer who was also chief lobbyist for the National Rifle Association), languished again—until the Depression, when drill pay
earned by Guardsmen became a new source of patronage for governors, and of bitterness for men on relief who could not get appointed
to the Guard. In World War II, the Guard's performance once again
was controversial and mixed. The December 1941 issue of *Fortune*
said that the National Guard, untrained and unprepared as it was,
could not be reorganized, because it had become "a political hornet's
nest." Other branches of the military, in any case, were not impressed with it. When New York's Twenty-seventh Division of the
Guard, for example, was put under marine command at Saipan, Marine Lieutenant General H. M. Smith found that while his own
units advanced about ten miles each day, the Guard division, composed mainly of New York politicians and their friends and relatives, invariably stayed put. The marines would have to drop back
each night to maintain a line. Finally, General Smith replaced every
single officer of the Twenty-seventh—creating a terrific scandal
back home in New York. An entire Guard division from the Midwest, on the other hand, was wiped out at Corregidor, and New
Mexico Guard tank units at Bataan were annihilated, leaving towns
in the states from which they came bereft of their entire populations
of young men. To avoid a recurrence of these regional disasters, and
to circumvent the ineptitude of Guard officers, Guard divisions

were broken up. Of eighteen National Guard division commanders at the beginning of World War II, only two retained command at the end. One general of the regular army began calling the National Guard Bureau itself "an organizational monstrosity." In 1944 Lieutenant General Lesley J. McNair, commanding general of the army ground forces, said, "The training experience of this headquarters for nearly four years has its most important lesson in the inadequacy of the National Guard in practically every essential.... One of the great lessons of the present war is that the National Guard, as organized before the war, contributed nothing to national defense."

General McNair recommended that the Guard be abolished. So did his successor, Lieutenant General Ben Lear. National Guard General Ellard A. Walsh, the adjutant general of Minnesota, who was head of the Guard lobby in 1944, was quick to respond. He spoke of the regular army's "undiluted and undisguised hate of us" and of "a diabolical attempt to destroy a great citizen force." He recommended more, newer, and fiercer lobbying. It worked. In 1948, National Guardsmen became, by law, completely exempt from the draft. (The token Guard units that were federalized for service in Korea required seven to nine months to train—as long as regular draftees who had received no training before.) Although the states had traditionally financed their own militias, until the years when the local businessmen started to, the federal government began to pay 97 percent of the cost of the Guard. A Guardsman now receives, for a half day's drill, the equivalent of a regular army soldier's full day's pay. And despite the existence of a regular army reserve, the fiction is still maintained—in Congress, in the Guard, in the Department of Defense—that the National Guard is the first line of reserve for some future war, and that training its men for war is what the Guard ought primarily to do.

There exist, in Guard archives, fairly riveting accounts of more or less recent Guard tactical maneuvers, like 1960's Operation Big Slam/Puerto Pine ("In this exercise there was a notable 'first,' the movement, on short notice, of a National Guard Artillery Battalion from Utah to Puerto Rico, in 'off season' for the part-time soldiers, and their speedy inauguration of a realistic field training program in unaccustomed surroundings"); Exercise Dixie ("The map problem set up for study involved defense of the Southeastern United States against an Aggressor airborne and seaborne attack in the vicinity of Mobile Bay, Alabama. The first phase consisted of the Aggressor successfully invading the Florida Peninsula by airborne and water-borne units, which were met by XII Corps troops. In addition to the invasion of Florida, Aggressor agents worked constantly to upset the civilian population"); and Operation Vikings Thrive in Arctic Cold ("The purpose was for the Minnesota Guardsmen from the 47th 'Viking' Infantry Division to learn how to ski and to overcome the handicaps of cold weather"). Air National Guard units (which, since Guardsmen almost immediately after Kitty Hawk could afford their own planes, have often predated regular air force units, and which now consist largely of air force veterans, civilian pilots, and men who just like to fly) are allowed to fly brief cargo missions to Vietnam and elsewhere. One recent Air Guard "combat" mission to Vietnam turned out to be Operation Yuletide—a ferrying over of Christmas presents to servicemen.

Sixty-three percent of young Guardsmen in a recent survey ac-knowledged that they had "joined the Guard because it offered least interference with your personal plans"; 49 percent that they had joined "because you knew you would be drafted if you did not"; 71 percent that "some individuals you know joined the Guard to avoid service in Vietnam." Only 19 percent thought that they might reen-list in the Guard when their time was up or that their second lieu-tenants were capable of combat leadership. Waiting lists for Guard units, since the Vietnam War began, have been so long that they are often closed, and the persistence of professional athletes, movie stars, relatives of politicians and of people with political influence in Guard units (as well as the reminiscences of young men who have recently completed their service in the Guard) yield the impression that the waiting lists are seldom impartially administered. Despite what was meant to be an intensive program for recruitment of blacks after the Detroit riots of 1967, the percentage of blacks in the Army Guard actually went down, from 1.18 percent to 1.15 percent, between 1968 and 1969. The percentage of blacks in the Air National Guard, it is true, went up—from 0.77 to 0.90.

The adjutants general of the National Guard in all but two states (South Carolina, where the highest Guard officer is elected by the public, and Vermont, where he is chosen by the legislature) are appointed by the current governors. They, like all Guard officers, are meant to meet standards set by the federal government, but as early as 1948 the army's Director of Personnel and Administration complained that "experience since the war has demonstrated that governors will not accept the decision of a Federal Recognition Board." National Guard General Walsh himself complained, in 1948, that Governor Earl Long had fired a Louisiana adjutant general because of political pressure from a Plaquemines Parish constituent, Leander Perez. In six states today, the adjutant general of the National Guard is also the Director of Selective Service. National Guard officers sit on almost all draft boards—which is a bit like asking the leaders of the draft-avoiders (or, as friends of the Guard prefer to put it, the "draft-motivated") to administer the draft impartially. In a recent *Congressional Quarterly* survey, only twenty-two U.S. senators and representatives actually said they had sons or grandsons in the reserves or the National Guard. But of the 234 draft-eligible sons and grandsons of members of Congress, 118 had received other sorts of deferment since the Vietnam War began. Only twenty-six served at all in Vietnam. None were missing or killed. One—Captain Clarence D. Long III, son of a representative from Maryland—was wounded.

One hundred and twenty-two U.S. senators and representatives (more than a fifth of the members of Congress) currently hold commissions in the reserves or the National Guard, and an organization of young Guardsmen and reservists, called the Reservists Committee to Stop the War, has filed suit against the secretary of defense on the ground that the Constitution specifically forbids U.S. congressmen from holding "any office" bestowed by, or under the control of, the executive branch of government.

In "In Pursuit of Equity: Who Serves When Not All Serve?"—a report prepared in 1967 by the National Advisory Commission on Selective Service, under the chairmanship of Burke Marshall—recommendations for draft reform included something on the order of a draft lottery, which we now have, and the abolition of the National Guard as a draft haven, which may follow of itself, in December 1970, when the draft lottery has gone completely into effect. There may then be National Guard problems of an entirely other kind.

A chronology of domestic duty by National Guard units since World War II reads like a history of the country transposed into a rather special key. In 1945, there were only three call-ups, all local—one for an industrial dispute in Indiana, two for reasons now forgotten, labeled in Guard histories "unknown." In 1946, there were five call-ups, all for nothing much, three of them "unknown." Between 1947 and 1950, there were nine, including five "industrial disputes," one "threat to local sheriff" (Loudon, Tennessee), and, in Puerto Rico, one "uprising against government." In 1951, there was just one call-up, a "race riot" in Cicero, Illinois. In 1952, there were three: two "prison riots" and a "student riot," at Columbia, Missouri. In 1953, there was nothing. In 1954 and 1955, two "crises in law enforcement" (Phenix City, Alabama; Gulfport, Mississippi), three "prison riots," one "industrial dispute," and (in Whiting, Indiana) a "natural disaster." In 1956—two years after the Supreme Court decision to integrate the schools—there were three "integration crises" and one memorable "teenage riot" (on the beach, at Daytona, Florida). There were four "civil disturbances" in 1957 (in Benton, Prentiss, Marion, and Simpson Counties, Mississippi), one "industrial dispute" (in Portsmouth, Ohio), and—from September 6 to September 20—the federalization of the National Guard in Little Rock, Arkansas, with which the first phase of the most recent period of the Guard begins.

In September 1957, Governor Orval E. Faubus called out the Arkansas Guard to prevent the enforcement of school integration. President Eisenhower federalized the state Guard to ensure enforcement and sent in some regular army troops as well. From then on, the Guard was engaged for some years in protecting civil rights, during what Guard archives started calling "racial disturbances," in the South. In 1958 and 1959, the Guard was called up for eight "racial disturbances" (all of them in Mississippi); also for one "prison riot" and three "industrial disputes." In 1960, there was just one call-up: the Rhode Island Guard for a "civil disturbance" (jazz festival) at Newport. In 1961, there was one "teenage riot," one "prison riot," three "racial disturbances," and two mysterious "sabotages of microwave stations" (in Utah and New Mexico).

In 1962 and 1963, there were suddenly three federalizations of the Guard: one each for "integration crises" at the University of Mississippi and the University of Alabama, and one after the bombing of the four young girls in a church in Birmingham. These federalizations of the National Guard in the southern states gave the regular army a chance to shake up and reorganize (as in wartime) some of the most patronage-ridden state units in the country. The Guard reforms were much like the changes that southern offices of the FBI underwent, under pressure from the Justice Department, in the same years. The army officer in charge of Guard federalizations and reform was General Creighton W. Abrams, who is now Commander of U.S. forces in Vietnam. In 1963, too, there was a call-up of Guard troops by the Washington, D.C., commissioners for what Guard archives call simply a "civil-rights demonstration" in Washington— the one in which Martin Luther King's "I have a dream" speech was heard at the Lincoln Memorial. In September 1963, Governor George Wallace called out the Guard, as Faubus had done six years earlier, to prevent compliance with the law in the school "integration crises" at Birmingham, Mobile, and Tuskegee. President Kennedy federalized the Alabama Guard, and General Abrams shook the Guardsmen up again. In 1964, there wasn't much. Nineteen sixty-five begins with a federalization of the Alabama Guard, and the addition of some regular army, for the march from Selma to Montgomery; has a little call-up for a "motorcycle riot" in June (at Weirs Beach, New Hampshire); and ushers in another era in August, with the rioting in Watts.

There followed what might be called the period of the urban disasters—in which, having been for eight years primarily a peace-keeping force, the National Guard was suddenly in the position of killing people. In Watts, 13,393 California Guardsmen were called. Four thousand blacks were arrested, several hundred were hurt, and thirty-four were killed. National Guardsmen do not have the authority to make arrests, but they do carry arms, and, as the National Advisory Commission on Civil Disorders, under Governor Otto Kerner of Illinois (in a report more valuable for its substantive descriptions of events than for its philosophical generalizations), subsequently put it, of those thirty-four dead blacks "several...were killed by mistake." In July 1966, there was the Filmore race riot in Chicago (4,300 Illinois Guardsmen called out, three blacks killed, including a thirteen-year-old boy and a fourteen-year-old pregnant girl) and the Hough race riot in Cleveland (2,000 Ohio Guardsmen called out, four blacks killed, and several children injured, as in Chicago, by "stray bullets"). In state after state, Guardsmen were called out to deal with urban looting and rioting—with tanks, guns, and training designed for waging war against an organized, armed foreign enemy. In July 1967, in Newark, 4,400 New Jersey National Guardsmen were called out. The New Jersey adjutant general, James F. Cantwell, was at the time, and still is, president of the National Guard Association. When order was restored, there were twenty-three dead, twenty-one of them blacks, two of them children. Later that month, in Detroit, when 10,253 Michigan Guardsmen were called and then federalized, the disturbance ended with forty-three blacks dead. There began a period of serious deliberation about the Guard. It became as clear as anything about the National Guard ever gets that Guardsmen were performing duties other than those of a "first line of military reserve," and the possibility arose that in civil disturbances much, if not most, of the tragedy and nearly all of the deaths were attributable to forces called out to restore order. Detroit was a crisis in the history of the National Guard.

Looking back on previous urban riots—the "killed by mistake" of Watts, the "killed by stray bullets" of Filmore and Hough—officials of the departments of Justice and Defense began to find the performance of Guard units, state by state, surreal. Guardsmen were in the habit of arriving by tank or truck, weapons loaded, and shooting out street lamps at night, for protection, then deluding themselves that the sound of their own shots in the dark was "sniper fire." Since their aim, moreover, was bad, the rounds of ammunition required to dispatch a single street lamp often injured people in apartments blocks away or in cars on other streets. The first person killed by Guardsmen in Newark, for example, was a small boy in a family car being driven home from a restaurant. In Newark, coordination between the local police and the New Jersey Guard was so bad that Director of Police Dominick Spina told the Kerner Commission, "Down in the Springfield Avenue area, in my opinion, Guardsmen were firing upon police and police were firing back at them."

Police Director Spina, who was tried and acquitted of charges arising out of alleged Mafia operations two years ago, and who was dismissed from his job on July 1 of this year, emerges, in the Newark riots of 1967, as something of a hero, on the order of *High Noon*. According to the Kerner Commission:

> On Saturday, July 15, Spina received a report of snipers in a housing project. When he arrived he saw approximately 100 National Guardsmen and police officers crouching behind vehicles, hiding in corners and lying on the ground around the edge of the courtyard.
>
> Since everything appeared quiet and it was broad daylight, Spina walked directly down the middle of the street. Nothing happened. As he came to the last building of the complex, he heard a shot. All around him the troopers jumped, believing themselves to be under sniper fire. A moment later a young Guardsman ran from behind a building.

The Guardsman said that he had fired the shot to scare a man away from a window, that his orders were "to keep everyone away from windows."

Spina said he told the soldier: "Do you know what you just did? You have now created a state of hysteria. Every Guardsman up and down this street...thinks that somebody just fired a shot and that it is probably a sniper...."

By this time, four truckloads of National Guardsmen had arrived, and troopers and policemen were again crouched everywhere, looking for a sniper.

The Director of Police stayed at the scene for three hours. The only shot he heard was the one fired by the Guardsman.

Nevertheless, at six o'clock that evening two columns of National Guardsmen and state troopers were directing mass fire at the Hays Housing project in response to what they believed were snipers.

On the 10th floor, Eloise Spellman, the mother of several children, fell, a bullet through her neck....

Suddenly, several troopers whirled and began firing in the general direction of spectators. Mrs. Hattie Gainer, a grandmother, sank to the floor.

A block away Rebecca Brown's 2-year-old daughter was standing at the window. Mrs. Brown rushed to drag her to safety. As Mrs. Brown was, momentarily, framed in the window, a bullet spun into her back....

And so on, in Newark. The result of calling in National Guardsmen began to seem, in retrospect, frightened Guardsmen, frightened police, and a toll of babies in distant bassinets, grandmothers in distant kitchens, mothers with their backs to windows, idle spectators, and unarmed citizens of every sort. But Detroit was the worst.

Governor George Romney, to begin with, was extremely reluctant to issue an official request that the Michigan National Guard be federalized—although local police, supported by the Guard under state control, were exhausted and had been unable to cope with rioting and looting for several days—because federalization of the Guard implies an "insurrection," which exempts insurance companies from paying damages to holders of insurance policies. Governor Romney repeatedly made urgent, unofficial requests for federal help to Deputy Secretary of Defense Cyrus R. Vance, who (according to his subsequent report of events in Detroit) felt that he had to reject them on the ground of their unofficial language. Deputy Secretary Vance, Attorney General Ramsey Clark, Supreme Court Justice Abe Fortas (not in his capacity as Supreme Court justice but as friend and political adviser to President Johnson), Defense Secretary Robert McNamara, and others were pacing with President Johnson on the White House lawn, discussing their own reluctance to federalize the Guard, or to send in more competent regular army troops, because they preferred to avoid the precedent of a liberal administration's sending troops to cope with urban rioting, in an action that might be construed as repressive or racist. In response to more urgent requests from Governor Romney, President Johnson sent Deputy Secretary Vance and a team of officials from the departments of Defense and Justice to Detroit, to study the situation and to discuss it with Mayor Jerome P. Cavanagh and other local citizens. While legal and philosophical deliberations concerning federalization were going on, the number of incidents in Detroit continued to climb. At 2310 hours on July 24 (about twenty-four hours after Mayor Cavanagh and Governor Romney had first telephoned Attorney General Clark about the emergency), Deputy Secretary Vance recommended to President Johnson that the Michigan National Guard be federalized and put under regular army command. Ten minutes later, the President federalized the Guard, under the command of Army Lieutenant General John L. Throckmorton, and sent in regular army troops as well.

The Guard's behavior until the President's move, and after, was a revelation and a nightmare. Some of the Guardsmen had traveled two hundred miles and been put on duty for thirty hours straight—most of which they spent firing. Guardsmen in Detroit fired off more than 13,326 rounds of ammunition, compared with 201 rounds fired off by the regular army. Some Guard units got lost in the city, and panicked. Two Guardsmen assigned to an intersection on Monday were still there on Friday. Guardsmen kept pulling up in tanks, shooting out streetlights, scaring themselves with the sound, and then blasting out the walls of whole buildings. At four o'clock one morning, a regular army unit went to the rescue of a Guard troop crouched behind a high school, claiming to be pinned down by sniper fire. The army colonel, hearing no shots at all, ordered all lights in an adjoining building turned on. The residents were terrified and unarmed. The Guardsmen had shot out every window. Mistaking a lighted cigarette in one window for a sniper, two Guard tanks drew up and a machine gunner opened fire, nearly severing the arm of a young woman and killing her four-year-old niece.

General Throckmorton, whose soldiers were doing fine without much shooting, thought tension might be reduced by less firing, and ordered ammunition removed from all weapons. The Guardsmen apparently never received the order. The Kerner Report continues:

> Without any clear authorization or direction, someone opened fire upon the suspected building. A tank rolled up and sprayed the building with .50-caliber tracer bullets. Law enforcement officers rushed into the surrounded building and discovered it empty. "They must be firing one shot and running" was the verdict.

Julius Dorsey, a black private guard, was trying to defend a market from looting. He fired three shots from his pistol into the air. The police radio reported, "Looters. They have rifles." Three National Guardsmen arrived and, seeing a distant crowd of fleeing looters, opened fire. They killed Julius Dorsey. The only soldier killed in Detroit in 1967 was Larry Post, a National Guardsman caught in a cross fire between two units of National Guardsmen.

After Detroit, it became clear that something would have to be done about the National Guard. In most states, Guard units—on the "first line of military reserve" theory—received no riot-control training at all, and in states where they did receive it, it was short and not uniform. There seemed, at the time, to be three basic positions about the Guard. One, that it was inevitably a corrupt, ungovernable mess of untrainable incompetents, and that it should be abolished as a peacekeeping force; local police forces should be better trained, and on those rare occasions when civil disturbances became extreme emergencies, the regular army, which has training and discipline, should be called in. Two, that nothing is perfect, that the Guard had done as well as could be expected, and that people in an area where there is rioting (even if they happen to be in their bathrooms or bassinets), though they may not merit the death penalty exactly, are in some sense "asking for" whatever they get. Three, that the Guard should be buffered with some immediate riot-control training, and that since the regular army soldiers, many of whom were blacks, had done so much better than the Guard, the Guard should immediately recruit as many blacks as possible.

The history of blacks in the American army and militia is a kind of absurdist tale of its own. The South drafted some slaves, and the North drafted some freedmen for its 150 regiments of blacks in the Civil War. But when the North took Louisiana, a southern black unit was caught in the middle and ultimately became the Union's Corps d'Afrique. Black militia briefly terrified some southern states in the early years of Reconstruction; then the black units were disbanded and the white southern militias started terrorizing blacks again. In New York City, Colonel William Hayward started a black National Guard regiment, the Fifteenth New York Infantry (Colored), with its own armory in Harlem and tried vainly to get it attached to any American unit in World War I. Finally, the unit simply attached itself to a division in the French Army, and served with considerable distinction throughout the war. In World War II, black divisions were still segregated, and although one of them, the Ninety-second Infantry (Buffalo) Division, took part in the liberation of Italy, most black soldiers were in service or maintenance units. After President Truman desegregated all divisions of the armed services, the black soldier—in Korea and, of course, still more in Vietnam—came militarily into his own. There have been, not surprisingly, hardly any black National Guardsmen since the National Guard began.

The group that favored a Guard buffered with some riot-control training and some blacks won out. Each Guardsman in each state was to receive thirty-two hours of such training, and blacks were to be recruited intensively. Some administration officials who did not agree with this policy quietly quit. The Guard had become, in their view, a crucial issue that had to be uncompromisingly met. The strength of the country, they argued, had always lain in the ability of liberals and conservatives to police their extremes. Now neither left nor right was willing to cope with the question of the Guard—the right (which was currently out of federal office anyway) because of a belief in states' rights and a feeling that people who got in a Guardsman's way probably deserved what they got; the liberal left, which was in power, out of a fear that facing the issue of law and order in civil disturbances would further alienate the radical left, and also because of a reluctance to tinker with the haven of the draft-dodger. The regular army and the National Guard, in any case, preferred to pretend that civil-disturbance duty was not the major responsibility of either of them but, rather, devolved upon local police officers— who, in turn, preferred to think of themselves as delivering babies and solving ordinary crimes. The civil disturbances were not exactly revolutionary. They were simply anomalous—flash reactions against urban conditions and inequities that had not been resolved.

For a year or more after the crash patchwork job on the Guard, all seemed to go well. The black-recruitment program was a failure and the hours of training in riot control went down, in most states, to less than six. There was no uniform procedure from state to state about whether to put ammunition in weapons, or what sort of weapons to use. But the "long, hot summers" never materialized. There were all sorts of civil disturbances (including one, at Grambling College in Louisiana, which Guard archives describe as a "riot for academic excellence"). But in the 1967 march on the Pentagon, Guard units behaved, under heavy provocation, extremely well; and nobody was killed by Guardsmen in any of the urban riots, in April 1968, over the assassination of Martin Luther King, Jr. It looked all right, as far as National Guard behavior was concerned. Even at the Democratic Convention in Chicago (August 1968), nobody was killed.

Guard duty in 1969 began with a blizzard in Pender, Nebraska, and went on through floods, train wrecks, downed planes, tornadoes, ice storms, forest fires, power failures, a hurricane (in Apalachicola, Florida), a "collapsed dam" (in Wheatland, Wyoming), "haul water" (in Berry and Oakman, Alabama), "flood" (in Soldotna, Alaska), "civil disturbance" (in Zap, North Dakota), and "searches for missing persons" (in such places as Rice Patch Island, North Carolina; Tallapoosa City, Alabama; and Tofte, Minnesota). True, there were "college disturbances" at Berkeley and Dartmouth, but the Guard did all right—as it did in the Moratorium March on Washington in October and, for that matter, at a Stamp Dedication Ceremony for the late Dwight David Eisenhower, in Abilene. The National Guard began again to stress its role in the national defense, and National Guardsmen, by 1969, were running 40 percent of the country's (militarily obsolete but still functional) Nike and Hercules missile sites.

A Harvard graduate, class of 1962, came to New York the summer after his graduation and took a job in a bank. His employer asked how he planned to fulfill his military obligation. The young man didn't know. The bank gave him two letters of recommendation. Within a month, he had risen to the top of the waiting list at the

Seventh Regiment Armory and begun his six months' basic training, before returning to the bank. A young advertising executive, a friend of whose mother was the wife of a veteran of Squadron A, got into the squadron just before he received his draft notice, and about a year before Squadron A became defunct. "It's a total joke," he said of his Guard training. "It's a farce. It's a stupid movie. It's just one constant snafu after another. At the armory drill, you just get into what they call a 'skirmish line.' Militarily, it's obsolete. The equipment is all bad. They're all badly trained. They're all stupid. At scenic Camp Drum, in your tank, they wait till the end of the afternoon to issue ammunition. There's no way to give it back. You have to get rid of it. So you just keep firing and firing until the gun barrel gets red— shells that cost the taxpayer ninety dollars apiece, guns that will knock down a whole building. Once, somebody made a mistake and started firing his machine gun at us, round after round, before he could stop it. He just said, 'Uh-oh.'"

A Guardsman who participated in what was intended to be the first of sixteen hours of riot-control training at some abandoned army barracks in Southern California said, "It was chaos. It was total confusion. We were divided in half—half 'rioters,' half 'riot controllers.' Nobody knew what to do. We raced around shouting. Then both sides started just destroying the buildings. We kicked in doors and smashed windows. After twenty minutes, the officers started blowing their whistles. They barely got people under control. Even at Guard drills now, discipline is on very thin ice. Every unit has lawyers, and officers know that dissident Guardsmen can make full use of the law. Marksmanship practice is a joke. The unit wants to look good. The rule is: everybody passes. There is a tremendous difference between the troops and the officers. The troops are better educated. The old guys just don't want to know it, but if there were a war now these boys simply would not go."

Right after the shootings at Kent State—when it was still thought that the Guardsmen's tear gas had run out, that they were sur-

rounded, that they had been pelted with rocks, that some were injured, that it was simply a question of panic—friends of the Guard
deplored the tragedy, while opponents of the Guard said the Guard
had all along been a "farce" and a "scandal." But friends and opponents agreed that the fact that there had not already been many
Kent States seemed to them "a miracle."

"No, we're not, we're just not bloodthirsty," Colonel W. D. Mc-
Glasson of the National Guard said to a recent visitor, in the National Guard Association's office at 1 Massachusetts Avenue, in
Washington. "Why, I remember when you didn't have the draft to
send you everybody. There was a time when having horse shows and
whatnot was the only thing that kept the Guard together. Harry
Truman once said that he used to have to pay twenty-five cents a
drill for the privilege of drilling at his hometown armory. Now
we have become, in reality, a federal force. They can shift us all the
way to the North Pole if they want to. The waiting lists have fallen
off a bit in the last two, three months, what with the lottery for the
nineteen-year-olds. But these kids that come in for six years and
then leave, they're not Guardsmen in spirit. People who liked the
hiking and the training, those were always the heart and soul of the
Guard. Defense Secretary McNamara wanted to reduce us to a force
of three hundred and forty thousand, but when he asked the adjutants general and the governors, state by state—well, we wound up
with approximately half a million. Now with this Kent State thing,
the newspapers are against us. Probably seventy-five percent of the
press are not like that. It's the large-circulation ones, mostly. But
then, you know, we never killed a soul in all those April riots over
Dr. King, all over this country. And national defense is really the
Guard's primary responsibility. As for civil disturbances, nobody
has found an ideal solution. In this country, we're so accustomed to
the idea that if we have a problem there must be a way to resolve
it. Well, there isn't always a solution. And the problem has been"
—Colonel McGlasson shook his head regretfully—"just when the

racial thing was starting to simmer down, the antiwar movement popped up."

"You know, a Guard unit is not a unit. It's a rabble of men," said Arnold Sagalyn, former senior vice president of the International Criminal Police Organization (Interpol) and now a consultant on urban affairs and a member of the President's Commission on the Causes and Prevention of Violence. "They have no sniper or gas teams, no discipline, no army sequence-of-force procedure—where first you give a warning, then you fix your bayonet, then you load your rifle, and so on. They're forbidden even to carry out civil-disturbance training in summer. In some cities, they've fired at shadows, fired at ricochets. In North or South Carolina, I forget which, Guardsmen were clearing a school, and they went through the doorway too close and started bayoneting each other. What we ought to have is some regular force—it would take just a fraction of what we spend on highways—ready to get to a disturbance fast, trained for it like a firefighter, trained to contain it, every man ready to file a report whenever he fires his weapon. Right now, a few militants making trouble in more than one city could put whole states out of action. The only answer is nonlethal weapons—make people sick, make them uncomfortable. It's better than killing them. When the draft lottery gets so that the only people who join the Guard are the ones who really *want* to be in it, you're going to get the wrong kind of people, the people who like to break heads. When I think of the way it is now, when I just think of the power of death that we entrust to them!"

"Now, Guard procedures vary from state to state," Lieutenant Colonel James Elliott, of the National Guard Bureau, said recently to a visitor in the Pentagon. "Now, in New York State, I believe, the Guard in civil disorders is not issued ammunition. I am not aware of the procedures in all the other states. But Ohio. Well, I guess that's one state where they elect to lock and load."

"I believe that the Guard has no purpose," said Paul Warnke, former Assistant Secretary of Defense for International Security Affairs. "And to the extent that it has a purpose, I don't agree with it. Now, McNamara and Vance, after Detroit, they thought if you have a disturbance you just smother it in people. I think what you do is you train the police to see that it doesn't spread. That's the only function that's essential. Now, if I were a major-league shortstop I wouldn't want to be drafted, either. But if this country has become so Vietnamized that we need Regional Forces and Popular Forces to deal with domestic disorder, well, I certainly don't think it has. And we already have three and a half million men under arms. But if this country is really at a stage where we need a special Guard to deal with domestic disorder, then I don't think we need a Guard anyway, because if we were at that stage, then I wouldn't give a damn."

"The army prefers the police in domestic disorders," said Colonel Dan Henken, a public-affairs officer of the Defense Department. "Frankly, we at the Defense Department want no part of it. In Detroit, though, we had to wean the citizens off the regular army. A lot of our men were black, and people were bringing them sandwiches and asking them not to leave. Saying, 'We don't want trouble, we just don't want those troublemakers around here.' But that's a police problem. If you send in the army, the voters get upset. What we ought to learn, though, is that you don't shoot. You make people uncomfortable. There was a terrific fuss when we used eight canisters of tear gas at the Pentagon in 1967. Eight canisters. The public now accepts the use of tear gas. The National Guard, you know, is primarily for the national defense. And anyway, they have a state-to-state jurisdictional problem. I shudder to think what would happen if there were a civil disturbance on the Belt Parkway between Virginia and Maryland."

In general, people's despair of the National Guard as a troop of lethally armed, untrained state anachronisms tends to correspond with a fear of extremists, right or left. People who are most sanguine about the country tend to think the Guard is one more evidence of the kind of muddling, and mix-up, and loophole, and bungling that makes the country work.

"Look, they said we couldn't break up the caste system and the Klan in the South," said a former official of the Justice Department. "They said, 'You can't turn the FBI around.' The FBI at the time was hunting Communists. Well, there weren't many Communists in Mississippi, so it was a pretty sleepy Bureau. The Justice Department started doing its own investigating for civil rights. And the FBI's pride got involved. And one day they were sending all their best men down there. The South got to be the proudest assignment an FBI man could get. Well, now, you throw yourself at a problem and if you can't break it you throw yourself at it again, and if you still don't break it—well, the next guy will. Now somebody's got to throw themselves at this National Guard Bureau. Somebody's got to say, 'I don't care about the patronage, and I don't care about the draft-dodging, and I don't care how elusive the problem is, I'm going to shake up that Guard Bureau.' And when the Bureau's shaken up and there are some good men in there, they're going to start shaking up the National Guard in every state right along the line and make something of it. After Detroit, nobody wanted to tackle it, because it looked like bad public relations. But now somebody's got to tackle it or we're going to have killings. At least the President's Commission on Campus Unrest has subpoena power. Now somebody has just got to tackle the Guard Bureau in Washington."

"The Bureau is just the purse strings of the National Guard," said Lieutenant Colonel James Elliott at the Bureau offices in Washington. "We just do what the Department of Defense tells us to do, and we are a liaison between Washington and the governors and adjutants general of the states. We think our performance in civil disturbances is adequate, but of course it varies from state to state. In August, when the American Legion held its annual convention in Oregon, the state authorized sixty hours of civil-disturbance training for its Guard, and there was no disturbance. But that was the state of Oregon."

The *New York Times* of Friday, July 24, published an FBI finding that the National Guardsmen at Kent State were not surrounded, had not run out of tear gas, had not been hit by rocks or subjected to sniper fire, and were not in any way injured when they killed four students and wounded thirteen others on May 4. The Justice Department's report found that six Guardsmen might be liable to criminal prosecution. It seemed at first astonishing that there should be an FBI report so rapid, so candid, and so devastating about any branch of the U.S. military. But the agent in charge of the investigation that led to the report was Joseph A. Sullivan, one of two Bureau chiefs who in the early sixties turned the Mississippi FBI to the cause of civil rights.

The Guard having passed, in its domestic duties since World War II, through four not quite discrete phases—civil defense, protection of civil rights, intervention in urban disorders (primarily looting) from Watts through Detroit to the King riots of 1968, and what appeared to be a phase of disturbance on campuses—Arnold Sagalyn, who was becoming less sanguine every minute, had become extremely concerned that the Guard was taking no interest in nonlethal weapons, particularly the chemical agent CS, which he advocates in lieu of deadly firearms. He pulled out from his desk a report he had prepared for the Kerner Commission two years ago.

"Its effect on rioters in Washington," he had written of CS, "was described by one police official as 'phenomenal.' Those exposed to this nonlethal control agent were strongly deterred from any activity which would risk another dose. Some police officers reported that they found it to be so effective that if they merely tossed an ordinary beer can, which resembled the CS container, a crowd would quickly break up and scatter.... It was found that dropping it inside a store that had been broken into immediately deterred future rioters from entering." Mr. Sagalyn put down the report. "When you have half a million Guardsmen armed to the teeth, with no uniform leadership or policy," he said, "and you bear in mind that *civilians*—farmers, hunters, Panthers, vigilantes, extremists, housewives—have more guns than all the other military combined, you pray that the situation isn't as volatile as it looks."

In mid-September, the National Guard Association of the United States, the lobbying group to which virtually all Guard officers belong, held its ninety-second annual convention, at the Americana Hotel in New York. The association, which goes by its acronym, NGAUS, had among its guest speakers General William C. Westmoreland, Chief of Staff of the United States Army; Dr. Curtis W. Tarr, director of the Selective Service System; General Lewis B. Hershey, former Director of the Selective Service System (to whom NGAUS was giving an award); Mayor John V. Lindsay of New York (whom various peace groups had tried to persuade not to speak); and Senator John C. Stennis, of Mississippi, chairman of the Senate Committee on Armed Services. Major General James F. Cantwell, adjutant general emeritus of the New Jersey Guard and still president of NGAUS, was scheduled to open the convention, but since he was currently under indictment in New Jersey (for putting Guardsmen on active duty to work in remodeling his house), he did not attend. Major General Sylvester T. DelCorso, adjutant general of the Ohio National Guard (and a member of the NGAUS executive council), did not attend, either.

There was a bomb scare on the first day of the convention, and some Guard officers discussed the possibility that a convention of the Guard at this time, with these speakers, at the Americana Hotel, might be construed by radicals as a provocation of some sort. But the convention quietly endorsed several resolutions, some military, some having to do with holding next year's convention in Hawaii, where, the adjutant general of Hawaii assured them in a tape-slide travel lecture, they would find "some of our *aloha* spirit, which is so needed now." But the major concerns of the conference were three: how to get less obsolete military equipment from the federal government in what most Guardsmen predicted would be a "weapons fallout" from the reduction of fighting in Vietnam; how to get combat veterans to enlist in the Guard, and six-year enlistees to reenlist for another term; and, most important, how to profit from the "Laird Memorandum," issued in early September by Secretary of Defense Melvin Laird. The Laird Memorandum proposed, in essence, an all-volunteer professional army, a "zero draft," and a better-trained, better-armed National Guard and Reserve to constitute, instead of draftees, the genuine first line of reserve in the country's defense.

Guard officers were dreamy, ecstatic, and characteristically muddled about what the Laird Memorandum would mean in terms of Guard recruitment—but they were unanimously certain that it would mean better arms, M-16 rifles instead of the old M-1s, helicopters, planes, perhaps missiles, the best technology. "We're tickled to see the Laird Memorandum," Major General Winston P. Wilson—known throughout the Guard as Wimpie, and, since 1963, chief of the National Guard Bureau—said on the morning General Westmoreland arrived. "We're going to have progress from the fallout of troop reduction in Vietnam. We're going to get rid of the Korean-vintage equipment. Why, out West, sometimes someone still has to bring their own shotgun. Now we're going to have a smooth escalation."

Asked about equipment for civil disturbances, General Wilson, who has served forty-one years as an Arkansas National Guardsman, twenty of them rising through the Bureau in Washington, said that he thought the Guard's equipment for such duty was adequate. "But we would like to have anything," he added vaguely. "We didn't really wake up at Watts. Now we would like to have batons, water cannons—you know, bulletproof vests, a little better dispensers for gas, bullhorns, bird shot, face masks that go on the helmet." He paused. "But on the local level there still is a judgment factor. There's a lot of sympathy just now for batons, but"—he paused again—"the rifle is still primary."

Asked whether the zero draft might result in zero motivation to join the National Guard, he explained, as Guard officers often explain, that the Laird Memorandum would simply restore the National Guard to the "first line of military reserve" status it held before the draft exemptions of 1948. Asked whether the Guard had opposed the draft exemptions of 1948, he explained that the Guard had in fact supported them. "You see, at the time, we had a recruitment problem," he said. Asked whether it was not precisely that recruitment problem that might now recur, he explained, as Guard officers often explain, that the National Guard was frequently accused of being the haven of the draft-dodger, whereas, on the contrary, it was a place where "draft-motivated" young men could perform their military obligation without being subject to the draft. This line of questioning among Guardsmen is never a productive one, and General Wilson returned with evident pleasure to an anecdote he had been telling all day, about his visit the evening before to the Persian Room of the Plaza, where he had witnessed a performance by Joey Heatherton. "She invited us to her room," he said amiably to anyone in sight, "and she gave me a great big buss..."

By five o'clock on the last afternoon of the convention, a small group of demonstrators were quietly picketing opposite the entrance to the Americana on Seventh Avenue. It was rumored, inside and outside the convention, that Vice President Agnew might attend the States Dinner, the formal closing banquet of the convention, that

night. General Wilson had flown to Washington, to return with
Senator Stennis in time for the dinner. Earnest discussions among
younger Guard officers were taking place in the Americana's bars.
Whether an army of mercenaries, supplemented by a force of citizen-
soldiers, was really what the Constitution had in mind. Whether, as
someone suggested, if a "Seven Days in May" situation should arise,
with the professional army holding the President captive, the National Guard might prove the country's only defense against its mercenaries, in the Laird Memorandum's terms. Whether, with a zero
draft, anyone but rednecks and martinets would join the Guard at
all. How curiously characteristic of the American system it is that *no*
branch of the military cares to confront civilians in civil disturbances. Whether an army composed in part of draftees was not a
greater restraining and liberalizing force than a combination of mercenaries and citizen-soldiers. There was talk of an anecdote from Dr.
Curtis W. Tarr's speech of the day before. "A small minority question why they should do anything for their country," the director of
the Selective Service System had said. "One young man put his question bluntly: 'If I don't want to go into the armed forces, don't want
to try to argue that I am a conscientious objector, don't want to go to
jail, and don't want to go to Canada, what can I do?' My answer did
not please him one bit: 'Somewhere you must find a society to which
you will feel willing to contribute.'"

By six-thirty on the last night of the NGAUS convention, most
of the officers were in full dress uniform—black for Army Guard,
white for Air Guard—and their wives were in evening dresses. Many
of the older men had medals from World War II, but the invitation
to the States Dinner, in a bungle perhaps typical of the Guard in
things military, omitted a rather important "hours." "The President
of the Association," it said, "earnestly requests all guests to be seated
by 1930." Guardsmen and their wives, looking like figures from the
antebellum South, occasionally wandered, drinks in hand, onto the
steps of the Americana to look at the demonstrators, under police
surveillance, across the street. One lady said she preferred to watch
through a window. "Come on, Joanie," another lady said. "Don't be

chicken." A photographer from the *New York Post* photographed a Guard sentry outside the banquet hall, sound asleep.

The States Dinner itself passed like any other convention banquet in the Americana's Imperial Ballroom. There were speeches, a clatter of butter plates, reunions of old friends, some tipsy conversations. Then, just before Senator Stennis spoke, there was an apparently annual ceremony. The sergeant at arms announced the presentation of "the various flags of our Union, in order of admittance," and the state flags were brought in, with appropriate music ("Maryland! My Maryland!" for Maryland, "East Side, West Side" for New York), one by one. People sang along with the songs they knew, but as the flag-bearers came in (many of them presenting also the first black faces of the convention), the officers from each state rose to their feet or stood on their chairs to cheer, waving their yellow Americana napkins over their heads. Hawaii, which gives the best parties, got a standing ovation from everyone. (So did the chaplain-escorted wife of an Air Guardsman missing in action over Vietnam.) But Mississippi, Ohio, Puerto Rico, Wisconsin, and Oregon were also roundly cheered. Yellow napkins were waving everywhere. Then Senator Stennis spoke, rather hawkishly about Vietnam and rather doubtfully about the Guard's capacity to recruit with a zero draft. The banquet became solemn again. Vice President Agnew did not appear. Outside the Americana, by 11:30 P.M., the demonstrators had long disappeared, but there were an inordinate number of horse-drawn carriages of the sort that go through Central Park. Asked whether so many hansoms were normal even for a convention of tourists at the Americana, a New York cabdriver said they were not. "I've never seen so many of them," he said. "What's going on in there?" Told that it was a convention of the National Guard, he said that explained it.

The New Yorker
October 3, 1970

LETTER FROM BIAFRA

IT IS ALMOST impossible to fly into Biafra now, or out of it. The relief organizations (Caritas, World Council of Churches, Nord Church Aid, Canadian Air Relief) that still fly to Biafra from the Portuguese island of São Tomé have formed a single operation, Joint Church Aid, which flies about five planes a night, sometimes two flights per plane, sometimes three, depending on the availability of pilots and the condition of planes. Always at night. Ever since a plane of the International Red Cross was shot down on June 5, by day, by Nigeria, and the International Red Cross suspended its relief flights to Biafra entirely, Joint Church Aid has decided not to fly into Biafra with anyone who, if a plane were to be shot down again, might appear to be on a mission other than church relief. The island of Fernando Po, once a base for Red Cross flights, has been closed off by Equatorial Guinea. The French Red Cross still flies a single plane, sometimes once, sometimes twice a night, from Libreville, Gabon, but it, too, is reluctant to take in passengers; and Biafra, worried that observers might spot incoming flights of arms, does not like to issue visas by way of Libreville. Well-meaning eccentrics used to fly to Biafra from time to time (Abie Nathan, the maverick Israeli pilot, who cooked what food he brought in for refugees himself; an anonymous lady who gave one iron pill to every child she met), but journalists and even doctors are now turned back in São Tomé, to catch the twice-weekly flight to mainland Angola and home again. It is possible that the blockade will soon cut off not only food coming in but reports coming out of this unprecedented war.

The population of São Tomé is one-tenth Portuguese police. The other citizens are mostly contract labor, imported not entirely voluntarily from the Cape Verde Islands, farther off the coast of Africa. A Portuguese island is, in any case, an incongruous place to fly to Biafra from, and there is something about the discontinuity of events and the day-to-day reporting of news that always seems to make either too simple or too mystifying the altogether anomalous predicament of Biafra. Meaningless datelines (Owerri, Emekuku, Awomama, Mbano), scarcely mapped and incessantly changing war fronts, strange friends (Haiti, Tanzania, Ivory Coast, Zambia, Gabon), strange enemies (England, Russia, Egypt, Chad), pictures and statistics no longer automatic in their meaning or credibility, the muddy, bungling, endlessly preoccupying catastrophe in Vietnam, even a sense of Africa derived from Kipling and Waugh—the narrative line for Biafra gets lost. Biafrans do not easily fit any stereotype of martyrdom or ideology. I asked a young Biafran just whose children it is who are dying, and he replied quite seriously that it is the children of villagers who are not strong enough to trek nearer the front to buy what food there is more cheaply and trek back to market to sell it more dearly, for a little profit to support their families. It takes a high tolerance for the sheer, bitterly comic ugliness of human suffering to care much for these survivors out of Bertolt Brecht. Editorial writers for the Western press, unlike reporters on the spot, often treat the Biafran position as morally ambiguous, as though the years from 1939 to 1945 had never existed, and as though killing and dying existed on a single plane of atrocity. It is possible that another ethnic population will be decimated before modern intelligence completes its debate about the extent to which the greatest crimes can be said to be the fault of the victims.

The relief flights from São Tomé take off just before dark, fly with lights off in the darkness over Federal Nigeria, and approach Uli Airport (a widened stretch of what was once a road) in the dark. The blue lights of the runway are flashed very briefly, and then turned off again as the planes begin to land. This is the rainy season in Biafra, but Uli, according to James W. Anderson, one of Joint Church Aid's hired pilots (who earn between $4,000 and $5,000 dollars a month), is "the only place in the world you can fly into and you hope the weather's bad." On clear nights, Nigerian planes, flown by Egyptian or East German pilots, attempt to bomb the runway. They have never hit it yet, and it is a disputed question whether they really want to hit Joint Church Aid planes, but even relief flights quite often miss the darkened landing, and take off abruptly to approach again and again. The pilots, whose professional history usually includes assignments like flying personnel to oil fields in ice storms in Alaska, or flying arms to Israel in 1948, seem fairly sanguine about risk. Last month, a Canadian plane crashed when it apparently received signals, by mistake, from another, more camouflaged Biafran airport. A second crew forgot to lower its landing gear and, when landing without wheels jammed the doors, had to slide down from the cockpit by means of emergency ropes. A few weeks ago, Joint Church Aid headquarters in Geneva made a last-minute exception to admit Eric Pace, of *The New York Times*, and since it seemed that two reporters would no more compromise a single relief flight than one, and since bad weather had limited bombings by what is euphemistically called the Intruder, the local church workers decided to let me go in as well.

On Saturday night, Captain Anderson's plane approached the runway at a right angle (a compass was broken), missed twice, and then landed smoothly in lightning and drenching rain. These trips are entirely calm, perhaps because they lack the unspoken agreement on commercial airlines (the meals, the movies, the silence of engines) to pretend that one has been on the ground all the time, or because they fly into a place suspended from one's personal experience so utterly. The plane, an American C-97, was cleared of its cargo of stockfish and corn-soya-milk extract in seven minutes, and took off for two more trips to São Tomé. The crews were planning three flights that night in order to have one less on Sunday, when they were hoping to hold a barbecue at the rather grim hotel where they are based. Stockfish is now Biafra's main source of animal protein. It was popular before the war in the land that is now Biafra; but when the blockade began, consumption of stockfish was so drastically reduced that the currency of Iceland, a major exporter, had to be devalued, until the United States, by purchasing stockfish for Biafran relief, gave the currency some support.

The tons of fish, in burlap bags, were loaded quickly into lorries. A bearded English relief worker named Graham dashed about in the dark and cold rain, which fogged his glasses. He picked up the passengers and their baggage (distinguishable on the runway by dim strips of yellow masking tape), and drove nearly blindly, with dimmed headlights, among a series of checkpoints manned by armed Biafrans and each consisting of a thatched hut and a branch extended across a road to a steel drum. One of the branches was lifted and the car drove to a building called State House for entry formalities in earth-floored rooms, by the light of four kerosene lamps. An important shipment of something was clearly expected from Libreville, because Arthur Mbanefo, a Biafran government official, and Professor Ben Nwosu, a Biafran nuclear physicist educated in California and now head of the Biafran Directorate of Research and Production, were gathered in the office of a Major Akigabu, who is in charge of immigration at State House, and who was once a teacher of Virgil in secondary school. Major Akigabu, a middle-aged man in battle fatigues, was quoting in near darkness from Book II of the *Aeneid*. "When you read it, you will shed tears," he said. "You have to shed tears."

The sense here is of a people about to die in isolation and pretending not to know it—convinced in any case by their recent history that they have no choice. Victims are seldom pure, or even entirely attractive, and a case can certainly be made against any victim of murder before some higher court of absolute irrelevance. But Biafrans, fighting a war, in a sense, for a position argued in Hannah Arendt's *Eichmann in Jerusalem*, are determined to avoid at least the accusation of passive complicity in their own destruction and resist, trusting their own interpretation of what the risks of capitulation and the costs of survival might be. Once the foremost advocates of Nigerian unity, they have been persuaded by a series, both before and since the war, of broken accords, systematic exclusions, and outright massacres, both total and selective (including the killing of all males over ten years old in a captured Biafran town whose civilians did not leave), that Nigeria intends to eliminate the peoples of the region that is now Biafra, and that the intention of genocide is not one that you test, passively, until the last returns are in. In the massacres of summer 1966, nearly a full year before Biafra's secession from Nigeria, thirty thousand natives of the Biafran region were murdered.

"I have just been reading *Exodus*," Professor Nwosu told a group of friends, some time after his night of waiting at State House. "Before the war, a novel to me was a trivial thing. But I should have known the West would not be impressed by thirty thousand. Some of you literary people should have told me."

In 1966, pressure to withdraw from Nigeria came mainly from the Ibo people, who make up the majority of the population of the Biafran region, and it was the Ibo intellectuals, spread out over Nigeria and the world, who wavered. Now the situation is different. The intellectuals have returned from their jobs in the outside world to Biafra, to extremity, and to a people with whom, in their own worldliness, they were not even entirely familiar. An Ibo civil servant, educated elsewhere in Nigeria, when he is asked the word in Ibo for a sash in which local women carry their babies on their backs, does not know, until it is pointed out to him, what you are talking about. He certainly does not know the word. English has always been Biafra's intertribal language, but conversations even in Ibo are interspersed now with English expressions, and the Biafran fondness for euphemism has a British ring. The war is everywhere referred to as "the crisis," areas of Biafra destroyed or occupied by Nigerian forces are always called "disrupted" or "disturbed."

The elite are leading now, as perhaps in war they always do. But Ibo society is, by tradition, individualistic and ruled by tribal consensus. The leaders and their ministries are unprotected to a degree uncommon in a country at war. If the people did not support their leaders, they could, being armed almost to a man, overthrow them. Biafrans now prefer the bush to the risks of Nigerian occupation, and Nigerian troops entering Biafran towns now find them empty. What defections there are, like that of Dr. Nnamdi Azikiwe, an Ibo who was once president of Federal Nigeria and who recently turned from the Biafran to the Nigerian side, preoccupy Biafrans continually—perhaps because there have been so few of them. A betrayal in 1967, by Brigadier Victor Banjo, who had been put in charge of all Biafran forces in the Midwestern Region, recurs in war-inspired songs all over Biafra. (Dr. Azikiwe's case is complicated by the fact that he had spent several months in London, in a state that his physicians described as "delayed shell shock," before going to Lagos and, when his extensive Nigerian properties had been returned to him, denouncing Biafra.) The favorable reaction in the American press to Dr. Azikiwe's claim that Biafran fears of extinction are a "fairy tale" presumably gave the Nigerians confidence to resume, a few days after the first editorials, their civilian air raids, bombing and strafing an orphanage at Ojoto. Dead: one nurse and fourteen children, miles from the nearest battle zone.

The former Eastern Region of Nigeria, which since May 30, 1967, has called itself Biafra, has always been the most densely populated region in all of Africa—and, in recent times, the most highly developed and educated black country there is. Its present population is about ten million; present size, ten thousand square miles; war dead in two years, one and a half million civilians by air raids and starvation, half a million more soldiers and civilians killed in actual combat zones. There are several hundred thousand refugees in Biafran refugee camps, millions more living with distant relatives in the traditional Ibo stress claim of the "extended family," seven or even twenty persons to a room. Biafran roads, before the bombings the best roads in Nigeria, are pitted now, interrupted by checkpoints and occasional rows of tree stumps to impede enemy landings, eroded further by the intense rains, sometimes hollowed under the tarmac to stop heavy-armored vehicles, but crowded in the late and early hours of darkness by lines of people—trekking, with burdens on their heads, to relatives, to markets, to shelter or hospitals. Kwashiorkor, the ugly, mortal protein-deficiency disease, which had almost been stopped when Red Cross flights were running at strength, is afflicting children again, and the people on the roads include a high proportion of adults damaged, bandaged, or in pain. Because the Biafran government is not recognized by any major country, Biafra is denied legal access on the international market to, among other things, morphine. In terms of statistics, loss of life, displacement of persons, the war has already taken a greater toll than Vietnam; and yet people on the road inevitably return smiles, and life in this enormous ghetto under siege seems determined to proceed almost normally.

As always in war, unless one happens to be at the front and be shot at, or caught in an air raid, there is nothing but a set of symptoms—distortions of peace—to give one a sense of war and its losses. Premature or simply inaccurate Nigerian claims of areas captured have often sent observers to battle zones to find that they are not simply at the front—they *are* it; and four journalists have already been killed while reporting from the Nigerian side. But the strange image-consciousness of Biafrans makes them highly scrupulous about not sending reporters where Biafran soldiers have not arrived. Biafran information officials will try reporters with the strangest evasions, from subjects as knowable and precise as whether there is or is not a Biafran Telex (there is not), or whether there are in fact flights from Libreville, to subjects as hard to know in wartime as the exact population and casualty rate. But they are deeply concerned for the safety of foreigners. "Why do you choose to fly into this volcano?" an Ibo doctor, exhausted with work, asked a foreign visitor. "You have no right or obligation to die here." When the foreigner replied, "I think it is a shared right," the doctor said, "Thank you." There is everywhere this crazed, articulate, sometimes even irritable courtesy, in the face of an absolute desolation closing in.

Foreigners flying into Biafra now bring their own food and, if the pilot permits it, their own gasoline in jerry cans. What fuel there is in Biafra is made in little roadside refineries, which consist of a thatched hut over firewood and an arrangement of pipes and steel drums beside a brook, like a still. A loss of fuel can be as dire in Biafra now as the shortage of food, since the army must be mobile to reach any stress point on the completely encircling front. The symptoms of war are evident in everything from the sound of mortars miles from the front to the fact that all markets have moved under camouflage in the bush and that children at feeding centers can get only one meal a day. Yet one subject Biafrans hardly ever talk about is the front, the actual progress of the war. Asked about this strange reticence, Biafrans will say the front is "irrelevant," or "We have no place to go. They take Owerri, we retake Umuahia. If we lose it all, we will fight without towns, from the bush." Another subject hardly mentioned in ordinary conversation, without laughter, is food, or even the starving of the children. If pressed, a Biafran will say he finds the subject "painful." Genocide, however, comes up again and again, and Biafrans will talk about a friend, a relative, a town, a personal flight from a mob before or in the war with a precise attention to dates and the most gruesome detail. Bombing raids on markets, churches, orphanages, and hospitals are recounted by families and in palm-wine bars with a kind of awe of their modern European quality, as though by dying on purely ethnic grounds Biafrans had established their place in modern history. One thing one hardly sees in Biafra is cemeteries. The dead are buried all over the third of the country that remains.

Nigeria, in what was originally described by the Nigerian government as a "quick surgical police action" that would last forty-eight hours and that has already lasted more than two years and cost more than two million lives, was armed for the war with highly sophisticated equipment by the British, who wanted, as did nearly everyone else at one time, a strong and unified Nigeria. Reporters like Frederick Forsyth in his book *The Biafra Story*, one of the few cogent accounts of what took place, attribute the subsequent disaster to the Labour Government of Harold Wilson, who took the advice of civil servants that it would all be over quickly, that it was all a question of Ibo intransigence. Most of Nigeria's oil fields are in the Biafran region, and the oil companies had their doubts. They had personnel in the field who knew the people and who had witnessed the events of the preceding years. But the civil servants prevailed, and when it was not all over quickly, the Labour Government vastly increased its shipments of arms to Nigeria, and covered up at home.

When, in August 1968, after thirteen months of war, the extent of the British commitment became clear, there were expressions of outrage in Parliament and in the press. The Government, no longer able to conceal the size of its arms shipments, began to argue that it was more merciful in the long run to let Biafrans starve and be bombed into submission than to remain neutral, that the alternative was a tribal "Balkanization" of all Africa, that the Ibo leaders were, in any case, exaggerating and prolonging the misery of their people in order to nationalize and abscond with the oil and consolidate their own leadership. In 1967, the Russians began sending heavy arms to Nigeria, and it was argued that it was important to compete with Russia in arming Nigeria for the sake of Nigeria's goodwill. It is now likely that Nigeria's debt to Russia is such that if Nigeria wins, the oil will go at least in part to Russia, and Russia will have its first important ally in black Africa. Biafrans claim their own guerrillas will see to it that, in the event of their defeat, no oil will flow at all. It is not clear what will happen to the oil if Biafra wins, although Biafran loyalty to anyone who gives them any help or recognition just now is strong. President Nixon expressed sympathy for Biafra in a campaign speech on September 9, 1968, but nothing as strong since. The only official expression of support from any Western power came last year, from President Charles de Gaulle.

In 1960, when Nigeria became independent, it was the Northern Region that kept threatening secession, and the Eastern Region, now Biafra, that most strongly wanted unity. The North, inhabited by the Muslim Hausa-Furlani, had been ruled by the British through local emirs, who kept the region feudal and underdeveloped. The Western Region, inhabited by the less militantly Muslim Yorubas, was ruled through local tribal chieftains and remained underdeveloped, too. (The Yorubas, traditionally a peaceful people, are now being recruited by the Hausas for the war, which solves some of the internal problems in what remains of Federal Nigeria.) The Eastern Region, traditionally governed under chiefs by tribal consultation, with chiefdoms often shifting among ruling families by popular agreement, was far more egalitarian and more difficult to rule. The British imposed "warrant chiefs" on the region, but after riots at Aba in 1929, which protested the imposition of rulers, they left the area to the missionaries—mainly the Anglican Church Missionary Society and the Roman Catholics. England's role in the war, as opposed to the support of Catholics in Caritas, has created a crisis of faith among Biafran Protestants, many of whom now attend predawn Mass in Owerri, in an uncompleted Catholic cathedral camouflaged by palm fronds, in the rain. The Ibos, who traditionally believed in one god, and worshipped him through idols, took to Christianity easily, and to Christian education. Communities sent bright children to schools abroad. By secession in 1967, Biafra had more doctors, lawyers, and engineers than any other country in black Africa. Of six hundred Nigerian doctors before the war began, five hundred were Biafrans. The crowded conditions in the Eastern Region, and their own education, sent Ibos all over the rest of Nigeria. They took part in all Nigerian institutions, but their living quarters were segregated, in ghettos called *sabon garis*. As early as 1953 at Kano, they faced pogroms.

Northern animosity toward Easterners, and suspicion of them, was so great well before independence that the North continually threatened secession unless it could dominate the Nigerian legislature. As early as 1947, Mallam Abubakar Tafawa Balewa, a Northerner who was later to become prime minister of Nigeria (and whom the Sardauna of Sokoto, a Hausa ruler, used to refer to as his "lieutenant" in Lagos), opposed unity and independence with the statement "I should like to make it clear to you that if the British quitted

Nigeria now at this stage, the Northern people would continue their uninterrupted conquest to the sea."

In the years after independence, there was a series of rigged censuses, rigged elections, and murders of members of the major political party of the Eastern Region by members of the major party of the North. On January 14, 1966, there was a military coup, which killed Prime Minister Balewa and the Sardauna of Sokoto, and which is sometimes described as the Ibo move for domination that started it all. The coup did end with General Johnson Thomas Umunakwe Aguyi-Ironsi, an Ibo, in power. But it killed only twelve officers, three of whom were Ibos; it was joined by Hausa and Yoruba factions of the army; and it was opposed by, among other Ibos, Lieutenant-Colonel Chukwuemeka Odumegwu Ojukwu, now the head of state of Biafra, and General Ironsi himself.

Six months later, the Northerners staged their coup. In view of the present Nigerian claims for a unified Nigeria, the code word that set off the operation is key: *araba*, the Hausa word for "secession." In his first broadcast after the coup, Lieutenant Colonel Yakuba Gowon, the Northerner who is now head of state of Nigeria, said that Nigerian unity could not stand the test of time, that "the base for unity is not there." Three weeks later Gowon was still flying the flag not of Federal Nigeria but of the Northern Region at his headquarters in the garrison at Ikeja. At a constitutional convention in Lagos in September 1966, the Northern delegates insisted on a clause reading "Any member state of the Union should reserve the right to secede completely and unilaterally from the Union."

But the world, including, at that point, the Biafrans, still believed in one Nigeria, and the Northerners who were then in power began to see the advantages of it. The army became uncontrollable. There followed a series of massacres of Ibos and broken agreements with the Eastern Region. Gowon's announcement to the press, for example, of accords between the Eastern and Northern Regions reached in Aburi, Ghana, in January 1967, differs in almost every detail from tape recordings of those accords subsequently released by Ojukwu. The Northerners had agreed to protect Easterners in the other regions on their passage home, to make financial provisions for the homeless refugees, and to give the Eastern Region a degree of autonomy. Gowon did not mention the refugee agreements, and denied the accord on autonomy. Over a million Ibos had already fled for their lives to the Eastern Region. In early May 1967, Gowon blockaded all communications to the East. On May 26, the Consultative Assembly of Chiefs and Elders gave Ojukwu, who had been for about a year and a half the military governor of the Eastern Region, a mandate to withdraw from Nigeria. The next day, Gowon published a decree that, among other measures, divided the Eastern Region into three small states, with Port Harcourt and the Eastern oil fields to be excised from the Ibo region. (Port Harcourt had been built by Ibos and was inhabited almost entirely by them. The oil fields, which had only begun producing just before Nigerian independence, had not been a factor in the dispute before.) On May 30, Ojukwu issued a Biafran Declaration of Independence. On July 6, 1967, with the slogan "One Nigeria!" Nigerian forces invaded Biafra, and soon afterward entered the Ibo town of Nsukka, where they set fire to the university and destroyed all its books.

Surprisingly—since most Ibo members of the Nigerian Army had been technical and administrative personnel, and since Biafra was very lightly armed—the Biafrans nearly won their independence in the first three months. Then the heavy British equipment came in. The Biafrans lost the coast and their major towns, although they had considerable success against the heavy equipment with homemade booby traps manufactured in Professor Nwosu's Research and Production Directorate. By April 1968, their agricultural and river areas were cut off, and people began to die of starvation in numbers that, at their peak, were estimated at ten thousand a day. Caritas, the World Council of Churches, and the Red Cross began sending in small amounts of food on Biafran mercenary arms flights. On October 12, Dr. Herman Middelkoop, of the World Council of Churches, sent a telegram to Secretary-General U Thant of the United Nations requesting UN humanitarian aid for Biafra. On October 19, the Secretary-General told the press that the telegram had not arrived and that the war was, in any case, an internal affair, in which the United Nations could not become involved.

In July 1968, the Red Cross asked General Gowon for permission to fly specially marked relief planes into Biafra. Gowon replied that Nigeria would shoot them down. They flew anyway, and the churches, having obtained the code for landing at Uli Airport, flew in, too. In June of this year, after endless negotiations over relief routes, with Nigeria arguing alternately that all relief must pass through Lagos and that there could be no relief, since total siege is a legitimate instrument of war (although the idea of total siege has traditionally been applied to cities and not to an entire ethnic population of ten million), the Red Cross plane was shot down. Since the shooting, it has been argued with increasing insistence that the situation has changed entirely, and that it is only the Biafran leadership that is making impossible, at great cost to its own people, the dream of a peaceful and unified Nigeria. Biafrans have come to argue that there never was a Nigeria, except as defined by the British colonial presence; that if the colonial "nations" of Africa were in fact to break up along tribal lines, not much would be lost except some unstable, colonial boundaries; and that a new force—local, indigenous, tribal, unaligned—may yet be brought forth into the world. As for defectors and the charge that the Biafrans are exaggerating their own danger of genocide, Biafrans reply that every ethnic group marked for extinction has had sincere and misguided collaborators with the enemy. Their own experience of tribal slaughters and world indifference or unconsummated sympathy has made them determined not to rely to the last man on Nigeria's new good faith.

On Sunday, at Owerri market, which is now a little cluster of wooden tables and benches, reached by a thin track of red earth marked by the imprint of sandals and bare feet, in the bush, a five-year-old girl sat on the ground meticulously gathering and blowing sand off each seed of breadfruit she had dropped on the ground. The price of a scruffy, dazed, and twitching hen was eight pounds (nearly twenty dollars); a leg of goat, fifteen pounds; a two-inch bony river fish, a bush snail, or a cigarette, nearly half a pound; a third of a cup of salt, or a cup of *garri* (ground cassava, the only food most Biafrans can get), one pound. The salary of a soldier or a beginning civil servant is fifteen pounds a month. A woman was preoccupied with keeping her entire wares, four minuscule bush snails, from crawling away. No one was buying anything but *garri*, and very little of that.

Suddenly, a shrieking, giggling band of eleven young men and three boys passed through the market, as though carried away by some enervating, mocking joke. These were some of the "artillery cases" one sees all over Biafra—people claiming some local variant of shell shock and traveling always in packs. They were treated by other citizens with a kind of care. Three at Owerri market were given a melon seed or a nut, which sent them into screams of laughter again. Medical comments about them vary. Dr. Fabian Udekwu, head surgeon at a hospital in Emekuku, insists that their disorder is genuine. "The reason their voices are so shrill is that their hearing is impaired," he said. A young military matron at the Armed Forces Hospital in Nkwerri was less sympathetic. "They are putting it on," she said. Most of the artillery cases are treated at a psychiatric hospital in Ekwereazu. It takes about two months to cure the symptoms.

At nine-thirty Sunday morning, in a bullet-scarred bungalow of what was once the Advanced Teachers' Training College in Owerri (Owerri, fifteen miles from the front, was taken by Nigerian forces last September, retaken by Biafra in April; it is now Biafra's provisional capital), I asked Elizabeth Etuk, who is in her twenties, chairman of the Biafra Youth Front, and a member of the Ibibio, a minority tribe, how many times she had been a refugee since she fled from Lagos just before the war. She began to count.

"Mark you," she said, "I'm now in a village I never heard of before." Miss Etuk, who received her doctorate in child psychology from Columbia University in 1967, gave up her study of "the intellectual development of our children" (almost all Biafran schools have been closed since the crisis) to form the Youth Front, which so far consists of a few thousand young people in about fifty villages, who administer feedings ("lunch, when there was a lunch"), catch lizards, sausage flies, and snails by night for their protein content, process cassava into *garri*, allot the little salt that is brought in by relief flights, perform and compose songs for the refugee camps, and organize play groups for the children who are not too weak with misery or kwashiorkor.

"They always play war games," she said earnestly. "Nobody wants to play the Nigerians. Sometimes the play is violent. It is the strain." She became very cheerful about the new Biafran songs that mix local languages. "The crisis has mixed the country up," she said. "You find refugees shouting when they hear their language, then other refugees in the same camp shouting when they hear their own." Her youth group has brought back some traditional dances that were beginning to die off. "Before the crisis, you know, some of us were very worried," she said. "We knew how to dance the waltz." I asked her whether women had always had much influence in the Eastern Region, and she became quite grimly militant. She described the Ibo women's part in the 1929 riots, and a more recent protest. "A committee went to His Excellency," she said, referring to Ojukwu. "And they told him, '*We* are the ones who have lost children. We are the ones who have lost husbands. We are the ones who lost our homes. Some of us are too old to have children again. Ojukwu, give us guns!' When the women start these things, the men know they are not joking. But they were very adamant. They said it had not come to that." A friend tried to distract her with a joke about soups from the Ibibio area of Biafra, and she laughingly told him that, since the population mix-up, Ibos would have to acknowledge that Ibibio soups were the best.

At lunchtime, Miss Etuk and her friend having refused to stay, I cooked some canned soup over a kerosene stove in my bungalow in Owerri and then went to a building called the Overseas Press Service, where it turned out two French journalists, who were about to leave Biafra, had run out of food. They ate in the press cafeteria. The menu, headed "Progress Hotel Umuahia" (Umuahia was captured in April by Nigeria) and restamped "Owerri": Boiled Yam, Mixed

Vegetables (apparently a kind of grass), Sliced Pineapple (a quarter of a single slice per guest).

Sunday afternoon, at the Victoria Palace Hotel, a palm-wine bar (Biafra is full of palm-wine bars called, and sometimes serving as, hotels: Hotel de Gabon, Hotel de Tanzania, Hotel de Haiti, Hotel DeGaulle, Hotel Tranquillity), the palm wine, a mildly alcoholic drink with the taste of oiled lemonade, had run out. There was still Biafra Gin, Biafra Sherry, and Biafra Stout Beer (one-half bottle, seven pounds). The place was filled with soldiers, in uniform and armed with pistols made in France. There were also a few civilian women and some artillery cases, who swarmed around the soldiers without shrieking and yet seemed to embarrass them. The aging proprietor of the Victoria Palace said that he had begun, in pre-crisis times, by trading salt, soap, and shoes to accumulate money to buy his hotel but that the "vandals" had looted his hotel when Owerri was disrupted. "Vandals" is the almost universal word in Biafra for Nigerians.

Just after dark on Sunday, in the house of N. U. Akpan, who is Chief Secretary to the Military Government, head of the Biafran civil service, a Presbyterian elder, and a member of the minority Ibibio tribe, the lights went out. The water in Owerri had been shut off some time before. Kerosene lamps were brought in. It was cold, and the rain outside looked bleak. I asked Mr. Akpan whether anyone in Biafra advocated simply giving up. (These questions always seemed to me awful, but Biafrans seemed to mind if they were not asked. Women at markets looked worried if notes were not made of every answer; and one is asked everywhere in Biafra to sign a guestbook, as though simply writing things down—names, comments—would someday give evidence that there had been a Biafra at all.) "If you said that," Mr. Akpan said quietly about giving in, "you would be beaten up. If I said it, I would be lynched."

I asked what the politics of Biafra, whose enemy had been armed after all by both the Russians and the British, might be after the war. Mr. Akpan said it would be unaligned in terms of ideology. "Only let us be unaligned," he said. "Let us look inward." He paused a long time in the near darkness. "The West brought us good tidings, but it wouldn't let us expand on them. Now we are suffering this strange mercy killing at the hands of the British, and it has brought out qualities we did not know we had. Nigeria, you see, has mortgaged its future to the Soviet Union, but we would wish after the crisis that they would be stable. We wouldn't wish a confused and unstable neighbor." He paused again. "Mark you," he said, "when Nixon was campaigning, Nigeria became jittery."

When I asked whether de Gaulle's expression of sympathy might have been a case of enlightened self-interest, he denied it vigorously. "France spoke for us when we had lost the oil, when we were nearly finished," he said. "Some of us, you see, thought last September was the end. But here we are."

At the dinner hour on Sunday, I again saw Elizabeth Etuk, with Austin Ogwumba (head of Biafran Security), Dr. Pius Okigbo (a Biafran economist, and former representative of Nigeria to the European Common Market), and some other guests, at the home of Godwin A. Onyegbula, the former Nigerian chargé d'affaires in Washington, now permanent secretary of the Biafran Ministry of Foreign Affairs and Commonwealth Relations. (The word "Commonwealth" in the title of Mr. Onyegbula, who is essentially the Biafran foreign minister, dates from a time when Biafrans still had hopes for the British, but it now refers only to "the commonwealth of nations.") I asked whether Biafrans felt comfortable with recognition by, of all nations, Haiti. François Duvalier went to school with several young Ibos in Michigan, long before he became Papa Doc, when he was still a young liberal medical student. Mr. Onyegbula laughed, averted his eyes, and entered that tangle of reasoning with which Biafrans express their loyalty to any of the strange partners with whom they now find themselves.

"Well, you know, when Haiti recognized us, I began to doubt all the things I had ever heard about it," he said. "I have never been there myself, but, you see, Haiti was, after all, the world's first black republic. Perhaps when your brother is suffering you have a telepathic experience." Mr. Onyegbula seemed relieved to let the subject drop. Conversation turned to the failure of Biafra to capture the imagination of black Americans. "Yes, yes," Dr. Okigbo said. "How can we get to them?" The guests began a very informed discussion about American black leadership, and whether it might be better to have the support of Mrs. Martin Luther King, Julian Bond, and Jesse Jackson or to enlist the "crisis mentality" of black radicals, who now seem to seek their identity with the descendants of Muslim slave traders—most recently at the Pan-African cultural conference in Algiers.

"It doesn't matter," Dr. Okigbo said, laughing. "After all, we are all on the same train without a ticket."

Late Sunday night, a Biafran rock group called the Fractions, who had brought their own generator for their guitars and against the darkness, were playing to a very crowded dance floor in the hall of the Advanced Teachers' Training College. Most of the young people were dancing Western style, some were doing the Highlife, and a few were discussing the news of Dr. Azikiwe's defection in Lagos. "In war, you always have Lord Hawhaw," a bearded young man said. "It doesn't reflect the core, the generality of opinion." Many of the dancers were soldiers. Two were solemn workers from Caritas. After the dance, in a rain that seemed almost total, on the Owerri-Orlu road, among the trekkers, almost all of whom were barefoot and shivering, and many of whom were naked children carrying basins or articles of furniture on their heads, a little boy put a large machete on top of his head to free his hands to rub his eyes. The driver of a State House car, who had already nearly hit a goat and a chicken, almost ran him down.

On Monday, at 9 A.M., in Owerri, the High Court of Biafra was in session in what was once a school, under Chief Justice Sir Louis Mbanefo, a former judge of the World Court, who as an Ibo justice in Nigeria in 1962 had reduced the sentence, for treason, of Chief Anthony Enahoro, whom he faced again last year in unsuccessful negotiations for peace in Biafra. All the judges and attorneys wore black robes and curled, yellowing wigs. On the table nearest the attorneys was a gray volume, *Reports of the High Court of the Federal Territory of Lagos*. The steps by which messengers climbed to the justices' bench consisted of rusted mortar containers, still marked "Explosives/UK." On the docket was an appeal of a sentence of murder (*Chief Amagwara Achonye v. the State*), but the case under discussion was a complicated one, which had already passed through native and higher courts, concerning the right of a man to build on the communal land of his family. The appellant had been in possession of the land since 1921, planted fruit trees and constructed a fence, but there were legal issues that entailed a distinction between "possession" and "ownership," and also issues of tribal law, which elicited phrases like "By native custom, My Lord, a man may not build on the ruins of his father's house unless the line has become extinct" and "If a man should have a house, My Lord, and what is commonly called a yard. . . ." The appellant and members of his family were in attendance, but silent. At one point, Justice Mbanefo asked one of the attorneys, a bearded young man with a severe cold and with thumbprints on his glasses, whether the case might be adjourned until Wednesday. "I don't know, My Lord," he replied. "I have to come all the way from Ihiala for these appeals. The problem of transportation will be—that is, unless my learned friend can . . ." Finally, the court did adjourn. An usher cried, "Court!" Everyone rose, and the justices left the room.

Later, in his office, in what had once been a little classroom, the chief justice remarked that the case should have been tried in 1967, "but the land in question, you see, was disturbed until now. So the matter of ownership was for some time academic." I asked Justice Mbanefo about the accommodation of British and native law. "We are still in the process of sorting it out," he said. "Mark you, the native courts consist of local men of impeccable integrity. We would not reverse the ruling of the customary courts unless it was patently against good conscience, equity, and justice." I asked Justice Mbanefo about the strange history of his two encounters with Chief Enahoro of Nigeria. "Ah, you see, under other circumstances it might have been different," he said, and he pointed out that a brother of Chief Enahoro is now in exile in Norway, where he makes fervent speeches on behalf of Biafra. "Mind you," he said, "only yesterday one of my own nephews, who was commanding a company, found some supplies left by Nigerian forces in retreat. Some of the company drank the beer left behind, and it was full of arsenic. Four men are dead. It is tragic, the loss of life. I don't think the British are acting in this out of a desire to see Biafrans killed. They are like all good imperialists. Human lives don't matter. Political expediency—this, I think, is really behind it."

Mr. Onyegbula came in to ask Justice Mbanefo, who is also an official of the Biafran Petroleum Commission, for an allotment of fuel for the Foreign Ministry. Justice Mbanefo could only give him half of what he asked. "I believe the Nigerian soldiers are fighting for the spoils," the justice said quietly. "You see, our refugees leave everything behind. We are fighting for our homes. With us, oil was never an issue. But now, of course"—he paused and nodded to himself several times—"you cannot ignore it."

On Monday afternoon, Chinua Achebe, the Biafran novelist (author of *Things Fall Apart* and *No Longer at Ease*), arrived in Owerri several hours late for an appointment because of a broken axle on the road from Oguta, where, having been five times a refugee from a series of disturbed areas, he now lives. Mr. Achebe is chairman of the Biafra National Guidance Committee, a group of Biafran intellectuals who go out and interview the people in the countryside to keep the government in touch with what the people are saying. Ordinary Biafrans speak freely of the Guidance Committee, and freely register their grievances at its meetings, but the government (presumably for fear the committee might acquire an image of repressive interrogation) is extremely reticent about it. The sun was out briefly in Owerri. I asked Mr. Achebe, whose novels are preoccupied with problems of the modern breakdown in Ibo tradition, about Ibo relations with the minority tribes—the Efiks, Ibibios, Ijaws, Annangs, Ogojas, and Cross River people (most of them Christians)—who comprise a bit less than half of Biafra's population and about half of the Consultative Assembly of Chiefs and Elders. The assembly consists of ten men, six elected and four appointed by the government, from each of the more than thirty districts of pre-crisis Biafra, and it includes, among representatives of labor, business, professional, and women's groups, such local elders as the Amanyanagbo of Kalabari, the Amanyanagbo of Bonny, Chief J. Mpi of Ikwerre, Douglas Colonel Jaja of Opobo, the Obi of Onitsha, Uyo Clan Head of Okwu Itu-Itam, the Onyiba Enyi of Ohaozara in Abakaliki, and the ninth Eze Dara of Uli. Members of Eastern minority tribes have often been killed along with Ibos, and many of the minorities who once chose to remain in disturbed areas and risk Nigerian occupation have since taken refuge in Biafra. General Ojukwu has frequently asked for a plebiscite, under international supervision, to determine the minority tribes' view of Biafran independence. "The crisis has now thrown everyone together," Mr. Achebe said. "It seems a very curious way to forge a nation."

On Monday evening, Patience Nwokedi, a twenty-two-year-old nurse in the Red Cross hospital at Awomama, hitchhiked the fifteen miles to Owerri to spend her one day off a week with her husband, Ralph, a twenty-eight-year-old civil servant, to whom she has been married for six months. They were going to wait until after the crisis to marry, but after two years decided not to wait. Mr. Nwokedi, who was educated at the Ibo university at Nsukka, used to write advertising for Federal Nigeria, which appeared in newspaper supplements abroad. In Biafra now, he supports his wife's mother, who was recently caught for some days in the bush behind enemy lines ("We are recuperating her," he said), his own mother, his own sixty-six-year-old father and his stepmother and their five children, who live in Nimo, two miles from the front, and a friend and five brothers and sisters who now all live in Mr. Nwokedi's two-room house with him. In good times, he can afford about a cup of *garri* per person per meal. He has four brothers in the army who help. "For a young man not to have served in the army, even if he is on essential services, is very painful to him," he said. "But without me my poor old dad would starve."

Ralph and Patience Nwokedi, who are Protestants, found a car for a visit to an old friend, Father Michael Conniff, at the Caritas mission for the Owerri diocese. Father Conniff, like most white men who have served in Biafra since the crisis, has a frantic, nearly crazed look about his bloodshot eyes. There are thirty-one parishes in the Owerri diocese. With the reduced relief flights, Caritas receives a shipment of food only every other night. "We don't know what we are getting," Father Conniff said. "Often we have to wonder, Is this worth dividing into thirty-one places? We cater for seven hospitals. The Red Cross used to cater for sixty-four. West German relief has fallen off ninety percent since the Biafran Air Force bombed an oil installation in the Midwest. All day long we are worried by wounded soldiers. Now they have nothing to eat. What are we to do?"

I asked him whether the diocese feeds only Catholic children.

"We take every child that comes," he said. "The only distinction is a special diet for the sicker ones." Three children had died in one of his sick bays the night before. Father Conniff patted a mongrel dog named Buster, fed on whatever leaks out of the burlap sacks of fish. "This is not a place everybody would want to come to," he said, in a voice that was by now cracking. "There are a lot of things to kind of scare a fellow from living here. When the area was retaken, there were a lot of bodies smelling. We buried them. Some of them were not pushed down too far. There's two in the yard, six under my window, one officer in the flower garden. The bush closed in. That brought mosquitoes bigger than fowl, rats, snakes. A lot of corpses are in this place."

I asked him what his prayers were like.

"More planes," he said vaguely. "More planes. Bigger planes. More planes." Not far from the mission, there was still a billboard reading, "Pepsi, the Big One."

Ralph Nwokedi's father had trekked all the way from Nimo for a three-week visit to his son. He would also visit Ralph's mother, twenty miles farther on. Although Christian, the elder Nwokedi is a polygamist. The elder Nwokedi, a tall, distinguished man, with long bare feet and a long maroon robe over a faded collarless shirt, ceremoniously broke a kola nut for his family and guests, in their dark living room. Kola nuts are full of caffeine, and are supposed to make water drunk after them taste very sweet. The kola nut, about three inches long, broke into six natural pieces, and the elder Nwokedi sliced these into halves and passed them around. He said a prayer, and then everyone chewed, and drank water from the house's only glass.

"When the first refugees come," the elder Nwokedi said, "we begin to harbor them, begin petting them, say, 'Be quiet, be quiet, peace will come.' Now we have to break off, finished. If I am young, I should go inside the battlefield and fight. Now I see how I try to keep my household together. We take cover each time, and our hearts run each time. I was a big man, but now I shall never weigh ten stone again." He was silent for a very long time. "When I become a Christian as a boy, I get a small book, and when I have children they should learn to read and write. The war breaks in and it turns my heart. It should be college now. Of all the time of my life, this is the misery."

Later, at the dinner hour, in the house of Dr. Ifegwu Eke, commissioner of information, who studied at McGill and at Harvard, where he earned his doctorate in economics, with a dissertation entitled "Study of the Productivity of Water," few of the guests showed up, because of the intensity of the rains. The conversation turned again to the defection of Dr. Azikiwe. "He was with us," Dr. Eke said. "But when Aba, Owerri, and Okigwe fell in rapid succession, he didn't want to come back."

I asked Dr. Eke whether much was known about the history of the Biafran region before modern times, and he said that there was material for research in European libraries but that no one had had time to get at it yet. "I lost all my own manuscripts when Enugu was disrupted," he said. "But Port Harcourt was the saddest fall. People were weeping that they should leave a town they had so long defended. At the last minute, the roads were full, miles of nothing but people trekking."

I asked whether Biafrans heard much of the news outside Biafra, and he said that people listened anxiously to any available transistor radio, that it made them feel they belonged to the world. "Ask a small boy about the moon," Dr. Eke said. "He will rattle off everything." He spoke of the front. "In many places, the mud comes to your waist in the rainy season, so everybody stays where he is." I asked about Biafran guerrilla activity in disrupted areas, and he laughed. "Call it infiltration," he said. "But whatever it is, we are there."

I had been told by several Ibos that Dr. Eke's time in America had not been happy, but he did not speak of it. He only spoke rather skeptically of the Red Cross and starvation ("They always overestimate or underestimate," he said. "When they needed two million dollars, they said two million children would die by February") and of the general indifference of the world. "You know how it is with any tragedy," he said. "After the first two floods, contributions will decline. People will simply say, 'Why don't they move?'"

Before dawn on Tuesday morning, a State House car, which had already nearly run over several hitchhikers who tried, with a kind of limp-wristed motion, to flag it down on the road to Mbano, picked up A. Kalada Hart, the young Biafran secretary of the Ministry of Energy and Mineral Supplies. "I don't seem to have any now," he said. The day was hot and not rainy for a change, and at Angara Junction, of the Okigwe, Owerri, Umuahia, and Orlu roads, there were trekkers who looked particularly desolate. The driver looked rigidly at the road. "Sympathy is such a silly sentiment," he said. At a compound in Mbano, Dr. Bede Okigbo, who was once dean of agriculture at the University of Nsukka, who studied at Washington State University and Cornell, and who is now coordinator of a farming directorate called the Land Army, discussed the problem of raising poultry in the part of Biafra that is left. "First, we have to see how much maize there is," he said. "We must minimize the competition between human beings and poultry for the maize."

Each community in Biafra must now donate a piece of land for farming by the Land Army, and each member of the community must spend a day each week on the Land Army farm. Half the produce remains with the community; the other half must be sold to the government. Land under dispute in the courts is frozen until after the crisis and planted. "Food scarcity here is not new," Dr. Okigbo said. "Before the war, there was often near famine. It is the soil, storage problems, and the insects."

I asked Dr. Okigbo how Biafran farmers reacted to the Land Army.

"The people are very individualistic," he said. "Each little farm used to grow a little of everything—twenty farms for twenty families. It is very hard to mechanize. First, we sent in boys to teach the local people, but the people were not much impressed. Now we are hoping to get them to ask for the experts." All the agriculture experts from Dr. Okigbo's faculty at Nsukka are now in the regular army, except the wounded or people with administrative jobs, who now work on the land. Dr. Okigbo looked at a government memo datelined "Enugu/Mbano." "We are studying plants which will not tempt people to eat the seedlings," he said. "We are studying the wild local vegetables for identification." A member of Dr. Okigbo's staff mentioned a soldier of the Madonna Commandos, who had volunteered to serve as a guinea pig for any vegetation the soldiers were afraid to try. (Biafran commandos, who are among the most respected Biafran soldiers at the front, travel along the roads in trucks with gray skull and crossbones on the windshields, quite unlike the more cheerfully decorated trucks other units travel in.) "We have learned we cannot establish targets for our farms," Dr. Okigbo said. "We have found our local pullets thrive better on less, on kitchen refuse, than imported pullets. But each time we plant, the enemy comes in. No matter how much target you establish, you see, you may not attain it."

On Tuesday afternoon, Moses Iloh, National Secretary of the Biafra Red Cross, sat in his headquarters in the bush at Abba, in a trailer with a broken wheel. "We have been disturbed so often," he said. "I don't see how we can move again." He spoke of people who had died from trekking, mothers who had miscarried, pneumonia, tuberculosis, malaria, orphans too young to know their names found with people moving in the bush. "And so many have lost their minds," he said. "The worst time was last year—May, June, July, August, September. Now the kwashiorkor is beginning again. A child who has had this thing twice shrinks. There is the brain damage. We have lost a hundred thousand people over fifty-five from shortage of bulk carbohydrates. You cannot fly in bulk carbohydrates. What will happen when there is nobody to tell us of the past, nobody to inherit the future?"

Mr. Iloh and I went to a Red Cross orphanage near Abba, where about twenty children were sitting quietly on their beds, which consisted of metal frames and bamboo pallets, some covered with blankets, some not. The children were led outside under a frangipani tree, a baby was placed on the ground in the center, a nine-year-old girl put her hands together in an attitude of prayer, a five-year-old clung to the hand of a matron, and the children began to sing, to the tune of "O Du Lieber Augustin," "When we are together, together, together, when we are together, the happier we will be. On your face, on my face, on your face, on my face…" Suddenly, the children switched to a song in Ibo, and I asked what the words meant. "They are asking Gowon to stop killing them," Mr. Iloh said. The children switched to English again:

> "Solomon the king.
> Solomon the judge.
> Solomon the peacemaker."

And then, very deliberately and grimly:

> "Solomon passes sentence."

Most of the children would stay at the orphanage. A few would be sent to Gabon for the duration of the crisis. Some would be sent to São Tomé, to be fed properly for a while, and then returned to

Biafra. And Mr. Iloh, who had already adopted one in addition to his own two children, was about to adopt another. "It is wonderful, wonderful," he said. "You can't tell the difference."

We went on to a World Council of Churches sick bay at Isu. A naked child hunkered outside, with the swollen stomach and utter lassitude of kwashiorkor. Mr. Iloh gently pulled down its lower eyelid. The interior was dead white. "Almost a hundred-percent anemia," Mr. Iloh said. I asked him whether kwashiorkor children were in pain, and he said, "Not unless the liver is affected."

There were victims of kwashiorkor and scabies, all with somehow intensely old-looking faces, on the beds and mats inside. The "severe" cases were separated by a raffia partition from the less severe, although I could not tell the difference. Some were coughing; some did not seem to have the energy. The matron, a young midwife, apologized that some beds had only one occupant. "We used to admit two in a bed," she said, "when we could feed them."

On the road to the Red Cross sick bay at Ezeoke, we passed St. Paul's parsonage of the Church Missionary Society, a thatched shop called the Live and Let Live Volkswagen House (empty), and another shop, which displayed one small wooden coffin. A notice was posted on the hospital wall: "On admission, girls on duty should find out the following facts: (1) If the child is an orphan; (2) If the child is motherless; (3) If the child is fatherless..." It was nap time, but the children, all of whom were dressed in clothes of the same material, were lying, sometimes two or three to a bed for companionship (there was a bed for every child), silent and wide awake.

A refugee camp nearby, in what had been the Holy Rosary School and Church Hall, had few occupants, although there were hundreds of pallets and bundles of personal belongings on the floor of a single room, with rain coming in through windows without panes. Most of the adult refugees were out looking for food. The ones who remained seemed to come from everywhere in Biafra. Some had moved more times than they could remember. On the wall, in chalk, there were still attendance figures for the last day of school, in 1967. Nobody seemed to know where the nearest children's feeding center was, except a girl from the local Red Cross detachment, her hair neatly tied in the nine longish pigtails one often sees in Biafra. "We gave out food yesterday," she said. "So there won't be any tomorrow."

On Tuesday evening, in his car on the road to Emekuku, Dr. R. N. Onyemelukwe, who is Biafra's chief health officer, spoke of his problems when the Biafrans retook Owerri. "Sanitation was a very formidable problem," he said. "It was all littered with corpses and night soil. The water supply, you may have noticed, was disrupted. All equipment was broken. All wires were cut. I think they were at war with books." He said that the bush and the snakes had begun to close in, although he himself had not yet seen a cobra. "Before the crisis, we were developing sanitation-consciousness in our people," he said. "We even anticipated problems of air pollution." He laughed. "Although, of course, the crisis has now reduced the number of vehicles." He spoke of burials, sewage, mass immunization. "There was not a single civilian living in Owerri when it was disrupted," he said. "I had one hundred workers, cleaning up. Of course, there was no market, so I had, ha-ha, to feed them. I imagine the population of night snails was depleted. In two weeks, Owerri was ready for the return of our civilians. Two white Red Cross workers, you know, were shot when Okigwe was disrupted. Every home has lost someone in this war."

Later that night, at the residence of Dr. Fabian Udekwu, head surgeon of the Teaching Hospital at Emekuku, a game of draughts, on a homemade board, was going on. A chair was littered with cartridge tapes—Bach, Mozart, Stravinsky. Dr. Udekwu, who studied at Johns Hopkins and did his residency at Cook County Hospital in Chicago, had worked for a time in a hospital in Ibadan, in Western Nigeria, fled through the bush when a friend of his, another Ibo surgeon, nearly lost his hands in a massacre in 1965, returned for some months to Ibadan, and, after another outbreak of killings, returned at last to Biafra. Since then, he has moved several times, as areas were disrupted. "It is terrible, you know," he said, "to come home and keep on running." I asked a friend of Dr. Udekwu's how the mobs had recognized Ibos in the massacres, and the friend replied that they were better dressed and that there was a distinctive Ibo facial structure (Ibos, to me, looked very different from one another). Their names were also characteristically Ibo; to find Ibos in cars, Hausa colleagues often kept checklists of license numbers.

Dr. Udekwu took me on a quick tour of the Emekuku hospital, where six hundred patients, mostly wounded soldiers, lay in kerosene-lamp-lighted wards, on beds and on pallets on the floor. They greeted the doctor cheerfully as he pointed out the results of operations; a Steinmann pin, consisting of a sterilized nail through an injured limb, with a bag of pebbles for traction at the foot of the bed; a splint made of scrap metal and screws for bad fractures. "We are born to improvise," he said. Most of the patients at Emekuku arrive at night. It takes them about forty-six hours' travel from the farthest front. The hospital's four senior surgeons and twenty doctors perform between fifty and a hundred operations a day.

"We need plastic surgeons, orthopedists, neurosurgeons, pediatricians," Dr. Udekwu said. "Then, of course, there's no sense operating on them if we can't feed them. And storage and malnutrition of donors creates a problem with blood donations. But the worst are the victims of the white phosphorus bombs. Have you seen one? Some of them are still smoking on the operating table." He said that he was able to treat them with hydrogen peroxide, and that he hoped never to see war again.

At Dr. Udekwu's dinner table, with several guests—including Dr. Onyemelukwe; Dr. Anezi Okoro, a dermatologist turned surgeon; and Mrs. Bede Okigbo, wife of the head of the Land Army (Mrs. Okigbo is in charge of food at Emekuku)—Dr. Udekwu said, "Let us pray." Dinner consisted of vegetable *ukwa* soup (rich, somebody said, in sulfur-bearing amino acids), a paté called *moi-moi* ("Why do we call it *moi-moi?*" Dr. Okoro said. "That is the Yoruba word. The Ibo is *mai-mai*"), and chicken, the bones of which, even in the half-light, were picked clean. Dr. Udekwu was worried about Biafran medical students whose education had been interrupted by the crisis. He favored rotating them for study abroad, in crash programs. "There are already eighty Biafran doctors abroad," he said. "But one must consider the overall situation. Forty-five percent of our population is under fifteen. We don't want to run the risk of losing our students. If we die, they can carry on." Dr. Udekwu began to talk about the work of the Biafra Relief Services, of New York, in resettling two Biafran leper colonies whose area had been disturbed. "The lepers are like the prisoners," he said cheerfully. "When an area is disrupted, they will flee and report to the next prison along the line."

After dinner, over glasses of palm wine, a young guest told a story of trying to get a job with Shell BP, the major oil company in the Eastern Region, before the war. He had been selected, out of hundreds of candidates, for one final interview. They asked him what he thought of Shell BP. He told them he thought the company was taking more out than it was putting into Nigeria. They did not hire him. (It seemed somehow characteristically Biafran to find this funny and surprising.) Dr. Udekwu began to talk about recent studies of starvation. "We used to think that people lived for a while off their fatty tissue," he said. "But now we realize it attacks the vital organs. Brain damage, of course, is irreversible. Mercifully, the worst cases will pass on."

Dr. Onyemelukwe and Dr. Udekwu bantered a bit about peptic ulcers, and Dr. Okoro shyly brought out a sheaf of poems. The first line of the first poem was "It was high tide in casualty." Later, as his guests left, Dr. Udekwu said, "I hope you don't think we eat like this every night. I am embarrassed." His guests thanked him and said they were embarrassed, too.

On the drive back to Owerri, Dr. Onyemelukwe initiated a discussion of the new government recommendations for cooking cassava leaves. Plucking the leaves kills the tubers, which creates problems for the survival of cassava. Boiling the leaves, which are hairy, for only fifteen minutes, as recommended, conserves their vitamin content but does not quite eliminate the cyanide they contain. A dilemma. "Just watch a goat," Dr. Onyemelukwe said, as we passed one. "And whatever a goat eats, you won't die. Pluck it and eat it." Before going to his own home, the chief health officer spent some time pushing a young man's stalled car through the rain.

I spent the rest of Tuesday night, with a flashlight, rereading Frederick Forsyth, and a report by some British anthropologists and diplomats familiar with the Eastern Region very quietly asking that the West reconsider its position on Biafra. I was scared in the dark, not of violence (I had not really seen any) or of disease (I had only a kind of muzzy cold from the rain) but of not being able to get out. I was convinced that there would be no planes, or no room for me on them. I became obsessed, like other journalists and Biafrans, with the question of the Telex. Biafra does have a radio connection with Gabon, and finally access to a real Telex in Geneva, but the insistence that there was one right *there*, in Biafra, was quite comprehensible in the dark, and seemed by its own logic to explain more serious questions: for example, censorship. There is, in effect, no censorship in Biafra, but Biafrans have to give some reason why journalists cannot take their cables directly to the Telex office. They claim they must censor the cables, and then they simply radio them, altering perhaps a word or two, to Gabon. They prefer the idea of censorship to the idea that there is no wire, no solid link to the world outside. So did I. One of the two other reporters left in Biafra that night (two weeks later, there were none), imagining that he heard a snake or a person rustling in his food, had thrown his jackknife, frightening himself more with the sound.

Just before dawn on Wednesday, a small congregation was attending a Mass at St. Paul's in the village of Isu. After Mass, an elderly woman pressed something into the hands of Father Gerard Gogan, a white priest, with the characteristic vagueness and despair about his eyes. "What is this?" he said, apparently startled by being approached or spoken to at all. "It is a letter for you," she replied. "I will read it," he said, more calmly, and put it in his cassock. In a black kettle, over a very smoky fire in a little thatched hut, some workers were boiling ten stockfish to feed over a hundred children. A kettle of medicinal leaves was being boiled for an eighteen-year-old malaria victim who stood nearby.

A little later, in the office of Major General Philip Effiong, an Efik, who is Chief of the General Staff, at Defense Headquarters (a camouflaged location in the bush), a copy of *The Geneva Convention Relative to the Treatment of Prisoners of War* lay on the table. On the walls were pictures of the mangled victims of Nigerian bombing raids. A young government worker was talking intensely about the problems Biafra might face after independence. "It will be freedom won through blood," he said. "There will be this background of sorrow, violence, and hatred. What will be the expectations? There will be a second struggle, for order and the fundamental freedoms. Will the people say, 'Where is it, the goal?' Will they have the energy?"

General Effiong walked in, a humorous, most unmilitary-looking man. He went to a wall map stuck with pins and wood slivers (round or square, orange, red, blue, pink) and gave a short briefing about the front. "Onitsha, active. Okigwe, off and on. Ikot Ekpene, changed hands half a dozen times. Umuahia, static, lots of raids by our guerrillas. At Onitsha, they are trying to break through to Nnewi, His Excellency's hometown, but we are almost inside Onitsha to the Savoy Hotel. Port Harcourt, all these areas must begin to feel the pressure. Many of our men at the front are without boots, but when there are gaps we do go through. At the beginning, we had no artillery and no mortars, not a single piece. We had a few helicopters and our famous B-26 [an old plane, from which a mercenary pilot used to kick bombs through a door]. Mark you, between August and October last year we had our most precarious moment. The fall of Umuahia was very depressing. I think we revived very well. There is optimism, and not without reason. You know, they lost three thousand men on the road to Onitsha. I know they have suffered terribly. It is a colossal war," he said. "It is a very, very colossal war."

I asked General Effiong to what extent the Biafran Army has been forced to resort to conscription.

"In a war of this kind," he said, "our people don't like it. We tried it for three months and found we had to stop. Our people couldn't see the point."

I asked whether the recent lessening of air raids was due entirely to the weather. "This has been puzzling us for some time," he said. "Perhaps it is our little homemade rockets popping. And our air force has been up again, nothing to write home to Mummy about but quite a little baby."

General Effiong showed me some captured military weapons, British antitank guns used against people (Biafra has no tanks), Russian napalm, machine guns from countries all over Europe, and some marked "U.S. Gov't Property/Army."

"If we fail, you see," General Effiong said, "then the black man in Africa is going to fail, and the minority man wherever he is. One would think we had done enough against all this to prove that we deserve to live."

At noon on Wednesday, in the Armed Forces Hospital at Nkwerre, which is run by Colonel Miller Jaja (who was once a Fellow of the Royal College of Surgeons in London, and who is a descendant of the Jaja of Opobo, who led a revolt against the slave trade in the early 1860s), Major Dennis Umeh, a thirty-one-year-old surgeon who enlisted in the army on the day before the war, said the hospital had been twice strafed and bombed by MiGs. "We didn't complain," he said. "This is a military hospital." There are two thousand patients in the hospital, which was once St. Augustine's Grammar School, and five thousand more in a large complex across the road. The matron, Major Mary Onyejiaka, is a thirty-four-year-old nurse who once served in the Nigerian Army. She makes the rounds of the enormous complex twice a week.

"I happen to have had the luck to be in the first unit at Nsukka," Major Umeh said. "We got the wounded well and back to the war zones very quickly." He paused and nodded. "Most who are still alive would agree that this is so." Now, he said, because of the malnutrition, recoveries are slower, but only three or four casualties die per ward per month. "They are a pitiable lot," he said. "But they linger on and they make it. I think it is battalion pride." He laughed. "And the food at the front is better." There are only nine qualified doctors and four medical students at Nkwerre, and only one operating theater, with four operating tables. Quite often, when the hospital has to ease conditions on the heavy fronts, casualties are lined up to wait outside the theater. "It increases the morbidity but not the mortality," Major Umeh said; that is, patients stay sick longer, but they do not die. I asked how families in Biafra receive word of wounded soldiers, and Major Umeh spoke of Noticas (Notice of Casualties), which sends couriers to the parents and the units of the hurt.

Major Umeh took me through the huge wards, named for their ailments, and a few tents of wounded outside. Some people in Fractures were singing; Dental seemed rather miserable. He pointed out delicate makeshift operations like Dr. Udekwu's, and he paused in a little X-ray room to warn a technician not to tell a patient of some harmless mortar particles left in his leg. "They are so sensitive," he said, "that if you tell them they will suffer." But he was most proud of the hospital's pharmacy, in which some young scientists were producing dextrose, extracting painkillers and tranquilizers from mixed pills (for the tetanus and artillery cases), analyzing native remedies ("It is like deciphering a code," a young scientist said), and making pills in test tubes. The pharmacy cannot produce antibiotics yet, but not, the major emphasized, for lack of knowledge, only for lack of facilities. "Give us two years of peace and we will do it," he said. "The lowered resistance of our patients to germs sometimes puts us back to square one."

I asked whether the pharmacy could produce enough painkillers for the front, and he said, "Oh, yes. Most of them should be asleep when they get here."

A major from one of the battle zones was in the hospital, visiting his men. I asked what unit he was from, and how many of his men were in the hospital, and then realized he could not tell me. Major Umeh was preoccupied. "The world ought to see us in our goodness," he said. "We value life. We have always done well on exams. We only want to have a peaceful life and contribute something to humanity."

On Wednesday afternoon, in the office of the Directorate of Research and Production, at Isu, Professor Ben Nwosu, tired and angry, asked me to understate the accomplishments of his team of scientists. "In the white world, they would call them inventions," he said. "Because we are black, they call them improvisations. Some time before the crisis, a handful of us just thought, If this thing starts, we want to be ready." Since then, the directorate has produced fuel, soap, rockets, booby traps, armored cars (out of tractors), gunboats, and civilian products of various kinds. People bring all sorts of scrap and spare parts to Professor Nwosu's directorate, but "the supply problem still advances upon us," he said. He was extremely bitter about the world's suspicion of the real intentions of Biafra. "We don't woolly-woolly. We didn't have to come back here. I wonder why people in the outside think we came back here. We are struggling because we want to save our lives as a people, and our children's lives."

I asked how his mechanics could possibly manufacture sophisticated arms without having centralized factories, which would be subject to bombings. "It is simple," he said, abruptly. "If you have ten lathes, you diffuse them in ten places. The result is the same."

On Thursday morning at seven, Sister Mary Joseph Theresa, daughter of the Eze Dara of Uli and sister of both a lady barrister and an engineer in Professor Nwosu's directorate, left the Ihioma Convent and went to the Queen of the Holy Rosary College, a school she had run at Onitsha (now disrupted) and started again at Orlu, with refugee children from all over Biafra. Sister Mary Joseph had also been a refugee, successively, from Onitsha, Port Harcourt, Owerri, and Nguru. "Running from my friends," she said. "I call them 'my friends.' I have nothing against them. We are all human beings. We are fighting because the Devil is there."

Sister Mary Joseph comes from one of the finest families in Biafra, and looks it—tall, frail, and radiant with intelligence, dressed somehow, in the mud and still-spattering rain, in a habit of immaculate white. Most children in Biafra have lost two years of school now, and Sister Mary Joseph recruited six teachers out of fifteen from her school in Onitsha (two are in the army, one is in the Directorate of

Research and Production, and one in the police) to teach in a section of a refugee camp at Orlu. "The children have a long way to trek," she said. "Many have heard of us, and they are coming." Children, some with, some without shoes and umbrellas, were arriving in the chilling downpour of early morning.

I asked Sister Mary Joseph whether the school could give them any breakfast or lunch. "My goodness, what would I give them?" she said. "What would I give?"

I asked whether all her students were Catholics. "Now, we don't ask them about religion," she said. "We just say Biafra."

There was a brief morning assembly, with hymns in English and in Ibo, and Sister Mary Joseph asked her teachers, whom she had called together, whether they had heard the newest Biafran hymn. "I've only heard it in the last two or three days," she said. "It is the best song yet." One teacher remarked that new songs travel quickly, since most of Biafra is within fifty miles. "It's more than that," another teacher said quickly. Sister Mary Joseph was riffling through an attendance book. "I can't believe that so much of Biafra is still in our hands," she said. "They've all learned now that there is a God. They can't deny that."

Classes began, separated from one another by raffia partitions, and the youngest class, from eleven to thirteen years old (depending on the loss of those two years), was learning geometry and French. "*Bonjour, monsieur*" and "*Asseyez-vous la classe*" and Euclid rang through the refugee home, where adult refugees were staring out at the rain from an adjoining room. "Anyone here know a song, any song?" Sister Mary Joseph asked the geometry class, and they sang "God, the Creator, Preserve and Guide Biafra." She asked the second class whether they knew any writers. Jane Austen. Any *Biafran* writers? Chinua Achebe. Had they read him? Yes. They returned to the study of cell structure and the soil.

The third class was learning English expressions ("They don't care tuppence," "A yes-man"), and Sister Mary Joseph asked them whether they knew anyone in America. One had a "senior brother" in Baltimore. One had a sister-in-law in California. One had a pre-crisis pen pal in Greenlawn, New York. All of them, in all classes, were extremely eager to answer questions, but Sister Mary Joseph said the fourth was the keenest class. They were all girls. Boys of fifteen in Biafra are eligible for the army. The fourth class had written essays, on lined paper the school had found for them, on "The Horrors of the Nigeria-Biafra War." ("No place is safe. No one is safe." "We might appeal to God to make both sides see reason." "It was also at night that one once felt safe in Biafra.") Sister Mary Joseph, who served her novitiate in Dublin (she has a trace of an Irish accent), recalled that when she was a child her father, Eze Dara of Uli, had insisted that the whole family learn to read, and so she had learned in the same class with her uncles. She thought that if the loss of schooling in Biafra now continued, there might have to be intergenerational classrooms again after the war. She enumerated all the American representatives who had expressed sympathy for Biafra: Candidate Nixon, Senator Eugene McCarthy, Senator Charles Goodell, Senator Edward Kennedy, Representatives Donald E. Lukens and Allard K. Loewenstein, Ambassador C. Clyde Ferguson—even Senator Richard Russell, of the South. She told the story of a young English lady working in Nigeria who had been caught behind Biafran lines. "The Inspector General detained her," Sister Mary Joseph said. "Mind you, it was right after the Eighteen [fourteen Italians, three West Germans, and one Jordanian arrested as Nigerian spies]. Poor Sally. The Inspector General didn't know what to do about her." Sister Mary Joseph had taken care of the English lady, and accompanied her on the flight to Libreville. Sister Mary Joseph asked me, and even an old friend of hers, to sign the inevitable guestbook. She mentioned another old friend, whom she had not seen in a long time. "I would need about two days to look for him," she said, "since we are all so dispersed now."

At a checkpoint on a particularly bad road full of stalled cars twenty miles from Owerri, an official of State House gave the code word in Ibo for General Odumegwu Ojukwu, and was told by the guard, in

English, "He passed here at a quarter to eight." Driving on, the official recalled the circumstances of His Excellency's delivery, on June
1 this year, of a speech on the second anniversary of Biafran independence, in the town of Ahiara. The speech, now referred to as "the
Ahiara Declaration," or "Ahiara," or even just "June First," had an
enormous impact in Biafra. It is twenty-one dense pages long. It includes thoughts as complicated in their expression, and as characteristic of General Ojukwu, as the dedication to his first book (which
will be published in November): "To the many sons and daughters
whose fathers toiled and tramped with me, and are gone." Another
sort of leader might have said, "To the Biafran orphans." The Ahiara
Declaration recounts some of Biafra's recent history and concludes
that the reason the two-year war has not won more of the world's
unambivalent sympathy is that the Biafran people are black. But it
deplores insufficient idealism within Biafra, and its political philosophy might be endorsed by anyone from Thomas Jefferson through
Fidel Castro to Senator John Sherman Cooper ("The Biafran revolution believes in the sanctity of human life and the dignity of the
human person . . . the reign of social and economic justice, and the
rule of law"). And yet there is the sense of something new, something genuinely humanist and indigenously African about it. Also
pride, religion, and despair.

In a military compound, heavily camouflaged, about fifteen
miles from Owerri, several chiefs and elders, in long robes and still
engaged in conversation, were coming out of the office of General
Ojukwu, past a sentry at the door. In a reception room with a blue
rug, flowered curtains, red chairs, green walls, and a little white Madonna on a coffee table (altogether more like a room in an inn, made
livable by transients, than like part of a military installation), a few
young associates of General Ojukwu were waiting for him. Some of
them seemed abject and ingratiating, others full of high spirits and
a sense of argument. General Ojukwu himself, thirty-six years old,
bearded, not slim, educated at Oxford and, much later, at Warmin-
ster, came in and slumped in a chair. He looked sad, ready for a joke,
and thoughtful, with a brooding gentleness pushed to an extreme

that could make a war leader out of a doubting, nonviolent man. He seemed to have the quality of the sort of person who can make people in a church sit still and be decent when all the exits are burning. His father, Sir Louis Odumegwu Ojukwu, who began in poverty, became a small investment banker, and died one of the richest men in Nigeria, had objected to almost every stage in his son's career, from his two years of work as a lower-echelon civil servant in the Eastern Region to his insistence on going to military school. The Nigerian Army was one of the few regionally integrated institutions in Federal Nigeria. When, after the coup of January 1966, military governors were appointed for all the regions of Nigeria, Lieutenant Colonel Ojukwu was appointed governor of the Eastern Region. After the massacres of May 1966, still believing in a unified Nigeria, he appealed to Eastern refugees from the Northern Region to go back, assuring them that their lives and property were now safe. He has regretted this decision, in view of the massacres that followed, ever since.

I asked him what the meeting that had just dispersed had been about. "It's my regular powwow with the chiefs," he said. "A morale-boosting session." I asked him how often he met with them, and he said as often as he could. I asked him what they talked about. "Everything from air raids to the distribution of salt," he said. "The war situation. The internal situation. Their own personal problems, what the people are thinking, how much of government policy has got down, ways this war has to be fought. Everybody wants to have said something." He smiled. "Chief Mpi held the floor."

I asked how the morale actually was, and he said, "Generally, this is the time for low morale. The rains. The cold. The war usually crawls. People ask, 'What's wrong with the army, is it food they want? Is it possible they enjoy this war? Tell me what they need.' Another position is 'Is there nothing else we can do, is there no other way?' Of course, there are those who are more angry than yourself."

I asked him whether he felt that the returned intellectuals were rediscovering their own people, and he nodded. "They used to look outside themselves," he said. "There was even a conscious effort to obliterate their own origin, looking down on those who stayed at home. Now it's time to come down to earth a bit."

He felt the Ahiara Declaration had expressed the real feelings of the people only as "an articulation in international terms." "I've always been aware of one thing, that I've never really stood an election," he said. When I asked him why he thought the Ahiara Declaration had not had much of an impact, particularly among American radicals, abroad, he said it was not the sort of speech to invite "that sort of dramatic response." He laughed, and said that people had told him they were surprised that "you have managed to mean so much to everyone at the same time." He spoke of the black "secret admirers" of Biafra, who feared the great unknown and could not believe that Biafra might succeed. I asked him how this compared with the white liberal position, and he said he thought white liberals were more openly sympathetic. "They say, 'This would be wonderful if it really succeeded.' They don't say we won't succeed." I asked whether by success he meant the establishment of the first viable black republic, able to compete on an equal basis with white nations of the world, and he said that was exactly what he meant.

I wondered what the postwar politics of Biafra might be in the world, and he said, "There is no doubt in my mind that to survive we must remain uncommitted." He said he believed that little nations either existed as ideological vacuums or opened up to let the two great ideologies flood them, and that he hoped, in sequels to the Ahiara Declaration, to establish a bulwark position that would do neither. "All conflict, of course," he said, "arises from the desire to dominate. The way to avoid conflict is to accept the rights of other men. But I do not believe that another ideology would solve the foreign problem."

I asked him about his book, and he said it was based on "speeches, random thoughts, random subjects, and a frantic period trying to find the underlying thoughts." I asked him what stake the world had in Biafra, and he said, "This is the worst system—this colonial, this neocolonial fraud. It can only yield short-term results. There is no logical case against Biafra. There is no properly argued case against Biafra. There is only fear, and the nuisance of having to reevaluate. They do not know what this phenomenon is." General Ojukwu's stenographer, as in all the general's negotiations and interviews, was writing down each word. When I left, the chiefs who had been talking in the corridor were gone.

On the way back to Owerri, the State House driver ran over a chicken, and did not stop. A small boy raised his one arm in a salute. At the airport, a Biafran crew was loading a strange cargo of sacks of cocoa beans and two old English refrigerators on the French Red Cross flight back to Libreville. The car passed a wake, with mourners singing, in Ibo, "He is dead. Got to bury him. He died in a state of courage. We shall all be there sooner or later. May his soul rest in peace."

The New Yorker
October 4, 1969

A YEAR IN THE DARK
INTRODUCTION

BEING film critic for *The New York Times* for a year (fourteen months, really) was for me a particular kind of adventure—with time, with tones of voice, with movies, with editing, with the peculiar experience it always is to write in one's own name something that is never exactly what one would have wanted to say. The job came to me at an odd time. I had begun at *The New Yorker* as a book reviewer, until I no longer saw the point of reviewing other people's books unless the books themselves were so important that one would want to make them known. There were not at that time enough books to explain a regular critic's job, and I do not believe in professional criticism anyway, as a way of life. I turned to reporting, and it seemed to make more sense. Selma, Harlem, Mississippi, the New Left, group therapy, pop music, the Sunset Strip, Vietnam, the Six-Day War—I wanted very much to be there and accurate about these things. I particularly detested, and detest, the "new journalism," which began, I think, as a corruption of a form which originated in *The New Yorker* itself. After a genuine, innovating tradition of great *New Yorker* reporters (A. J. Liebling, Joseph Mitchell, St. Clair McKelway, Lillian Ross, Wolcott Gibbs) who imparted to events a form and a personal touch that were truer to the events themselves than short, conventional journalism, determined by the structure of the daily news, had ever been, there sprang up almost everywhere a second growth of reporters, who took up the personal and didn't give a damn for the events.

There began, apparently, to be a taste for this. The facts dissolved. The writer was everything. It is hard enough to define hard fact, but we were starting to get, in what looked like quite respectable contexts, a new variant of sensational or yellow journalism—that corroding thing, the news or some distortion of the news, as entertainment. I remember particularly a reporter for the then "lively," dying *Herald Tribune* who would charge up to people in Alabama with extended hand, introduce himself, and beginning "Wouldn't you say...?" produce an entirely formulated paragraph of his own. Sooner or later somebody tired or agreeable would nod, and the next day's column—with some intimate colloquialisms and absolute fabrications thrown in—would attribute its quotes and appear, as a piece of the new journalism.

The finest reporters I met at the time were *Times* men in the South. While others were rushing frantically about, desperate and verbal about deadlines, dangers, reputation, the problems of safely reaching a telephone, Paul Montgomery, Gene Roberts and Roy Reed more or less sloped from place to place, getting the story with true ear and straight into the next edition of the *Times*. They were entirely free of self-importance or punditry, rather like great short-order cooks. The harassed ones are never any good. It seemed almost a question of making it look easy. My idealization of the *Times* in this respect was much later modified, in the Paris disturbances of May. (The bureau, with one exception, was always in a terrific huff. They were normally shallow and about a day behind events. And they seemed always trying to recoup, with stories headlined "Parisians Have Second Thoughts About...," some particularly inadequate story of the day before. All such a headline ever meant was that the reporter himself had changed his mind.) But most *Times* reporters still seem to me the best I know.

In October, 1967, when the *Times* suddenly, almost incidentally, offered me Bosley Crowther's job, Mr. Crowther had been reviewing for twenty-seven years. Anything one man has done in his own way for that long becomes unoccupied in a truly vacant sense. People form strong ideas about how it should not be done; yet it is not at all clear what the job, apart from the man who has done it almost as long as it exists, might be. Like nearly everyone, I had always gone to the movies a lot and liked to go to them. It so completely blotted out the content of much of life and yet filled the days, like dreaming. (It later turned out that my favorite screening time was eight in the morning, when the change to the movie world was entirely smooth.) I had done a few movie reviews before, at *The New Yorker* for a month, and once for *Life*, but I had never read much film criticism—except by writers who interested me on other grounds. Reviewing movies seemed not at all like reviewing books, more like writing about events, about anything. And although there was wide access in the *Times* (a lot of people seem to read movie reviews), there was not, except in foreign films, the seriousness of making or ruining a film, as there can be with plays or books. I trusted my judgment enough to think I would know what distinction there was, and try not to harm it.

I bought quantities of film criticism in the months before the job began, Agee, Arnheim, everybody: the angry trash claimers (writers who claim some movie they have enjoyed is utter trash, and then become fiercely possessive about it); the brave commercialism deplorers (writers forever saddened that some popular movie has failed to realize the high aesthetic possibilities they might have envisioned for it); the giddy adjectivalists, stunned, shattered or convulsed with hilarity every other day by some cinema experience; the severe traditionalists, usefully comparing any given film to one which had gone before; the cement solid positivists, whose essays were likely to begin, "The screen is a rectangle," and, although the exposition rarely got much deeper, seemed to feel most comfortable with formulations about the Medium. The best criticism I read was still by writers who simply felt moved by film to say something about it—without reverent or consistent strategies, putting films idiosyncratically alongside things they cared about in other ways.

In those months, I also began to go to the movies all day long, drive-ins, Spanish theaters, Chinese, Forty-second Street, museums, etc., and then I stopped. It began to produce a sensation of interior weightlessness, of my own time and experience drifting off like an astronaut's. It was not at all the private reading binges that take place at home. It was more like travel, dislocating, among strangers, going into a public dark for dreams and controversy. On January 1st last year, the job began. Or more accurately, on Friday, December 29th, when the Sunday piece for January 7th was due. This was the first indication I had of the absolute exigencies of scheduling. From that moment, it was like catching your sleeve in a machine. The final, immutable deadline for Sunday pieces turned out to be the small hours of Tuesday morning—which created occasional disastrous coincidences, like a piece on violent suffering written just before Senator Robert Kennedy was shot and published the Sunday after he died. But the grinding calamity could be the daily pieces, whose simple mechanics were these: a screening, perhaps the day of the opening, perhaps a few days before, copy due at six in the afternoon, to appear when the paper is printed at 9:30 P.M. The pieces were typed with nine carbons, and edited in hurdles. The idea at the *Times* is that reviews are not edited at all, but the reality was a continual leaning on sentences, cracking rhythms, removing or explaining jokes, questioning or crazily amplifying metaphors and allusions, on pieces that were not that good in the first place. The first hurdle was the young editor of what was called the Cultural News Department, whose major contributions were to divide paragraphs in unlikely places, losing the sense (there is an ancient newspaper tradition that paragraphs more than one or two sentences long "look terrible"), and to point to as many sentences as possible and ask what I meant by them. I fell for this every time, would explain at length, and then receive that absolute nightmare of editorial replies, "Well, why don't you come right out and say it?"

After a few months, this transaction became untenable and I was permitted to submit pieces directly to the second hurdle, the Obituary and Culture Desk (Obit), where all culture pieces are edited. Here, sentences were often reversed (there was rarely the conception that in doing sentences a writer chooses among options), the timing of remaining jokes undone, and meanings "clarified." Little things could occur on Sundays: "unavailing work" one week became "unavailable work"—quite a difference, after all—and a movie's reference to Jean-Sol Partre was helpfully explained in a parenthesis to be "a pun on the name of Jean-Paul Sartre." But the Sunday section, under a kind, harassed, intelligent editor, Seymour Peck, was edited slightly and for good reason. In the daily, after regular, protracted and yet tentative argument (one is never, even in the face of pure inanity, that certain about editing), there would be spasms, for days on end, of drastic changes whose source was never clear. At one point, lower echelon editors were coming over the hills like the Chinese, with queries and suggestions, until it occurred to me that I could complain. That worked. It stopped. The only defense against the sourceless spasms, though, was to keep a vigil on editions of the paper until 1 A.M., call the Obit Desk and quarrel, threaten to resign (on February 11, 1968, I did resign; nobody paid much attention), or to ask for the intercession of a major editor. Arthur Gelb, Abe Rosenthal, Clifton Daniel, all the major editors of the *Times*, were, and are, after all writers themselves and very patient about writers' problems, but it seemed hardly possible—the importance of other things in the world considered—to ask them often to intercede in prose and culture wars. In the end, I just stopped reading the paper, in order not to know.

The spatial context of writing at the office was peculiar. I sat, for the first few months, at a desk among rows of desks in what is called the culture pool. Looking up from my typewriter to think, I would often be staring directly into the eyes of Hilton Kramer, who was thinking too. Phones rang incessantly on every side. When it was possible, I wrote at home. On a particularly grumpy day, several months after Bosley Crowther had left the *Times* for Columbia Pictures, I decided, out of pure grumpiness really, that it was time to move into his office. All first-string critics' offices at the *Times* are glass enclosed, and late one night, working on a Sunday piece—with Grace Glueck, who also worked late, typing nearby—I began to scrub the words Movie News off what had been Mr. Crowther's door. The letters had always looked unseemly to me. I tried to slide them around into Movie Snew, but that didn't work, and I finally removed them altogether and felt fine.

From the first, the job had sides I had not quite anticipated. For one thing, it turned out to be extremely public, more like a regular, embarrassed, impromptu performance on network television than any conception of writing I had ever had. The film reviewer writes more frequently than anybody else at the *Times* except Clive Barnes, who did theater and ballet, and who writes gladly, naturally. I don't; one of the reasons for trying daily journalism was to see whether it would get any easier. The Movie News staff at the time consisted of three other reviewers, Vincent Canby, whom I liked and admired a lot, and Howard Thompson and Abe Weiler, whom I liked too. In principle, I had the choice of which movies to review, but for a while I reviewed them all, sometimes two or three in a day, trying to get the rhythm of the job. The paper thought it important that I should establish a position vis-à-vis Mr. Crowther at the start so that readers would have some context for what they were reading then. That led to the first long piece on violence, and later, to one about *The Graduate*. I thought it a bad idea, supposing that what shift there was from Mr. Crowther might be clear without returning to specific issues at once for differences. Near strangers were always telling me whether they agreed or disagreed with me. (This usually produced an evening of doubt, with a particular violence of tone in the review of the following day.) Conversations around me hardly ever seemed to be about anything but films any more.

Some odd, incidental things began to happen in my life outside. On February 17th, for example, there was the awards dinner of the Directors' Guild. Normally, I tried to stay clear of occasions of that kind, but a friend was getting an award, and he had invited his friends. For some days before the event, a lady from the Guild kept calling alarmingly, demanding to know who my escort for the evening would be. It turned out this was only for place cards—which were little gilded director's chairs with each guest's name engraved on them. The dinner itself, 700 people at the Americana, was not alarming in any way. We sat next to the director of "Dark Shadows," a television soap opera about vampires, which I happened to watch from time to time, and we later moved to a table of close friends.

Then, without having drunk very much or anticipated it in any way, as soon as the presentation of the awards began, I became completely hysterical with giggles, very high, hee hee, and very loud. A speaker would no sooner begin to praise a nominee, or to thank all the people who had made his award possible, than I was off again. The speeches became very brief. I couldn't leave the room either. It would have seemed an even greater fuss. It went on for more than an hour, part mirth, part crack-up. I wondered whether I would have to be led away.

An early surprise was the number of utterly deadly films that came out, tolerable to sit through, nearly impossible to discuss. I enjoyed reviewing the spiritedly awful ones, *The Power, Dr. Faustus, Survival 1967, Broken Wings*, and I kept returning compulsively to the ones I liked. But a news event of comparable insignificance to, say, *The Impossible Years*, would receive no coverage in the *Times* at all. I felt we should simply mention that such a movie had opened, and let it go at that, or perhaps, as somebody suggested, appraise in some very practical consumer way the movie's proper price: first half hour worth fifty cents; second hour, minus four dollars; net loss in going, three-fifty plus baby sitter. Another solution was to try to broaden the context a little, move as far and as fast away from consumer service inventories as possible and, except for the plot (it is very difficult to discuss a film at all without telling what it is "about" in the narrative sense), skip performance, direction, choreography, and so on, unless they *meant* something—and try to go on to details or tangents that did. I tried that sometimes.

For some reason, "the industry" was continually upset. This was puzzling. In all of 1968, Hollywood produced scarcely any movies of any value, scarcely anything that moved people, captured their fantasy lives, made them laugh, or even diverted them a little. It seemed to have lost even the knack of making artful trash. "The industry," as compared to other characteristically American industries, was bewildered, inefficient, antiquated, also not much in touch with art. (I suspect, with all the talk of audiences under twenty-five, children are beginning to lose the movie-going habit entirely.) But I was certainly not costing them any money. People, including me, will apparently still go to movies no matter what. Although I am now convinced that the old movie factory is going to lose its audience and become a mere feeder for unindustrialized countries and television, while the movie audience fragments, becomes more particularized, and attends only the films of artists in control of their work, I did not think so then. I rather liked the industry. It was not enough. The producer of a creaky leviathan wanted not only his own millions but François Truffaut's reviews. The third-generation, imagination-depleted moguls wanted to be treated like auteurs.

There began to be constant rumors that I was fired or had quit, that the industry had applied pressure. The pressure rumors were silly. The *Times* might be besieged, unhappy at moments, conciliating, but certainly unpressurable. They seemed rather glad about controversy. They did not give a damn about the industry. I got a memo from Abe Rosenthal once, asking me to use the words "very" and "boring" less often. Arthur Gelb once or twice reminded me that readers see reviews before and not after films. Members of the bull pen, another editing hurdle, whose function I never did quite understand, often loathed what I was doing. But the major editors were unfailingly steadying. There were lots of cheery memos, and after the twelfth week, a call from Mr. Gelb to say that the trial period was over and it was all right. I guess we all knew I wasn't going to do it for a hundred years. As for the early quitting rumors, they probably had to do with a certain cycle of misery—particularly at low points, like a piece on Music, or the Death piece, which I never did get quite right—when the articles themselves were so bad I got desperate. At other times, there were cycles of fun.

There was once a full-page ad in the *Times* not liking the reviews, and *Variety* used to point out as factual errors things that often were and occasionally were not factual errors I had made. Strom Thurmond once denounced the *Times* in Congress for my review of *The Green Berets*, which he read into *The Congressional Record*, along with Clive Barnes's review of *Hair* (I was a liberal Republican, I think, when Senator Thurmond was still a Southern Democrat).

But the only direct contacts I had with the industry (since the *Times* said I could avoid contact with public-relations people if I liked) were two, one over *Star!* one over *Funny Girl.* The *Funny Girl* episode was a drink, at which the producer complained—about the distinction of his film, about the execrable quality of the *Times* review. I made as many sympathetic noises as I could. In a while, a box arrived, containing a gilded broccoli. I had written that William Wyler's attitude toward Barbra Streisand in *Funny Girl* seemed to be simultaneously patronizing and grandstanding, as if he were firing off a gilded broccoli. I was touched by the gift, although (since I had twice postponed this apparently unavoidable interview) it was a few days old and rather smelled. I laughed. Then the producer, apparently quite seriously, asked me why I had implied that Miss Streisand was a whore. Nothing had been further from my mind, and I asked him wherever he had gotten that idea. "You called her a broccoli," he said. I said that whoredom and broccoli were truly not associated in my mind. He said they were in his and, as though there could be no doubt whatever about this, in the reader's. It seemed to me the interview was not going well and I asked him, out of courtesy really, whether I might keep the gift. "On one condition," he said. I asked what the condition was. He asked why I didn't trust him. I said I did, but that it would be nice to know what the condition was. We discussed this a while. Finally, he said the condition was a kiss. It seemed unsporting to say no, and I said all right. It turned out the kiss had to be right there, at Sardi's, in the drinking hour. I said that the *Times* kissing a producer at Sardi's might be bad form. He lost all interest in the matter after that. Normally a private anecdote, except that it would have been so clearly public had it gone the other way.

At the screening of *Star!*, in the first act, I went to the ladies' room and was sick. No fault of the film's. Flu. Back in the screening room, not wanting to step over many feet, I took up a different seat, near the aisle. A *Times* reviewer, out of fairness, is never supposed to walk out of anything, but when I started to be sick again, I decided it was ridiculous to stay. I particularly waited until after the intermission, so that when the house lights went on, and then off again, I would still be clearly in my seat (one of the myths of the *Times* film reviewer's power is that if the *Times* looks unhappy at something, the other reviewers will hate it). I waited a half hour more, and then tiptoed out. I saw the rest of the film at the last preview. A terrific fuss ensued. The PR man from Fox, finding himself at the end without the *Times*'s elbow to grasp or fanny to pat, called and asked for an explanation. I explained. Suddenly, a deluge of letters from Darryl Zanuck to the *Times*. I had left, for no reason, before the intermission. Therefore my review was short and, he felt, unkind. Mr. Daniel patiently replied. Mr. Zanuck wrote again. It went like that. Outrage. Patience. That was all.

The people I did hear from a lot were readers—about six letters a day. "Our reader," particularly as conceived by the culture editor, was a hypothetical, highly serious person, hanging from a subway strap, who had never read a book or seen a movie, used an obscenity or slept with anyone, but who was desperately anxious that every character, however minor, involved in any way with the making of a film should be identified by some parenthetical reference to his prior work. I began to throw in such identifications maniacally for a while, referring to winners of the Silver Arena at Pula or supporting roles in films like *Three*, but nobody seemed to find that funny except me, and so I stopped. "Our readers" came up a lot, particularly in truisms about good writing being simple writing and so forth, until one day I said, rather mildly I thought, that I didn't give a damn about our reader, and the crisis passed. Speaking of damns and who gave them, there was always a little compulsion—shared by most writers for family publications I think—to sneak a little obscenity into the *Times*. Once, in reviewing *The Killing of Sister George*, I tried to say that it had some good Anglo-Saxon expletives ending in "off" and meaning "go away." An editor who was always fair in these matters did make me give up the "ending in off." It was some similar, though awful compulsion, I think, that made me put in some really grotesque errors in matters I knew perfectly well: type in an extra name, for example, in just copying the letters off a credit sheet, or write of the moments when the earth moved in *The Bridge of San Luis Rey.* It was like planting mines for oneself when one is feeling guilty about expressing so many opinions about everything.

The readers I guess I was writing for, and whom I presumed I had been hired for, were people fairly like myself, or specific friends I had had somewhere along the way. It varied a bit, depending on whom I had seen or lately read. I don't think it is possible to write for people completely unlike yourself. I tried not to be completely negative, except about films I considered reprehensibly rotten, and the readers I heard from were often kind—although certainly not always. After the *Green Berets* review, among highly imaginatively obscene or physically threatening mail, there was an anonymous soul who sent me each week, addressed to Red Renata Adler, his losing tickets from Aqueduct. After several pieces attacking the Left, there were similar letters from the other side. And of course, there were always highly intelligent critical letters as well—and eleven humorous ones after the San Luis Rey debacle. I tried to answer all of them, although, being fairly messy with bills and papers, I lost a few. There was naturally some crazy mail, which I tried to answer seriously too. Just once, at a low time, I used the senatorial gambit for writing to weird vituperative constituents: "Dear Sir, I think I ought to inform you that some preliterate lunatic has been writing me letters and signing your name." Inevitably, I chose the wrong case. I got an immediate reply. The reader answered that, though he had perhaps been a bit harsh, he was certainly no lunatic, and he hoped that I bore him no ill will. The nicest mail was from people who wrote as though they thought I was having a hard time.

In a way, I guess I was. What I wanted to do with the job was to try, as a just-under-thirty person then, of fairly contemporary experience, to review films in earnest (or in fun, depending on the film) with a bit more tension and energy than the traditional paper way. I was trying to shorten and tighten the daily pieces from what they had been before, and expand the range sometimes. In particular, I wanted drastically to change the redundancy of the Sunday articles. (It seemed absurd to rephrase every Sunday the reviews I had done on weekday afternoons.) None of this quite worked out. One continual problem was control. I was forever trying to do in a line something that should have been a piece, and making a piece out of what might have amounted to a line, and frazzling tone. I never seemed able to get it right. There was a special complication with what I can only call the easy victories. That is, I have a personal suspicion of critical writing that comes easily, of felicitous accidents. In criticism, I think there ought to be evidence of time taken, trouble ironed out, of a kind of American Gothic zeal for suffering. It makes the doing of criticism have some risks of its own and it seems more fair. Yet what would happen is that the dashed-off pieces, the unearned lines almost always worked out best. It was like being told, as people often are, that a shoddy piece of work is the best thing they have ever done. It leaves one somehow off-stride with fate. And often, I did wind up recapping in Sunday pieces, either because it was late Monday night and I did not have a thought in my head, or to go back to films and try to get the proportion right, or because repetitions somehow became inadvertent rest stops in my mind.

Some of the nicest times were when events in the outside world were allowed to impinge—the strikes in Paris and Cannes, the Evelyn Waugh disturbances in Venice, meeting the Czech directors, their doubts in the spring, their absolute despair in France and Italy in summer, meeting artists in those weeks, following them about and doing criticism of some films that mattered a bit. The little dramas of solid *Times* reporting came up then too: having to cross borders in hired cars to phone stories for deadlines during strikes; barricades; and, when I knew I couldn't possibly face another Sunday piece, Cuba—where, though it turned out the international desk had been banned for a year, the culture desk was not. It was in travelling too that I discovered that, in newspaper terms, the culture copy desks had been treating me, when I was at home, with their own version of restraint. A story of marathon private strike meetings in Paris, on which the desk really got its chance, was rewritten top to bottom, with mistakes. The Cuba pieces presented problems of their own. Since regular *Times* reporters were still banned, the stories got treated a little as though they were news (the first piece, for instance, appeared on the front page), and it was a kind of writing I was only trying to learn about. But politics at other times (in a year when notoriety and power, media performance and political act, were becoming confused from Washington to Columbia) seemed to occur in writing about movies anyway.

In time, in just struggling with the pace and form, I think there began to be a kind of continuity—not the continuity exactly of criticism or prose, but a record of what movies come out in the course of a year, what movies there actually *are,* and what it can be like for somebody to go to nearly all of them. With all the truisms about the glamour and vitality of the medium, reviewing it daily turned into a kind of journal, with spells of anger, friendliness, ideas, just being tired—the movies themselves coming over the hills in swarms, so many of them nearly undistinguishable, some of them really fine. I have cut little except the purest redundancies, and left some of those. I thought I'd like to record the balance of films just about the way it was for one year, from Elke Sommer and Norman Mailer through festivals, George C. Scott, Truffaut and theaters like the Lyric and the Amsterdam. About a film every other day. I guess I believe things now, about film sex, horror, plot, satire, empathy, foreign languages, old prints, criticism, audio-visual aids, inter-generational dirty jokes, cinémathèques, color films, the reviewable quality of TV commercials and so on, that I hadn't thought about before, but they are in here somewhere without any logic except that of newspaper space and time. I am still taken with a thought about plotless absurdism and its relation to a new value system in which the quality of events is regarded as neither desirable nor undesirable—in which it is desired only that *something* should happen, no matter what. The happening as a value. I think it runs deeply counter to existentialism, and that it is dangerous to life. It occurred to me at the end of my first review of *Faces*—a film which, incidentally, because of schedulings, I reviewed four times. But a year in the dark consisted far more truly of stories and actors, directors and theaters, and seeing them to write really entailed about 160 collisions of one's own experience with Doris Day's, Jean-Luc Godard's, Kahlil Gibran's or

Sidney Poitier's. And here it is, not an encyclopedia of movie statistics, or selected critical essays, but the whole peculiar year.

Some pleasant things happened near the end: a screening of *Yellow Submarine* at which so many of the under-forty reviewers were resolutely seeing it through once with pot that a police raid would have seriously diminished the number of reviews next day; a movie desk memo saying that Roberto Rossellini's *Axe of the Apostles* would be screened that afternoon; and a meeting of the New York Society of Film Critics, for the annual awards. I had never gone to its meetings before. (I had seen most of the critics at screenings throughout the year, of course.) This was different. As the voting went from what I thought was mediocrity to mediocrity, as it began to be clear that criticism is everybody's personal word and certainly not a court or a democracy, I decided to walk out. I had never done anything remotely like walking out of something to resign and I didn't do it very well. Stefan Kanfer of *Time* and Richard Schickel of *Life* whispered kindly that I should sit down again, since they were planning to walk out too, and had a statement prepared. I sat down and sent a note to Vincent Canby, who agreed. The statement, Mr. Schickel's, I think, was read. There were expressions of outrage, and of regret. Joseph Morgenstern of *Newsweek* said he had walked out once, but discovered that it made no difference. It seemed to me, though, that if *Time, Life* and the *Times* walked out, there would be, in effect, no New York Society of Film Critics. In the end, we all settled for a change of rules, and thought we might resign later, one by one, more quietly. I did realize that a lifelong member of a society of film critics was not something I would like to be. I had known for some time that a year at the movies—at a time when I was at the end of a tether of some kind, wanted to drop out of life for a bit and yet try to cope, about as audibly as some new journalist, with things I cared about—was fine for me, but that it was about enough.

March 1969

ON VIOLENCE
FILM ALWAYS ARGUES YES

THE MOTION picture is like journalism in that, more than any of the other arts, it confers celebrity. Not just on people—on acts, and objects, and places, and ways of life. The camera brings a kind of stardom to them all. I therefore doubt that film can ever argue effectively against its own material: that a genuine antiwar film, say, can be made on the basis of even the ugliest battle scenes; or that the brutal hangings in *The Dirty Dozen* and *In Cold Blood* will convert one soul from belief in capital punishment. No matter what filmmakers intend, film always argues yes. People have been modeling their lives after films for years, but the medium is somehow unsuited to moral lessons, cautionary tales or polemics of any kind. If you want to make a pacifist film, you must make an exemplary film about peaceful men. Even cinema villains, criminals and ghouls become popular heroes overnight (a fact which *In Cold Blood*, more cynically than *The Dirty Dozen*, draws upon). Movies glamorize, or they fail to glamorize. They cannot effectively condemn—which means that they must have special terms for dealing with violence.

I do not think violence on the screen is a particularly interesting question, or that it can profitably be discussed as a single question at all. Every action is to some degree violent. But there are gradations, quite clear to any child who has ever awakened in terror in the night, which become blurred whenever violence is discussed as though it were one growing quantity, of which more or less might be simply better or worse. Violence to persons or animals on film (destruction

---

Originally titled "The Movies Make Heroes of Them All"

of objects is really another matter) ranges along what I think is a cruelty scale from clean collision to protracted dismemberment. Clean collision, no matter how much there is of it, is completely innocent. It consists, normally, of a wind-up, a rush, and an impact or series of impacts; and it includes everything from pratfalls, through cartoon smashups, fistfights in westerns, simple shootings in war films, multiple shootings in gang films, machine gunnings, grenade throwings, bombings, and all manner of well-timed explosions. Most often, thorough and annihilating though it may be, a film collision has virtually no cruelty component at all. It is more closely related to contact sport than to murder, and perhaps most nearly akin, in its treatment of tension, to humor. I am sure that such violence has nothing to do with the real, that everyone instinctively knows it, and that the violence of impact is among the most harmless, important, and satisfying sequences of motion on film.

Further along the cruelty scale, however, are the individual, quiet, tidy forms of violence: poisonings and stranglings. Their actual violence component is low, they are bloodless but, as any haunted child knows, their cruelty component can be enormous. The tip-off is the sound track; abrupt, ingratiating, then suddenly loud, perhaps including maniacal laughter—the whole range of effects that the radio-and-cinema-conditioned ear recognizes as sinister—to approximate the nervous jolt of encounters with violence in reality. Further yet along the scale are the quick and messy murders with knives or other instruments (some uncharacteristically ugly impact scenes also fall into this category) and finally, the various protracted mutilations.

I do not know whether scenes of persons inflicting detailed and specific physical sufferings on other persons increase the sum of violence in the world. There are probably saints who dote upon amputations, and certainly sadists who cannot stand the sight of blood. But I think the following rules are true: violence on the screen becomes more cruel as it becomes more particular and individual; and it is bad in direct proportion to one's awareness of (even sympathy with) the detailed physical agonies of the victim. What this amounts to, of course, is a belief that films ought to be squeamish. In life, it is different: awareness of the particular consequences of acts is a moral responsibility and a deterrent to personal cruelty.

The difference between film and life on this point, I suppose, is this: that an audience is not responsible for the acts performed on screen—only for watching them. To be entertained by blasts, shots, blows, chairs breaking over heads, etc., is not unlike being entertained by chases, bass drums, or displays of fireworks; to be entertained by their biological consequences is another thing entirely. An example, again from *The Dirty Dozen:* in one scene, a demented soldier, rhythmically and with obvious pleasure, stabs a girl to death; in another, a château full of people is blown up by means of hand grenades dropped down gasoline-drenched air vents, and nearly everyone else is mowed down by machine-gun fire. In real life, or in ethics seminars, one person dying slowly is less monstrous than a hundred blowing sky high. Not so, I believe, on film, for none of the deaths was real, and only one was made cruel and personal. The style of the Armageddon was most like the style of an orchestra; the style of the stabbing was too much like violence in fact. And while I don't suppose that anyone will actually go out and emulate the stabbing, I don't think dwelling on pain or damage to the human body in the film's literal terms can ever be morally or artistically valid either. Physical suffering in itself is not edifying, movies celebrate, and scenes of cruel violence simply invite the audience to share in the camera's celebration of one person's specific physical cruelties to another.

The New York Times
January 7, 1968

THREE CUBAN CULTURAL REPORTS
WITH FILMS SOMEWHERE IN THEM

HAVANA

IN THIS year of severe rationing and shortages of nearly everything material, Cuban cultural life is particularly active, and under stress. With so little else available, Cubans spend a lot of what free time there is on the arts, and cultural priorities within the revolution have always been extremely high. Dance, writing, theater, painting, films and poster art travel in "itinerant exhibitions" to the remote provinces, Oriente and Camaguey. The jury for the Casa de las Americas prize in art and literature has gone this year, for symbolic reasons, to deliberate in an agricultural settlement on the Isle of Pines, where students from the Havana Art Institute are already spending their forty-five days cutting sugar cane.

Cuban art, conscious of the experience of socialist realism in the Soviet Union, appears relatively free so far of what the Cubans call *panfleto,* that is, flat propaganda work. But the arts in Cuba are, after all, administered by the Cuban Cultural Council, which is an agency of the government, and although its various bureaus—cinema, publishing, theater and so on—have so far determined on their own what degree of artistic freedom is admissible, there are forces gathering to suppress work that does not entirely reflect a propaganda line. At Havana's Teatro García Lorca, the Cuban National Ballet, directed by the internationally known choreographer Alberto Alonso, and starring Alicia Alonso and Maya Plisetskaya's brother, Azari Plisctski, is now staging a production of *Romeo and*

Juliet. Set to electronic music and jammed even in rehearsal by enthusiastic crowds, the production ends with a little speech explaining the moral of the story: Two lovers cannot oppose the system alone. It requires a united effort of the people.

A solid production with just a fillip of political commitment has become characteristic of much of Cuban art in the last ten years, and has developed certain stylistic values of its own. But some ideologues are beginning to demand a more thorough political orientation. A series of four pseudonymous articles last fall in the military magazine *Verde Olivo* attacked the "depoliticalization" of much of Cuban art, particularly two works, a book of poems, *Outside the Game* by Heberto Padilla, and a play, *Seven Against Thebes* by Anton Arrufat, which won the prizes of the Cuban Artists and Writers Guild, UNEAC, last year. The articles suggested worthy future subjects— heroism during Hurricane Flora, for example—for revolutionary art and deplored less committed work as counterrevolutionary. The attack went unanswered for three months. Mr. Padilla, whose poetry was denounced for its "pessimism" (his poems imply that individuals are inevitably crushed by historical forces), had already lost his job at *Granma,* a government newspaper, and has not been granted the trip abroad that is part of the guild prize. The contested book of poems also includes these lines: "I live in Cuba. Always / I have lived in Cuba. These years of wandering / through the world, of which they have spoken so much / are my lies my falsifications. / Because I have always been in Cuba."

Mr. Arrufat's play, denounced for its "pacifist" elements (all war is depicted in horrible terms), has not been produced, but both *Seven Against Thebes* and Mr. Padilla's *Outside the Game* have been published in a UNEAC edition—with two conflicting introductions. The first, by writers who belong to UNEAC, disclaims the poems and play but defends the freedom to publish them. The other, by members of UNEAC's international jury, defends Padilla's poems in the strongest terms. Earlier this month, Haydée Santamaria, a heroine of the revolutionary battle of the Moncada who is now head of the Casa de las Américas (an institute for Cuban cultural exchange with the rest of Latin America), suggested that the UNEAC jury consist only of Cuban writers in 1969.

Cuban filmmakers are now preparing to publish a position paper of their own—which will be the first public answer to the *Verde Olivo* line of attack. The six-page "Declaration of the Cuban Cineastes" will deplore equally the "clean hands" and "pure vocation" of liberal writers, who, in trying to prove their independence of ideology, produce "reactionary" art, and the "timid and bureaucratic" dogmatists, who, in trying to control development of the arts, occupy a "masked" counterrevolutionary position as well. The young filmmakers will advocate free artistic expression, not too "lazy" to take the aims of the revolution into account; their guardedly liberal statement is expected, in the intellectual community, to bring the controversy to a public crisis of some kind.

The last time the issue of artistic freedom arose in Cuba on a major scale was in 1961 when a documentary film, *P.M.*, which showed drunkenness and decadence in Havana nightclubs, was suppressed. Cuban artists and intellectuals protested vigorously, until Premier Fidel Castro, in a famous speech to the intellectuals, stated his position on freedom in the arts: "What are the rights of revolutionary writers and artists? Within the revolution, everything; against the revolution, no rights whatsoever."

Among the writers opposing the suppression of *P.M.* was Guillermo Cabrera Infante, then editor of *Lunes de Revolución,* a Cuban cultural journal. The journal was discontinued, and Mr. Cabrera Infante, who has since left Cuba, is now conducting an important correspondence in an Argentine periodical, *Primera Plana,* protesting Cuban censorship. It was after praising *Tres Tristes Tigres,* a book by the emigrant Cabrera Infante, as the best Cuban novel since the revolution, and after dismissing as unimportant a book by Lisandro Otero, vice president of the Cultural Council, that Mr. Padilla lost his job at *Granma.*

It might be assumed that artists who have not left Cuba after ten revolutionary years are demonstrably "within the revolution," but the present crisis seems a kind of testing of the still ambiguous and contradictory grounds, to determine whether Cuba is about to undergo what seems to many a historically inevitable tightening of control. The situation this year is different from 1961: Problems in the arts are ironically complicated by the fact that, except for the economic blockade—which many Cubans credit with having strengthened the country and unified the people—pressures from the United States have become less apparent. They appear, more subtly, as a Cuban internalization of the values of American culture itself. At every cultural level, for a newly literate people, past and present are learned together, and the weight of cultural history as well as the weight of contemporary art naturally falls on the side of peoples who have been literate for some time. A generation too young to remember Batista, the early struggles, illiteracy or real underdevelopment is growing up. And there exists a contingent of youth that Cuban intellectuals refer to as "snob"—bored with revolutionary discipline and fascinated by American life styles, American films, American rock (a Beatle-like group called Los Meme is greeted with screams; a Havana youth newspaper reports solemnly that the Mamas and Papas are breaking up), and what an official for Cuban television calls the American "Queen for a Day Psychology." Minor leanings in this line are tolerated, but students who drop out too firmly or too conspicuously are likely to be expelled from the schools and sent to the provinces for "agricultural re-education."

"In the early days of the revolution," a Havana University student said, "the important words were 'blockade' and 'imperialism.' People used to explain personal troubles, even nightmares, in terms of *imperialismo*." The crucial words now, he said, are "Third World" and "underdevelopment," with Cubans trying desperately to identify themselves with underdeveloped countries, to divorce themselves from the culture ninety miles away. It is out of lack of confidence that Cuban artists are developing in definably Cuban ways, he said, that a dogmatist approach takes form.

There are certainly fields in which Cubans are developing art and cultural dilemmas of their own. In the early days of the revolution the Cuban Institute of Film Art and Industry, ICAIC, fought a battle over posters against bureaucrats who argued that representational, essentially socialist realist art was the only means of communicating to the people. ICAIC held out for art, and now professional and amateur artists in Cuba design posters with such style that even the political agencies are producing graphics of distinction and originality.

On the lawns of what was formerly the Havana Country Club, a Cuban architect, Ricardo Porro, has designed the Havana Art Institute (a school for children between twelve and seventeen), consisting of rounded structures, like Gaudí in brick, with bulbed dome windows on top and long columned walks along the windowed sides. It is one of the most pleasant, least institutional schools imaginable. The prefabricated houses replacing peasant huts all over the country, on the other hand, are flat, infinitely reduplicated rectangles. Cuban theater, since the Arrufat issue arose, has been largely limited to imaginative productions of Bertolt Brecht, or inventively staged choral readings from the Cuban poet and patriot José Martí. Vicente Revulta, one of the best-known theater actors and directors in Havana, has temporarily moved to the more liberal film institute.

Out of a concern about underdevelopment, a Youth Congress of Artists and Writers, which met recently in Havana, will meet again later this month, with delegates from all the provinces, in Camaguey. The young people want to discuss how, as active revolutionary workers, they can find time and access to materials, instruction, and outlets for the artwork they would like to do. A genuine cultural problem, acknowledged by the government, lies in bringing books, film, art, and information to a generation of new intellectuals emerging from the schools, and being sent, for the most part, to settle in the provinces. The old propaganda vehicles, newspapers and television, are not suited to new sensibilities. Hard news of the outside world, even in Havana, scarcely exists.

The writer who introduced the word "underdevelopment" on the intellectual plane is Edmundo Desnoes, whose novel *Memories of Underdevelopment* (now a highly popular film in Cuba, and for some reason published in the United States as *Inconsolable Memories*) uses the word ironically to apply to a writer who is not entirely convinced by the revolution, who is not in fact entirely convinced by anything. Mr. Desnoes, a tall, blond man of thirty-eight, who worked until recently as an editor of books, now works for the Cuban propaganda agency COR in charge of coining slogans—rather like the poet Vladimir Mayakovsky in the Russian Revolution. Before the revolution in Cuba, Mr. Desnoes, who describes himself as having been for years completely alienated from society, lived on a boat in the Bahamas. In 1961 he returned to Cuba, expecting an invasion and expecting, he says, to die. Asked whether as an intellectual, highly skeptical writer, he found that the revolution gave or cost him energy, he said, "For me, it is always an effort to remain alive." Asked whether he believed in progress at all, he said that formerly he did not, but that looking at Cuba fifty years ago, "a country of pimps and prostitutes," and looking at Cuba now, it is difficult to maintain his skepticism about it.

Mr. Desnoes, like nearly every other able-bodied Cuban, spends about a month each year cutting sugar cane. He acknowledges that he hates it. "As an intellectual, you have a certain idea of nature," he said. "Landscapes, something impressionistic. But the cane is alienating, overwhelming. Conversation becomes absolutely crude and elementary. Bending down to the coffee plants, I suppose, is physically more difficult. But the cane never seems to end." Mr. Desnoes, who has lived in the United States and who has traveled a great deal abroad, said he would not leave the country now until the sugar harvest of ten million tons, projected by Premier Castro for 1971, was in.

Before the revolution, books by Cuban writers were not published in Cuba except at the writer's own expense, and Mr. Desnoes published his own first novel, in an edition of five hundred copies, himself. The Cuban bourgeoisie under Batista, he said, read mainly *Life* and *Reader's Digest*. "Now, for the first time, a Cuban writer has an authentic audience," he continued. "He does not have to look abroad for international acclaim. It entails certain responsibilities." Asked about the characteristics of that new audience, he said it was perhaps still too accepting, too uncritical. "The problem is to understand them, not to project," he explained. "In all the new education, we cannot be sure what the people know. It may be that with all the ideology about Latin America people have no idea what Latin America is. Or any country. Or a continent."

He said that the revolution had so far proceeded pragmatically, reactively, without any rigid ideological system, and attributed this to the instincts of Premier Castro. Asked how the revolution would go without Mr. Castro, he said, "Perhaps Stalinism, no? But it is not right to protect your ideas against the future. It might become a nightmare or a dream." In a late-night discussion between Mr. Desnoes and some friends in Havana's Hotel Nacional it was mentioned that the United States had not, after all, invaded Cuba, where it might once have succeeded, and had, instead, gone to Vietnam, where it had fewer interests and could not win. It was suggested that this might be construed as a colossal blunder of idealism. Mr. Desnoes said that in coming to grips with America, a colonial writer must also come to grips with the fact that it has also helped to form his own idealism. "If the country is so powerful that with a flick of its finger it could extinguish Che in Bolivia," he said, "one must also understand the things it has not done." On the subject of how the United States might react to a full recognition of its loss in Vietnam, Mr. Desnoes said, "I hope it will not be like Moby Dick. A bewildered monster who flicks his tail and wipes us off the island."

Humberto Solas, twenty-seven-year-old director of *Lucía*, the most popular film in Cuban history, works six months a year on films and six in the agriculture or at other jobs, which he does not mind. "The year has twelve months," he said, and when it was remarked that the content of the experience of American intellectuals is often only other intellectuals, he said he was certain his contact with the people in his months away from film helped in his work.

Mr. Solas, who is reading a Soviet polemical history of Stalinism distributed by the Cuban government to intellectuals (a few special books, called Polemical Editions, are occasionally circulated only among intellectuals, for discussion purposes), is very much concerned with the dogmatist position on Cuban art. "They do not understand the revolution," he said. "Now, after ten years, everybody is thinking. This is a popular revolution. We have a strong secret service to deal with real counterrevolutionaries. We don't need a populist-dogmatist bureaucracy."

Mr. Solas is also very much worried by a rumor that a book called *The Hard Years*, by Jesús Díaz, will become a reflection of a cultural line. "It is a study of the years before the revolution," he said. "But it is important to realize that 'the hard years' are now." He much admires a recent Colombian novel, *One Hundred Years of Solitude*, by Gabriel García Marquez—"very revolutionary, very deep," he said. "The populist position is, 'I did not want to put the bomb, but I was told to, and I did.' The deep position is, 'I was told to, and then I thought, and perhaps I didn't put the bomb.'" Solas was convinced that young people "of talent and sensibility would not accept a populist approach. But if, as he thinks unlikely, the hard line should win out, he would stay in Cuba and wait for a better time. "If I could not make my kind of films, I would rest," he said. "In the end, the question is who is more revolutionary, which side of the controversy produces better art."

The New York Times
February 10, 1969

HAVANA

At the time of the revolution, Cuba's contribution to world cinema consisted mainly of cheap tropical locations, facilities for dubbing, and, in Havana's Chinatown, the three most famous pornographic theaters in the world. Starting virtually from nothing, Cuban filmmakers—most of whom are in their late twenties or early thirties— have now developed the most widely discussed, persuasive, and controversial medium in the country. Films now reach far more extensively than television (which broadcasts mainly propaganda and old films monitored from stations in Miami) every place where Cubans meet.

In early 1959, three months after the revolution, the Cuban government founded ICAIC (Instituto Cubano del Arte e Industria Cinematográficos), a film institute instructed to form and document the revolutionary experience of the people, while creating films as art. Under the direction of Alfredo Guevara, a former guerrilla, who, in exile in Mexico City, had served as an assistant to the Spanish director Luis Buñuel, the film institute took over all film production, distribution and collection in the country and began to move, rather like the new roads and schools, into the countryside. Since modern equipment was unavailable, the institute created a kind of spare-parts cinema, refurbishing the one hundred commercial theaters in Havana and the four hundred in the rest of the country, founding a 3000–film cinémathèque, and sending all films, Cuban and foreign, to villages all over the country in mobile units, which show films in fields, community centers, and schoolhouses. According to an official of ICAIC, every Cuban now has access to about two films a week. The pornographic film houses have been closed.

The budget varies considerably from year to year, but the government supplies the institute with what filmmakers call "means"— that is, props, locations, theaters, access to places, transportation, technicians, and actors temporarily released from national theaters. Since Mr. Guevara has long been a personal friend of Premier Fidel Castro, filmmakers are relatively independent of the national Cuban Culture Council, which nominally administers all the arts in Cuba. As a result, the film institute is regarded by Cuban intellectuals as one of the major sources of information and relative liberalism.

American films made since 1960 are not exported to Cuba and, since the blockade, Cuban films have not been admitted to the United States. But among the most widely and seriously discussed foreign films in Cuba now is the Czechoslovak *Closely Watched Trains*, Jiří Menzel's story of a young boy who thinks himself impotent, sleeps with an older woman and, the next day, blows up a Nazi train. The crucial point for young Cubans is that the woman who brings the boy the bomb, and who sleeps with him, is an artist. "In any Russian film of the forties," Humberto Solas, a twenty-seven-year-old Cuban director, said over lunch in the Hotel Habana Libre (formerly the Hilton), "the woman would have brought the boy the bomb and sung him the Internationale. In Menzel's film, it is just as important for her to go to bed with him. It is something new. It is human.

Mr. Solas himself has just directed *Lucía,* the most popular and enthusiastically discussed film in Cuban history. Already seen by more than a million people, *Lucía* tells the story of a woman's problems in Cuba in three historical periods, 1895, 1932, and now. In the first episode, Lucía, played by Raquel Revuelta, falls in love with a Spaniard, who turns out to be married. She is persuaded to run away with him and reveals to him the location of the *cafetan,* the revolutionary headquarters. He turns out to be a Spanish spy as well, and brings the Spanish soldiers in. She murders him. In the next chapter, Lucía, played by Eslinda Núñez, is drawn by a boyfriend out of her rather F. Scott Fitzgerald set into guerrilla sabotage in which the boyfriend is killed. Both episodes are done with a remarkable sense of style and period, but it is the third, the contemporary, chapter that causes the greatest excitement in Cuba now.

Lucía, played by Adela Legrá, is young and married. She wants to work and to learn to read in the country's alphabetization program, but her husband has the traditional Latin quality of *machismo.* His pride and his sense of manhood require that his wife be completely dependent on him and remain at home. He is enormously suspicious of anyone who wants to take her out of the house and into the revolution. A leader of the local agriculture settlement—a lovely, wizened, officious black woman who unconsciously imitates Premier Castro's mannerism of repeating an important sentence now and then, with bent knees and index finger pointing toward the ground—tries to reason with him. It is no use. Lucía leaves him. They have a sad and hopeless meeting on the beach, and the question of *machismo* is left unresolved.

Cuban audiences, whose members include even the most clearly *machista* men, adore the film, laughing at all the parodistic touches, particularly at the Premier Castro imitation and at elderly farmers being appalled by miniskirts. But young intellectuals tend to prefer the first two chapters for their style and to have reservations about the third for its simplicity, although they respect the sense of doubt and ambiguity at the end. Cubans acknowledge that *machismo* is a problem for the revolution—resisting the liberation of women and even affecting the use of modern machines. A man's pride in his strength and in the work of his hands can bring him into conflict with a tractor or a piece of factory equipment.

"Yet the problem is difficult," Mr. Solas, a tall, gentle young man, who became a guerrilla in the mountains at the age of fourteen, said of this chapter of his film. "It is, after all, the *machista* spirit that creates revolutionaries. *Machismo* is simply not suited to social relations. It can also be a factor in the government's relation to the people. Maybe it will be overcome now that everybody studies." Asked whether, for example, a *machista* spirit in government might be what inhibits young people in boarding schools (many of whom object to the system of fifteen days' confinement to school, with one day off) from registering any form of protest now, he said that it might. "For me, as a boy, fighting Batista was easier," Mr. Solas said. "He was hated. It was simple. Now the young have a complex of admiration and fear. The men of the revolution are Greek statues to them, and to say that the marble might be flawed or the statue might be missing one arm is difficult."

Mr. Solas described *Lucía* as an exercise in which he rid himself of the influence of international directors he admires—Luchino Visconti, Ingmar Bergman, Roberto Rossellini, and Buñuel. His next film will be completely Cuban, examining in greater depth the problems of Cuba now, the contradictions, the people who have somehow been left outside the revolution. "It is important not to regard them as monsters," Mr. Solas said. "There is a tragic aspect. Even people who don't understand the revolution are giving everything." As examples, from his next film, he mentioned a guerrilla who, after the revolution has succeeded, becomes a functionary and misses the excitement of his life. Or a mother who is committed to the revolution because her sons are revolutionaries, but who secretly longs for them to become doctors or to have some other form of bourgeois success. Or an opportunist who becomes an interpreter for foreign visitors only to have contact with the products they bring in. Mr. Solas believes that these revolutionary dilemmas will disappear as the revolution develops.

Another vital and controversial film in Cuba now is *Memories of Underdevelopment*, directed by Tomás Gutiérrez Alea, and based on a prize-winning novel by Edmundo Desnoes that was published in the United States as *Inconsolable Memories*. More than 600,000 people have already seen the film, which is a highly intellectual study of a writer living in affluence at the time the revolution comes. The writer's wife and friends leave Cuba, and he is unable to hear their voices when they step to the other side of the window in the airport waiting room. His life is full of Scarlatti, Botticelli, dry martinis, and girls, and he has doubts whether his love of the revolution does not derive from an artist's hatred of the bourgeoisie. Mr. Desnoes himself appears in the film in a panel discussion, which ends when Jack Gelber, the American playwright, asks why, "if the Cuban revolution is really a total revolution," there should be a roundtable format "about issues with which I am familiar," instead of an open discussion with the people. "The American is right," the narrator says, a psychologically difficult sentence in Cuba these days.

The film is full of documentary footage, interior monologues, flashbacks, abrupt cuts and avant-garde touches. Cuban audiences seem extraordinarily receptive to avant-gardism of every sort—electronic music, surrealism and absurdist comedy. Cuban intellectuals explain this in two ways: Before the revolution the masses in Cuba had not been exposed to art of any kind and, since tastes had not been "deformed" by popular art, avant-gardism seems quite natural. And most artists struggle consciously to keep the artistic and political vanguards together, against the "populist" idea that only representational art can reach the people.

In describing a fiction film in progress, a Cuban filmmaker is likely to begin with an abstraction—and sometimes leave it at that. Jorge Fraga, a twenty-three-year-old director, explained, for example, that his film *The American War* is about "two forms of violence, active and passive, generated in two brothers by the inevitable ambience of colonial war." Pressed about the actual content of the plot, Mr. Fraga revealed an intensely dramatic story of rape, cowardice and murder, but the original equation was clearly uppermost in his mind.

While shooting *The American War,* Mr. Fraga's crew stayed at a former resort hotel, now a convalescent home, in the village of San Diego, which is in Pinar del Río, the nation's westernmost province. The home is near a spa, whose waters are still believed to be medically restorative. It was not a cheerful place—a murky swimming pool surrounded by plaster swans; eggs and an unidentifiable soup for lunch; people in ragged bathrobes wandering about; a salon, whose furniture consisted of two facing rows of seventeen slatted rocking chairs. But the crew of fifteen actors and technicians did not seem to mind.

The actual shooting took place in a remote area at the end of a pitted road, on the Hacienda Cortina, the estate of a pre-revolutionary senator. This is near the site of one of the tourist resorts being built for Cuban workers, who, in their twenty days' yearly vacation, have no place outside Cuba to go. The filming, like all filming, consisted mainly of waiting—for the sunlight to be right and for the old Zeiss 16-mm. camera to be properly set up. Vicente Revuelta, the brother of one of the Lucías and himself one of the best-known Cuban theater actors and directors, was wandering about making jokes. Since the situation in Cuban theater is not just now as liberal as in cinema, Mr. Revuelta has temporarily moved to the film institute.

A great many jokes were made about a truly hideous dog that was staggering around the crew. From the conversation, it was clear that the dog had nearly died in the night and that its owner, because of anxiety, had refused to eat. The dog, which was white, had a red band of what appeared to be medication around its neck, covering what seemed to be a hairless rash. It seemed for a moment to reflect all the misery of Latin America that such a repellent creature should exist, and that even its owner could care whether it survived. Then it suddenly became clear that the dog was in the film. There was no rash. The red band had been painted on because one of the characters in the film was supposed to strangle the dog. On the preceding afternoon, Mr. Fraga explained, he had injected the dog with a drug so that it would lie with its tongue hanging realistically out. Mr. Fraga had given the dog an overdose that had almost resulted in its death. The dog was fine, merely slightly looped, as it wandered about. It was still not handsome; its health still did not inspire much confidence, but it was waking up. The red band would be washed off when the shooting was done.

The New York Times
February 11, 1969

HAVANA

From the early days of the Cuban revolution, the priority of films, and particularly documentaries, has been so high that the government's first law dealing with cultural matters established a national film institute, ICAIC, in March, 1959. Film-projection crews began to move, in twenty-five-day trips, to the remotest villages. In addition, documentary filmmakers were instructed to overcome the influence of Western "films of a commercial nature which are ethically disgusting and artistically dull," to "serve as a narrator and protagonist of the revolution," and to bind city and countryside together in a revolutionary consciousness. Cuban television has never been of much importance, partly because the *campesinos* do not have sets and partly because it is not suited to public places, where people gather and discussion takes place. Television is still steeped in propaganda of the crudest sort. (A recent program reported that the reason Israeli forces were so strong in the Middle East was that they were led by Nazi generals.) Since television, which existed before Fidel Castro's revolution, is ideologically single-minded and technically archaic, it is films that are taken with the greatest seriousness as national sources of information and of art.

The quantity of propaganda in Cuban newsreels and documentaries is roughly comparable to the amount of advertising in American television, with the difference being that Cuban films advertise only one product, socialist revolution, and that propaganda is now integrated in what has become a distinctively Cuban style. Films characteristically cut, with great suddenness, from the pure study of a subject, with great respect for the quality of the subject's life, to an extremely blunt and remote political point. There is also a wider surreal and sometimes consciously comic conception of the relation between life and revolution. Cubans say that Cuba was the only socialist country to show *Morgan,* the irreverent English treatment of insanity and Marxism.

Among the most prolific, simultaneously folk and surreal filmmakers of ICAIC is Santiago Álvarez, who, since 1959, has made 437 newsreels and twenty documentaries. The forty-nine-year-old Mr. Álvarez now produces newsreels at the rate of one a week. At the time of the revolution, he was a music archivist for Cuban television who had never thought of making films. Asked how he happened to become a director, he said he had been caught up in creative revolutionary activism, "the same way Fidel became a *guerrillero.*"

Mr. Álvarez's films contain strong elements of what, to a foreign observer, seems absolute *panfleto,* that is, pure propaganda work. But Cuban filmmakers say that although in the present struggle over artistic freedom the socialist realist, "populist" forces will try to claim Mr. Álvarez for their side, he will place himself firmly on the side of relative liberalism.

An Álvarez documentary about North Vietnam, called *Hanoi: Tuesday, December 13,* is one of the most beautiful films ever made about Asia, capturing, with the delicacy of a scroll, the rhythm of Vietnamese life, the hats, nets, fish, rice shoots, rivers, water buffalo. But intercut with a kind of poem about patience and tragedy ("We turn our hatred into energy," a Vietnamese says, in preparing for a bombing raid), with a surprisingly contemporary narration from a children's book about Indochina, by the turn-of-the-century Cuban poet and patriot José Martí, are scenes of what seems like crude and dissonant propaganda. President Johnson is suddenly introduced with literal, breech birth scenes of a woman and a cow. Asked whether he had put these scenes in out of personal artistic necessity or for didactic reasons, Mr. Álvarez replied that his reasons were emphatically personal. "I have to put them in. They are what I feel," he said.

Except for *Lucía* and *Memories of Underdevelopment,* which are the most important of Cuba's few fiction films, the most distinctive films in Cuba are still documentaries—nearly all made with Álvarez-like juxtapositions of fact, with a strong, unpolitical sense of human misery, and the most blatant ideology. Looking at Cuba's documentaries is like watching ten years of Cuban history—the Bay of Pigs invasion, Hurricane Flora, the 1961 literacy campaign, speeches by Premier Castro, a film in which Major Ernesto Che Guevara appears, scarcely able to speak because of his asthma. ("We had to splice it together in a few days," Mr. Álvarez said, "to give the people something after the death of Che.") In the film institute's 1,500-seat cinémathèque, however, there are quantities of American films made before 1960, and subsequently nationalized. And there are frequent retrospective exhibitions of Hollywood films, including a recent retrospective of Marilyn Monroe.

The parodistic sense in Cuban films is so strong and so deadpan that it is not always possible to tell when it unambiguously exists. There is a completely solemn film, for example, about the artificial insemination of cattle, with shots of three men at a kind of console behind a pane of glass, as a cow, flopping one idle ear, is inseminated with a single pill—coded blue, green or red, according to the breed of the bull. The seriousness of the Cuban cattle-improvement program seems here to run into a strong sense of ribaldry.

Another documentary, a kind of athletic *Potemkin* in style, shows Cuban athletes arriving by boat in Puerto Rico to protest being barred from the Central American games. (Acceptance in competition in capitalist countries or contexts plays a large role in many Cuban films.) They were ultimately admitted, and won many gold medals, but the film shows a Cuban athlete throwing up into the sea and another being cuffed on the ear by the coach for having responded to the jeers of the anti-Cuban crowd. The film called *Cerro Pelado,* after the name of a battle and the boat itself, shows streets of stores in San Juan, which audiences instantly and delightedly recognize as the stores of Cubans who fled. The climax of the film is a grand melee, in which Cubans tear down a Soviet flag that Puerto Ricans had run up a flagpole to mock the Cuban victories.

There seems also to be a sense if not of satire then at least of cheerful inconsistency, when—at a time of a virulent anti-Israel campaign—a film called *Now*, venomously anti-West, is accompanied almost completely by a rendition, set to Spanish words, of the Hebrew song "Hava Nagila."

Two of the most moving and poetic documentaries in Cuba now were made by Octavio Cortázar, who is thirty-one, and who describes his films as "testimonies" to a Cuba that his son will never see. The first film, *About a Person Whom Some Call St. Lazarus and Some St. Babalou*, is about a pilgrimage that takes place each year on November 16, near Santiago in the province of Oriente. The pilgrims are black, descendants of slaves from the Yoruba tribe in Dahomey; and the Christian St. Lazarus has merged in their beliefs with Babalou (of the song "Babalou Aye") in the voodoo cult of Santero. For twenty-four hours they crawl, either on their stomachs or backward, in sitting positions, some with weights dragging from an injured limb, some with sick children on their backs, many groaning, to the Lazarus-Babalou shrine. Mr. Cortázar interviews priests, psychiatrists, workers, students, the Tata Nganga (the local Santero leader), and the pilgrims as they crawl, about what can be the meaning of such a pilgrimage, in the middle of a socialist revolution, on the part of people who would otherwise consider themselves Marxist-Leninists.

"I was shocked when I saw them," Mr. Cortázar, a tall, sensitive man, who studied for two years at the film school in Prague, said of the pilgrims. "The contradiction, the superstition. I cannot speak for the new generation and say that they will not be religious. I cannot say that they will not believe in God. But I know that with literacy, in the new Cuba, this pilgrimage will not exist." The film ends with shots of some very healthy, modern schoolchildren doing exercises on a beach.

Mr. Cortázar's other testimony to a disappearing Cuba is *For the First Time,* a film about one of the film institute's mobile units bringing Charlie Chaplin's *Modern Times* to villagers in the Baracoa Mountains of Oriente. Mr. Cortázar interviews the villagers, who had never seen a film before, about what they think film is. "It is like a party," one of them says, "with couples and beautiful girls." Another, an immensely dignified, wrinkled lady, wearing a handkerchief over her hair, says film "is something you show in a cinema—very important thing. Very good." A young woman gets frightened and bursts into tears. At night, carrying torches, a little audience arrives for its movie, and sits in folding chairs in a field. The faces are amused, not awed, and radiant. The children eventually yawn and go to sleep. ICAIC's directors say that film is one of Cuba's few windows to the outside world. *For the First Time* catches, simply and respectfully, a moment, the first viewing of film, that will probably never occur in Cuba again.

The New York Times
February 12, 1969

HOUSE CRITIC

A NOTE BY THE AUTHOR

In the 1960s and '70s, Pauline Kael was not only the most powerful movie critic in America. She had become the most powerful reviewer in any medium. And her influence extended, not just to criticism of all kinds, but to journalism, to academic writing, to the appointment of faculty to film departments at universities throughout the country. Writing every week for six months of the year in *The New Yorker,* and publishing regular collections of her pieces, she generated admiration (for some years deserved), and then—gradually, surprisingly—fear. She had colleagues and filmmakers she liked, and others she didn't. Her likes and dislikes became dogmatic, remorseless. She had her cliques and imitators, including a more or less servile cult, known as the *Paulettes.* They chattered, laughed, whispered, loudly gossiped and sneered during previews and screenings, then went back to their various publications and tried to outdo one another in agreeing with Kael.

Meanwhile, almost without anyone's taking notice, Pauline Kael's interest in movies was declining, even as her writing style became more and more excessive. She began less to write than to rule. The titles of her books, in their redundant, unfunny naughtiness, should have given it away. *I Lost It at the Movies, Kiss Kiss Bang Bang, Deeper Into Movies.* The joyless, fake ordinariness of it all, the aging, essentially humorless woman reveling in unimaginative talking dirty—we didn't notice, prize committees of various kinds did

---

Originally titled "The Perils of Pauline"

not notice the underlying quality of what we were endorsing, year after year.

But her influence was great, her exercises of power remarkably effective. What we might characterize as unconscious Pauline Kaelism was contagious, and now pervades the culture, wherever second-rate prose can be found.

A biography, *Pauline Kael: A Life in the Dark* by Brian Kellow has just been published. Library of America has just published an anthology of her writing. Both books are worthy and have been widely and seriously reviewed. In 1980, Renata Adler, at the time a *New Yorker* writer—author of two novels, and five books of essays and reporting, including, as it happens, *A Year in The Dark*, an anthology of her own pieces as former chief film critic of *The New York Times*—reviewed Kael's *When the Lights Go Down* for *The New York Review of Books*. That review created an enormous fuss, consternation, the taking of sides.

Adler's review itself was reviewed and discussed in newspapers and magazines at the time. It has remained a subject of controversy to this day.

There were rumors: a committee had collaborated to write it; Mr. Shawn, editor of *The New Yorker*, had secretly commissioned it; Adler was pursuing a vendetta generated by some incident or series of incidents years before. None of this, as it happened, was true.

Even Kellow, in his biography, gets it wrong. He writes that Adler, at a meeting of the New York Film Critics Circle, "stormed out," saying she "had to see her analyst immediately." Adler had no analyst, and she had not "stormed out." When she did, in fact, walk out, several other critics, including Stefan Kanfer of *Time*, walked out with her. As they left, Kael said, "Do you realize how offensive you're being?" That tone and that question were provoked by Adler's, Kanfer's, others' (including Vincent Canby's) quiet disagreement with a consensus which Kael was trying to create and enforce. Adler was, at the time, relatively young, the chief film critic of the *New York Times*. (That position was widely thought to be so desirable that advertisements for a department store read "Some people think

Renata Adler's job is like being paid to eat bonbons.") Adler had no reason to be hostile to Kael, and was not. In fact, until she was asked to review Kael's collection, Adler had admired Kael's work.

Renata Adler's "Pauline Kael piece" generated a lot of fuss and controversy. Through the years, it was mentioned so often in articles about Kael, including virtually all her obituaries, that people who had never read the piece had the strongest possible views of what they thought was in it. The reviews of Kellow's biography and the Library of America volume often mention the piece in some way.

What follows is what the famous or infamous piece actually said.

2015

THE JOB of the regular daily, weekly, or even monthly critic resembles the work of the serious intermittent critic, who writes only when he is asked to or is genuinely moved to, in limited ways and for only a limited period of time. Occasionally, a particularly rich period in one of the arts coincides with a prolific time in the life of a major critic; or a major critic—Edmund Wilson, Harold Rosenberg—takes over a weekly column and uses it as the occasion for an essay. After a time, however, even Edmund Wilson no longer wrote frequently and regularly about books. He also wrote, all his life, on other subjects. Harold Rosenberg wrote continuously on subjects other than painting. Normally, no art can support for long the play of a major intelligence, working flat out, on a quotidian basis. No serious critic can devote himself, frequently, exclusively, and indefinitely, to reviewing works most of which inevitably cannot bear, would even be misrepresented by, review in depth.

At most publications, staff critics are cast up from elsewhere in the journalistic ranks—the copy desk, for instance, or regular reporting. What they provide is a necessary consumer service, which consists essentially of three parts: a notice that the work exists, and where it can be bought, found, or attended; a set of adjectives appearing to set forth an opinion of some sort, but amounting really to a yes vote or a no vote; and a somewhat nonjudgmental, factual description or account, which is usually inferior by any journalistic standard to reporting in all other sections of the paper. On the basis of these columns, the reader gets his information and, if he is an art consumer, forms his own judgment and makes his choice.

Serious publications, however, tend from time to time to hire talented people, educated, usually young, devoted to the craft of criticism, at least as it entails fidelity to an art and to a text under review. What usually happens is that such a critic writes for some time at his highest level: reporting and characterizing accurately; incorporating in whatever is judgmental evidence for what he's saying (a sign of integrity in a critic, as opposed to an opinion monger, is that he tries for evidence; in reviewing prose forms, for example, he will quote); and producing insights, and allusions, which, if they are not downright brilliant, are apposite. What happens after a longer time is that he settles down.

The consumer service remains the professional basis for the staff reviewer's job; fidelity, evidence, and so forth are still the measures of his value, but the high critical edge becomes misplaced, disproportionate when applied to most ordinary work. The staff critic is nonetheless obliged, and paid, to do more than simply mark time between rich periods and occasional masterpieces. The simple truth—this is okay, this is not okay, this is vile, this resembles that, this is good indeed, this is unspeakable—is not a day's work for a thinking adult. Some critics go shrill. Others go stale. A lot go simultaneously shrill and stale. A few critics, writing quietly and well, bring something extra into their work. Arlene Croce, a fine ability to describe. John Russell, a piece of education in art history. Hilton Kramer, something in the realm of ideas. A few others bring a consistent personal voice, a sort of chat whose underlying proposition is: This is what happened in my field today; here's what I have to say about it; draw what conclusions you will, on the basis of your familiarity by now with my style, my quality of mind, and the range of my association, in short with who I am. Some staff critics quit and choose to work flat out again, on other interests and in intermittent pieces. By far the most common tendency, however, is to stay put and simply to inflate, to pretend that each day's text is after all a crisis—the most, first, best, worst, finest, meanest, deepest, etc.—to take on, since we are dealing in superlatives, one of the first, most unmistakable marks of the hack.

Movies seem to invite particularly broad critical discussion: To begin with, alone among the arts, they count as their audience, their art consumer, everyone. (Television, in this respect, is clearly not an art but an appliance, through which reviewable material is sometimes played.) The staff movie critic's job thus tends to have less in common with the art, or book, or theater critic's, whose audiences are relatively specialized and discrete, than with the work of the political columnist—writing, that is, of daily events in the public domain, in which almost everyone's interest is to some degree engaged, and about which everyone seems inclined to have a view. Film reviewing has always had an ingredient of reportage. Since the forties, *The New York Times* has reviewed almost every movie that opened in New York—as it would not consider reviewing every book, exhibit, or other cultural event, or even every account filed from the UN or City Hall. For a long time it seemed conceivable that movies could sustain, if not a great critic, at least a distinguished commentator-critic, on the order, say, of Robert Warshow, with the frequency of Walter Lippmann. In the late fifties and early sixties, it seemed likely that such a critic might be Pauline Kael.

Writing freelance, but most often in *Partisan Review*, Ms. Kael seemed to approach movies with an energy and a good sense that were unmatched at the time in film criticism. In France, young people were emerging from the archives of the Cinémathèque to write reverently for film publications and, later, to make the films that became the *nouvelle vague*. Here, movie critics were so much the financial and spiritual creatures of the industry that, in 1962, Judith Crist was counted new and brave for having a few reservations about *Cleopatra*. Magazines had staff movie critics; but no one paid much attention to them. Newspaper movie critics were, in general, writers of extended blurbs for high-budget films. Out in San Francisco, though, there was this person, writing as frequently as she could manage to sell pieces. In 1965, a book appeared, something mildly off in the coarse single *entendu* of its title, *I Lost It at the Movies*, but, as a collection of movie reviews, interesting. Ms. Kael continued to write, freelance. One began to look forward, particularly if one had already read a lot about a picture, to reading what Pauline Kael had to say.

Then, briefly at *McCall's* (where, braver even than Ms. Crist, she panned *The Sound of Music*) and, beginning in 1968, at *The New Yorker*, Ms. Kael acquired a staff critic's job and a strong institutional base. Nothing could be clearer—the case of John Simon comes to mind at once—than that such a change is by no means always fortunate. A voice that may have seemed, sometimes, true and iconoclastic when it was outside can become, with institutional support, vain, overbearing, foolish, hysterical. Instead of the quiet authority of the this-is-who-I-am, and here's-what-I-have-to-say, there is the somewhat violent spectacle of a minor celebrity in frenzy, weirdly intent on what he/she is going to "do to" whatever passes for his/her weekly text. For a year or two, Ms. Kael, however, continued to write fine pieces. If there were many weeks when she seemed far from her best, nothing could be more natural; no writer is always at his/her best. She tended to write rather too long for what she had to say each week, and there was something overwrought in her tone. Here, of course, there was a difference from a serious intermittent critic—whose tone and length reflect, not the rote pressures of a deadline but a real pitch and interval of thought. For some time, however, the effect was only this: One could not look forward, always and to the same degree, to reading what Ms. Kael had to say.

Then there began to be quirks, mannerisms, in particular a certain compulsive and joyless naughtiness. Not just conscious, heavy allusions of the sort that recurred in her titles, *Kiss Kiss Bang Bang; Deeper into Movies*, etc., but an undercurrent of irrelevant, apparently inadvertent sexual revelation. It seemed that editing, especially *New Yorker* editing, would have caught this tendency at its most awkward and repetitive. It was possible that precisely the columns most nearly out of all control were episodes in a struggle against *The New Yorker's* constraints—not always an unworthy struggle. But there was also, in relation to filmmaking itself, an increasingly strident *knowingness*: Whatever else you may think about her work, each column seemed more hectoringly to claim, *she certainly does know about movies*. And often, when the point appeared most knowing, it was factually false. Ms. Kael, for instance, berated George Roy Hill, at length and in particularly scornful, savvy terms, for having recorded the outdoor sequences of *Butch Cassidy and the Sundance Kid* indoors, in a studio: "Each ... comes out ... in the dead sound of the studio. There is scarcely even an effort to supply plausible outdoor resonances." As it happens, Mr. Hill had insisted on recording outdoors, at great expense and over heavy objections from the studio, which had predicted (accurately, at least as regards Ms. Kael) that no one could tell the difference. When informed of such errors, Ms. Kael never acknowledged or rectified them; she tended rather to drag disparaging references to the work of filmmakers about whom she had been wrong into unrelated columns ever after.

Still, there were often fine columns that could be the work of no one else. When one struck a long bad piece, or a lot of long bad pieces, one could consider them off-weeks, lapses. Moreover, as there had once been fan clubs for movie stars, and then cults of directors and authors, there were, by the late sixties (as reflected even in names featured on movie marquees), cults of movie critics; a critic with a cult is a critic under peculiar stress. Ms. Kael still seemed to feel extremely strongly about most films she reviewed. Somehow, particularly in bland movie times, that seemed a kind of virtue. It hardly occurred to one that holding too many very strong opinions about matters of minor consequence might elsewhere be the virtue of hucksters and demagogues. A semblance of passion enlivened a weekly column. It was possible to think of each off-column as an exception. I, for one, continued to believe that movie criticism was probably in quite good hands with Pauline Kael.

Now, *When the Lights Go Down*, a collection of her reviews over the past five years, is out; and it is, to my surprise and without Kael- or Simon-like exaggeration, not simply, jarringly, piece by piece, line by line, and without interruption, worthless. It turns out to embody something appalling and widespread in the culture. Over the years, that is, Ms. Kael's quirks, mannerisms, tics, and excesses have not only taken over her work so thoroughly that hardly anything else, nothing certainly of intelligence or sensibility, remains; they have also proved contagious, so that the content and level of critical discussion, of movies but also of other forms, have been altered astonishingly for the worse.

To the spectacle of the staff critic as celebrity in frenzy, about to "do" something "to" a text, Ms. Kael has added an entirely new style of ad hominem brutality and intimidation. The substance of her work has become little more than an attempt, with an odd variant of flak advertising copy, to coerce, actually to force numb acquiescence, in the laying down of a remarkably trivial and authoritarian party line.

She has, in principle, four things she likes: *frissons* of horror; physical violence depicted in explicit detail; sex scenes, so long as they have an ingredient of cruelty and involve partners who know each other either casually or under perverse circumstances; and fantasies of invasion by, or subjugation of or by, apes, pods, teens, body-snatchers, and extraterrestrials. Whether or not one shares these predilections—and whether they are in fact more than four, or only one—they do not really lend themselves to critical discussion. It turns out, however, that Ms. Kael does think of them as critical positions, and regards it as an act of courage, of moral courage, to subscribe to them. The reason one cannot simply dismiss them as *de gustibus*, or even as harmless aberration, is that they have become inseparable from the repertory of devices of which Ms. Kael's writing now, almost wall to wall, consists.

She has an underlying vocabulary of about nine favorite words, which occur several hundred times, and often several times per page, in this book of nearly six hundred pages: "whore" (and its derivatives "whorey," "whorish," "whoriness"), applied in many contexts, but almost never to actual prostitution; "myth," "emblem" (also "mythic," "emblematic"), used with apparent intellectual intent, but without ascertainable meaning; "pop," "comic-strip," "trash" ("trashy"), "pulp" ("pulpy"), all used judgmentally (usually approvingly) but otherwise apparently interchangeable with "mythic"; "urban poetic," meaning marginally more violent than "pulpy"; "soft" "(pejorative); "tension," meaning, apparently, any desirable state; "rhythm," used often as a verb, but meaning harmony or speed; "visceral"; and "level." These words may be used in any variant, or in alternation, or strung together in sequence—"visceral poetry of pulp," for example, or "mythic comic-strip level"—until they become a kind of incantation.

She also likes words ending in "ized" ("vegetabilized," "robotized," "aestheticized," "utilized," "mythicized"), and a kind of slang ("twerpy," "dopey," "dumb," "grungy," "horny," "stinky," "drip," "stupes," "crud"), which amounts, in prose, to an affectation of straightforwardness.

I leave aside for the moment Ms. Kael's incessant but special use of words many critics use a lot: "we," "you," "they," "some people"; "needs," "feel," "know," "ought"—as well as her two most characteristic grammatical constructions: "so/that" or "such/that," used not as a mode of explication or comparison (as in, for example, he was so lonely that he wept) but as an entirely new hype connective between two unrelated or unformulated thoughts; and her unprecedented use, many times per page and to new purposes, of the mock rhetorical question and the question mark.

Because what is most striking is that she has, over the years, lost any notion of the legitimate borders of polemic. Mistaking lack of civility for vitality, she now substitutes for argument a protracted, obsessional invective—what amounts to a staff cinema critic's branch of est. Her favorite, most characteristic device of this kind is the ad personam physical (she might say, visceral) image: images, that is, of sexual conduct, deviance, impotence, masturbation; also of indigestion, elimination, excrement. I do not mean to imply that these images are frequent, or that one has to look for them. They are relentless, inexorable. "Swallowing this movie," one finds on page 147, "is an unnatural act." On page 151, "his way of pissing on us." On page 153, "a little gas from undigested Antonioni." On page 158, "these constipated flourishes." On page 182, "as forlornly romantic as Cyrano's plume dipped in horse manure." On page 226, "the same brand of sanctifying horse manure." On page 467, "a new brand of pop manure." On page 120, "flatulent seriousness." On page 226, "flatulent Biblical-folk John Ford film." On page 353, "gaseous naïveté." And elsewhere, everywhere, "flatulent," "gaseous," "gasbag," "makes you feel a little queasy," "makes you gag a little," "Just a belch from the Nixon era," "you can't cut through the crap in her," "plastic turds."

Of an actress, "She's making love to herself"; of a screenwriter, "He's turned it on himself; he's diddling his own talent." "It's tumescent-filmmaking." "Drama and politics don't climax together." Sometimes, one has the illusion that these oral, anal, or just physical epithets have some meaning—"*Taxi Driver* is a movie in heat," for instance, or "the film is an icebag." But then: "*Coma* is like a prophylactic." One thinks, How, how is it like a prophylactic? "It's so cleanly made." Or a metaphor with a sadistic note that defies, precisely, physical comprehension. "The movie has had a spinal tap."

The degree of physical sadism in Ms. Kael's work is, so far as I know, unique in expository prose. What is remarkable, however, is how often, as a matter of technique, she *imputes* it. She writes, in one review, that a female character regards another female character as "a worm for squishing"; in another review, that a male character sees another male character as "a trivial whitey to be squished"; in a third review, of a female character, that "she'd crunch your heart to clean a pore"—without perhaps being aware that all the squishing and crunching attributed to characters, actors, anyone, is entirely her own idea.

"You half expect her to shove that little bug away and stamp on him," she writes, in yet another review, of Candice Bergen. More in a moment about who that "you" might be; but the tactic is perfect.

"You" have a violent expectation. Ms. Bergen would "shove" and "stamp on" the "little bug" (another actor). While Ms. Kael is just out there, writing it all down.

"You want to wipe it off his face." "You want to kick him." Your "guts are squeezed." Guts appear a lot, in noun, verb, or adjective form: "The film's discreet, gutted sensitivity," for instance, "is self-sufficient." What?

"You are caught up emotionally and flung about the room." Thirty pages later, "we" are caught "by the throat" and "knocked about the room." All this, of course, is standard, blurb copy. What is less usual is the attention to a specific limb or organ: the "maggot in his brain"; the filmmakers who "should stop lighting candles in their skulls, they're burning their brains out"; the "punishment in the sinuses," "punched too often in the vocal cords," "vocal cords...you might think...had survived a rock slide." All right, still in the realm of the usual, routine. But then, a pure Kaelism. Having described a scene in which a character "holds her hand over a fire until it is charred and bursts," still apparently unsatisfied, Ms. Kael adds this joke: "(Did Altman run out of marshmallows?)"

I do not mean to suggest that this style, this cast of mind, is pathological—only that it is not just idiosyncratic, either. It has become part of a pattern, an instrument to a purpose—quite remote by now from criticism or even films. Another such instrument is the mock rhetorical question, the little meditation with the question mark. In this book, there are literally thousands of them, not just of the jokey, marshmallow sort, but of every sort, in tirades and fusillades, in and outside parentheses. An apparently limitless capacity to inquire:

> Could it be that he's interiorizing his emotions, in response to Schrader's conception of the emptiness of Jerry's life, and doesn't realize how little he's putting out?

> Has he been schooling himself in late Dreyer and Bresson and Rossellini, and is he trying to turn Thackeray's picaresque entertainment into a religious exercise?

Yet can we be meant to laugh at his satisfaction with his own virulence after we've seen Florence Malraux's name on the credits as assistant to the director, and remembered that Resnais is the son-in-law of André Malraux, who died a few months ago after a long illness?

(Is Cimino invoking the mythology of Hawkeye and the great chief Chingachook?)

Is it just the pompadour or is he wearing a false nose?

How can the novelist have pain in his bowels when *Providence* has no bowels?

Have you ever bought a statue of a pissing cupid?

Were these 435 prints processed in a sewer?

Didn't Alda recognize that his material is like kapok?

Why doesn't he hear her voice first . . . and be turned on by it? And wouldn't he then look to see whom it belonged to? And does she know who he is when she bawls him out? And if she does wouldn't this affect how she speaks to him? And if she doesn't when is the moment she finds out?

Why are we getting these union speeches now? Were the outsiders directing the strike? Were the pros working out strategy? Have we been conned? Have people become so accustomed? . . .

Why didn't anyone explain to him that he needn't wear himself out with acting?

Why is Doc in an unholy alliance with the Nazi villain, Szell?

Shouldn't the movie be about *why* he imagines what he does?

Who is this hitchhiker on the road of life?

Allied Artists and Bantam Books, why are you doing this?

(Is it relevant that Bertolucci's father's name was Attilio?)

How can you have any feeling for a man who doesn't enjoy being in bed with Sophia Loren?

How can the Count's arrival and his plea for a hasty marriage have any vibrations?

Why then does it offend me when I think about it?

And what is Sally doing when she holds out her arms to her husband?

Where was the director?

Does the cavalry return?

Who—him?

You shouldn't risk losing thoughts like that. Has the tape recorder been stored in a safe place?

But, oh, God, why isn't it better? Why isn't there the daring and the exaltation that our senses fairly cry out for?

And so on.

It is difficult to convey the effect of hundreds of pages of these questions. Those that have answers—Yes. No. What? I don't know, sweetie; you're the one who saw the movie—badger the reader, who is courteously inclined to *think* when addressed with question marks, into a mindless, degrading travesty of colloquy or dialectic. Others are coy, convoluted displays of erudition. Ms. Kael wants us to know, for instance, that she knows that Resnais is related to Malraux, and that Malraux is dead; also, that she knows the first name of Bertolucci's father. Others still, addressed, like script-margin annotations, to the film itself ("Shouldn't the movie be about *why*, etc.?"), are proprietary, prescriptive. Ms. Kael, having lost any notion of where the critic sits, wants to imply that she was at the story conference, that the film is somehow hers. And others still, in particular the outcries—to God, and Allied Artists and Bantam Books—are meant to demonstrate that she *cares*, cares more than anybody. It is overwhelmingly clear, however, from the reviews in this book, that one thing Ms. Kael has ceased to care about is films.

She hardly praises a movie any more, so much as she derides and inveighs against those who might disagree with her about it. ("Have you ever bought a statue of a pissing cupid?") And, like the physical assaults and sneers, the mock rhetorical questions are rarely *saying* anything. They are simply doing something. Bullying, presuming, insulting, frightening, enlisting, intruding, dunning, rallying. The most characteristic of these questions, in its way, is the one about Alan Alda and the kapok. Had it been phrased declaratively—Alda doesn't recognize that his material is like kapok—it would still be uninteresting; but it might raise a question of its own. How, in what sense, is it like kapok? (In the same way, perhaps, as *Coma* is like a prophylactic?) Or if the question had been, at least, addressed to Alda—Alda (God, Bantam Books), didn't you recognize that your material is like kapok?—it would be clear what is being asked. I would point out, however, that the question (which permits only a yes or no) is still so framed as to compel assent: Yes, I did recognize; No, I didn't recognize, etc. But to address the question to the *reader* effectively conceals what is being said (namely, nothing), and attempts to enlist him in a constituency, a knowing constituency—

knowing, in this instance, about Alda's ignorance about this nothing. The same with "Why didn't anyone explain to him that he needn't wear himself out with acting?" and all the other trivial, inane interrogations. They express what are not views or perceptions, but blunt devices to marshal a constituency—of readers, other reviewers, filmmakers if at all possible—which has, in turn, no views but a coerced, fearful, or bemused falling in line.

I do not mean for a moment to imply that every Kael review is in the vituperative or inquisitional mode. There are meditations of all kinds and, quite often, broad cultural allusions:

> The images are simplified, down to their dramatic components, like the diagrams of great artists' compositions in painting texts, and this, plus the faintly psychedelic Romanesque color, creates a pungent viselike atmosphere.

A word heap, surely. The quality of observation may be characteristic of people who insist that films be discussed in *visual* terms. I am not certain that Ms. Kael has a clear idea what a "Romanesque color" might be, particularly in the "faintly psychedelic" spectrum, and even in the most "pungent, viselike atmosphere"; but I'd like to stay for a moment, in two simpler sentences, with the visual, the cinematic eye.

On page 398, there is an "upper lip pulling back in a snarl" to reveal "yellow teeth like a crumbling mountain range." On 436, on the other hand, there are "jagged lower teeth that suggest a serpent about to snap." Now, the vision, it's true, is consistent. But surely the mouths are peculiarly observed, or both the mountain range and the serpent are upside down.

There are allusions as well to literature. Ms. Kael likes to mention Dostoevsky, Tolstoy, and Shakespeare's fools. "It's like a classic passage in Tolstoy," she writes, and before one can wonder Really? Which? she has dropped the subject. "We're given the components of a novel at a glance," she writes elsewhere, and fortunately drops that, too. But then:

It's true that one remembers the great scenes from the nineteenth-century Russian novels, not the passages in between; but...there's a consistency of vision in Turgenev or Dostoevski or Tolstoy.

One pauses. Can it be that there is actually a thought coming? Yes. It's this:

We're told what we want to know.

I'll spare you further references to literature and Tolstoy. I'll skip most of the recurrent, indescribable reflections on "art" and "artists": "When artists are raging, straining to express themselves," or "If De Palma were an artist in another medium." Their intellectual content ranges from "An artist can draw a lot of energy from obsessive material"—unarguable, certainly, and not carried further—to this baffling Kaelism: "They are not plagued by the problem of bourgeois artists. They have loose foreskins."

Historically, it is hard to know what to make of the little italicized *eureka* in "Truffaut is romantic *and* ironic"; "romantic irony" occurs so early and often in any liberal education. But even in the cultural province she claims most confidently as her own, Ms. Kael can go puzzlingly astray. When she calls *King Kong* "marvelous Classics-comics," for instance, it seems almost pedantic to recall that Classics Comics were, in fact, condensations of classic books, the Bible, say, or her beloved Tolstoy, not at all the genre that she seems to have in mind. As for allusions to racial or social developments, they tend to take a jokey form. "He's an equal opportunity fornicator."

There are also, however, ruminations of the highest order:

For those who are infatuated with what they loathe the battle with themselves never stops.

Too true. Several reviews later:

And when your slavemaster is your father and he wants to kill you for your defiance that defiance must kill everything you've ever known.

Perhaps less true.

I'd like to say here that I didn't expect to find this, and I wasn't looking for it. I now think that no one has looked at the *meaning* of these sentences, or at their intellectual quality, in many years. I have also postponed, in some ways I would rather have avoided, Ms. Kael's critical characterizations of specific performers and specific films. These are always largely matters of personal taste. In addition, the mere mention these days of a specific movie can distract movie-goers, with the sheer vehemence of widely held opinions, from what is actually being said, and by what methods and techniques. That situation is only partially a result of Ms. Kael's efforts. Most writing about films now contains a degree of overstatement, mean-inglessness, obfuscation. I won't dwell on the advocacy, if that is the word, of Peckinpah, De Palma, Coppola, but turn to very quiet ground:

> In repose, Lily Tomlin looks like a wistful pony; when she grins, her equine gums and long, drawn face suggest a friendly, goofy horse.

I'm not sure this is an insight worth restating, or amplifying, three times in a single sentence ("pony," "equine," "horse"). I am quite sure it is not an insight, it is wrong, to write of the characters in *The Deer Hunter*, that "they're the American cousins of hobbits." Then:

> George C. Scott has to be dominating or he's nothing.

It's hard to know what to respond—except *Petulia*. Maybe Ms. Kael thought he was "nothing" in that film. Certainly, he was not "dominating" in it. Or:

In *Nashville*, Keith Carradine's voice insinuates itself; that tremolo makes it seem as if he were singing just to you.

This, I submit, is no longer a matter of doubt. The whole point of what was probably the most beautifully thought-out and acted scene in *Nashville*, and perhaps in any movie since, was that Carradine could have been singing to nobody but Lily Tomlin. Each of the female characters who mistakenly believed that he was singing to her—not, however, because of any tremolo, but because he had slept with her—was portrayed as smugly but touchingly obtuse. Each soon recognized that he was singing to somebody else—again, not on the basis of his tremolo but from the direction of his stare.

The only reason this matters in the slightest is that if any "you" would be led by Carradine's voice to the mistake made by specific female characters in that scene in *Nashville*, then there is no reason why those specific characters, and they alone, should have made it. The scene utterly loses its point.

About *Coming Home*:

Later, we watch her face during her orgasm with Luke; this scene is the dramatic center of the movie. The question in the viewer's mind is, What will she feel when her husband comes home and they go to bed? Will she respond, and if she does, how will he react?

No one, I think, would disagree with Ms. Kael that the scene is the dramatic center of the movie; but it seems just as clear that one question that is *not* in the viewer's mind is the one (or the two) Ms. Kael suggests. The question, if any, is another one, which has persisted almost from the movie's start, and which Ms. Kael would have seemed uniquely designed, by temperament, to spot: What is it that Luke, the paraplegic, does in making love? This essentially clinical question is one that the movie deliberately suggests and then, I believe, dishonestly blurs throughout. Be that as it may, I don't think a viewer in the world has in mind in that scene the question Ms. Kael ascribes to him. I happen not to have liked the movie, either. But, given the physical circumstances, I don't think even Ms. Kael could have taken a cheaper shot, or one less apposite, than the last line of her review: "Are liberals really such great lovers?"

Let's leave all that. Let's leave her unusually many uses of the form so/that, such/that—from "so haughty that her name should be 'Anastasia,'" "so endearing...that he should be billed as Richard 'Cuddles' Dreyfuss," "so grasping that the film should be called 'Tentacles,'" through this sort of meander-hype connective:

> ...so eerily sensitive that your mind may easily drift to the terrible (true) accounts of how people on the street sometimes laughed at Virginia Woolf.

> ...so lusciously, ripely beautiful in her peach-blond wig that her trained, accomplished acting suggests an intelligent form of self-respect.

Let's leave aside her humor: "you feel she needs a derrick to lift her lids"; "each repositioning of her features requires the services of a derrick"; "you fight to keep your eyes open"; "people were fighting to stay awake"; "but after a while I was gripping the arms of my chair to stay awake"; "the audience was snoring"; "the only honest sound I heard...was the snoring in the row behind me," etc. Let's leave even her favorite deep/surface dichotomy, or paradox, or whatever she thinks it is: a director, "deep on the surface"; a film, "deep on the surface"; "deep without much surface excitement"; "rough on the surface but slick underneath." Let's leave aside, in short, all the relatively harmless mannerisms and devices.

A more important, related stratagem recurs constantly in her work, and by no means in hers alone. I don't know how to characterize it, except as the hack carom—taking, that is, something from *within* the film and, with an air of triumph, turning it *against* the film or a performer. "Gere looks like Robert De Niro without the mole on his cheek," for instance, "but there's more than that missing." More than the mole. About a scene with a burning candle, "someone should have taken a lighted wick to [the scenarist's] ideas." About an actor's expression within a role, "His face is stricken with grief and humiliation; that should be [his] face for what [the writer and director] do to him." About a scene of begging for absolution, that the writer and director "ought to be the ones kneeling in penance." Ms. Kael revels in this sort of thing. The only reason the device has any significance is the unpleasant, even punitive overtone—the notion that a film or a performer is not merely undistinguished, or unimportant, or untalented, but actually *guilty* of something. The image of filmmakers penitent is particularly congenial to her work. She speaks often, in this carom mode, of being "betrayed" and of what she (or "we") can or cannot "forgive." ("A viewer could probably forgive everything that went wrong"; "the script seems like a betrayal, of them, and of us.")

Films and performers may be guilty. They may or may not be absolved. Audiences are also at risk. People who do not share, for example, her infatuation with the more extreme forms of violence are characterized as "repressive," "acting out of fear, masked as taste," "turned philistine," "trying to protect themselves from their own violence," "surely with terror and prurient churnings underneath?" "What may be behind all this," she actually writes at one point, "is repression of the race issue." An occasional film may be forgiven (really) as "not the sort of failure you write an artist off for." But those fearful, repressive, philistine, secretly violent, racist, prurient people in the audience are not going to be forgiven until they come around.

Which brings me to the "we," "you," "they," "some people"; "needs," "feel," "know," "ought"—also to a structural mechanism I have seen in no other writer's work. The structural mechanism first. Although it is true that Ms. Kael can hardly resist a restatement, or a repetition, or a meaningless amplification ("ditsey little twitches," "ruthless no soul monsters"; "incomprehensible bitch," "obnoxious smartass"); although she seems at times to have a form of prose hypochondria, palpating herself all over to see if she has a thought, and publishing every word of the process by which she checks to see whether or not she has one; it is also, equally, true that she can hardly resist any form of hyperbole, superlative, exaggeration: "poisonously mediocre," "wickedest baroque sensibility at large in America."

These predispositions—to restate and to overstate—make it all the more curious structurally that Ms. Kael withholds until the sixth long paragraph of one review the words "it's Jack Nicholson's best performance"; to the middle of the third paragraph of another the claim that Sophia Loren "has never looked more richly beautiful or given such a completely controlled great-lady performance"; to late in the fourth paragraph of yet another that Laurence Olivier "has the power to find something he's never done before, in any role"; and to so unobtrusive a place that I could hardly find it when I looked for it again, the word that Paul Newman "gives the performance of his life—to date." Now, it's true, as I have remarked, that Ms. Kael rarely spares us an afterthought, or a forethought. But the structural reason for reserving these superlatives until so late in a piece becomes clear from the last example. Paul Newman's "performance of his life—to date" was in *Slap Shot*. A film directed by George Roy Hill (whom she had mistakenly accused of failing to trouble to record *Butch Cassidy and the Sundance Kid* outdoors). What is operating here is the structure of spite.

"We" and "you" can occur, of course, in any writer's work, in moderation. For the first two hundred pages, it seems that Ms. Kael means a sort of scolding nanny "we," or a flirting schoolmarm's, or a nondirective therapist's, or a tour guide's, or a prison matron's. Consistent with the nanny, miffed, are remarks like, "She consented, but I was offended for her"; "I can't help feeling that the audience is being insulted, although the audience doesn't think so." Also the repeated threats of what will happen "if" an actor, or a director, or a film "doesn't pull" him or itself "together." But then, there is something so pervasive and remorseless in that "we"—"we want," "we resent," "we feel," "we're desperate for," "we don't know how to react," "we know too well what we're supposed to feel," "we want it, just as we wanted," "we all *know*"—that the "we" becomes a bandwagon, a kangaroo court, a gang, an elite, a congregation, which readers had better join, or else be consigned to that poor group of deviants, sissies, aesthetic and moral idiots who comprise "some people," "many people," "a lot of people," "those people," "they."

"You," normally, is the individuated "we." "You may wonder, Are these boys being naughty because they're old enough not to be?" "You feel that some of your brain cells are being knocked out." "You want the director to stop all the nonsense." Sometimes, the "you" seems the subject of a hypnotist: "You feel that you understand everything that's going on"; "You don't feel embarrassed by anything that Clint Eastwood does." But "you" is most often Ms. Kael's "I," or a member or prospective member of her "we." As for "feel," "needs," and "know," Ms. Kael uses "feel" variously, but most fervently in the emotional sense. She has, however, an odd view of what "emotion" is: "the one basic emotion he needs to show—sexual avidity." So I'm not always certain what she means by "feel." "Needs": "He needs a little Terry Southern in his soul." "Jimmy needs to be an exciting, violent, emotional man . . . the pianist/gangster split as a heightened, neurotic metaphor for Everyman—a Dostoevskian Everyman." "Know": A film "doesn't seem to know that that's its theme"; a director "doesn't seem to know what actors are for"; but "we all know" quite a lot of things; and "James Mason knows. God, does he know." "Know" also often goes with a sort of culinary "needs"; "The film doesn't seem to know that it needs a little playful sado-masochistic chemistry." I think I'll just skip "ought."

Ms. Kael's work has been praised as "great . . . a body of criticism which can be compared with Shaw's" (*Times Literary Supplement*). She has won a National Book Award. So far as I know, apart from a personal statement by Andrew Sarris, which appeared in the *Village Voice* as this piece was going to press, the book has received uniformly favorable reviews. *The New Republic* describes it as consisting of "all peaks and no valleys." A Kaelism, surely. None of this is Ms. Kael's fault. It is only symptomatic. The pervasive, overbearing, and presumptuous "we," the intrusive "you," the questions, the debased note of righteousness and rude instruction—the whole verbal apparatus promotes, and relies upon, an incapacity to read. The writing falls somewhere between huckster copy (paeans to the favored product, diatribes against all other brands and their venal or deluded purchasers) and ideological pamphleteering: denouncings, exhortations, code words, excommunications, programs, threats. Apart from the taste for violence, however, which she takes to be a hard, intellectual position, there is no underlying text or theory. Only the review, virtually divorced from movies, as its own end:

> If there is one immutable law about movies it may be that middle-class people get hot and bothered whenever there's a movie that the underclass really responds to.

No matter that the sentence is clearly false. (Think of *Shaft*, for instance.) No matter even that "one immutable law" manages wonderfully to combine Kaeline authoritarianism with Kaeline hype. The sentence is plainly inconsistent with what Ms. Kael writes elsewhere—when it is the elitist mode that suits her: the "mass audience" she derides frequently; the audience she "couldn't help feeling...was being insulted, although the audience doesn't think so"; the "many people," of whom she writes, in yet another piece, who "resist quality" because "they're afraid of being outclassed." All that the one immutable law about movies amounts to is that Ms. Kael will not brook disagreement. Personally. And not just with her enthusiasms—which might be a form of generosity in a critic. Also, more vehemently, with her revenges and dislikes. "Did these people stand up and cheer to get their circulation going again?" she writes of even the smallest film she fears might become a hit. She likes to ban.

Three last quotations, as another kind of symptom:

> It's quite possible that [he]...wasn't fully conscious that in several sequences he was coming mortifyingly close to plagiarism.

> It's as crude as if [he] had said, "Things were really bad in Berlin in '23," and, asked "How bad?," he had replied, "They were so bad even a black man couldn't get it up."

> Paul Schrader may like the idea of prostituting himself more
> than he likes making movies.... (For Schrader to call himself
> a whore would be vanity: he doesn't know how to turn a trick.)

Now, it doesn't matter whom these quotations are "about"—although the middle one concerns Ingmar Bergman. They are not "about" anything. Each marks a kind of breakthrough in vulgarity and unfairness. Look at the "It's quite possible" in the first, and the "mortifyingly." Look at the "as if" in the second, and the "even." Consider, in the third, the "would be." All three involve a perfectly groundless imputation to another (plagiarism, racism, corruption) and a pious personal recoil (mortifyingly, crude, vain). The strategy is characteristic of Ms. Kael's work. I can hardly imagine a reader who would sit through another line.

Cumulatively and in book form, these reviews have an effect different from anything that was even intimated on a weekly or desultory basis. It occurred to me when I had read a few hundred pages that the book assumes an audience composed partly of people who know nothing about the movies, and partly of people who read only film reviews. Accept the claim that she *cares*, and/or remember that it's only a movie; and there's no need to pay attention to the rest. But what I think has happened is this: an extreme case of what can go wrong with a staff critic. Prose events that would, under ordinary circumstances and on any subject other than movies, have been regarded as lapses—the sadism, slurs, inaccuracies, banalities, intrusions—came to be regarded as Ms. Kael's strong suit. Ms. Kael grew proud of them. Her cult got hooked on them. Readers generally skipped over them. There was always the impression, unfounded but widely held (I held it), of liveliness. And it was not clear how radical an imposition each mannerism and device would become when the reviews appeared weekly, and with a strong institutional base.

The New Yorker, as it happens, is an institution of unique civility and patience, dedicated absolutely, although it may not always look that way, to leaving writers free to write what, and at what length, they choose. In recent years, it was having insuperable problems with its other movie critic. Editors of weekly magazines, moreover, work—no less than staff critics—under the pressures of a deadline. The result is that, of practical though not spiritual necessity, staff critics have special institutional support. *The New Yorker* could not devote its energies, every week, to a bitter struggle over movie columns—which, incidentally, were growing so long that other pieces, on which serious intermittent writers had worked for years, were being overwhelmed.

With intermittent writers, when there is a disagreement, a piece can always be postponed. In this way, of course, editors can exert strong, legitimate pressure. It may be your piece; but it's their magazine. With a staff critic, that mild form of blackmail is reversed. Editors cannot, professionally, often postpone a weekly piece. So *The New Yorker* had either to fire Ms. Kael (which would, for many reasons, including the problems with the other critic, have been a mistake; anyway, *The New Yorker* doesn't fire people) or accommodate her work. The conditions of unique courtesy, literacy, and civility, of course, were what Ms. Kael was most inclined by temperament to test. The excesses got worse.

Then an odd thing happened: Ms. Kael went out to Hollywood. For a critic preoccupied with metaphors for selling out, this seemed an extraordinary move. The *New York Times*, for instance, is so acutely aware of the possibilities for conflict of interest in film reviewing that it forbids its critic to write screenplays. When Ms. Kael returned from Hollywood, I, among others, felt strongly that *The New Yorker* should take her back. I hadn't read this collection. She was the critic people knew and talked about. I believed she was lively and that she cared. Anyway, in her absence, it had become clear that nobody else at *The New Yorker* wanted to be the staff movie critic. She did come back.

She writes as she has written these past five years, but at least her column is no longer weekly. Criticism will get over it. Once the tone and the ante, however, have been pumped up to this awful frenzy, it becomes hard—even in reviewing Ms. Kael's work—to write in any other way; or, in the typographic clamor, to detect and follow a genuine critical argument. What really is at stake is not movies at all, but prose and the relation between writers and readers, and of course art.

The New York Review of Books
August 14, 1980

THE JUSTICES AND THE JOURNALISTS

OF ALL writing in this society, the writing of courts—in particular, the Supreme Court—has the most immediate powers and consequences. Men go to jail or are released, great corporate structures are dissolved or left intact, laws are upheld or overturned, men regulate their future conduct on the basis of what judges write. Most writing, of course, aspires to be or to appear original, to tell something new. This is true in scholarship and art. It is especially true, almost by definition, of journalism, where what is old, self-evident, or well-known is simply not the news. The writing of judges, however, aspires to just the opposite effect. Perhaps because of its unique powers, judicial writing rests very largely on citing precedents, on saying: What we say today is more or less what we have always said, or should have said; it's what our citizens have tacitly agreed; it's what the Constitution meant; it's obvious. Every Court decision clearly contains some new element, or there would be no need to make it. What creativity there is, however, goes mainly into saying why it ought to come as no surprise.

When serious investigative reporters confront the Court, there is thus a profound clash of aspirations. It is compounded, for Bob Woodward and Scott Armstrong in *The Brethren: Inside the Supreme Court*, by another problem. The Court, more than any other public institution, explains itself, identifies its sources. A dictator can say: This is the law because I say it is. A journalist can say: These are the facts and I need not tell who told me so. The Court says: This is the law as applied to facts ascertained in a public forum, and, under our system, we are obliged to tell you why. To attempt, as Woodward and Armstrong have done, to go behind the Court's explanations over a period of six terms (1969 to 1975), and to find insights, or even secrets, of any importance whatsoever is an enormously ambitious undertaking. There are intimations, as early as page one of their introduction, that the authors may not be ideally equipped for it.

"And because its members are not subject to periodic reelection, but are appointed for life," they write, "the Court is less disposed to allow its decision making to become public."

Now, however long you may study that sentence, and whether or not you are a lawyer, you will realize that the connection between its two facts—if they are facts, if there is a connection—cannot be "because." If there were a connection, it would more logically be "although." But there is no connection. And looked at more closely, the two facts linked by that "because" are not quite facts. It is true that all federal judges are normally and constitutionally appointed "for life." The Constitution just happens to phrase it "during good Behavior." This distinction might seem unimportant—were it not that the authors later devote pages to efforts made to impeach Justices Douglas and Fortas. There could have been no such efforts if Justices were so simply and unequivocally appointed not during good Behavior but for life. And, since the "decision making" of Justices is, in the most obvious sense, precisely what *is* public, the authors can be alluding only to the Justices'—and, now, the clerks'—reticence about what goes on in conference (where clerks are not present) or in chambers.

What the authors promise, however, and not just in their subtitle, "Inside the Supreme Court," is revelations per se, disclosure of secrets on a grand, even unprecedented scale. Their information, they claim, is "based on interviews with more than 200 people, including several Justices, more than 170 former law clerks, and several dozen former employees of the Court."

A question immediately suggests itself. The custom of protecting the identity of sources, in daily journalism at least, has become extremely widespread. I happen to believe that, except when actual, identifiable harm would result, to the source or to some other worthy cause or person, that practice can be unprofessional, a serious impediment to journalism of all kinds. It makes stories almost impossible to verify. It suppresses a major element of almost every investigative story: who wanted it known.

But even if the identity of sources ought, almost invariably, to be protected, is there any tradition of reporting which requires that their *number* be protected as well? "More than 200 people," "several Justices," "more than 170 law clerks," "several dozen former employees." Well, how many? Two hundred and one people or 299? Three Justices, or five? What in the name of journalism would be compromised if we knew?

By the next page, we learn that the authors had "filled eight file drawers with thousands of pages of documents from the chambers of 11 of the 12 Justices" who served in the period under investigation. Then there is an apotheosis: "In *virtually every* instance [of what, they do not say] we had *at least one, usually two,* and *often three or four* reliable sources in the chambers of each Justice" (italics added). Apart from an occasion to smuggle that word "reliable" into what appears to be a quantitative statement, what can these vague enumerations mean? They mean that, at least as regards number, the authors prefer their own pointless secret (how many) and implications of massiveness to precise statements of simple fact.

A related preference appears in more trivial contexts: "'No way,' Justice Rehnquist shot back, adding a mild obscenity for emphasis." By this point in the book, page 395, the authors have attributed to one Justice or another almost every obscenity I know. Are the identities of even "mild obscenities" now to be protected? Eight Justices were allegedly in the room when Justice Rehnquist said whatever it was, so there can be no question of needing to protect a source. But again, the authors prefer a knowing-sounding secret to a simple fact.

Most of the facts in this book, however, are far from simple. I have not meant to imply that this is a light or even unimportant work. It is only that, in this first, extended confrontation—at book length, outside an actual lawsuit—between the Court with its secrets, whatever they are, and investigative journalists with their secrets, such as they are, the journalists' own technique seems unexamined, and often very far from sound.

The Brethren, as it happens, contains no scandals and, although the authors clearly do not know it, no revelations that would astonish any lawyer or other student of the Court. Nonlawyers, I think, will find the book extremely hard to read. Since early in this century, most American law students have been taught in what is called the "case method" by textbooks called "Cases and Materials": essentially very heavy compilations of appellate decisions in Contracts, Torts, Procedure, and so on interspersed with some expository matter by the author/compiler, and even a few questions at the chapter ends. Whatever the pedagogic value of these textbooks, every law student would concede that they are among the world's most boring books. *The Brethren* is, in some ways, Woodward and Armstrong, "Cases and Materials on the Supreme Court." The cases, however, are not appellate judgments but journalists', not lawyers', summaries; and the materials are meditations—and an odd form of gossip that the authors seem to regard as investigative scoops.

The gossip most characteristically takes the form of a declarative sentence about a frame of mind. "Burger was furious." "Harlan was furious." "Brennan was furious." Innumerable paragraphs begin with the information that one Justice or another was "furious," "delighted," "upset," "especially upset," "exceedingly upset," "happy," "not happy," "also unhappy," "disturbed," "worried," "pleased," "not pleased," "both pleased and frightened," "glad," "troubled," "tormented," "elated," "despondent," "overjoyed," "shocked," "as usual more amused than shocked," "once again enraged," "crestfallen," "flabbergasted," and so forth.

Not only do the Justices ride these gusts of mood and feeling; all the more, the clerks. My favorite piece of American judicial history may be the news (page 326) that "Marshall's clerks were miffed."

The book also chronicles less subjective states of mind: realizations, for example; also vows. "Burger vowed to himself that he would grasp the reins of power immediately." Since the authors admit that Chief Justice Burger refused all contact with them, it is hard to know how they can write this quite so categorically. Justice Burger may, of course, have confided his vow to someone else, who then anonymously passed on the information that Justice Burger said he had vowed something to himself. But it is precisely the weakness of this kind of journalism that, because there is no way to check almost any of its assertions, the journalists themselves are sooner or later drawn into some piece of irresponsibility or idiocy; and one has to read every one of their assertions, from the most trivial to the most momentous, with the caveat "if true." Justice Burger "vows" again, 312 pages later, this time "to his clerks." The content of that vow: "that he would hold his ground." As for realizations. "When Nixon was informed of the investigation, he realized," they actually write, "that Fortas' actions were perhaps criminal and perhaps not."

In fairness to the authors, one ought to raise the possibility that the above sentence reflects editing by lawyers—not good lawyers certainly, not constitutional lawyers but lawyers who did not think Justice Fortas a "public figure" within the meaning of *New York Times v. Sullivan*, and who also thought, rather incredibly, that a libel, if libel there was, would evaporate with the addition of two "perhapses" and one "not." There arises, then, the question of *The Brethren* and the law—which the authors treat confidently, seriously, and at length. In small things and in large, with surprising frequency, they get it wrong. They don't seem to know, for example, the difference between appeal and certiorari, or even what an appeal is. This leads them to major misstatements in their first explanation of the steps by which the Court decides to take a case: "1. The decision to take the case requires that the Court note its jurisdiction or formally grant cert. Under the Court's procedures, the Justices have discretion in selecting which cases they will consider." The second sentence is plain wrong. The Justices have such discretion only when the issue is whether to grant cert; they do not have that discretion when a case comes to them on appeal. The first sentence, of course, does not mention appeal.

There are small matters: Justice Douglas, for example, confined to a hospital bed, asking another Justice to be his "*best friend* [authors' italics] and swear out a writ" to get him out. Now the ancient legal locution happens to be "*next* friend"; the only reason, apart from the knowingness implied by those italics, that this is not just a slip too inconsequential to mention is what it implies about the authors' ear for dialogue. In a journalistic enterprise that relies so heavily on a sort of telephone game—Justice, for example, who confides to clerk, who tells reporter—a demonstrably inaccurate ear may be a handicap. It casts doubt particularly on extended conversations that the authors reconstruct, unqualifiedly, in quotes.

As it happens, the way the Justices treat one another's illnesses, aging, reluctant retirements, death is a genuinely moving subtext of the book. The authors, and especially the clerks—because another serious subtext is the patronizing, self-infatuated trivialization, by recent clerks, of the relation of clerkship—have a tendency to reduce the Justices' concern with mortal fallibility to the news that Justice Douglas smelled, in conference, because he had become incontinent.

There are also large, quite complicated mistakes of law, which should startle and confound lawyer and nonlawyer alike. I'll mention just one, before returning to another sort of gossip, which, finally, constitutes the "Materials" of the book. "Moreover, Stewart felt trapped," they write, "by a phrase Rehnquist had convinced him to add to a 1971 opinion (*Roth v. Bd. of Regents*). Though it had seemed harmless to Stewart at the time, the phrase said that due process should be invoked only for rights specifically created by governments."

Roth v. Bd. of Regents came down in 1972, not 1971; but that is not the point. The point is that if Justice Stewart *had* ever written that "due process should be invoked only for rights specifically created by governments," he would have abrogated the Constitution—letter, spirit, and Preamble. Among the truths which the Framers held to be self-evident, the reader will remember, was that certain, emphatically not government-created rights—life, for instance, and liberty—are inalienable. If Justice Stewart had written a phrase to the effect that citizens could, without due process, be deprived of life or liberty, that would be news indeed. Of course, that is not what he wrote. What he wrote was that due process should not be invoked for *property* rights other than those created by government. That view is problematical, controversial, and probably, in spirit, unconstitutional enough. But nothing like what the authors say.

Their discussion of the abortion cases is also, for its length, remarkably askew and superficial; their summary of *Alexander v. Holmes County*—a wonderful case in which the Court reversed a decision of the heroic Fifth Circuit, to that lower court's eternal credit and surprise—shows they have not even a minimal understanding of civil-rights litigation in the South. The reason they cannot address in any depth even the important questions of which they are aware lies in their unusual preoccupation with a very odd kind of gossip: who voted how and when, and whose vote changed; who thought what about whose earlier drafts; but, above all, who liked or disliked whom.

One would have thought the matter of earlier drafts could have been disposed of in a second. No writer, least of all an investigative reporter working on a book, wants to be held accountable for his early drafts. But, "'If an associate in my law firm had done this,' Powell told a clerk [of Chief Justice Burger's draft in a busing case], 'I'd fire him.'" "White thought Blackmun's drafts [in the abortion cases] were dreadful." "Stewart told his clerks that the Chief's initial draft of the decision [in the Nixon tapes case] would have got a grade of D in law school." Hardly anyone, I think, would contend that even the final opinions of the Court very often reflect the work of nine, or even any, distinguished draftsmen. To the caveat "if true" about this sort of news, in short, one is inclined to add "So what?" But Woodward and Armstrong endlessly return to who thought what of drafts.

Another subject that fascinates them is shifting votes. Now it must be obvious, on a moment's reflection, that it is desirable—even essential to the judicial process—that the Justices be able sometimes to persuade one another to change their minds. The authors do have evidence in support of two old and interesting rumors. The first, that Chief Justice Burger often reserves (or repeatedly and perhaps disingenuously changes) his vote, in order to retain the prerogative of assigning a majority opinion, is not too serious. The result, most often, is only that he joins in a majority position more liberal than any he would have taken on his own. The second, that the Chief Justice has tried to alter certain traditions of the Court—to assign from the minority even when he is in the majority; or to permit re-hearing of a case when no member of the deciding majority has voted to rehear—would strike lawyers as more disturbing. Except that, under protest from other Justices, these efforts failed.

More than drafts, however, more than vote changes, the authors are concerned with the popularity, within the Court, of Justices. Their villain is, beyond doubt, Chief Justice Burger. He is character-ized, in terms attributed to other Justices, as "grossly inadequate," "overbearing and offensive," "tasteless," "without substance or integ-rity," "intellectually dishonest," "abrasive," "asinine," a "blustery braggart," and so on. Other Justices are also characterized in terms attributed to their colleagues: Justice Marshall, for instance, as "pet-ulant"; Justice White as "not particularly likeable," "an enigma" who cheats at basketball. But every Associate Justice, according to this book, has something disagreeable to say about the Chief Justice. This may or may not be true. If true (as everyone who has ever worked in an office with even a beloved boss will know), it may or may not have any meaning. But on page 323, in another apotheosis, there may be a kind of clue. "The Justices found themselves entering the clerks' long-standing debate: Was the Chief evil or stupid?"

"The clerks' long-standing debate." There have been countless other clues on this order: "The language remained Blackmun's; the more rigorous analysis was the work of the clerk." "How, Powell asked his clerks, did Marshall turn out such a masterpiece so quickly? The clerks were frank. Marshall's clerk was first rate...."

"The clerks were frank," to the same effect, it seems, quite often. On page 279, this achieves an almost wonderful fatuity. Justice Rehnquist has allegedly brought to conference an issue of the *National Lampoon*, which depicts all members of the Court in obscene postures: Justice Brennan, for instance, opening his robe in front of two little girls; Justice Blackmun sodomizing a kangaroo. Justice Brennan, the authors say, thought he alone was portrayed as innocent. "His clerks decided they owed it to him to explain 'flashing.'" Justice Blackmun claimed not to know what he was supposed to be doing to the kangaroo: "The clerks drew straws to see who would tell him."

Oddly enough, and for reasons of which the authors seem to have no notion, this is the only "Materials" scoop they have: the fact that clerks spoke to them; the precise number who did; the apparent smugness and foolishness of what they said; and the fact that (although they clearly believed otherwise, else why speak to investigative reporters?) the clerks knew no important secrets at all.

The origins of Supreme Court clerkship are recent—the turn of the century. Justices White, Rehnquist, and Stevens are, in fact, the only former Supreme Court clerks to have become Justices. There used to be one clerk per Justice; even in the late years of the Warren Court, when there were two, the relation was close. A clerk was, for a year, an apprentice, a son, research assistant, ghostwriter, friend. His real importance to the Court, if any, was, as a student recently graduated from law school, to bring the views of law faculties to the attention of Justices. Whatever it was, it was a unique and fine relation. Now, with the mushrooming of clerkships (four to each Justice), there is a possibility that they have become a bureaucracy like any other—with confidences to violate, surely; but with fewer secrets, because the Court explains itself, than others have to tell.

The authors' "Materials" scoop, in other words, would have had to do with what has happened to clerks and the relation of clerkship. Their "Cases" scoop, for not unrelated reasons, would have had to do with Justice Rehnquist and his work. As clearly as Chief Justice Burger is their villain, Justice Rehnquist is very much their man. Their inquiry about how he came to be appointed, compared with their discussion of the appointment of other Justices, is remarkably uninquisitive. Here's how he is characterized, however, as a member of the Court: "jolly," "jovial," "sincere," "thoughtful," "remarkably unstuffy," "good natured," "aware of Burger's faults," of "crisp intellect," "diligence," and "friendliness toward clerks," "hard not to like." "Rehnquist and his clerks," the authors typically write of him, "chuckled quite a bit."

It is true that they also quote other Justices to the effect that Justice Rehnquist is "slow even to correct an outright misstatement," that he "misrepresented the legislative history," "twisted the facts," used "disingenuous scholarship," made "misuse of precedents," tried an "underhanded attempt to slip through a major policy shift." But they seem unaware that these adverse characterizations, if true, are of an entirely different order from any others they have made. Even if the clerks did have a "long-standing debate" as to whether the Chief Justice, for instance, was "evil or stupid," that debate, those adjectives, would have no legal or other substance.

The Court, after all, is an ongoing body, committed to the Constitution and its own history. If the Burger Court had allowed certain critical rights to erode (the right, for example, in all criminal trials to a jury of twelve and to a unanimous verdict), it has also (in the first abortion decisions) made some of the most radical and humane judgments in the history of the Court. Even *Alexander v. Holmes County*—in which the *Brown v. Board of Education* integration formula, "all deliberate speed," was superseded altogether by "at once ... now and hereafter"—was hardly ineloquent or unradical. These were, however, questions about which reasonable men, and honorable Justices, might differ. But Justices, whatever their views, are supposed to be committed, in the exercise of their profession, to straight facts and valid precedents in law.

This has nothing to do with ideology. There should, there must, at all times, be conservatives on the Court. But if there were a Justice who did "twist facts," "misrepresent ... history," "misuse precedents," and so on—if there were a Justice somewhat unconcerned not only with what is humane or just (matters, arguably, of rhetoric) but even with what is *apposite*—such a Justice would be fundamentally unserious. If there were a Justice who had few thoughts or even arguments but only positions and strategies (like a teething Jesuit or Talmudic scholar), such a Justice would represent not the judicial mind at all but the legal mind at its most trivial and base—making, in the name of advocacy, arguments that it is precisely the business of the judiciary to cut through. It is possible that the Court has just such an unprecedented casuist in Justice Rehnquist—not a "constructionist" or even a "conservative" at all, except in caricature.

It sometimes seems that if a genuine conservative, of real distinction, were ever on the Court, one would find Justice Rehnquist in dissent.

The authors' partiality for the youngest Justice makes his influence on their book considerable, as considerable in its way as (and analytically more important than) the influence of the clerks. Their error, for instance, about what Justice Stewart wrote in *Roth*—no due process for non-government-created rights, instead of no due process for non-government-created *property* rights—originates, in all probability, with Justice Rehnquist, who (in consistently eliding liberty and property rights) gradually *has* been trying to obscure precisely the distinction Justice Stewart made. In *Arnett v. Kennedy*, which most lawyers would agree was his worst opinion (although the authors cite two others as his "worst"), Rehnquist further managed, by a characteristic piece of analysis, to deprive due process of any meaning—as was noted by his colleagues, including Justices White and Powell, but not by the authors here. In their rapport with the youngest Justice, the authors miss the essence of just such attempts to "slip through a major policy shift."

If the book fails—in its legal analysis, in its efforts to find and disclose important secrets, as an account of the Court in any significant or coherent sense—why is it an important book at all? Because of who the authors are and the very extent of their ambition: *Inside the Supreme Court.*

The relation between the press and the courts, in our society, is rarely devoid of interest. It is an important event in the history of both institutions when highly regarded journalists approach the nation's highest Court. The trouble is, it turns out to be futile to approach the subject in this way. It is not unusual for people to misapprehend the nature of the institution and make more or less misguided approaches to Justices. Chief Justice Burger himself made at least one unjudicial approach, in the matter of the bombing of Cambodia, to President Nixon. This story, however, is not the authors' scoop but Mr. Nixon's, in *RN*.

What does the failure mean? It means that certain techniques, perhaps well suited to investigation of breaking stories of a criminal nature, are entirely unsuited to extended, serious analysis of other matters. The only scoop there could possibly be about an institution as public as the Supreme Court *would* be a revelation of crime or corruption—of which Woodward and Armstrong, at least, found none. It may be that an analytic mind and an integrating theme—an instinct for which facts have meaning, which are meaningless, and which are not even facts—are more suitable than an investigative reporter's sheer persistence, and obsession with keeping (his own) and breaking (others') secrets, to pursuing certain kinds of stories. Most stories—apart from affairs of the military, of crime, and sometimes of the heart—are not, after all, secrets *as such*. Anticipation of this book was high, in journalistic and in legal circles. The Court, with the possible exception of the relation of clerkship, survives—no more nor less public than it ever was. Investigative reporting, perhaps, might think again.

New York Times Book Review
December 16, 1979

THE EXTREME NOMINEE

THE WORDS "strict constructionist," "judicial restraint," "judicial deference," "original intent," "laissez-faire," and even "conservative" have acquired in recent years at least three entirely distinct sets of meanings. In one, which is traditional and legitimate, the words accurately characterize the views of almost all serious constitutional scholars, and of all honorable and competent federal judges—whose work is, after all, not merely bound but defined by a solemn oath to uphold and apply the Constitution. In another, the words are mere code or buzzwords, used almost mindlessly and without meaning but with highly polemical intent; that is, to characterize the views one holds or wishes to applaud, and to disparage all opposing views with yet another, accusatory buzzword: "judicial activist." Finally, the same words have been appropriated by holders of views so extreme, so coercive, so intrusive, and so radically at odds with tradition, with legal precedent, and with the whole text, history, structure, and meaning of the Constitution that they serve actively to conceal rather than to express positions, and have come to mean their precise and Orwellian opposites. In modern political history, this sort of transformation is not at all unusual. The most extreme agendas and regimes often adopt the terms of legitimacy and moderation.

When President Reagan announced his nomination of Judge Robert Bork, of the Court of Appeals for the District of Columbia Circuit, to the seat on the Supreme Court that had been vacated by Justice Lewis Powell, news publications and spokesmen of every

Originally titled "Notes and Comment" in The Talk of the Town

kind used that vocabulary of "strict constructionism," "judicial restraint," "judicial deference," "original intent," "laissez-faire," and
"conservative" as though it applied especially, or at all, to issues now
posed for the Senate by that nomination. This was not surprising.
President Reagan, Attorney General Edwin Meese, and Judge Bork
himself had used that vocabulary to characterize the positions of the
nominee. They were also trying to frame the terms of the debate for
all three constituencies of those words—the legitimate, the polemical, and the ideologically extreme to a degree almost unprecedented
in the history of the American federal courts. This left most people
who had not actually read Judge Bork's published articles and his
opinions, both for the Court and in dissent, uncertain of and not
overly worried by which set of meanings was intended.

The Supreme Court for more than two decades has been in no
sense and by no stretch of the imagination a radical or a liberal, or
even a Democratic, court. On the day Justice Powell announced his
resignation, the Court consisted of two Justices appointed by Democrats and seven appointed by Republicans. Justices Powell, William Rehnquist, and Harry Blackmun were appointed by Richard
Nixon, Justices Sandra Day O'Connor and Antonin Scalia by Ronald Reagan. Justice John Paul Stevens was appointed by Gerald
Ford, Justice William Brennan by Dwight Eisenhower.

Justice Byron White, who was appointed by John Kennedy, has
voted so consistently with Justice Rehnquist on what has been until
now the right wing of the Court that he is no longer mentioned as a
swing, or even a moderate, vote. Justice Thurgood Marshall, who
was appointed by Lyndon Johnson, is the sole liberal Democratic
appointee.

It is this Court, and its continuity with its predecessors in almost
every major decision upholding an individual constitutional right
against the powers of the state, over a period of more than thirty
years—going back to *Brown v. Board of Education* and beyond—
that Judge Bork has repeatedly and consistently accused of deciding
"lawlessly" and "without principle," and of "creating rights," and of

imposing "value choices" and "preferences," and of "lacking candor," and of being "unprincipled," and of producing a line of precedents "as improper" and "as intellectually empty" as *Griswold v. Connecticut*—a 1965 case in which the Court upheld a married couple's right to use contraceptives, a decision to which Bork has returned obsessively and scornfully again and again, and one that he would clearly vote to overrule. He has accused the Court, including on major occasions Justices Oliver Wendell Holmes, Louis Brandeis, Felix Frankfurter, Potter Stewart, and Lewis Powell, with whom he prefers on other occasions to be identified, of being, unaccountably but consistently less principled, less competent intellectually, and less committed to the Constitution than Judge Bork believes himself to be.

It goes without saying, although we all seem to feel obliged to say it, that a man who is nominated for the Supreme Court is entitled, like every other citizen, to his views, his judgment, his character, his history, his temperament, his intellectual quality, his personality and predilections. We know of Judge Bork, for instance, that he was a professor of law at Yale; that he was Solicitor General under President Nixon; and that he fired Special Prosecutor Archibald Cox, an act that was subsequently found by a federal court to be unlawful but that he now defends as having saved the "viability" of the Justice Department. We know that he has been a judge on a federal appellate court; that some of his friends regard him as witty; that he smokes, and likes martinis; that he did not pay certain taxes he had owed in New Haven since 1972, but paid them in July 1987, the day before the New Haven *Register* broke the story.

We know that he had been about to resign from the bench and resume private practice (he had hired no new clerks) when President Reagan announced his nomination for the Court. All this seems to leave open the possibility that he is an open-minded man, experienced in legal scholarship and in public office, who might affect the "balance" but would in no way threaten either the continuity, collegiality, and integrity of the Court itself or the entire constitutional structure—the separation of powers, the system of checks and balances—with which the republic was founded, and which has endured and developed over the past two hundred years.

From most of the reaction to his nomination so far, one might think: Well, some blacks oppose him, and some gays oppose him, and some women who oppose sex discrimination and believe in the right to abortion oppose him, and some woolly-headed liberals who believe in a right to privacy, or even believe that the First Amendment protects speech, oppose him, but those groups don't always speak with one voice—or for the whole decent, centrist consensus of the country. On the other hand, the right wing supports him. And even some members of the establishment, including the academy and the press, support him, or at least are reconciled to him. And Roosevelt, after all, had his Court-packing scheme. So unless there is some "smoking gun," the Senate might as well confirm him and get it over with. That's the way the system works.

But that's not how the system works. The Court-packing plan, for instance, failed. It was defeated by the Senate. The vast majority of the House, the Senate, and the electorate, moreover, were of President Roosevelt's party, and supported his social policy, at a time of genuine economic and political disaster. The present House and the Senate, many of whose members were elected as surely as and more recently than the current President, are not of his party. There is no crisis, except in extreme constituencies, and that is a crisis of ideology. But Judge Bork has made it so clear how he would decide nearly all major constitutional cases that have come before the Court, not just in the last thirty years but long before, that certainly for the first time in this century, and perhaps in the history of the republic, the Senate is being asked not to confirm a man but to establish on the Court a doctrine and a set of concrete decisions, most of which are reversals of established law and precedent. And Bork's published work seems to set forth methods, certainties, and positions that, while they may be consistent with what Bork calls "representative democracy," are so radically at odds with the Constitution as to amount to a rigid ideological system of his own.

What Bork has been looking for, and believes he has found, is above all a theory, a simple axiom, or principle, or formula, that the Court can—in fact, must—apply in constitutional adjudication to all cases that come before it. This "theory," developed at length in an article in the *Indiana Law Journal* in the fall of 1971, does not initially acknowledge the existence of "rights" at all but speaks instead of competing "gratifications," "pleasures," "preferences," but repeatedly and above all "gratifications": "Every clash between a minority claiming freedom and a majority claiming power to regulate involves a choice between . . . gratifications," and "There is no principled way to decide that one man's gratifications are more deserving of respect than another's or that one form of gratification is more worthy than another."

The innumerable "lawless," "utterly specious," and "unprincipled" decisions—in fact, the perpetration of "limited" judicial "coups d'état"—that Bork thinks he discerns particularly, but by no means only, in the Warren Court seem to him, however, to "establish the necessity for theory." To be a "principled" judge "means," in fact, to "have and rigorously adhere to a valid and consistent theory." And "the Court's power is legitimate only if it has . . . a valid theory . . . of the respective spheres of majority and minority freedom." Bork believes that, while he does "not offer a complete theory of constitutional interpretation," he has found the best one by far. It is essentially this:

There are two classes of constitutional "rights"—or, rather, claims to "gratification." (He notes in passing, and with disdain, "rhetoric" to the effect that any "rights . . . inhere in humans.") The first class of rights consists of those which are "specified"; namely, those which the "Framers" can be found literally and "actually to have intended," and which are "capable of being translated into principled rules." And the second class consists of "secondary," or "derived," rights, which "are located in the individual *for the sake of a governmental process*" (italics added). "They are given to the individual because his enjoyment of them will lead him to defend them in court and thereby preserve the governmental process." In all other cases, the Court must simply administer the "majoritarian" "will," or "preferences," as these are expressed in law. This Judge Bork believes to be the doctrine of "strict constructionism," "laissez-faire," and "original intent."

There are many difficulties with this theory. In the first place, the constitutional command that the courts consider only specific "cases" or "controversies" has precluded them from proclaiming "theory"—either philosophical or "advisory" or in advance of any set of facts. That is how constitutional adjudication works. The law is discovered in the cases, and not the other way around. That is why Justice Powell, in a long interview in the *Times* after his resignation, took the trouble to say, "I never think of myself as having a judicial philosophy. . . . I try to be careful, to do justice to the particular case, rather than try to write principles that will be new, or original, or whatever."

Secondly, the notion that "rights . . . inhere in humans," which Bork dismisses as some new, modish rhetorical development, was held so firmly by the founders of the republic that the second paragraph of the Declaration with which they proclaimed their independence began, "We hold these truths to be self-evident, that all men are created equal, that they are endowed by their Creator with certain unalienable rights." The Constitution itself was drafted with three clear aims: to create a compact to form a republic, which would unite the separate states; to establish a structure by which that republic would be governed; and to protect precisely the individual rights of citizens against majoritarian intrusion and coercion by the state.

That the Framers regarded these rights as inhering in the individual, and not as in any sense "derived," either from any document or from any trivial, utilitarian "governmental process," is clear, and not just from the Bill of Rights—which Judge Bork, in the same article, brushes aside as a "hastily drafted document upon which little thought was expended." It was thoroughly thought out again, after the Civil War, when the Fourteenth Amendment extended the core of the Bill of Rights, along with due process and equal protection, to the citizens of all the states. But Bork treats this amendment rather dismissively as well, speaking of the "value choice (or, perhaps more accurately, the value impulse) of the Fourteenth Amendment." He writes of the "men who put the amendment in the Constitution" that "many or most of them had not even thought the matter through."

"Courts must accept any value choice the legislature makes unless it clearly runs contrary to a choice made in the framing of the Constitution," Bork writes. And: "It follows, of course, that broad areas of constitutional law ought to be reformulated." And: "The distinction between rights that are inherent and rights that are derived from some other value is one that our society worked out long ago with respect to the economic market place. . . . A right is a form of property. . . . The modern intellectual argues the proper location and definition of property rights according to judgments of utility. . . . As it is with economic property rights, so it should be with constitutional rights relating to governmental processes."

The notion that the individual or his rights exist for the state, and to serve its "judgments of utility," is the basis of Bork's ideology. A notion more antithetical to the whole purpose and structure of the Constitution can hardly be imagined. "There is no principled way in which anyone can define the spheres in which liberty is required and the spheres in which equality is required." But the Constitution does not speak of "spheres," and the founders of the republic discerned so little of the tension that Bork consistently finds between "liberty" and "equality" that the same sentence of the Declaration which speaks of "liberty" as one of men's "unalienable rights" includes the statement "All men are created equal."

"It is emphatically the province and duty of the judicial department," Justice John Marshall said in 1803, in the great case of *Marbury v. Madison*, "to say what the law is." To that end, insulated by life tenure from the majoritarian pressures to which members of the two other branches, and of the state legislatures, were subject, the federal courts were empowered—indeed, obliged—to protect, from the prospect of "tyranny" by any of these majoritarian bodies, individual constitutional rights. The Constitution is complicated, intricate, difficult to understand and apply. That has been part of its continuing vitality. But two hundred years of decisions by the Court have understood ever more clearly that it was the intention of the Framers to make very difficult—to require the state to give fairly compelling justifications for—any attempt to take any of those individual rights away. And the reason Judge Bork's whole formulation is more disturbing than the mere ruminations of an ideologically extreme, revisionist professor is that he misapprehends the nature of "strict construction" in such a way as to compel him, as a "principled" judge, to abdicate the judicial duty "to say," on behalf of the individual constitutional right against the state, or on behalf of one branch of the federal government bringing suit against another, "what the law is." And yet nothing could be more apparent from his writings than that he is and intends to be a highly "activist" Judge, concerned less with theory than with results, and with reaching what he considers certain desirable outcomes.

The consistent form of his activism has so far been repudiation. Sometimes, particularly in congressional hearings, he rather tepidly and ambiguously repudiates prior positions of his own. But when it suits him, and if the result he wishes to reach requires it, he repudiates, without hesitation, the clear text of the Constitution itself. Thus, if the Constitution says explicitly, "Congress shall make no law... abridging the freedom of speech," Bork writes, "Laymen may perhaps be forgiven for thinking that the literal words" are what is meant, and that any legislation seeking to censor or repress that speech bears the burden of explaining why an exception should be made. "But what can one say of lawyers who think any such thing? Anyone skilled in reading language should know that the words are not necessarily absolute....We are, then, forced to construct our own theory of the constitutional protection of speech."

Having set aside, in other words, "original intent" as it is expressed in a specific provision of the Constitution, he proceeds to attack also, as "deficient in logic and analysis as well as in history," the "clear and present danger" standard that was first developed by Justices Holmes and Brandeis in the years after World War I. He wishes to overrule all the free-speech cases that elaborated and refined that standard, and then to apply instead the test set forth in his "own theory," which leaves constitutionally protected only what he calls "explicitly political speech," a category that he defines so narrowly as to exclude not only what most people mean by "speech" but also what is generally meant by "political." If Judge Bork's narrow conception of "explicitly political" speech had prevailed against the sermons, marches, boycotts, and sit-ins that advocated violation of what the federal courts eventually found to be bad and lawless state laws, those laws would never have been found unconstitutional, and there would still be Jim Crow in the South.

What he clearly wants, and clearly intends on the Court to vote to achieve, is to overrule as well many other important lines of cases—concerning, for instance, the right of privacy. Bork believes quite simply that no such right exists: that it is a "court-created right"—or, rather, an imposition of the "unprincipled preference" of the judges for the "gratification" of that "minority" which, for instance, wishes, as in *Griswold*, to be free to use contraceptives, over the "gratification" of that majority which wishes to be free not only *not* to use contraceptives but to prevent anyone else from using them. He does not acknowledge, or appear to perceive, a difference in the order of "freedom" embodied by choosing to do or not to do something and "freedom" to prevent anyone else, even in private, from doing or not doing whatever it is. In fact, Bork routinely uses the vocabulary of coercion to describe choices of the private citizen, and the language of "loss of liberty" or "loss of freedom" to describe the position of the majority whose intrusion the private citizen is trying to resist.

In the name of "freedom," he wants to overrule, for instance, *Shelley v. Kraemer*, a 1948 decision, thereby allowing states to enforce "a racially restrictive covenant." And to overrule *Skinner v. Oklahoma*, a 1942 decision, and thereby uphold the right of the state to sterilize robbers. He thinks that the Supreme Court decision forbidding the poll tax was wrongly decided, since the poll tax in question was "not discriminatory" and was "very small." And so on. There are, of course, cases about which men of good will reasonably disagree—having to do, for example, with capital punishment, with the one-man, one-vote reapportionment cases, and with the "exclusionary rule," which forbids the state to use in criminal trials evidence that was illegally seized. Of the last, he has said in an interview that it seems to him that "the conscience of the court ought to be" at least as much "shaken by the idea of turning a criminal loose upon society" as by the idea of admitting illegally seized evidence.

It might be worth examining by Judge Bork's own reasoning the kind of "majoritarian" statute he would feel compelled to uphold. The only individual right that he finds in the Fourteenth Amendment, albeit "derived," is the right to be protected from state action that enforces "racially invidious classification." So there is nothing to prevent a majoritarian preference from being expressed, for instance, in a statute requiring everyone, of every race, to be blond. And nothing—perhaps this is more serious—to prevent the state from enforcing a majoritarian preference that all single mothers should be sterilized. Or all women with an IQ below 130. Or all mothers under eighteen.

Bork has repeatedly called *Roe v. Wade*, the 1973 decision recognizing the right to abortion, "an unconstitutional decision," a "judicial usurpation of state legislative authority." This has a different significance altogether from calling it a mere mistake, which arguments for the continuity and predictability of the Court's decisions could leave undisturbed. If it is "an unconstitutional decision" and a "judicial usurpation," then Justice Bork would be obliged by his constitutional oath not to reaffirm it. And overruling *Roe v. Wade* would permit the recriminalization of abortion by the states.

On the other hand, since there is no right of privacy in the matter, one way or the other, there is nothing to prevent a state from *imposing* abortions, as long as that imposition is expressed in a "racially neutral" law.

Bork would doubtless reply that no such statutes could be passed anywhere in this country, and that we should have more faith in "majoritarian" "preferences" than that. But there have been totalitarian states in this century, as "majoritarian" as any in history, which have passed very extreme statutes of that order. For that matter, for decades in the South there were statutes of a related kind.

In a simultaneously impassioned and derisive article published in *The New Republic* of August 31, 1963, Bork left no doubt of where he stood. What he opposed at the time was "legislation by which the morals of the majority are self-righteously imposed upon a minority." He also said, "The simple argument from morality to law can be a dangerous non-sequitur." He was not writing about *Griswold*, or *Roe v. Wade*. The dangerous "majority" in this instance included, among many other individuals and institutions, Congress, then about to pass the Interstate Public Accommodations Act, which became Title II of the Civil Rights Act of 1964.

Bork was so exercised at the prospect of this majoritarian "mob coercing and disturbing other private individuals"—the "mob" presumably composed of Rosa Parks, religious elderly people, schoolchildren, sedate college students at lunch counters, and perhaps even those brave, mostly Republican judges of the Fifth Circuit, Elbert Tuttle, John Minor Wisdom, Richard Rives, John Brown, and others who supported them—that he referred no fewer than four times to the impact of the proposed law on barbers, though barbers were explicitly excluded, in public hearings before Congress, from enterprises covered by the act. Although he warned of "the danger of violence," he gave no indication that he knew which side the violence was on, or was aware that the "private individuals" he described as being "coerced" were really mobs armed with baseball bats and ax handles, and troopers with dogs, clubs, and water hoses, and that though there was "violence"—bombings, beatings, shootings—not one incident of that kind, in all the years of the desegregating transformation of the South, was perpetrated by the people whose conduct he so deplored.

In as recent a case as *Dronenburg v. Zech*, 1984, Judge Bork repeated many of the views he had expressed in *The New Republic* in 1963 and the *Indiana Law Journal* in 1971. *Dronenburg* was a case that should have been—and, in a sense, was—decided in a single paragraph, to the effect that there was ample precedent for upholding a policy that permitted the military to discharge an officer for homosexuality. But Judge Bork, speaking for the Court, used the occasion to write one of what have become known as his Ed Opinions, or Ed Notes, or Letters to Attorney General Meese—in effect, job applications, reiterations of commitments he had made concerning what he would do as a member of the Supreme Court.

"The principle of such legislation," Bork once wrote, "is that if I find your behavior ugly by my standards, moral or aesthetic, and if you prove stubborn about adopting my view of the situation, I am justified in having the state coerce you into more righteous paths. That is itself a principle of unsurpassed ugliness." These lines were not part of any opinion having to do with privacy, say, or abortion, or censorship, or freedom of speech. They were written to describe the desegregation provisions embodied in Title II. The "principle of unsurpassed ugliness" that so exercised him was desegregration.

For at least the past thirty years, no American institution has served us better than the federal courts. For almost twenty-five years, Bork has staked his career on repudiating and denouncing the decisions of those courts. He has expressed his views so forcefully, and for so long, that he has become the nominee because of them. A senator faithful to his own constitutional oath cannot lightly or blandly vote to confirm the nomination unless he is prepared to endorse those views.

The New Yorker
August 3, 1987

CANARIES IN THE MINESHAFT
INTRODUCTION

ALONG with every other viewer of television during Operation Desert Storm, the Gulf War of 1991, I believed that I saw, time after time, American Patriot missiles knocking Iraqi Scuds out of the sky. Every major television reporter obviously shared this belief, along with a certainty that these Patriots were offering protection to the population of Israel—which the Desert Storm alliance, for political reasons, had kept from active participation in the war. Commentators actually cheered, with exclamations like "Bull's-eye! No more Scud!" at each such interception by a Patriot of a Scud. Weeks earlier, I had read newspaper accounts of testimony before a committee of the Congress by a tearful young woman who claimed to have witnessed Iraqi soldiers enter Kuwaiti hospitals, take babies out of their incubators, hurl the newborns to the floor, and steal the incubators. I believed this, too.

Only much later did I learn that hardly a single Patriot effectively hit a single Scud. The scenes on television were in fact repetitions of images from one film, made by the Pentagon in order to persuade Congress to allocate more money to the Patriot, an almost thirty-year-old weapon designed, in any case, not to destroy missiles but to intercept airplanes. In his exuberance, a high military official announced that Patriots had even managed to destroy "eighty-one Scud launchers"—interesting not only because the total number of Scud launchers previously ascribed to Iraq was fifty, but also because there is and was no such thing as a "Scud launcher." The vehicles in question were old trucks, which had broken down.

What was at issue, in other words, was not even pro-American propaganda, which could be justified in time of war. It was domestic advertising for a product—not just harmlessly deceptive advertising, either. The Patriots, as it turned out, did more damage to the allied forces, and to Israel, than if they had not been used at all. The weeping young woman who had testified about the incubator thefts turned out to be the fifteen-year-old daughter of the Kuwaiti ambassador to Washington; she had not, obviously, witnessed any such event. Whatever else the Iraqi invaders and occupiers may have done, this particular incident was a fabrication—invented by an American public relations firm in the employ of the Kuwaiti government.

During Operation Desert Storm itself, the American press corps, as it also turns out, accepted an arrangement with the U.S. military, whereby only a "pool" of journalists would be permitted to cover the war directly. That pool went wherever the American military press officer chose to take it. Nowhere near the front, if there was a front. Somehow, the pool and its military press guides often got lost. When other reporters, trying to get independent information, set out on their own, members of the pool actually berated them for jeopardizing the entire news-gathering arrangement.

It would have been difficult to learn all this, or any of it, from the press. I learned it from a very carefully researched and documented book, *Second Front: Censorship and Propaganda in the Gulf War*, by John R. MacArthur. The book, published in 1992, was well enough reviewed. But it was neither prominently reviewed nor treated as "news" or even information. A review, after all, is regarded only as a cultural and not a real—least of all a journalistic—event. It was not surprising that the Pentagon, after its experience in Vietnam, should want to keep the press at the greatest possible distance from any war. It was not surprising, either, that reporters, having after all not that much choice, should submit so readily to being confined to a pool, or even that reporters in that pool should resent any competitor who tried to work outside it. This is the position of a favored collaborator in any bureaucratic and coercive enterprise.

What was, if not surprising, a disturbing matter, and a symptom of what was to come, was this: The press did not report the utter failure of the Patriot, nor did it report the degree to which the press itself, and then its audience and readership, had been misled. This is not to suggest that the press, out of patriotism or for any other reason, printed propaganda to serve the purposes of the government— or even that it would be unworthy to do so. But millions of Americans surely still believe that Patriots destroyed the Scuds, and in the process saved, or at least defended, Israel. There seemed, in this instance, no reason why the press, any more than any person or other institution, should be eager to report failures of its own.

Almost all the pieces in this book have to do, in one way or another, with what I regard as misrepresentation, coercion, and abuse of public process, and, to a degree, the journalist's role in it. At the time of the Vietnam War, it could be argued that the press had become too reflexively adversarial and skeptical of the policies of government. Now I believe the reverse is true. All bureaucracies have certain interests in common: self-perpetuation, ritual, dogma, a reluctance to take responsibility for their actions, a determination to eradicate dissent, a commitment to a notion of infallibility. As I write this, the Supreme Court has, in spite of eloquent and highly principled dissents, so far and so cynically exceeded any conceivable exercise of its constitutional powers as to choose, by one vote, its own preferred candidate for President. Some reporters, notably Linda Greenhouse of *The New York Times*, have written intelligently and admirably about this. For the most part, however, the press itself has become a bureaucracy, quasi-governmental, and, far from calling attention to the collapse of public process, in particular to prosecutorial abuses, it has become an instrument of intimidation, an instrumentality even of the police function of the state.

Let us begin by acknowledging that, in our public life, this has been a period of unaccountable bitterness and absurdity. To begin with the attempts to impeach President Clinton. There is no question that the two sets of allegations, regarding Paula Jones and regarding Whitewater, with which the process began could not, as a matter of fact or law or for any other reason, constitute grounds for impeachment. Whatever they were, they preceded his presidency, and no President can be impeached for his prior acts. That was that. Then the Supreme Court, in what was certainly one of the silliest decisions in its history, ruled that the civil lawsuit by Paula Jones could proceed without delay because, in spite of the acknowledged importance of the President's office, it appeared "highly unlikely to occupy any substantial amount of his time." In 1994 a Special Prosecutor (for some reason, this office is still called the Independent Counsel) was appointed to investigate Whitewater—a press-generated inquiry, which could not possibly be material for a Special Prosecutor, no matter how defined, since it had nothing whatever to do with presidential conduct. Nonetheless, the first Special Prosecutor, Robert Fiske, investigated and found nothing. A three-judge panel, appointed, under the Independent Counsel statute, by Chief Justice William Rehnquist, fired Fiske. As head of the three-judge panel, Rehnquist had passed over several more senior judges, to choose Judge David Bryan Sentelle.

Judge Sentelle consulted at lunch with two ultra-right-wing senators from his own home state of North Carolina: Lauch Faircloth, who was convinced, among other things, that Vincent Foster, a White House counsel, had been murdered; and Jesse Helms, whose beliefs and powers would not be described by anyone as moderate. Judge Sentelle appointed as Fiske's successor Kenneth W. Starr. North Carolina is, of course, a tobacco-growing state. Kenneth Starr had been, and remained virtually throughout his tenure as Special Prosecutor, a major, and very highly paid, attorney for the tobacco companies. He had also once drafted a pro bono amicus brief on behalf of Paula Jones.

The Office of Special Prosecutor—true conservatives said this from the first—had always been a constitutional abomination. To begin with, it impermissibly straddled the three branches of government. If President Nixon had not been in dire straits, he would never have permitted such an office, in the person of Archibald Cox, to exist. If President Clinton had not been sure of his innocence and— far more dangerously—overly certain of his charm, he would never have consented to such an appointment.

The press, however, loves Special Prosecutors. They can generate stories for each other. That something did not happen is not a story. That something does not matter is not a story. That an anecdote or an accusation is unfounded is not a story. There is this further commonality of interest. Leaks, anonymous sources, informers, agents, rumormongers, appear to offer stories—and possibilities for offers, pressures, threats, rewards. The journalist's exchange of an attractive portrayal for a good story. There we are. The reporter and the prosecutor (the Special Prosecutor, that is; not as often the genuine prosecutor) are in each other's pockets.

Starr did not find anything, either. Certainly no crime. He sent his staff to Little Rock, generated enormous legal expenses for people interviewed there, threw one unobliging witness (Susan McDougal) into jail for well over a year, indicted others (Webster Hubbell, for example) for offenses unrelated to the Clintons, convicted and jailed witnesses in hopes of getting testimony damaging to President Clinton, tried, after the release of those witnesses, to jail them again to get such testimony. Still no crime. So his people tried to generate one. This is not unusual behavior on the part of prosecutors going after hardened criminals: stings, indictments of racketeers and murderers for income tax offenses. But here was something new. Starr's staff, for a time, counted heavily on sexual embarrassment: philandering, Monica Lewinsky. They even had a source, Linda Tripp. Ms. Tripp had testified for Special Prosecutor Fiske and later for Starr. She had testified in response to questions from her sympathetic interlocutor Senator Lauch Faircloth before Senator D'Amato's Whitewater Committee. She had testified to agents of the FBI right in the Special Prosecutor's office at least as early as April 12, 1994. An ultra-right-wing Republican herself, she not only believed White House Counsel Vincent Foster was murdered, she claimed to fear for her own life. She somehow had on the wall above her desk at the Pentagon, where her desk adjoined Monica Lewinsky's, huge posters of President Clinton—which, perhaps not utterly surprisingly, drew Ms. Lewinsky's attention. Somehow, in the fall of 1996 Ms. Tripp found herself eliciting, and taping, confidences from Ms. Lewinsky. In January of 1997, Ms. Tripp—who by her own account had previously abetted another White House volunteer, Kathleen Willey, in making sexual overtures to President Clinton—counseled Ms. Lewinsky to try again to visit President Clinton. By the end of February 1997, Ms. Lewinsky, who had not seen the President in more than eleven months, managed to arrange such a visit. Somehow, that visit was the only one in which she persuaded the President to ejaculate. Somehow, adept as Ms. Lewinsky claimed to be at fellatio, semen found its way onto her dress. Somehow, Ms. Tripp persuaded Ms. Lewinsky, who perhaps did not require much persuasion, to save that dress. Somehow, the Special Prosecutor got the dress. And somehow (absurdity of absurdities), there was the spectacle of the Special Prosecutor's agents taking blood from the President to match the DNA on a dress.

Now, whatever other mistakes President Clinton may have made, in this or any other matter, he, too, had made utterly absurd mistakes of constitutional proportions. He had no obligation at all to go before the grand jury. It was a violation of the separation of powers and a mistake. Once again, he may have overestimated his charm. Charm gets you nowhere with prosecutors' questions, answered before a grand jury under oath. And of course, Mr. Starr had managed to arrange questions—illegally, disingenuously, at the absolute last minute—which were calculated to make the President testify falsely at his deposition in the case of Paula Jones. Whether or not the President did testify falsely, the notion that "perjury" or even "obstruction of justice" in such a case could rise to the level of "Treason, Bribery or other high Crimes and Misdemeanors," the sole constitutional grounds for impeachment, had no basis in history or in law.

One need not dwell on every aspect of the matter to realize this much: As sanctimonious as lawyers, congressmen, and even judges may be, most legal cases are simply not decided on arcane legal grounds. Most turn on conflicting evidence, conflicting *testimony*.

And this conflict cannot, surely, in every case or even in most cases, be ascribed either to Rashomon phenomena or to memory lapses. In most cases—there is no other way to put it—one litigant or the other, and usually both, are lying. If this were to be treated as "perjury" or "obstruction of justice," then, alas, most losers in litigation would be subject to indictment. Anyone who has studied grounds for impeachment at all knows that "high Crimes and Misdemeanors" refers, in any event, only to crimes committed in the President's official capacity and in the actual conduct of his office.

And now the press. Perhaps the most curious phenomenon in the recent affinity of the press with prosecutors has been a reversal, an inversion so acute that it passes any question of "blaming the victim." It actually consists in casting persecutors as victims, and vilifying victims as persecutors. *The New York Times* is not alone in this, but it has been, until recently, the most respected of newspapers, and it has been, of late, the prime offender. A series of recent events there gives an indication of what is at stake.

In a retreat in Tarrytown, in mid-September, Joseph Lelyveld—in his time a distinguished reporter, now executive editor of the *Times*—gave a speech to eighty assembled *Times* newsroom editors, plus two editors of other publications, *The New Yorker* and *Newsday*. The ostensible subject of the retreat was "Competition." Mr. Lelyveld's purpose, he said, was to point out "imperfections in what I proudly believe to be the best *New York Times* ever—the best written, most consistent, and ambitious newspaper *Times* readers have ever had." This was, in itself, an extraordinary assertion. It might have been just a mollifying tribute, a prelude to criticism of some kind. And so it was.

"I'm just driven by all the big stuff we've accomplished in recent years—our strong enterprise reporting, our competitive edge, our successful recruiting, our multimedia forays, our sheer ambition," Lelyveld went on, "to worry" about "the small stuff," particularly "the really big small stuff." "I especially want to talk to you," he said, "about corrections, and in particular, the malignancy of misspelled names, which, if you haven't noticed, has become one of the great themes of our Corrections column."

He might have been joking, but he wasn't. "Did you know we've misspelled Katharine Graham's name fourteen times? Or that we've misspelled the Madeleine in Madeleine Albright forty-nine times—even while running three corrections on each? . . . So far this year . . . there have been a hundred and ninety-eight corrections for misspelled given names and surnames, the overwhelming majority easily checkable on the Internet. . . . I want to argue that our commitment to being excellent and reliable in these matters is as vital to the impression we leave on readers, and the service we perform for them, as the brilliant things we accomplish most days on our front page and on our section-front displays."

Lelyveld recalled the time, thirty years ago, when he had first come to the newspaper (a better paper, as it happens, an incomparably better paper, under his predecessors, whom present members of the staff tend to demonize). "Just about everything else we do today, it seems to me, we do better than they did then." But, in view of "the brilliant things we accomplish most days" ("We don't just claim to be a team. We don't just aspire to be a team. Finally, I think we can say, we function as a team. We are a team"), he did want to talk about what he regarded as a matter of some importance: "Finally . . . there's the matter of corrections (I almost said the 'festering matter' of corrections). As I see it, this is really big small stuff."

A recent correction about a photo confusing monarch and queen butterflies, he said, might seem amusing—"amusing if you don't much mind the fact that scores of lepidopterists are now likely to mistrust us on areas outside their specialty."

And that, alas, turned out to be the point. This parody, this misplaced punctiliousness, was meant to reassure readers—lepidopterists, whomever—that whatever else appeared in the newspaper could be trusted and was true. Correction of "malignant" misspellings, of "given names and surnames," middle initials, captions, headlines, the "overwhelming majority" of which, as Lelyveld put it, would have been "easily checkable on the Internet" was the *Times*'s substitute for conscience, and the basis of its assurance to readers that in every other respect it was an accurate paper, better than it had ever been, more worthy of their trust. Stendhal, for instance, had recently been misspelled, misidentified, and given a first name: Robert. "A visit to Amazon.com, just a couple of clicks away, could have cleared up the confusion." Maybe so.

The trivial, as it happens often truly comic, corrections, persist, in quantity. The deep and consequential errors, inevitable in any enterprise, particularly those with deadlines, go unacknowledged. By this pedantic travesty of good faith, which is, in fact, a classic method of deception, the *Times* conceals not just every important error it makes but that it makes errors at all. It wants that poor trusting lepidopterist to think that, with the exception of this little lapse (now corrected), the paper is conscientious and infallible.

There exists, to this end, a wonderful set of locutions, euphemisms, conventions, codes, and explanations: "misspelled," "misstated," "referred imprecisely," "referred incorrectly," and recently—in some ways most mystifyingly—"paraphrase."

On September 19, 2000, "An article on September 17 about a program of intellectual seminars organized by Mayor Jerry Brown of Oakland, California, referred imprecisely to some criticisms of the series. The terms 'Jerrification' and 'pointy-headed table talk' were the article's paraphrase of local critics, not the words of Willa White, president of the Jack London Association."

On October 5, 2000, "A news analysis yesterday about the performances of Vice President Al Gore and Gov. George W. Bush of Texas in their first debate referred imprecisely in some copies to a criticism of the candidates. The observation that they 'took too much time niggling over details' was a paraphrase of comments by former Mayor Pete Flaherty of Pittsburgh, not a quotation."

On November 9, 2000, "An article on Sunday about the campaign for the Senate in Missouri said the Governor had 'wondered' about the decision of the late candidate's wife to run for the Senate. But he did not use the words 'I'm bothered somewhat by the idea of voting for a dead person's wife, simply because she is a widow.' That was a paraphrase of Mr. Wilson's views and should not have appeared in quotation marks."

On December 16, 2000, "Because of an editing error, an article yesterday referred erroneously to a comment by a board member," about a recount. "'A man has to do what a man has to do' was a paraphrase of Mr. Torre's views and should not have appeared in quotation marks."

Apart from the obvious questions—What is the *Times*'s idea of "paraphrase"? What were the actual words being paraphrased? What can "Jerrification," "pointy-headed table talk," "niggling," and even "A man has to do what a man has to do" possibly be paraphrases *of*—what purpose is served by these corrections? Is the implication that all other words in the *Times*, attributed in quotation marks to speakers, are accurate, verbatim quotations? I'm afraid the implication is inescapably that. That such an implication is preposterous is revealed by the very nature of these corrections. There is no quotation of which "Jerrification" and the rest can *possibly* be a paraphrase. Nor can the reporter have simply misheard anything that was actually said, nor can the result be characterized as having "referred imprecisely" or "referred erroneously," let alone be the result of "an editing error."

It cannot be. What is at issue in these miniscule corrections is the *Times*'s notion of what matters, its professionalism, its good faith, even its perception of what constitute accuracy and the truth. The overriding value is, after all, to allay the mistrust of readers, lepidopterists, colleagues. Within the newspaper, this sense of itself—trust us, the only errors we make are essentially typos, and we correct them; we never even misquote, we paraphrase—appears even in its columns.

In a column published in the *Times* on July 20, 2000, Martin

Arnold of the Arts/Culture desk, for example, wrote unhesitatingly that, compared with book publishing, "Journalism has a more rigorous standard: What is printed is believed to be true, not merely unsuspected of being false. The first rule of journalism," he wrote, "is don't invent."

"Except in the most scholarly work," Mr. Arnold went on, "no such absolutes apply to book publishing. . . . A book writer is . . . not subject to the same discipline as a news reporter, for instance, who is an employee and whose integrity is a condition of his employment . . . a newspaper . . . is a brand name, and the reader knows exactly what to expect from the brand." If book publishers, Mr. Arnold concluded, "seem lethargic" about "whether a book is right or wrong, it maybe [sic] because readers will cut books slack they don't give their favorite newspaper."

In this wonderful piece of self-regarding fatuity, Mr. Arnold has expressed the essence of the "team's" view of its claim: The *Times* requires no "slack." It readily makes its own corrections:

The Making Books column yesterday misspelled the name of the television host. . . . She is Oprah Winfrey, not Opra.

An article about Oprah Winfrey's interview with Al Gore used a misspelled name and a non-existent name for the author of *The Red and the Black*. . . . The pen name is Stendhal, not Stendahl; Robert is not part of it.

The Advertising column in Business on Friday misspelled the surname of a singer and actress. . . . She is Lena Horne, not Horn.

An article about an accident in which a brick fell from a construction site atop the YMCA building on West 63rd Street, slightly injuring a woman, included an erroneous address from the police for the building near which she was standing. It was 25 Central Park West. (There is no No. 35).

Because of an editing error, the Making Books column on Thursday... misstated the name of the publisher of a thriller by Tom Clancy. It is G. P. Putnam, not G. F.

An article on Monday about charges that Kathleen Hagen murdered her parents, Idella and James Hagen, at their home in Chatham Township, N.J., misspelled the street where they lived. It is Fairmount Avenue, not Fairmont.

And so on. Endlessly.

What is the reasoning, the intelligence, behind this daily travesty of concern for what is truthful? Mr. Arnold has the cant just about right. "Don't invent." (Pointy-headed table talk? Jerrification? Niggling? Paraphrase?) "Discipline"? "Integrity"? "Rigorous standard"? Not in a long time. "A newspaper is a brand name, and the reader knows exactly what to expect from the brand." Well, there is the problem. Part of it is the delusion of punctilio. But there is something more. Every acknowledgment of an inconsequential error (and they are never identified as reporting errors, only errors of "editing," or "production," or "transmission," and so forth), in the absence of acknowledgment of any *major* error, creates at best a newspaper that is closed to genuine inquiry. It declines responsibility for real errors, and creates as well an affinity for all orthodoxies. And when there is a subject genuinely suited to its professional skills and obligations, it abdicates. It almost reflexively shuns responsibility and delegates it to another institution.

Within a few weeks of its small retreat at Tarrytown, the *Times*, on two separate occasions, so seriously failed in its fundamental journalistic obligations as to call into question not just its judgment and good faith but whether it is still a newspaper at all. The first occasion returns in a way to the subject with which this introduction began: a pool.

On election night, television, it was generally acknowledged, had made an enormous error by delegating to a single consortium, the Voter News Service, the responsibility for both voter exit polls and calling the election results. The very existence of such a consortium of broadcasters raised questions in anti-trust, and VNS called its results wrongly, but that was not the point. The point was that the value of a free press in our society was always held to lie in competition. By a healthy competition among reporters, from media of every political point of view, the public would have access to reliable information, and a real basis on which to choose. A single monolithic, unitary voice, on the other hand, is anathema to any democractic society. It becomes the voice of every oppressive or totalitarian system of government.

The *Times* duly reported, and in its own way deplored, the results of the VNS debacle. Then, along with colleagues in the press (the *Washington Post*, CNN, the *Wall Street Journal*, ABC, AP, the Tribune Company), it promptly emulated it. This new consortium hired an organization called the National Opinion Research Center to undertake, on its behalf, a manual recount of Florida ballots for the presidential election. The *Miami Herald*, which had already been counting the votes for several weeks, was apparently the only publication to exercise its function as an independent newspaper. It refused to join the consortium. It had already hired an excellent accounting firm, BDO Seidman, to assist its examination of the ballots. NORC, by contrast, was not even an auditing firm but a survey group, much of whose work is for government projects.

The *Times* justified its (there seems no other word for it) hiding, along with seven collegial bureaucracies, behind a single entity, NORC, on economic grounds. Proceeding independently, it said, would have cost between $500,000 and $1 million. The *Times*, it may be noted, had put fifteen of its reporters to work for a solid year on a series called "Living Race in America." If it had devoted just some of those resources and that cost to a genuine, even historic, issue of fact, it would have exercised its independent competitive function in a free society and produced something of value. There seems no question that is what the *Times* under any previous publisher or editors would have done.

In refusing to join the consortium, the *Miami Herald* said the recount was taking place, after all, "in our own back yard." It was, of course, America's backyard, and hardly any other members of the press could be troubled with their own resources and staff to enter it.

The second failure of judgment and good faith was in some ways more egregious. In late September of 2000 there was the *Times*'s appraisal of its coverage (more accurately, the *Times*'s response to other people's reaction to its coverage) of the case of Wen Ho Lee.

For some days, there had been rumors that the *Times* was going to address in some way its coverage of the case of Wen Ho Lee, a sixty-year-old nuclear scientist at Los Alamos who had been held, shackled and without bail, in solitary confinement, for nine months—on the basis, in part, of testimony, which an FBI agent had since admitted to be false, that Lee had passed American nuclear secrets to China; and testimony, also false, that he had flunked a lie detector test about the matter; and testimony, false and in some ways most egregious, that granting him bail would constitute a "grave threat" to "hundreds of millions of lives" and the "nuclear balance" of the world. As part of a plea bargain, in which Lee acknowledged a minor offense, the government, on September 14, 2000, withdrew fifty-eight of its fifty-nine original charges. The Federal District Judge, James A. Parker, a Reagan appointee, apologized to Lee for the prosecutorial conduct of the government.

The *Times* had broken the story of the alleged espionage on March 6 of 1999, and pursued it both editorially and in its news columns for seventeen months. A correction, perhaps even an apology, was expected to appear in the Week in Review section, on Sunday, September 24, 2000. Two *Times* reporters flew up from Washington to register objections. The piece, whatever it had been originally, was edited and postponed until the following Tuesday. (The Sunday *Times* has nearly twice the readership of the daily paper.) Readers of the Week in Review section of Sunday, September 24, 2000, however, did find a correction. It was this:

An Ideas & Trends article last Sunday about a trend toward increasing size of women's breasts referred incorrectly to the actress Demi Moore. She underwent breast augmentation surgery, but has not had the implants removed.

In the meantime, however, on Friday, September 22, 2000, there appeared an op-ed piece, "No One Won the Whitewater Case," by James B. Stewart, in which the paper's affinity with prosecution—in particular the Special Prosecutor—and the writer's solidarity with the *Times* reporters most attuned to leaks from government accusers found almost bizarre expression. Stewart, a Pulitzer Prize-winning journalist and the author of *Blood Sport*, wrote of Washington, during the Clinton administration, as a "culture of mutual political destruction." In what sense the "destruction" could be deemed "mutual" was not entirely clear. Mr. Stewart praised an article about Whitewater, on March 8, 1992, written by Jeff Gerth (one of the original writers of the Wen Ho Lee pieces) as "a model of investigative reporting." He wrote of "rabid Clinton haters" who believed that Vincent Foster was "murdered, preferably by Hillary Clinton herself"; he added, however, the Clintons "continued to stonewall," providing "ample fodder for those opposed to the President."

"The Independent Counsel's mission," he wrote, "was to get to the bottom of the morass." No, it wasn't. What morass? Then came this formulation:

> Kenneth Starr and his top deputies were not instinctive politicians, and they became caught up in a political war for which they were woefully unprepared and ill-suited. The White House and its allies relentlessly attacked the Independent Counsel for what they thought were both illegal and unprincipled tactics, like intimidating witnesses and leaking to the press. Mr. Starr has been vindicated in the courts in nearly every instance, and he and his allies were maligned to a degree that will someday be seen as grossly unfair.

One's heart of course goes out to these people incarcerating Susan McDougal; illegally detaining and threatening Monica Lewinsky;

threatening a witness who refused to lie for them, by implying that her adoption of a small child was illegal; misleading the courts, the grand jury, the press, the witnesses about their actions. Persecuted victims, these prosecutors—"caught up," "woefully unprepared," "relentlessly attacked," "maligned."

> The investigation unfolded with inexorable logic that made sense at every turn, yet lost all sight of the public purpose it was meant to serve. Mr. Starr's failure was not one of logic or law but of simple common sense.

Quite apart from whatever he means by "public purpose," what could Mr. Stewart possibly mean by "common sense"?

> From early on, it should have been apparent that a criminal case could never be made against the Clintons. Who would testify against them?

Who indeed? Countless people, as the *Times* checkers, if it had any, might have told him—alleging rape, murder, threats, blackmail, drug abuse, bribery, and abductions of pet cats.

"The investigation does not clear the Clintons in all respects," Mr. Stewart wrote, as though clearing people, especially in all respects, were the purpose of prosecutions. "The Independent Counsel law is already a casualty of Whitewater and its excesses." What? What can this possibly mean? What "it," for example, precedes "its excesses"? *Whitewater*'s excesses?

> But as long as a culture of mutual political destruction reigns in Washington, the need for some independent resolution of charges against top officials, especially the President, will not go away. [A reigning culture of mutual destruction evidently needs another Special Prosecutor, to make charges go away.] After all, we did get something for our nearly $60 million. The charges against the Clintons were credibly resolved.

An extraordinary piece, certainly. Four days later, on Tuesday, September 26, 2000, the *Times* ran its long-awaited assessment, "From the Editors." It was entitled "The Times and Wen Ho Lee."

Certainly, the paper had never before published anything like this assessment. A break with tradition, however, is not an apology. What the *Times* did was to apportion blame elsewhere, endorse its own work, and cast itself as essentially a victim, having "attracted criticism" from three categories of persons: "competing journalists," "media critics," and "defenders of Dr. Lee." Though there may, in hindsight, have been "flaws"—for example, a few other lines of investigation the *Times* might have pursued, "to humanize" Dr. Lee—the editors seemed basically to think they had produced what Mr. Stewart, in his op-ed piece, might have characterized as "a model of investigative reporting." Other journalists interpreted this piece one way and another, but to a reader of ordinary intelligence and understanding there was no contrition in it. That evidently left the *Times*, however, with a variant of what might be called the underlying corrections problem: the lepidopterist and his trust. "Accusations leveled at this newspaper," the editors wrote, "may have left many readers with questions about our coverage. That confusion—and the stakes involved, a man's liberty and reputation—convince us that a public accounting is warranted." The readers' "confusion" is the issue. The "stakes," in dashes, are an afterthought.

"On the whole," the public accounting said, "we remain proud of work that brought into the open a major national security problem. Our review found careful reporting that included extensive cross-checking and vetting of multiple sources, despite enormous obstacles of official secrecy and government efforts to identify the *Times's* sources."

And right there is the nub of it, one nub of it anyway: the "efforts to identify the *Times's* sources." Because in this case, the sources were precisely governmental—the FBI, for example, in its attempt to intimidate Wen Ho Lee. The rest of the piece, with a few unconvincing afterthoughts about what the paper might have done differently, is self-serving and even overtly deceptive. "The *Times* stories

—echoed and often oversimplified by politicians and other news organizations—touched off a fierce public debate"; "Now the *Times* neither imagined the security breach nor initiated the prosecution of Wen Ho Lee"; "That concern had previously been reported in the *Wall Street Journal*, but without the details provided by the *Times* in a painstaking narrative"; "Nothing in this experience undermines our faith in any of our reporters, who remained persistent and fair-minded in their news-gathering in the face of some fierce attacks."

And there it is again: Wen Ho Lee in jail, alone, shackled, without bail—and yet it is the *Times* that is subject to "accusations," *Times* reporters who were subjected to those "fierce attacks."

The editors did express a reservation about their "tone." "In place of a tone of journalistic detachment," they wrote, they had perhaps echoed the alarmism of their sources. Anyone who has read the *Times* in recent years—let alone been a subject of its pieces—knows that "a tone of journalistic detachment" in the paper is almost entirely a thing of the past. What is so remarkable, however, is not only how completely the *Times* identifies with the prosecution, but also how clearly the inversion of hunter and prey has taken hold. The injustice, the editors clearly feel, has been done not to Dr. Lee (although they say at one point that they may not have given him, imagine, "the full benefit of the doubt") but to the reporters, and the editors, and the institution itself.

Two days later, the editorial section checked in, with "An Overview: The Wen Ho Lee Case." Some of it, oddly enough, was another attack on Wen Ho Lee, whose activities it described as "suspicious and ultimately illegal," "beyond reasonable dispute." It described the director of the FBI, Louis Freeh, and Attorney General Janet Reno as being under "sharp attack." The editorial was not free of self-justification; it was not open about its own contribution to the damage; it did seem concerned with "racial profiling"—a frequent preoccupation of the editorial page, in any case. The oddest sentences were these: "Moreover, transfer of technology to China and nuclear weapons security had been constant government concerns throughout this period. To withhold this information from

readers is an unthinkable violation of the fundamental contract between a newspaper and its audience." It had previously used a similar
construction, for the prosecutors: "For the FBI.... not to react to
Dr. Lee's [conduct] would have been a dereliction of duty." But the
question was not *whether* the FBI should react (or not) but *how*,
within our system, legally, ethically, constitutionally, to do so. And
no one was asking the *Times* to "withhold information" about "government concerns," least of all regarding alleged "transfer of technology to China" or "nuclear weapons security." If the *Times* were
asked to do anything in this matter, it might be to refrain from passing on, and repeating, and scolding, and generally presenting as "investigative reporting" what were in fact malign and exceedingly
improper allegations, by "anonymous sources" with prosecutorial
agendas, against virtually defenseless individuals.

There was—perhaps this goes without saying—no apology whatever
to Wen Ho Lee. "The unthinkable violation of the fundamental
contract between a newspaper and its audience" did not, obviously,
extend to him. Lelyveld, too, had referred to a Corrections policy
"to make our contract with readers more enforceable." What "contract"? To rectify malignant misspelling of names? This concern,
too, was not with facts, or substance, or subject, but to sustain, without earning or reciprocating, the trust of "readers." The basis of
"trust" was evidently quite tenuous. What had increased, perhaps in
its stead, was this sense of being misunderstood, unfairly maligned,
along with those other victims: FBI agents, informers, and all manner of prosecutors. No sympathy, no apology, certainly, for the man
whom many, including in the end the judge, considered a victim—
not least a victim of the *Times*.

That *Times* editors are by no means incapable of apology became
clear on September 28, 2000, the same day as the editorial Overview. On that day, Bill Keller, the managing editor of the *Times*,

posted a "Memorandum to the Staff," which he sent as well to "media critics," and which he said all staff members were "free to share outside the paper."

It was an apology, and it was abject. "When we published our appraisal of our Wen Ho Lee coverage," it said, "we anticipated that some people would misread it, and we figured that misreading was beyond our control. But one misreading is so agonizing to me that it requires a follow-up."

"Through most of its many drafts," Keller continued, the message had contained the words "of us" in a place where any reader of ordinary intelligence and understanding, one would have thought, would have known what was meant, since the words "to us" appear later in the same sentence. "Somewhere in the multiple scrubbings of this document," however,

> the words "of us" got lost. And that has led some people on the staff to a notion that never occurred to me—that the note meant to single out Steve Engelberg, who managed this coverage so masterfully, as the scapegoat for the shortcomings we acknowledged.
>
> My reaction the first time I heard this theory was to laugh it off as preposterous. Joe and I tried to make clear in meetings with staff...that the paragraph referred to ourselves....In the very specific sense that we laid our hands on these articles, and we overlooked some opportunities in our own direction of the coverage. We went to some lengths to assure that no one would take our message as a repudiation of our reporters, but I'm heartsick to discover that we failed to make the same clear point about one of the finest editors I know. Let the record show that we stand behind Steve and the other editors who played roles in developing this coverage. Coverage, as the message to readers said, of which we remain proud.

Bureaucracy at its purest. Reporters, editors, "masterfully directed" coverage, at worst some "opportunities" "overlooked." The buck stops nowhere. "We remain proud" of the coverage in question, only "agonized" and "heartsick" at having been understood to fail to exonerate a member of this staff. The only man characterized as "the scapegoat" in the whole matter is—this is hardly worth remarking—one of the directors of the coverage, some might say the hounding, of Wen Ho Lee.

Something is obviously wrong here. Howell Raines, the editor of the editorial page (and the writer of the Overview) was, like Joe Lelyveld, a distinguished reporter. Editing and reporting are, of course, by no means the same. But one difficulty, perhaps with Keller as well, is that in an editing hierarchy, unqualified loyalty to staff, along with many other manifestations of the wish to be liked, can become a failing—intellectual, professional, moral. It may be that the editors' wish for popularity with the staff has caused the perceptible and perhaps irreversible decline in the paper. There is, I think, something more profoundly wrong—not just the contrast between its utter solidarity, its self-regard, its sense of victimization and tender sympathy with its own, and its unconsciousness of its own weight as an institution, in the stories it claims to cover. Something else, perhaps more important, two developments actually—the emergence of the print reporter as celebrity and the proliferation of the anonymous source. There is an indication of where this has led us even in the *Times* editors' own listing, among the "enormous obstacles" its reporters faced, of "government efforts to identify the *Times*'s sources." The "sources" in question were, of course, precisely governmental. The *Times* should never have relied upon them, not just because they were, as they turned out to be, false, but because they were prosecutorial—and they were turning the *Times* into their instrument.

In an earlier day, the *Times* would have had a safeguard against its own misreporting, including its "accounting" and its Overview of its coverage of the case of Wen Ho Lee. The paper used to publish in its pages long, unedited transcripts of important documents. The transcript of the FBI's interrogation of Dr. Lee—on March 7, 1999, the day after the first of the *Times* articles appeared—exists. It runs to thirty-seven pages. Three agents have summoned Dr. Lee to their offices in "a cleared building facility." They have refused him not only the presence of anybody known to him but permission to have lunch. They keep talking ominously of a "package" they have, and telephone calls they have been making about it to Washington. The contents of the package includes yesterday's *New York Times*. They allude to it more than fifty times:

> "You read that and it's on the next page as well, Wen Ho. And let me call Washington real quick while you read that."

> "The important part is that, uh, basically that is indicating that there is a person at the laboratory that's committed espionage and that points to you."

> "You, you read it. It's not good, Wen Ho."

> "You know, this is, this is a big problem, but uh-mm, I think you need to read this article. Take a couple of minutes and, and read this article because there's some things that have been raised by Washington that we've got to get resolved."

And they resume:

> "It might not even be a classified issue. . . . but Washington right now is under the impression that you're a spy. And this newspaper article is, is doing everything except for coming out with your name . . . everything points to you. People in the community and people at the laboratory tomorrow are going to know. That this article is referring to you. . . ."

The agents tell him he is going to be fired (he is fired two days later), that his wages will be garnished, that he will lose his retirement, his clearance, his chance for other employment, his friends, his freedom. The only thing they mention more frequently than the article in the *Times* is his polygraph, and every mention of it is something they know to be false: that he "failed" it. They tell him this lie more than thirty times. Sometimes they mention it in conjunction with the *Times* article:

> "You know, Wen Ho, this, it's bad. I mean look at this newspaper article! I mean, 'China Stole Secrets for Bombs.' It all but says your name in here. The polygraph reports all say you're failing.... Pretty soon you're going to have reporters knocking on your door."

Then they get to the Rosenbergs:

> "The Rosenbergs are the only people that never cooperated with the federal government in an espionage case. You know what happened to them? They electrocuted them, Wen Ho."

> "You know Aldrich Ames? He's going to rot in jail!... He's going to spend his dying days in jail."

> "Okay? Do you want to go down in history? Whether you're professing your innocence like the Rosenbergs to the day they take you to the electric chair?..."

Dr. Lee pleads with them, several times, not to interrupt him when he is trying to answer a question: "You want me, you want to listen two minutes from my explanation?" Not a chance:

> "No, you stop a minute, Wen Ho.... Compared to what's going to happen to you with this newspaper article..."
>   "The Rosenbergs are dead."
>   "This is what's going to do you more damage than anything.... Do you think the press prints everything that's true?

Do you think that everything that's in this article is true?...
The press doesn't care."

Now, it may be that the editors of the *Times* do not find this news-
worthy, or that they believe their readers would have no interest in
the fact that the FBI conducts its interrogations in this way. The
Times might also, fairly, claim that it has no responsibility for the
uses to which its front-page articles may be put, by the FBI or any
other agency of government. Except for this. In both the editorial
Overview and the "Note from the Editors," as in Mr. Stewart's
op-ed piece, the *Times*'s sympathies are clearly with the forces of
prosecution and the FBI. "Dr. Lee had already taken a lie detector
test," the editors write, for example, in their assessment, and "FBI
investigators believed that it showed deception when he was asked
whether he had leaked secrets."

In the days when the *Times* still published transcripts, the reader
could have judged for himself. Nothing could be clearer than that
the FBI investigators believed nothing of the kind. As they knew,
Dr. Lee had, on the contrary, passed his polygraph—which is why,
in his interrogation, they try so obsessively to convince him that he
failed it. Even the editorial Overview, shorter and perhaps for that
reason less misleading, shows where the *Times*'s sense of who is victimized resides. After two paragraphs of describing various activities
of Dr. Lee's as "improper and illegal," "beyond reasonable dispute,"
it describes, of all people, Louis Freeh, the director of the FBI (and
Janet Reno, the attorney general) as being "under sharp attack."
Freeh was FBI director when agents of the Bureau, illegally detaining Monica Lewinsky, were conducting "investigations" of the same
sort for the Office of the Independent Counsel. Freeh was also advocating, not just in government but directly to the press, more Special
Prosecutors for more matters of all kinds.

But enough. The *Times* feels a responsibility to correct misim-
pressions it may have generated in readers—how names are spelled,
what middle initials are, who is standing miscaptioned on which

side of a photograph, which butterfly is which—is satisfied, in an important way, in its corrections. For the rest, it has looked at its coverage and found it good. The underlying fact, however, is this: For years readers have looked in the *Times* for what was once its unsurpassed strength: the uninflected coverage of the news. You can look and look, now, and you will not find it there. Some politically correct series and group therapy reflections on race relations perhaps. These appear harmless. They may even win prizes. Fifteen reporters working for one year might, perhaps, have been more usefully employed on some genuine issue of fact. More egregious, however, and in some ways more malign, was an article that appeared, on November 5, 2000, in the Sunday *Times Magazine*.

The piece was a cover story about Senator Daniel Patrick Moynihan. Everyone makes mistakes. This piece, blandly certain of its intelligence, actually consisted of them. Everything was wrong. At the most trivial level, the piece said Moynihan had held no hearings about President Clinton's health plan and no meetings with him to discuss welfare. (In fact, the senator had held twenty-nine such hearings in committee and many such discussions with the President.) At the level of theory, it misapprehended the history, content, purpose, and fate of Moynihan's proposal for a guaranteed annual income. It would require a book to set right what was wrong in the piece—and in fact, such a book existed, at least about the guaranteed annual income. But what was, in a way, most remarkable about what *The New York Times* has become appeared, once again, in the way it treated its own coverage.

The Sunday *Magazine*'s editors limited themselves to a little self-congratulatory note. The article, they reported, had "prompted a storm of protest." "But many said that we got it right, and that our writer said what had long seemed to be unspeakable." ("Unspeakable" may not be what they mean. Perhaps it was a paraphrase.) They published just one letter, which praised the piece as "incisive."

The Corrections column, however, when it came, was a gem. "An article in the *Times Magazine* last Sunday about the legacy of Senator

Daniel Patrick Moynihan," it began, "misidentified a former senator who was an expert on military affairs. He was Richard Russell, not Russell Long."

The "article also," the correction went on, had "referred imprecisely" (a fine way to put it) to the senator's committee hearings on President Clinton's health care. (Not a word about welfare.) But the Corrections column saved for last what the *Times* evidently regarded as most important. "The article also overstated [another fine word] Senator Moynihan's English leanings while he attended the London School of Economics. Bowler, yes. Umbrella, yes. Monocle, no."

No "malignant" misspellings here. But nothing a reader can trust any longer, either. Certainly no reliable, uninflected coverage of anything, least of all the news. The enterprise, whatever else it is, has almost ceased altogether to be a newspaper. It is still a habit. People glance at it and, on Sundays, complain about its weight. For news they must look elsewhere. What can have happened here?

"The turning point at the paper," I once wrote, in a piece of fiction, "was the introduction of the byline." I still believe that to be true. I simply had no idea how radical the consequences of that turning point were going to be. Until the early seventies, it was a mark of professionalism in reporters for newspapers, wire services, newsmagazines, to have their pieces speak, as it were, for themselves, with all the credibility and authority of the publication in which they anonymously appeared. Reviews, essays, regular columns were of course signed. They were expressions of opinion, as distinct from reporting, and readers had to know and evaluate whose opinion it was. But when a reader said of a piece of information, "The *Times* says," or "The *Wall Street Journal* says," he was relying on the credibility of the institution. With very rare exceptions—correspondents, syndicated columnists, or sportswriters whose names were household words, or in attributing a scoop of extraordinary historical importance—the reporter's byline would have seemed intrusive and unprofessional.

In television reporting, of course, every element of the situation was different. It would be absurd to say "CBS (or ABC, NBC, or even CNN) says" or even "I saw it on" one network or another. It had to be Walter Cronkite, later Dan Rather, Diane Sawyer, Tom Brokaw, Peter Jennings—not just because no television network or station had the authority of any favorite and trusted publication, but because seeing and hearing the person who conveyed the news (impossible, obviously, with the printed byline) was precisely the basis, for television viewers, of trust.

Once television reporters became celebrities, it was perhaps inevitable that print reporters would want at least their names known; and there were, especially at first, stories one did well to read on the basis of a trusted byline. There still existed what Mary McCarthy, in another context, called "the last of the tall timber." But the tall timber in journalism is largely gone—replaced, as in many fields, by the phenomenon of celebrity. And gradually, in print journalism, the celebrity of the reporter began to overtake and then to undermine the reliability of pieces. Readers still say, "The *Times* says," or "I read it in the *Post*" (so far as I can tell, except in the special case of gossip columns, readers hardly ever mention, or even notice, bylines), but trust in even once favorite newspapers has almost vanished. One is left with this oddly convoluted paradox: As survey after survey confirms, people generally despise journalists; yet they cite, as a source of information, newspapers. And though they have come, with good reason, to distrust newspapers as a whole, they still tend to believe each individual story *as they read it*. We all do. Though I may know a piece to be downright false, internally contradictory, in some profound and obvious way corrupted, I still, for a moment anyway, believe it. Believe the most obviously manufactured quotes, the slant, the spin, the prose, the argument with no capacity even to frame an issue and no underlying sense of what follows from what.

At the same time, a development in criticism, perhaps especially movie criticism, affected print journalism of every kind. It used to be that the celebrities featured on billboards and foremost in public consciousness were the movie stars themselves. For a while, it became *auteurs*, directors. Then, bizarrely but for a period of many years, it became *critics* who starred in the discussion of movies. That period seems, fortunately, to have passed. But somehow, the journalist's by-line, influenced perhaps by the critic's, began to bring with it a blurring of genres: reporting, essay, memoir, personal statement, anecdote, judgmental or critical review. Most of all, critical review—which is why government officials and citizens alike treat reporters in the same way artists regard most critics—with mixed fear and dismay. It is also why the subjects of news stories read each "news" piece as if it were a review on opening night.

There is no longer even a vestige or pretense, on the part of the print journalist, of any professional commitment to uninflected coverage of the news. The ambition is rather, under their bylines, to express themselves, their writing styles. Days pass without a single piece of what used to be called "hard news." The celebrityhood, or even the aspiration to celebrity, of print reporters, not just in print but also on talk shows, has been perhaps the single most damaging development in the history of print journalism.

The second, less obvious, cause of decline in the very notion of reliable information was the proliferation of the "anonymous source"—especially as embodied, or rather disembodied, in Deep Throat. Many people have speculated about the "identity" of this phantom. Others have shown, more or less conclusively, that at least as described in *All the President's Men*, by Bob Woodward and Carl Bernstein, he did not, in fact could not, exist. Initially introduced as a narrative device, to hold together book and movie, this improbable creature was obviously both a composite, which Woodward, the only one who claims to have known and have consulted him, denies, and an utter fiction, which is denied by both Woodward and Bernstein—the better writer, who had, from the start, a "friend," whose information in almost every significant respect coincides with, and even predates, Deep Throat's. But the influence of this combination, the celebrity reporter and the chimera *to whom the reporter alone has access*, has been incalculable.

The implausibility of the saga of Deep Throat has been frequently pointed out. Virtually every element of the story—the all-night séances in garages; the signals conveyed by moved flowerpots on windowsills and drawings of clocks in newspapers; the notes left by prearrangement on ledges and pipes in those garages; the unidiomatic and essentially uninformative speech—has been demolished. Apart from its inherent impractibilities, for a man requiring secrecy and fearing for his life and the reporter's, the strategy seems less like tradecraft than a series of attention-getting mechanisms. This is by no means to deny that Woodward and Bernstein had "sources," some but far from all of whom preferred to remain anonymous. From the evidence in the book they include at least Fred Buzhardt, Hugh Sloan, John Sears, Mark Felt and other FBI agents, Leonard Garment, and, perhaps above all, the ubiquitous and not infrequently treacherous Alexander Haig. None of these qualify as Deep Throat, nor does anyone, as depicted in the movie or book. Woodward's new rationale is this: the secret of the phantom's name must be kept until the phantom himself reveals it—or else dies. Woodward is prepared, however, to disqualify candidates whom others— most recently Leonard Garment, in an entire book devoted to such speculation—may suggest, by telling, instance by instance, who Deep Throat is *not*. A long list, obviously, which embraces everyone.

It is no wonder that Woodward, having risked the logic of this, would risk as well an account of a mythical visit to the hospital bedside of former CIA Director William Casey, who was dying and who, according to doctors, had lost all power of speech. Casey's hospital room was closely guarded against visits from all but his immediate family. Woodward claims to have entered the hospital room, asked Casey a question, observed him "nod," and quotes him as saying, "I believed."

There is more. Woodward now claims that the "anonymous source" for another book, *The Brethren*, was Justice Potter Stewart. Justice Stewart, perhaps needless to say, is dead. He was a highly respected and distinguished Justice. But that does not satisfactorily resolve the matter, because Justice Stewart can and does bear a sort of witness here. He *wrote* some important opinions. Some of the opinions most seriously misunderstood, misrepresented, and even misquoted in *The Brethren* are Potter Stewart's. And nothing could be more obvious from the book than the fact that, apart from the clerks, Woodward's primary source was in fact Justice Rehnquist.

The ramifications of this cult of the anonymous source—particularly as Deep Throat, this oracle to whom only a single priest, or acolyte, has access, have been, for journalism, enormous. No need any longer to publish long transcripts. Why bother? No need even to read them, or anything—public documents, the novels of Robert Stendahl. Two clicks to Amazon.com will give you spellings. And an "anonymous source" will either provide you with "information" or provide what your editors will accept as "cross-checking" for what you have already said. The celebrity reporter has created, beginning with Deep Throat, what one would have thought a journalistic oxymoron: a *celebrity* anonymous source. More than that: a celebrity anonymous source who *does not even exist*. As late as page 207 of Leonard Garment's book, *In Search of Deep Throat*, Mr. Garment actually writes:

> I was doggedly confident that Woodward, Bernstein, and, above all, their editor . . . would not have put themselves out on a long limb for a gimmick that would eventually be revealed and denounced as a journalistic fraud of historic proportions.

Not a gimmick. A device. When Woodward produced the noumenal encounter between the anonymous source and the celebrity reporter, it turns out, a religion was born, which has grown to affect not just journalism but the entire culture. In print journalism, you can usually tell, when such a source exists at all, who it is: the person most kindly treated in the story. And the religion, with all its corollaries, dogmas, and implications, has made of reporters not fallible individuals competing for facts and stories in the real world but fellow members of the cult. Whomever or whatever they go after—Wen Ho Lee, Whitewater, or "scandals" that did not pan out—or whomever they equally baselessly support—Independent Counsel Kenneth Starr, Chairman Henry Hyde of the House Judiciary

Committee, and FBI Director Louis Freeh—they tend to support dogmatically, and as one. Best of all, they like to consult and to write approvingly of one another and even, if need be, themselves. Administrations come and go. Quasi-governmental bureaucracies, with their hierarchies and often interlocking cults and interests, persist.

The convergence of the anonymous source with the celebrity reporter now has ramifications that could not have been foreseen. A certain journalistic laziness was perhaps predictable—phoning around as a form of "legwork," attributing information to "sources," in quotes, which no one was equipped either to verify or to deny. But the serious result, which no one could have foreseen, is this: The whole purpose of the "anonymous source" has been precisely reversed. The reason there exists a First Amendment protection for journalists' confidential sources has always been to permit citizens—the weak, the vulnerable, the isolated—to be heard publicly, without fear of retaliation by the strong—by their employer, for example, or by the forces of government. The whistleblower or the innocent accused were to be protected. Instead, almost every "anonymous source" in the press, in recent years, has been an official of some kind, or a person in the course of a vendetta speaking from a position of power.

More disturbing, in spite of what has been at least since Vietnam an almost instinctive press hostility to the elected government (an adversarial position that can be healthy in a free society), the press now has an unmistakable affinity with official accusers, in particular the Special Prosecutors and the FBI. And when *those* powerful institutions are allowed to "leak"—that is, become the press's "anonymous sources"—the press becomes not an adversary but an instrument of all that is most secret and coercive—in attacks, not infrequently, with an elected administration but also with truly nameless individuals, those who have neither power nor celebrity of any kind, and who have no means of access, least of all as "anonymous sources," to the press.

The press, in these matters, has become far more unified. There may be competition among those who will get the first interview of some celebrity or other, or first access to a treasured "anonymous source." But it is the *same* celebrities and the same sources that journalists pursue, not excluding interviews with one another. Even among the apparently most irate and shouting television personalities whom Calvin Trillin has so memorably characterized as "Sabbath gasbags," there is a sameness. Political views are permitted, routinely, along a spectrum from left to right; but the views of each participant, on virtually any subject, can be predicted from week to week.

The worst, however, is the mystique of the "sources." Citizens of a democracy require reliable information. How can they check "sources"? What possible basis is there for relying on them? The word of the celebrity reporter who cannot bring himself to name them? What sort of reliability, what sort of information, what sort of journalism is this? Especially since there seems to be, among "investigative reporters" and the institutions that support them, a stubborn loyalty to and solidarity with sources—even when a source (as in the recent case of Charles Bakaly of the Special Prosecutor's office) *admits* that he is the previously "anonymous source" in question, or, more puzzlingly, when the "source" has demonstrably deceived the reporter himself. In what may be a journalistic variant of the Stockholm syndrome (whereby hostages become extremely loyal to their captors), journalists and their editors defend and protect the anonymity, and even the reliability, of their sources, even when they have been most seriously misled. A sacred covenant, apparently. But what of the trust and "contract" with the reader? Forgotten, secular, a matter of spelling and perhaps the small stuff. There, for instance, is the *Times*, in its "assessment," trying to establish the basis for a now utterly discredited story as "cross-checking sources" and resisting "obstacles" posed by other people's having tried to "identify our sources." Would this not have been the occasion to name at least the sources who deliberately misled them? Are the identities of self-serving liars, and particularly liars of this sort, who use the newspaper story as a weapon of intimidation, to be protected? Four months later, in February of 2001, the *Times* again reappraised its coverage of Wen Ho Lee. The pieces somehow, under a lot of cosmic obfuscation, seemed to have missed their underlying points: (1) that there was no evidence of spying by anyone at Los Alamos; (2) that there was no evidence of any spying by Wen Ho Lee. The suspicion of him rested largely on two incidents: that he had once telephoned a man under suspicion of something undefined and offered to help him, and that he had once entered, uninvited, a meeting at Los Alamos, and hugged a major Chinese scientist there. Typical spy behavior: a phone call and a hug.

If so, then you are speaking inescapably of the instruments of a police state, with secret informers, and the press just one in a set of interlocking and secretive bureaucracies. The alternative, it seems to me, is to proceed in a more diligent way, one by one, in the press, on the street, in the academy, to look for information and try to draw reasonable inferences from it. A combination of research and thinking and consulting, if need be, a genuine source—that is, someone who has information and is willing to impart it. No professional ideologies that paradoxically combine political correctness with self-serving orthodoxies and an affinity for prosecutors. No faith in Delphic utterances from unidentified persons. In spite of what might have affected generations of aspiring reporters, no one is going to contrive an absurd set of signals for you, meet you secretly and regularly and undetected by others in a garage by night and tell you anything worth knowing.

Pools, informers, leaks from prosecutors, celebrity reporters with anonymous sources—all of these are forms simultaneously of consolidation and of hiding, facets of what the enterprise has become. Consider the celebrity reporter, the particular powers of celebrity in a celebrity culture, especially when his nominal profession, after all, is the purveying of information, the dissemination of what the society will know about itself.

Consider the prosecutorial affinity, which is both easy and immensely destructive. Wen Ho Lee, as it turned out, had nearly miraculous access, in the end, to good, pro bono lawyers. Most non-celebrity citizens simply have no such access—either to lawyers or to the press. They are not just truly anonymous. They are plain un-heard.

Consider as well the use of pools. Not the imposed pools of the military, but voluntary, self-satisfied, bonded bureaucracies and consortiums. To use saving money as an excuse for not having the independence, the interest, the curiosity and inclination to go out there and see for yourself—it is simply not reconcilable with any notion of the working journalist. Under the First Amendment, the press enjoys special protections so that the public will hear from many competing individual and institutional voices, and so that debate, as Harry Kalven put it, can be "free, robust, and wide open." Journalism has to be competitive or it is nothing. Television's mistake in using its consortium was understandable and should have been instructive. But television that night was in the business of *prediction*. In Florida, where something already existing is in dispute—in a state with sunshine laws specifically making facts available for public information—to send a surrogate institution is indefensible. For one thing, it virtually guarantees that the sunshine laws will atrophy. For another, it guarantees that the public will *never* know what the real count was. In lieu of NORC, it would have been better to send in, if not professional auditors, a group of diligent fourth-grade children who can count.

All monopolists collaborating in restraint of trade say they are cooperating to save everybody money. In this case, another unmistakable and crucial motive has been to hide. That hiding reflects fear. Fear of being alone, fear of being out of step with the prevailing view. Fear even of being right when everyone else is wrong. So hide yourself in an orthodoxy and a group. Let no independent reporters and, lord help us, no independent newspaper in there. Try to co-opt the *Miami Herald*. Let the sociologists from NORC handle it. The administration, the government, will not be offended. At least not with us.

Oddly enough, even the policy of Corrections is a form simultaneously of consolidation of power and of hiding. The orthodoxy is: We are so scrupulous we correct even the smallest thing. Therefore, you can trust us as you would Mao, the Scripture, the Politburo. It is a form of Fundamentalism, it protects the ideology. Nothing more clearly exposed the essence of that Corrections policy than the Editors' Note about Wen Ho Lee. They misrepresented what they had actually said. They defended, in glowing terms, what they did say. They gave themselves credit for "calling attention to the problem." Much like those charities a few years ago when the child, who had been photographed so movingly and had corresponded so faithfully with its "adopted" parents, who sent ten dollars a month, turned out to have been long dead or not even to exist. The charities, too, said, "We were just calling attention to the problem." If you do a textual analysis of what the *Times* did say, over a period of many months, and how its "accounting" or "assessment" now describes it, you have not just disinformation but an indication of what much of journalism has become. We were first, but we blame it on the *Wall Street Journal*, which was earlier, and on the misrepresentations of others, who came later. On the whole, we are proud. And the only one to whom we genuinely owe an apology is one of our staff, the editor of the series in question, "the scapegoat," whom we must now praise in the most extravagant terms. And about whom we are abject, agonized, heartsick.

I know nothing about the editor in question. I did read, months ago, his irate and patronizing response, defending those very articles, to someone who had ventured, in *Brill's Content*, to criticize them. There is, in general, in newspapers at least, almost no reliable, uninflected coverage of the news. No celebrity journalists seem even to aspire to it. There is opinion, a verdict, an assumption of the role—how to put it?—of *critic* to the day's events. A verdict. We do not need a verdict. We need an account.

That is where the absence of those once long, verbatim transcripts is of great importance. The transcripts permitted none of that judging or tilting or hiding. They were straightforward. They were some-thing that television, for example, with its scheduling and time constraints, could not do. Nor could tabloids.

Consolidating with others and going secret. From the anony-mous source, to the prosecutor's office, to the consortium, all are just steps. And correcting—either typos, or misspellings, or things ev-eryone knows already or that matter to no one, or that correct them-selves on a daily basis—is just the mask, the surface of the decay. One more indication of moral and factual authority—and, in conse-quence, another source of power. It may be, it is virtually certain, that newspapers, to regain their honor, will have to relinquish some-thing of their power and think again.

The whole constitutional system had been, for some time, under attack by all three branches of government. There has been the be-havior of the executive, as embodied not just by the President in his understanding of his office, but, paradoxically, by the Independent Counsel in his prosecutions. There has been the behavior of the leg-islature, in its lascivious travesty of the impeachment process. There has been the conduct of the Supreme Court, intruding on the prov-ince of the executive, the legislative, the states, and finally on the rights of every citizen. By making its decision in *Gore v. Bush*, explic-itly, unique—to be regarded as having no precedent and setting none—it undermined the whole basis of Anglo-Saxon law, which is grounded in the notion that the decisions derive their validity from being built upon, and in turn relied upon, as precedents.

The Supreme Court, in its power of judicial review, is regarded as nearly sacred within the system and beyond appeal—with one ex-ception: the press. Judicial review is trumped by press review. The Justices are highly aware of this. Judges who claimed to be conserva-tives, even as they struck most radically at the Constitution, the bal-ance of powers, federalism, the fundamental understandings of the society, played to journalists. Virtually the only decisions of this Court upholding freedoms, under the First Amendment, for exam-ple, have been decisions in favor of the press. The press seems less aware of this—still describing the most radical judges, obligingly, as "conservatives." Somehow, comfortable and serene as the system still seems to be, and as though political life were still in some sense normal, the whole question of legitimacy seemed to rest on so few public officials—until recently Senator Moynihan, for example, and now Justices Stevens, Ginsburg, Souter, Breyer. There is always the possibility that there will be heroes, or that the system is self-correcting. But it will not do for the press, with very few exceptions, simply to join all other bureaucracies, to correct spellings or give us their impressions about race (there are still "tensions") while, in the ultimate abdication, they miss the factual. Independent journalists have obligations of their own.

2001

SEARCHING FOR THE REAL
NIXON SCANDAL

ON THE weekend of Memorial Day 1976, at John Doar's farm near Millerton, New York, there was a reunion of what had been, in 1974, the House Judiciary Committee's impeachment inquiry staff. John Doar, who was Special Counsel for the inquiry, had since become a partner in a New York law firm, where he was in charge of a major antitrust case. Other members of the staff had returned for the occasion from their various jobs. Some had brought tents and sleeping bags. Others had rooms in the nearby motels and inns. A few were sleeping in the house. More than a hundred people in all showed up, also several dogs, including a small terrier called Credence and a huge English sheepdog, who had attended the original staff picnic, on August 15, 1974, in Washington. Thirty-nine former staff members had chartered a plane from Washington to Pittsburgh, where they were picked up by other former members of the staff. Supper, the first evening, was catered by the local Grange. People took motorcycle rides into the hills. Small bonfires were lit around the farm itself. Some of the youngest bounced on a trampoline or played basketball. From soon after supper until well after midnight, there was square dancing. A band and a caller had been brought in from Hartford. Nearly everyone took part in the square sets and in a virtually endless Virginia reel. In the wildest fantasies of San Clemente, no one could dream that such an event was taking place. And even in Millerton, one had the fleeting impression of dancing on a grave.

It was not a grave, of course. President Nixon had only resigned. After nearly two years, it was no longer clear what that resignation had meant, or even what the inquiry had had to do with it. Meanwhile, with every document published by the Senate Select Committee on Government Operations with Respect to Intelligence Activities (the Church Committee), it was becoming more clear that the case for the impeachment of Richard Nixon, in 1974, had fallen apart.

It all seemed, anyway, long ago, and difficult to remember in detail. In late July 1974, the House Judiciary Committee, under Chairman Peter W. Rodino, had voted to recommend three Articles of Impeachment to the House. Article I was essentially an obstruction of justice charge. Article II charged misuse of the agencies of government. Article III, in effect, charged contempt of Congress, in doctoring and in refusing to produce subpoenaed evidence. In view of the Church Committee's account of the conduct of previous administrations, including violations of law and abuses of power since at least 1936, the first two Articles seemed to dissolve. As for Article III, there had been disagreement about it from the start. Doar himself ultimately did not support it—on the grounds that requiring the President to produce this evidence, and thereby implicate himself in what would obviously become a highly serious criminal case, was reminiscent of the Star Chamber. Others argued that such a view implicitly endorsed claims of executive privilege, the national security, whatever, as camouflaged euphemisms for the Fifth Amendment; that if the President needed, in effect, to take the Fifth, he ought to be obliged, like any other citizen, to come right out and take it; and that a failure to pass Article III would add to all the other powers of the President a new power, to withhold evidence from the only process the Framers had established specifically to override such claims of secrecy: the impeachment process, the "Grand Inquest of the Nation," by which the President could be held, constitutionally, to account.

In any case, it didn't matter. Article III would never have passed, or even existed, without Articles I and II. The problem with all three Articles, and with their accompanying Summary of Information and Final Report, and with the thirty-odd volumes of Statements of Information, which were also published by the House Judiciary

Committee, is that, in spite of a valid perception the whole country shared of the integrity of the process at the time, all those volumes never quite made their case, or any case. And one result, which nobody on the staff could possibly have foreseen, was that, in light of the Church Committee report and other documents, what remains of the records of the impeachment inquiry would support not only a claim that Richard Nixon was hounded from office after all, but also, more strangely, the reverse: that the impeachment inquiry itself was just another phase in the continuation of the cover-up.

Neither of these claims, obviously, is right; yet they are not easy to dismiss. As there continue to be revelations of abuses of and by the CIA, the FBI, the IRS, the military, and officials at every level of government and corporate enterprise, in the remote as well as the immediate past, it becomes less and less clear why the Nixon presidency in particular had to end. This summer, the Senate voted overwhelmingly to establish a permanent Office of Special Prosecutor, as though what had seemed, in 1973, an extraordinary crisis, requiring extraordinary measures, was now perceived as a more or less permanent state of affairs in government—and as though such a permanently critical situation could be remedied by the addition of yet another watchman to the constitutionally established existing watchmen in the night. Another indication of the degree to which the specific Nixon case remains still unresolved is implicit in those theories that Nixon was driven from office by a conspiracy within government itself—more specifically, within the CIA. It is as though history already required, in explanation of Nixon's having left the presidency at all, an elaborate plot, in the form of a reconstruction from scraps of inconsistent evidence of an Agency cabal.

It seems certain, though, that the Nixon presidency, far from being continuous with those before, was in fact unprecedented; that, without the supposition of cabals of any sort, Nixon himself did something not only more than any of his predecessors but altogether else. And the reason why no investigation, by Congress, or the press, or in the courts, has so far managed to establish precisely what he did has to do, I think, both with the way the investigations were conducted and with what I now believe to be the very nature of the case. Putting together some of the circumstances of the impeachment inquiry with a few facts in those Church Committee documents—and trying to reconcile these with several, at the time apparently unaccountable, discrepancies and lapses in the conduct of President Nixon, his lawyers, and his aides—I think one does arrive at a bottom line, a plausible, even obvious explanation of why it was that the Nixon presidency had to end. It may have been for a time unthinkable; or we may have known it all along.

I. WHAT KIND OF CASE?

The inquiry. On the morning of March 27, 1974, Barbara Fletcher, who was in charge of most calls to the impeachment inquiry staff from congressmen and members of the press, received a long-distance call from a young man who claimed that in 1973, as he was walking down Wisconsin Avenue, President Nixon shot at him. For various reasons, few of the logs and records kept by the staff (and now sealed, for the foreseeable future, in the archives of the House Judiciary Committee) are altogether dependable or complete. The files of congressional committees are, in any case, notoriously inaccurate. But because of her diligence and the delicacy of her assignment in dealing with these calls, Miss Fletcher kept scrupulous and exhaustive logs. The young man said he had been wearing a shield. He asked to be given a lie detector test. He left two Milwaukee phone numbers, his mother's and his own. Miss Fletcher noted all this and said she would pass the information on. It was evident from the whole tone of the entry that the young man, like a lot of other callers—like the lady who brought in her garbage as evidence that she was being poisoned; like the many hundreds of people who sent in rocks, with the message that only he who is without sin should cast them—was not well.

But among the innumerable what-ifs of the inquiry, and of Watergate itself, the problem might not have been a minor one. What if the young man had been completely sane and right? The staff would have been unable to investigate his claim. There were no investigators on the staff. And it is far from clear that shooting at a man in the street is contemplated in the phrase "Treason, Bribery, or other high Crimes and Misdemeanors"—the only grounds on which a President can be impeached. Shooting at a political opponent, certainly, would fall within the constitutional standard, as a "political" crime, that is, a crime against the system and the Constitution itself. But an ordinary violation of the criminal statutes, no matter how serious, is probably not contemplated in the phrase. The astonishingly foolish, poorly reasoned, and poorly documented brief submitted by the White House argued that it is: that "other high Crimes and Misdemeanors" simply meant a literal, ordinary (though in deference to that "high," a serious) crime, committed in the President's "public, or official capacity." It was hard to think of any unlawful acts, apart perhaps from adultery or purse-snatching, which a President might commit in his private, or unofficial capacity. The White House brief was intended, of course, to limit to the narrowest criminal terms any definition of the grounds on which a President might be impeached. It went on to say that "high Crimes and Misdemeanors," as a term of art, had a unitary meaning, like "bread and butter issues"—a comparison which, in its peculiar vulgarity, exemplified something both slipshod and condescending in the work of the White House lawyers, under James St. Clair, by whom the President was at the time so oddly, badly served. It was true of the whole brief what one of the youngest members of the inquiry said of subsequent documents submitted for the White House: that sooner or later, at their characteristic level of effectiveness, in general and in detail, these lawyers seemed bound to produce a brief on behalf of their client, President Philip N. Nixon.

One effect of the White House brief on grounds for impeachment, however, was to draw attention from the quality of the brief produced by the impeachment inquiry staff. That brief, our brief, which was published on February 20, 1974, was the first indication of what kind of work would be done by a staff of nearly forty lawyers who came from both political parties and from all parts of the country and who had, or claimed to have, by 1974, when they were hired, no view one way or another about whether President Nixon ought to be impeached. "I will say that every staff member was questioned whether or not they had taken a position on impeachment," Special Counsel Doar told the Judiciary Committee on January 31, 1974, "and if they had, other than that there should be an inquiry, then they were not considered for the job." For seven months, both Doar and Chairman Rodino insisted that no member of the staff take any side whatever on the question. As late as July 23, 1974, when Minority Counsel Sam Garrison suggested that Democrats on the staff might all along have been inclined to favor impeachment, while Republicans might have tended to oppose it, Rodino said that if he had known Garrison took such a view he would have fired him.

While there were strong reasons for maintaining a bipartisan staff with this apparent viewlessness, in the first serious attempt to impeach a President in more than a century, the criterion is not one for putting together a firm of lawyers. It is more suited to selecting jurors—who are meant unprofessionally to weigh, but never to investigate or to assemble a case. Lawyers are advocates. The lawyers Doar hired were bright, loyal, discreet, and highly recommended. They represented as broad a cross section of the country as the congressmen on the committee. They worked under two ironclad admonitions: to maintain absolute confidentiality and to be "fair." At the same time, Doar had to proceed on the assumption that almost no one could be trusted. On January 2, 1974, I asked him how, in that case, he was going to keep perfect confidentiality in so large a staff of lawyers. "You work them very hard," he said, "and you don't tell them anything." The brief produced by such a staff was, predictably, deficient.

So were most of the other inquiry documents. It turned out to be unimportant. What was important was that, through months of tension, crises of morale, and professional frustration, the staff did manage to work hard and to keep silent. What they were working on, or thought they were working on, is another matter. Few of them, at the time or even two years later, seemed to have more than an intimation that, while what they were doing was essential, the only thing essential about it was that they be seen to be doing *something* in secret, day and night, for months. "Some of it was the worst time of my life," one of the junior lawyers said, more than a year after it was over. "What you had for the first few months, you see, was thirty lawyers, treading water." That "treading water" was his insight. That "for the first few months" was an understatement. The fact that underlay the ordeal was that most of the work, almost all the time by almost all the staff, was a charade. A valuable charade, in that a machine was seen to churn, while no circus took place, and the courts, and a smaller group of Doar's, and ultimately the congressmen themselves could do their work. But the machine itself, firmly required to be directionless, produced, naturally enough, no investigation and, in the end, no case. It is commonly said that "the case" is in those thirty-odd staff volumes. Only by people who have not read them; hardly anyone has read them.

Doar himself was working mainly with a smaller group of about seven people, five of whom were old friends who had worked with him before and who were not on the regular staff.' Much of what could be salvaged from or written into the lamentable brief on grounds, for instance, was the work at the last minute of these ad hoc irregulars—as was, for good or ill, the conduct of the inquiry, from the ordering of facts and strategies, through compiling the endless Statements of Information, Summary of Information, and Final Report, to the drafting of letters to the White House, of the actual Articles of Impeachment, and even of the statements of Chairman Rodino, from the opening of the inquiry, through the hearings, to the remarks with which he responded, in his living room, to the television broadcast of Richard Nixon's resignation speech.

There was never any doubt among Doar and this small group that, unless there was overwhelming evidence of Nixon's innocence (and the only conceivable circumstance in which, by 1974, there could be such evidence would have been a conspiracy among his aides to frame him, in which case, under a superintendency theory, he might have been impeached for that), the object of the process was that the President must be impeached. Doar had, in fact, been the second nonradical person I knew, and the first Republican, to advocate impeachment—months before he became Special Counsel, long before the inquiry began. There had to be such complete discretion on this point, and such constant, rote repetition of the words "fair," "fairness," "fairly," that there arose a temperamental hazard of inventing pieties and believing in them, against the evidence of your own purposes and your own sense—a hazard to which Nixon had obviously succumbed. Doar customarily spoke, however, in terms of "war" and "the Cause." It had to be so. To exactly the degree that impeachment is warranted, it is no less than urgent. Given the immense, lawful and (since in an impeachment a refusal to observe the restraints of law is precisely the point at issue) unlawful powers of an American President, it would have been unthinkable for Doar to have taken the job as less than an advocate. As late as this summer, 1976, however, most members of the staff and of the Judiciary Committee were still divided in their view of when it was that Doar reached his decision—whether it was in March 1974, as a result of the grand jury presentment, or on the morning of July 19, when, in one of the many completely imaginary stories generated by the inquiry's lore-manufacturing apparatus, Chairman Rodino was supposed to have shouted at Doar to force him to make up his mind.

All this by way of outlining the circumstances in which the inquiry was conducted. Doar, certain from the start that the President must be, under conditions of exemplary fairness, removed from office, could not, he thought, disclose that determination to the congressmen or to his staff. The situation created its own peculiar stresses. Secrecy and loyalty had been the Watergate virtues, after all. Apart from exercising these virtues, staff lawyers were occupied, for instance, in filling out, on the basis of documents already public, those endless and in terms of impeachment entirely useless "chron cards"— the minute-by-minute chronologies, which had been important in the Neshoba County Case of 1967 (in Doar's successful prosecution, as chief of the Justice Department's Civil Rights Division, of the murderers of Andrew Goodman, Michael Schwerner, and James Chaney), but which had no relevance at all to the case at hand. The congressmen, of necessity, became impatient. When the chron cards were replaced by flat, uninflected, numbered Statements of Fact, which Doar proposed that the staff read to the Judiciary Committee for a period of six weeks, beginning in May, the congressmen argued at length whether the statements could properly be designated *fact* at all—whether what was fact was not the sole prerogative of the committee members to determine. In the end what were read to them were called *Statements of Information*. And in the end, having understandably failed to see the point of all these statements (there was hardly any point, except to gain time and to present the committee with a tidy and impressive format), the congressmen's conduct was exemplary—leading to a President's departure from office, without any of the bitterly partisan recriminations which might have divided Congress and the country for many years.

A single episode, however, illustrates the virtual impossibility, at the time, of conducting almost any impeachment research project. It has to do with the 1976 report of the Church Committee. In the context of the 1974 inquiry, there arises the obvious question: If the conduct of past administrations bears, as it so evidently does, on the Nixon case, why did the inquiry not look into these matters and produce some such report? It tried. Doar, aware that such a report would be among the soundest and most obvious defenses for any President against impeachment, knew he had to commission, from outside the staff, a historical account of abuses of presidential power, in anticipation of any report the White House lawyers would produce. As it happens, the White House lawyers never undertook anything of the kind—an error, perhaps of over-confidence, so profound that it still seems hardly credible.

Doar's own report, by scholars under the direction of the distinguished Yale historian C. Vann Woodward, was supposed, like all other inquiry work, to be kept secret. When Congressman Charles Wiggins, for example, insisted that the inquiry's failure to make such a study was unforgivable, he was never told, nor were any other congressmen, that the project was already under way. Committee members, all of whom are lawyers, had already made it clear that they did not want any professors, Yale or other, to advise them on matters of law. In any case, whether secrecy caused the assignment to be phrased unclearly, or for whatever reason, the study was not what would have been required if the White House had produced such a study, which of course it didn't. Professor Woodward ultimately published the work (which does not appear among the inquiry volumes) elsewhere, in paperback.

A footnote to the story of that project concerns Minority Counsel Albert Jenner. As counsel for those Republicans who concurred in the majority vote of the committee, Jenner was a pivotal and historic figure, the pivot of the pivot, in a sense. Had he construed his job differently, had he seriously disagreed with Doar at any point, Jenner could have obstructed the process at every turn. It is by no means clear what the outcome, under those circumstances, would have been. But the fact is, he did not. Another fact is that he was absent a lot of the time, traveling and lecturing. Jenner still remarks, as he did frequently in the course of the inquiry, that Doar is an "administrator," while he, Jenner, is a "litigator." He says he was persuaded of the case against the President in March of 1974, with the grand jury presentment—at the same time, he adds, as Doar. Then, very amiably, he walks over to the shelves of his law office in Chicago, where his inquiry documents are kept. "This will interest you," he says, "although we've kept it top secret. It's something we relied on very heavily." And he removes from the shelf a bound copy of Professor C. Vann Woodward's study. The title is correct. The authorship is attributed to Vance Packard.

That's how things were, broadly, at the inquiry. And in spite of whatever it did accomplish, what it could not accomplish, or even really attempt, was an investigation of the case. What I am concerned with here is establishing a context for a set of initial assumptions, followed by a few facts from various sources, which led me to what I thought were going to be some wild speculations—about why our side, like their side, could not be doing what it appeared to be doing; about what happened and why, although it is all over, it still seems unsettled now; about what a real investigation, if circumstances had permitted one, would have found. It was evidently not a story of the inexorable processes of simple justice; or of their forces of darkness vanquished by our forces of light. Nixon's chosen successor has, after all, for two years held his office. He has retained the former President's unindicted accomplices and aides, and appointed some of the closest of them to positions—the command of NATO, for example—that ought to be unthinkable for men so utterly compromised. Nixon himself carries on as though the investigation never really reached him. And no revelation about him or, these days, any other holder of a public trust has any sense of finality to it. There never seems to be a truth with which it ends. Unless Nixon did something beyond what is known about him, or his men, or any of his predecessors, his departure from office seems random, arbitrary, and even incomplete. What I was left with finally was a set of questions and, I believe, a single inescapable inference—which would account, not so much in the detail of investigative reporting as in the very logic of events, for what I think must be the last fact, the bottom line.

In the early weeks of the inquiry, at about the time the brief on grounds was in the works, Doar considered a number of loose assumptions about what kind of case it was going to be. There was, in general, a Tip of the Iceberg theory: that whatever the inquiry might ultimately reveal, it could only be the small, visible part of what was actually there; the case would have to be made from that small visible part. There was a Narrow Escape theory: that Nixon and his aides, having made what amounted to an extremely radical analysis of the system (namely, that all its processes were meaningless and all its officials essentially corrupt), had begun to supersede the legitimate forms of government in what amounted to a revolutionary coup; the case would have to protect the country from that coup. There was a Robber Baron theory: that certain forms of corruption and violations of the system, like those committed by the robber barons, while they may have been tolerated for years, grow at some historic point beyond the tolerable; the case would have to bring such abuses of the presidency to an end. There was the Pattern of Conduct theory: that, while there may be abuses of power that a President might randomly, and perhaps by mistake commit, a pattern of systematic violations would provide grounds on which he ought to be impeached. And a Higher Standard of Conduct theory: that, since the President alone is required by the Constitution to "take care that the laws be faithfully executed," the Framers intended (as it is clear, from their letters and debates, they did intend) not to grant the President some "executive privilege" outside the law, but on the contrary, to hold him accountable, by some higher standard than any other citizen, to the law itself. There was the Superintendency theory: that the President, like any other civil or corporate officer, has a reasonable obligation to inquire and to inform himself of the acts of his subordinates, and be held accountable for them, particularly when those acts are crimes committed in his name, and solely for his benefit and on his behalf.

It is obvious that these informal assumptions combined hypotheses about the case with strategies for winning it. More directly in the line of strategy was what to look for and to try to prove. There was the Criminal Act under the Statutes theory, the one set forth in the White House brief, which everyone, from distinguished constitutional scholars to students of the problem in any depth at all, rejected. A Tax Fraud and Emoluments theory—which, for various reasons, including questions posed by the financial affairs of previous Presidents and present congressmen, was never seriously investigated by the staff. And there was a sort of nameless theory, which had to do with getting from the constitutional oath, faithfully to execute the office of President, to the unconstitutional acts, by way of the lies. There is nothing, of course, in the law or in the Constitution which requires anybody not to lie, except under oath. But the President, once he is in office, need not submit to being put under oath; he incurs no risk of perjury. He cannot anyway be indicted while in office; nor can there be an effective warrant to search his premises. The question was whether the President, notwithstanding his special constitutional oath, had a limitless power to commit unlawful acts and to conceal them, by means of a limitless right, in effect, to lie. It was some combination of the Oath-to-the-Acts theory with those in the preceding paragraph which led to the ultimate argument for impeachment, and to the form of the Articles themselves.

All these initial formulations and assumptions were, of course, addressed to the difficult question of what "other high Crimes and Misdemeanors" were. In February 1974, however, one of Doar's small group wrote, in a very short memo, "I think you're being too cavalier about bribery." It had been dismissed. In addition to the problems which followed from any Tax Fraud and Emoluments theory, bribery seemed just too difficult to prove. I remember, however, thinking as I read that memo in February that, if bribery was impossible to prove, then at least two parts of the impeachment provision of the Constitution were obsolete. Having so much occasion to read the phrase "Treason, Bribery, or other high Crimes and Misdemeanors," I thought that, as far as the presidency was concerned, there was no longer any circumstance in which treason could apply. With the technology of modern warfare, foreign policy—allying oneself, for example, on the instant, with a foreign power previously considered an enemy—was necessarily a matter of presidential discretion. There seemed to be no conceivable sense in which treason, by any definition, could be committed by a modern President.

II. THE DEFENSE

To turn now to those apparently unaccountable White House lapses, discrepancies, things that don't make any sense. I begin with a proposition that is arguable and that I don't at all require: that if

Nixon himself had been caught, red-handed, in the Watergate he would not have been impeached. Burglary is a literal crime, as required by the White House brief; and burglary of the offices of a political opponent makes it that "political" crime that would satisfy anybody's brief; but I think he could have explained it away. As for the cover-up, the obstruction of justice, if the President had been caught red-handed and lied about it, he would not have been impeached. There would, of course, have been an outcry. But an outcry is not an impeachment. There had to be many, many outcries, with two years of metaphoric bombshells, and massacres, and smoking guns, before the process was truly under way. The proposition is, anyway, unimportant. At the time of the break-in, President Nixon was at Key Biscayne. It is only to speculate that if he had been involved in the Watergate, personally, unarguably, and directly, he would have fared better than he did. Until November 1972, there was still, of course, the election to think about; there might have been a risk in that election. But not impeachment. Apart from his own acts, it took a lot of time, and people, and institutions, the press, the Special Prosecutor, the Ervin Committee, the courts, before the mechanism was even in place.

It is after he had won the election, however, by an unprecedented margin, that the odd progression of lapses and inconsistencies begins. Why, for instance, immediately or at least soon after the election, did the President not pardon Hunt and the other Watergate burglars and continue to comply with their demands? The money was there. The payments would have continued to be clandestine. There had been, then, no confessions by John Dean or Jeb Magruder, no accusation even by James McCord. There had certainly been no resignation by Attorney General Richard Kleindienst; no appointment of Elliot Richardson, bringing with him the Special Prosecutor, Archibald Cox; no Saturday Night Massacre, triggering resolutions of impeachment. The Ervin Committee hearings had not even begun. At least as late as March 21, 1973, the President could have pardoned all the Watergate defendants (thereby relieving the pressure of impending sentences by Judge Sirica) and simultaneously, vaguely, taken the blame for the whole affair himself. It might have been nothing to impeach him for. And, as we have since had good occasion to know, to pardon is the President's constitutional right.

Precisely because it would have been safe to pay, pardon, take the blame after the election, it may, however, have seemed safer not to. No politician would have been positively eager to take the blame. For a long time, I thought that was explanation enough. To turn, though, to another, more familiar set of whys: the tapes. Why not, when Alexander Butterfield revealed their existence, destroy the tapes? Why turn over to the House Judiciary Committee what were obviously doctored transcripts of tapes, the originals of which the inquiry staff already had? Why not record, and find, and turn over to the committee a single tape on which the President looked good? His defenders, if they had had the wit to do so, could at least have argued that, while there have been grounds to impeach any President, with Nixon there were, on balance, not only extenuating circumstances but strong, good grounds (the opening to China, peace, détente, whatever) to keep him on. Why not, having decided to turn over any tapes at all, simply *flood* the Judiciary Committee with tapes, masses of tapes, U-Haul truck after U-Haul truck? Every time the staff seemed to find incriminating evidence, the President's lawyers would have claimed to find further tapes with exculpatory evidence, all of which, in the name of being "fair," the inquiry staff would have been obliged to examine. That would presumably have drawn out the inquiry until at least November 1974—when, almost certainly, most members of the Judiciary Committee would have been defeated in the congressional elections, their constituents would have been so impatient with how slow they were. In January 1975, the process would have had to begin again and be drawn out— if anyone could bear to continue with it—until President Nixon had served out his term.

Instead of looking separately at those whys, there are two explanations people like to give for all of them: that Nixon was insane; that it was not his nature, as revealed by the whole history of his life, to yield an inch in anything. One problem with these answers is that, even if true, there is really nothing they explain. To account for apparent lapses in the conduct of a man who rose to great power at least twice, and fell from it, by claiming he was just intransigent or mad is to disregard the particular meaning of any of them. Whatever the state of his sanity or his nature, Nixon was doing all right with them until mid-1974. If there needs to be a single abstraction, or at least a sweeping word, to cover the detail of the mistakes made by and for him, I do not think that a word exists, for a middle way that is not only wrong; it is the only way that is wrong, a kind of dark side of the Golden Mean. Anything—more, less, everything, nothing—is sometimes better than that way. With the medium lie, the partial erasure, the half stonewall, the President and his lawyers were always finding their way into it.

But there doesn't need to be an abstraction, a policy or state of character, to explain those whys. Looking again, in terms of the substance of the tapes themselves, at just that initial question of the pardons, specific explanations do suggest themselves. It has always been an anomaly that whatever we know, from tapes or other sources, about the offenses that led to Nixon's departure from office is based, in one way or another, on what was known to John Dean. Although Dean knew a lot (the Huston plan, the burglary of Ellsberg's psychiatrist's office, the seventeen wiretaps, certain events that preceded the Watergate break-in, the essentials of the cover-up), he was, after all, a minor White House lawyer, who did not even have a conversation of substance with the President until September 15, 1972—when Nixon needed to have talked with Dean as a basis for covering him with a claim of executive, and for good measure, attorney-client, privilege. How little Dean was in the President's confidence is clear from the now-famous conversation of March 21, 1973, in which he "informed" Nixon of what Nixon already so well knew. And because that conversation subsequently acquired such importance (in terms of Dean's credibility, of Watergate, and of choices Nixon subsequently made), almost all subpoenas of presidential conversations were addressed to the matter of confirming or failing to confirm what John Dean knew—which, as far as the President was concerned, was confined almost entirely to conversations in the spring of 1973, about Watergate.

Except for September 15, 1972. And looking again at the transcript of that conversation, it becomes obvious why the President could not safely grant Hunt and the other burglars pardons: the House Committee on Banking and Currency, the Patman Committee. The problem was never the burglary of the Watergate. The problem was the source of the cash. As soon as hundred-dollar bills in the possession of the burglars had been traced via Bernard Barker's bank account to Mexico (i.e., within five days of the burglary), the course of events was set. The same account had cleared $89,000 in checks endorsed by a Mexican lawyer, Manuel Ogarrio. And the problem, from the moment the cash was traced to a Mexican bank account, was that the Patman Committee started to look into it— and that committee, unlike any subsequent investigative body, would have known how and where to look. In late 1969 and early 1970, the Patman Committee had held hearings about secret, numbered foreign bank accounts (in Switzerland, the Bahamas, and elsewhere) mainly with a view to the use of such accounts by organized crime. It had not considered their use in a political campaign. By September 1972, it was beginning to look into exactly that. When it was stopped.

Chairman Wright Patman had a list of witnesses concerning cash transactions related to the Watergate. On September 14, 1972, the first of the important witnesses declined to appear. Chairman Patman scheduled another meeting, for October 3, 1972, to proceed with the subpoena power. On October 2, 1972, Assistant Attorney General Henry E. Petersen wrote Patman a letter, hand-delivered, warning that the committee hearings might "not only jeopardize the prosecution" of the Watergate case but also "seriously prejudice" the defendants' rights. If Nixon had granted pardons, that argument would, of course, have fallen apart; hearings can hardly prejudice the rights of defendants when the President has already pardoned them. The Patman investigation could have gone ahead. In his conversation of September 15, 1972, the President wanted to ensure that it would not. He issued instructions that a number of people be sent to contact the committee with that argument from defendants' rights. He considered sending Attorney General Richard Kleindienst. Then he thought of John Connally. He finally settled on sending Congressman Gerald Ford. (President: "What about Ford?...This is, this is, big, big play...they can all work out something. But they ought to get off their asses and push it. No use to let Patman have a free ride....")

The Patman hearings were suspended. By October 31, 1972, the committee's staff had made a little headway all the same. Even without subpoena power, the staff had found enormous irregularities in the bookkeeping of, among others, the treasurer of the Finance Committee to Re-Elect the President, Hugh Sloan. And in the records of several banks where CREEP had its accounts. And in statements, written and oral, made to investigators about the sources of the cash, by the chairman of the Finance Committee to Re-Elect, Maurice Stans. The staff had also, almost incidentally, discovered a campaign contribution to CREEP via the Banque Internationale à Luxembourg. There was so much cash and so much irregularity, though, that without the power to subpoena records or to take testimony under oath, the committee lost the trail.

Secret foreign accounts as a source of laundered campaign contributions would not, in and of themselves, be enough to impeach a President, either. To turn then, for a while, to the questions raised by Nixon's treatment of the tapes. There can hardly be any doubt, in the logic of events, that Alexander Butterfield, who disclosed the existence of the taping system to the minority staff of the Ervin Committee and then to the full committee on national television, was a plant. The only question for a time was whose. Ever since he testified, Butterfield has managed to imply that he spoke reluctantly, that a question was put to him in such a way that he had to tell, or perjure himself, or compromise his honor, or whatever. This version—the reluctant witness, the clever investigator—has understandably not been disputed by the Ervin Committee staff. But the record, the only record that staff made of that interview at the time, simply does not bear that out. Butterfield volunteered. "I feel it is something you ought to know about," he said, "in your investigations." Having added, in that initial interview, "This is something I know the President did not want revealed," Butterfield went on to tell the full committee, on national television, that the tapes "are precisely the substance on which the President plans to present his defense." He went to considerable lengths then to emphasize—utterly misleadingly, as it turned out—the particular *clarity* of the tapes, and the care with which they were checked, both in the Executive Office Building and in the Oval Office. The EOB tapes were, in reality, so bad that the President himself (in his tape of June 4, 1973) complained of how hard it was to understand them; the group that produced the inquiry transcripts spent approximately one man-hour per minute trying to decipher them. I leave aside the question of whether Butterfield was an agent of the CIA—a rumor reported in *The New York Times* and elsewhere, and denied by him. Although his testimony ultimately backfired, it seems certain that Haldeman (and by extension, Nixon) sent him in.

As a character in all these events, Butterfield has never made much sense. Like Hugh Sloan, Earl Silbert, Henry Petersen, Alexander Haig, Fred Buzhardt, and even James St. Clair, he was one of what became an unlikely herd of self-styled victims of deceit, and then self-serving and improbable heroes of Watergate. Butterfield's wife had been Haldeman's wife's best friend at college. The Butterfields and Haldemans were friends. Butterfield's office was placed to control all access, by persons or documents, to President Nixon's office—surely a sign of an earned trust. When Haldeman needed somebody to hide the $350,000 secret White House fund of cash, the man he used was Butterfield. Butterfield subsequently became an informer, the informer, for the impeachment inquiry. But, apart from homey speculations about the Nixon marriage (he was, in every interview, the source of the story that the Nixons were not close), he never really said anything. His initial disclosure of the existence of the tapes was, after all, in the President's interest. Everyone who had spoken to the President was put on notice: No one could feel safe. With the misleading emphasis on clarity, people were warned all the more clearly. It is probable that, in three years of only normally syco-phantic conversation with the President, there was not a major fig-ure in government, from all three branches, the military, all the various bureaus, agencies, and departments (not to mention minor White House officials who might, like John Dean, have felt under pressure to testify), who did not feel compromised, or even impli-cated in a felony, on those tapes. The President had them, and had at the time no reason to think he must disclose any more of them than he cared to. The message in Butterfield's testimony was a perfect threat, at the very least, to every Nixon confidant and appointee.

To take just one domestic constellation: the Department of Jus-tice (in the person of Attorney General Richard Kleindienst) and the two major investigative agencies (in the persons of Acting FBI Director L. Patrick Gray and CIA Director Richard Helms) were intimately involved with the obstruction of justice on which the case for impeachment came to rest. When Senator Lowell Weicker, of the Ervin Committee, first suggested that the President might have been guilty of "misprision of a felony" in not reporting to any prop-erly constituted authority what John Dean had told him, and when the House Judiciary Committee considered, as part of its argument for impeachment, the same failure to pass the information on, Nixon may have thought his accusers were not sane. There could scarcely be any legal or constitutional obligation to report a crime to people who were in on it—and for whose complicity he thought he had, among other evidence, the tapes.

If the tapes as a veiled and planted threat did not entirely work, the reason may apply to most adversary situations, in public and in private life, in which both parties are lying and at fault. When peo-ple lie in concert, a single, simple truth can be impossible to prove— as in the case of finding, among only three suspects, the individual who produced the eighteen-and-a-half-minute gap. But when they lie in conflict, each liar, in indignation about the other, may begin to feel innocent. People who feel *wronged*, in particular, are likely to forget what regrettable thing it is they themselves did or said. It could be that, in their outrage, those people who were compromised on the tapes simply forgot. Or maybe the threat did work, and they did not forget. History, after all, is left with the remarkable fact that, to this day, nobody except John Dean has come out with testimony, borne out by the tapes or otherwise, that implicates President Nixon in any crimes. And here is the status of the tapes themselves: Although Congress has, by special legislation, impounded them (thereby foreclosing Nixon's access to the main weapon he thought he had against others and, simultaneously, precluding access to the best evidence against the man himself), the tapes remain, while the matter is appealed to the Supreme Court, in the EOB. Dr. James Rhodes, the national archivist, has written to Nixon's lawyers and to the White House to request permission to rewind the tapes—which he says are deteriorating because they are loosely wound. Dr. Rhodes has also asked to check which tapes, of what may be as many as five thousand hours of conversation, actually do contain a "signal," i.e., voices—a matter that can be very quickly checked. He has received no reply. It is possible that, among all the parties of interest in the tapes, only the national archivist is concerned with preserving them.

As for why Nixon would submit to the Judiciary Committee doctored transcripts of tapes the staff already had, that nearly worked. The White House released its thick book of doctored transcripts on April 30, 1974. The regular staff, at the time, was in such a daze of fairness that it simply could not find systematic discrepancies between the White House version and the true version of eight conversations that overlapped. When the EOB tapes turned out to be mostly garble, interrupted by hissing, buzzing, and tapping noises, Doar considered abandoning this form of evidence. The lore-manufacturing apparatus, at this point, introduces a blind lady, with miraculously sensitive ears. There was no blind lady. A blind man who listened to the EOB tapes couldn't understand them either. A member of Doar's small group insisted, threatening to resign over the question, that Doar permit him and a tape expert to re-record from originals at the White House, and later (when White House Attorney Fred Buzhardt withdrew access to originals) from the tapes in Judge Sirica's chambers. The tape expert and the member of the group who had threatened to resign found two others to "go into the mud," as they put it, for hundreds of hours, filling out each transcript, word by word. The rest of the small group initiated work on the discrepancies—weeks after the White House transcripts were released.

The grand jury had based its presentment, mainly, on the tape of the March 21, 1973, conversation in the Oval Office between the President and John Dean. St. Clair directed his whole case, such as it was, toward showing that the President had not unequivocally authorized the payment of hush money on that day. But the "I don't give a shit . . . I want you all to stonewall it, let them plead the Fifth Amendment, cover-up or anything else . . . save the plan" conversation, which persuaded Republican congressmen Thomas Railsback and Robert McClory to vote for impeachment, took place on March 22, 1973, in the EOB. It was deleted from the White House transcripts and unintelligible on the Special Prosecutor's. The grand jury never heard it. It is even possible that nobody at the White House ever heard it, that it was always mud. Barely possible. The recopying had just reached the tape of March 22, 1973, when Buzhardt cut off access to the tapes.

In this context, too, there is a particular point about the transcript of June 23, 1972—the tape that was supposed so profoundly to have shocked the President's defenders that it obliged them to persuade him to resign. The few, very few, Nixon associates who have not tried since his resignation to save themselves at his expense claim that both Buzhardt and St. Clair had read in May this transcript which so astounded them in July. Buzhardt has said that he knew all was lost when, in late July 1973, he listened for the first time to the tape of June 23, 1972, and heard the incriminating word "Gemstone." The inquiry's tape expert says it took months for him to be able to decipher that word. In any case, it is certain that both Buzhardt and St. Clair were familiar with the contents of the tape before the Judiciary Committee voted, and did not trouble to let any of the President's defenders on the committee know. Months later, during the trial of *U.S. v. Mitchell, et al.*, it became clear that this transcript also had been doctored; neither of Nixon's lawyers had called attention to those excisions in July when they had listened to the tape. When one recalls that the President, in the statement with which he released the transcript, made a special point of admitting that he had concealed it from his attorneys—when one realizes that the worst strangler, dope-pusher, child-molester, finds it unnecessary in adversity to apologize to his own counsel—it seems possible that in this little episode the President was framed. St. Clair felt that, before the case reached the floor of the House, he ought to show Congressman Wiggins, the President's major defender on the committee, that transcript of June 23, 1972. Having received what must have been a considerable shock when Wiggins, enraged, told him the transcript meant the case was lost (and that if the White House did not at once make the transcript public, he, Wiggins, would), St. Clair must have returned to his client with an assurance that the problem was not insuperable—as long as the President's counsel did not resign. St. Clair, however, would feel obliged to resign unless the President stated publicly that he had withheld from his attorneys the knowledge of this tape. The President believed, and did as he was told. And St. Clair was able to tell the press that he was not, after all, the first lawyer whose client had lied to him.

As for not having found and turned over a single tape the President looked good on, it is fairly clear, from the tape of June 4, 1973, that Nixon, with the concurrence of Ziegler and earlier Haldeman (and Haig, with his loving assurance, "Only you. Only you"), was under the impression that he sounded pretty good on most of them. On June 26, 1973, Nixon again listened to himself on tape. Within days, the Ervin Committee heard from Butterfield. And St. Clair, who liked to insist that he was defending the presidency, when he was actually using the presidency to protect a criminal defendant and then using the President himself to protect the President's lawyer's name, never did give a straightforward reply when members of the committee asked whether he had listened to any tapes at all. He could presumably have asked Buzhardt to find a good tape, but neither of the lawyers seems to have felt a necessity for finding one, they were so preoccupied with the minuscule questions posed by the tape of March 21, 1973. Finally, why not have flooded the committee, as is often done in antitrust cases, with unassimilable evidence? As well ask why the White House lawyers were remiss in almost everything. There was every reason, however, for President Nixon not to want to do it. And the inescapable inference, I think, consists in the explanation why.

III. WHAT'S MISSING?

A piece last year in *Esquire* raised the question of how it was that *The New York Times* at first missed the story of Watergate. One explanation was that *Times* reporters had been following leads on other stories—drug-taking by a high government official, and so on—stories that did not yield. Many papers ultimately made their contribution. The Washington *Star*, interviewing a gardener, discovered that a recent visitor at San Clemente had been Judge Matthew Byrne, of the Ellsberg trial; that broke the story of the offer to him of the directorship of the FBI. The Providence *Journal* broke the story of Nixon's income tax. The *Los Angeles Times*, Jack Nelson in particular, broke various stories. *Time* revealed the seventeen wiretaps. Other reporters uncovered important stories—as, of course, did *The New York Times*. But the reporting that led most directly to Nixon's departure from office was unquestionably Woodward and Bernstein's in the *Washington Post*. The author of the *Esquire* piece concluded that *The New York Times* had been remiss. It seemed more likely, though, that Watergate, and the important revelations it led to, were not the story. And I don't mean the tip of the iceberg here. I mean that, in spite of all the Watergate cover-up talk on the few known transcripts (out of three years, after all, of recorded conversation), Nixon simply did not think Watergate was the front he was vulnerable on.

If one bears with this line of thought, that Watergate was not the story, then the problem is what was. It is hard to sustain a belief in a conspiracy within his administration against him. It would be unreasonable to expect to drive from office, by means of tapes in his sole possession, the man who had appointed (and who presumably had compromising tapes of) the presumptive heads of any such conspiracy. Moreover, no evidence on a grand enough scale ever came *out* about President Nixon to support a view that the intelligence agencies had conspired to produce such evidence. Finally, it is clear from the Church Committee documents and from more recent, almost daily news reports that the agencies had problems enough with secrets of their own to preclude an interest in the removal from office of a chief executive—when that removal would lead, as it inevitably did, to investigations of the agencies themselves.

Even less convincing are theories that the offenses at the heart of the Nixon administration had to do with a Hughes connection, or with the Bebe Rebozo $100,000. So many people, Republicans and Democrats alike, have had some sort of Hughes connection. As for Rebozo, a memorandum of June 16, 1972, from Gordon Strachan to H. R. Haldeman, does report a complaint from Florida CREEP contributors that they had "already given through Bebe." But, as events in the intervening years, concerning kickbacks and financial-political scandal of all kinds and on all sides, demonstrate—and as the fact that no article of impeachment having to do with taxes or finances was ever passed confirms—the President could not have been impeached simply over money. Vice President Agnew did have to resign over money, but it seems beyond question that this resignation would not have occurred had it not been for Watergate—when the President viewed the prospect of Agnew's resignation as protection for himself.

The minds of assassination theorists run, perhaps, to murder: the shooting of Governor Wallace; or the crash of the plane bearing Mrs. E. Howard Hunt. But it is unlikely that the Nixon scandal had to do with murder—else why not have murdered a few more people, and those more key? One arrives suddenly at the territory of the florid killings, Jimmy Hoffa, Sam Giancana, John Roselli—and at the Church Committee documents—in a most unlikely way. Because what was happening in the name of intelligence activities provided, at least, a context for the way Nixon conducted his administration; and because the Church investigation itself provides an example of not wanting to know too clearly, or to state at all, what your own research unmistakably implies.

IV. TRANSACTIONS

The Church Committee's report on intelligence activities consists of seven volumes. Like most government documents, they are hard to read. The first volume, *Alleged Assassination Plots Involving Foreign Leaders*, was, politically, the right place to begin. A bipartisan majority of the committee could agree to investigate these matters—past and foreign—precisely and only because they were remote, indifferent, a subject in which nobody had anything politically to lose. If someone had really managed, in the early sixties, to assassinate Fidel Castro, the whole country probably would have been for it. There was, in those days, no Left to speak of. The rest, among investigators, press, citizens at large, was just consensus and hypocrisy. Consensus, because in the matter of old and failed assassinations, all parties could agree to a distraction from the real and serious questions: whether, for instance, the agencies were doing what they were authorized and paid to do, and at what price; whether there was any way to keep them, domestically, within the law. Hypocrisy, because everyone could agree to be outraged that such plots were ever contemplated—when it was, and is, by no means clear that they were not always part of what has been required, from time to time, of an intelligence agency.

One might even have thought naïveté compounded with consensus and hypocrisy, in that people could seriously entertain the idea that foreign interventions of a high and violent order could be undertaken by underlings, without the knowledge of the various Presidents. This would involve a misunderstanding of the presidency so profound that it brings in just the cast of mind that made it difficult to know what Nixon did: a bureaucratic logic of passing the buck downward, of presuming, in the name of "fairness," the ignorance of the man in power, beyond the farthest reaches of common sense. What did the boss know and when did he know it makes sense only as the question of a jury lawyer whose client is the boss. The presumption of innocence is, after all, a practical, moral convention for the conduct of fair trials. It was never meant to go any further, to suggest that truth itself, say, consists in the outcome of a conflict of legal strategies. And certainly not to express the Mafia ethic that the lowest takes the rap.

But when the Mafia itself, literally, was brought into the story, there was something in the details that began to obscure the drift. The collaboration of the CIA and the Mafia in a plan for a foreign assassination had its initial plausibility. The Mafia had had profitable operations in Cuba; it must have longed to have them back. Then, with Sam Giancana, John Roselli, even Judith Campbell Exner, Frank Sinatra, the rococo elements appear—giving rise to at least one speculation, and one certainty. The speculation: that the whole story is backward, that there might have been a White House connection with the Mafia, perhaps accidentally and carelessly. The connection would have come, inevitably, to the attention of J. Edgar Hoover—whose FBI cannot, as it claimed, have been bugging a Mafia phone, but must have been tapping the White House phones for many years, for the FBI director's purposes. There cannot have been any other reason to wait *fifty-four* weeks to bring the Roselli-Giancana matter to President John Kennedy's attention. To exactly the degree that a connection is dangerous to the national security, its termination, too, is presumably no less than urgent; it took Hoover more than a year to feel that urgency. It was obviously just a moment when, for whatever reason, Hoover felt he must deal this card. As for the CIA, when this Mafia connection, by whatever route, came to its attention, the White House might have said—as it said so recently, in the case of the burglary of Ellsberg's psychiatrist's office— Stay away from that. That's national security. The CIA's employment of the Mafia for purposes of assassinating Castro would have become the consensual fiction. Advantage to the Mafia: such private services as having the CIA break into the apartment, years ago, of the singer girlfriend of that jealous lover, Sam Giancana; tax relief; and relief from various other legal pressures, probably.

That would be a speculation. But a certainty is this: that, at some unspecified point in its history, the CIA began to include the investigation and control of narcotics traffic, without mandate or explanation, in its own interpretation of its intelligence work; that, in recent years, virtually every group that has newly claimed the control of narcotics as part of its mission (from Egil Krogh's Plumbers, through the units of John Caulfield and G. Gordon Liddy, when they came from drug-enforcement agencies) has used that claim as a cover for some crime; that the CIA, in the course of the Church Committee hearings, was unable to give any satisfactory account either of its dealings with the opium-running tribesmen of Southeast Asia, or for allegations of drug traffic by its own Southeast Asian airline, Air America. A report by the CIA's own inspector general concluded that there was "no evidence that the Agency… has ever sanctioned or supported drug trafficking *as a matter of policy*" (italics added). Those words in italics must constitute the weakest disclaimer of criminal activity by a governmental agency ever to be seriously presented in any public forum.

And looking back, then, at the alleged purpose of the association with Giancana and Roselli, there arises at least this question: Does it make sense for the CIA to have enlisted organized crime as an ally in a plan for an assassination of the highest importance, while, at the same time, it claims responsibility for suppressing traffic in narcotics, which is the most highly profitable enterprise for organized crime? Does either half of this proposition, which would make of the secret collaborator in one international enterprise the bitterest conceivable enemy in the other, make any sense? (The fact is, of course, that Castro was not assassinated. Narcotics traffic, on the other hand, has flourished, supporting not only organized crime but all those bureaucracies whose mission is to suppress it.) The reason the questions are not idle is that there is evidence, scattered throughout the Church Committee report, that, at least since its demoralization in the Bay of Pigs, the CIA has changed from a band of courageous and patriotic amateurs into another sort of band entirely.

Investigative reporting is not what I intended or what I have done here; my politics, such as they are, tend to be moderate. But one cannot help, in looking at documents which might establish a context for a last inference about the Nixon administration, finding signs, in government in recent years, of something, in economic terms at least, radically amiss—evidence of great improprieties involving immense sums of cash. There are, to take two examples, transactions involving two of the CIA's "proprietaries"—the businesses which the CIA says it must own, as a cover for its intelligence activities. The first is the sale of an airline, Southern Air Transport, which the CIA bought, in 1960, for use in Asia. The CIA bought the airline, which was based in Miami, Florida, for approximately $300,000, and held the shares in the name of a former board member of its other airline, Air America. In 1973, it sold Southern Air Transport, to its former owner, for approximately $6 million—several million dollars less than its book value at the time, and $2 million less than what had already been offered, in cash, by another buyer. The CIA's explanation for the sale was this: it sought "to avoid a conflict of interest." However complicated other aspects of the transaction may have been, one thing is clear: Selling to former associates, at a price millions of dollars below book value and below a competing cash offer, does not so much *avoid* as it quite openly declares the most direct and glaring conflict of interest.

A second case concerns a $30 million "insurance complex," which the CIA claimed it was obliged to set up abroad, as a result of the death of four agents in the Bay of Pigs. Leaving aside the question of whether it might not have been possible to compensate four surviving families by some means other than an enterprise costing millions, the CIA went on to claim that for reasons of "cover" the insurance complex had to make investments, in foreign and American stocks, and also to keep some "non-interest bearing deposits" in foreign banks. The only "issue" which a section of the report obviously written by the CIA itself could find in the matter of these deposits was that the selection of the banks was "non-competitive"—as though the Agency might have been showing favoritism in its choice of banks, or attempting to influence their policies. That is not, of course, the real issue at all. An "insurance complex," in foreign banks, with a portfolio of foreign and American stocks, and deposits on which it claims to get no interest, is not a necessary or even plausible "cover" for intelligence work but an opportunity—stated with a brazenness that insults the committee which investigates— for fraud on a scale that no private corporation could contemplate. Since the CIA refused, on grounds, it says, of national security, to disclose how much money it has at all, and since Congress has so far indulged that refusal, the Agency continues in its special capacity for making illegal profits and never having to account to anyone for them, or to give any explanation of who or what has that money now.

As for the FBI—as portrayed in the Church Committee report, it seems so locked in obsessions of its own that it hardly bears on the Nixon case. In federal government, it has always been vital interests such as defense (and more recently, medical care) which present special opportunities for impropriety, because of their intense importance to a public that, lacking expertise, is helpless in terms of oversight. All this by way of a cursory outline of situations which existed in government, quite apart from the Nixon administration; and to establish a context for what I think the Nixon scandal itself had to be. It would have to be of an entirely other order than any of these, as it were, more normal scandals; and it required not the most florid and aberrant explanation but the worst and perhaps the most obvious. And here's what I think, inescapably, it has to be.

V. BOTTOM LINE

People are accustomed to speak of the tragedies of Vietnam and Watergate, or of the post-Vietnam post-Watergate morality, as though they were linked only in some abstract, ethical sphere. Then, one looks at those transcripts once again. In his conversation of February 28, 1973, with John Dean, President Nixon discussed an allegation that, in 1968, at President Lyndon Johnson's insistence, the FBI tapped conversations between Agnew, the candidate for Vice President, and Anna Chennault, widow of General Claire Chennault and president of Flying Tiger Airlines. The rationale for this tap was supposed to be that Mrs. Chennault was urging the South Vietnamese to slow down or stop the peace negotiations in Paris, to help assure the election of a Republican administration, under which, she was supposed to be telling the South Vietnamese, they would get better terms.

Mrs. Chennault says she did not even know Spiro Agnew in 1968; but that is not the point. She says she knew Richard Nixon very well. On February 28, 1973, President Nixon was preoccupied only with whether there had been such a tap, not with the rationale behind it. One remembers that, less than a week before the 1968 election, the South Vietnamese did stop the negotiations cold. Less than a week. One remembers, too, the remarkable suddenness and, even for refugees, unprecedented hysteria and chaos with which the war, in March 1975, finally did end; and the apparently real fury and sense of betrayal President Thieu expressed when he so precipitately, and it seemed spitefully, gave up. And one cannot help thinking back on 1968 and believing that, in 1972, there must have been a deal. On October 26, 1972, two weeks before the election, Henry Kissinger said of Vietnam, "Peace is at hand." Peace is at hand. There can and could be no doubt that he sincerely meant it. Within the week, however, Alexander Haig flew to Vietnam. There was unprecedented bombing and the mining of Haiphong. After all that, in January 1973, when the accords were signed, the terms were in no substantial way different from the ones Henry Kissinger had gotten, months earlier, when he genuinely thought peace was at hand. Then, one remembers we were pouring huge amounts of money into South Vietnam; and that the government there, being famously corrupt, was getting a lot of it. One remembers that President Nixon himself was getting a lot of illicit campaign contributions, from a lot of strange sources, and diverting at least some of them to his personal use. And one can't help thinking that, in 1972, the South Vietnamese administration, not wanting peace to be at hand just yet, used some of the enormous amounts of money we were pouring in there to bribe our administration to stay in.

All right, it is difficult, monstrous; and, of necessity, only an inference, impossible to prove. But one looks back—thinking, not laundered money, foreign money. It is hard to recall the sums and characters, where they came from and where they went. But, early in the Ervin Committee hearings, there is the dim sound of the testimony of CREEP Finance Chairman Maurice Stans. He mentioned a contribution, $30,000 in cash, from a "Philippine national"—a contribution, Stans said at the time, he had been too fastidious to keep. Gordon Liddy's successor as counsel to the Finance Committee to Re-Elect, Stans said, had told him that it would not be legal to accept such money. So Stans had arranged, he said, with Fred Larue, an assistant to John Mitchell at CREEP, to return that $30,000 to its source. "Since then, and this is more irony, Senator," Stans went on, amiably, in the ensuing colloquy, he had learned from a Justice Department official that it would have been "perfectly proper" to accept that money from a foreign national, "so long as he is not an agent of a foreign principal." That is what Stans testified on June 12, 1973.

It would not, as it turns out, have been "perfectly proper" to accept a campaign contribution from a foreign national. It would have been illegal. But the sum itself is so trivial, $30,000. One wonders why Stans testified at such length about it. Hugh Sloan, the Finance

Committee treasurer, testified at length about it, too. It is not until *four volumes* later, in the records of the Ervin Committee hearings, that one finds any correspondence that deals with this transaction. It occurs in support of the testimony of Fred Larue, who had paid some of the hush money to the burglars, and who was by then negotiating his plea. Stans had not asked Larue to return any money to any source, it turns out, until May 9, 1973—more than a year after the Finance Committee had accepted it; but less than a month before the Ervin Committee hearings began. And even in his letter of May 9, 1973, Stans did not specify to whom the money was to be returned. Larue simply wanted to return the CREEP money in his possession. His counsel *did* specify, more or less. The $30,000, Stans's attorney finally wrote, in acknowledging a letter dated May 16, 1973, from Larue's attorney, was "paid" to Anna Chennault, for "return to foreign nationals"—nationality, Philippine or other, unspecified.

The only reason this trivial amount, this $30,000, came to light at all was that it was part of $81,000 in cash that Hugh Sloan was stuck with when the source of the cash in the possession of the Watergate burglars had been traced to those checks endorsed by the Mexican lawyer Manuel Ogarrio. And that, one recalls, was the cash that had interested the Patman Committee. At first, Stans had told the committee staff that the money came from Ogarrio; then, that he could not disclose whom it came from, since they were Texans to whom he had promised anonymity; finally, that he did not know who the donors were. The Patman Committee staff, having coincidentally discovered, at about the same time, that $700,000 in cash had come to CREEP, in a suitcase, from an American corporation by way of Mexico, was at first misled into thinking that the story had to do not with contributions by foreign nationals but with donations by American corporations and citizens (illegally and in secret) by way of foreign banks. As it turned out, the story was both: Americans and foreign nationals. But the committee, lacking its subpoena power, never got Stans or any other CREEP official under oath—as the Ervin Committee, so many months later, did. And that petty $30,000, within the $81,000 (which remained of the original Ogarrio $89,000), came back to haunt Stans, Sloan, Larue, CREEP, Mrs. Chennault, and the country as a whole. On June 23, 1972, Stans had instructed Sloan to give the $81,000 to President Nixon's personal attorney, Herbert Kalmbach, who gave it to Larue, who happened to use it as part of the hush money. And Larue plea-bargained. So, in whatever disjointed form, the $30,000 had to be accounted for. And it was foreign.

And thinking foreign, there are anomalies great and small, every-where one looks. Hugh Sloan explained to the Ervin Committee that he had been unable to give a proper accounting of CREEP funds between April and July 1972, because Kalmbach had been "abroad." Abroad. There is no reason why the President's personal attorney and principal fund-raiser should not travel abroad. The height of the political campaign just seems an odd time for his holiday. In his own testimony, Kalmbach always insists, and when he does, elicits sym-pathy, that he was deceived and "used." In the memorandum of June 16, 1972, however, there is Kalmbach, returned from abroad, re-questing assignments that are "tough and dangerous." Within days, he was raising, from domestic sources this time, the cash for the hush money. Kalmbach had already raised more than $12 million for the 1972 campaign. A political-matters memorandum as early as October 7, 1971, says, "Kalmbach keeps asking for tough, interesting assignments." On February 1, 1972, he is reported to have declared himself "willing to run the very high risk of violating the criminal provisions" of campaign-spending legislation.

And even in what remains of the records of CREEP itself—on file, as required under post-Watergate law, at the Federal Election Commission—one finds both foreign and domestic oddities. What was still until last year the Committee to Re-Elect the President is now called the 1972 Campaign Liquidation Trust. It reports an in-terest income of $80,000 a year, with this income annually exceeded by expenses—as might be expected in a fund that wants to liqui-date. It is only that campaigns normally end with deficits, and that an interest income of $80,000 reflects a lot of capital—which raises the question of who or what has that money now, and by what right. Some domestic curiosities: Until October 1976 the Campaign Liquidation Trust still had on its books a suit against John Dean and his attorney—for the return of $15,100, paid "on or about April 12, 1973." (The suit was settled with the return of that money to the Trust.) On a single day, May 3, 1973, six months after the President had, after all, been overwhelmingly reelected, the Committee to Re-Elect listed on its books seven separate payments of $3,000 and one of $2,500 to Maurice Stans, as "Salary"—making his salary for that day $23,500; four days later CREEP paid him another salary of $3,000. It paid Stans that sort of salary on a lot of days. More surprisingly, perhaps, CREEP was still paying Hugh Sloan—who made such an issue, before the Ervin Committee and elsewhere, of his resignation on the grounds of conscience, in July 1972, on account of Watergate—considerable sums every month until at least spring 1973. In January 1973, Sloan was still carried on the books as "Treasurer"; but his salary had become "Consulting Fee." By February, his title had become "Consultant." On February 15, 1973, Sloan's consulting fee was $1,320; on February 21, 1973, $1,080, and so on. Unlike John Dean, Sloan was never sued by the Committee to Re-Elect. But Sloan had, after all, handled enormous cash contributions, as treasurer to the Finance Committee, in the 1968 campaign as well; and, unlike Dean, he could be presumed to know in 1972, although he never really told, about the sources of the cash.

In the records of CREEP on file at the Federal Election Commission, there are only slim indications of contributions from any foreign source. On February 27, 1973 (again, months after Nixon's reelection), something called "Committee of United States Citizens in Asia for Nixon" did file a registration form. In answer to question (a) "Will this committee operate in more than one state?" the committee replied, "No—only internationally, outside the U.S." In answer to (d) "Will it support a candidate for President or Vice President in the aggregate amount of $1,000 or more during the calendar year?" the reply was "Yes." For (e) "Does this committee plan to stay in existence beyond the current calendar year?" another "Yes." And in answer to (f) "If so, how long?" there is "Perpetually." Under "Name of bank, repository, etc.," the reply is "None." And "List all reports required to be filed by this committee with states and jurisdictions" elicits another "None." Under a question asking the identity of the committee's "custodian of books and accounts," there is "Marshall Hendricks, Lewis Burridge, Anna Chennault." In its Statement of Affiliated and Connected Organizations, the committee listed "(a) Committee of United States Citizens in Hong Kong for Nixon (b) Committee of United States Citizens in Japan for Nixon (c) Committee of United States Citizens in Korea for Nixon," and so on.

There is, on the surface, no absolutely obvious reason why—in late February after the November in which a President, who is constitutionally precluded from serving more than two terms, has already been elected to his second term—citizens should not establish as many Asian branches for his reelection as they like, even listing no "bank, repository, etc." and with an intention (although this might suggest an echo of the Narrow Escape theory) to remain in existence "perpetually." But within a month—by March 22, 1973, in fact—the Asia Committee of CREEP and its affiliated committees found themselves, all together, unable to claim contributions in excess of $1,000. Having planned to stay in existence "perpetually," they nonetheless asked to be allowed to cease to report. The Asia Committee wrote to the Office of Federal Elections, seeking "the approval of your office to cease reporting, until such time in the future as we may have receipts in excess of $1,000," That a Nixon campaign committee in Asia should reserve to itself the possibility of such receipts at a "time in the future" raises questions about which one does not care to speculate.

But it is hardly new that there were irregularities everywhere in the finances of the 1972 campaign. Detail only obscures the logic of historical events. In thinking about international political contributions, the logic has normally gone the other way—contributions by the American government or by American corporations to officials, or parties, or governments abroad. But with the by now almost weekly revelations of payments by American companies to foreign officials in Europe, Asia, South America, and the Middle East, it began to seem highly probable in the very nature of secret cash transactions that some of that money was going to find its way back, and/or that some foreign interests rich enough to afford it were going to lobby, with cash, in America. Taking only defense matters, there was for instance Lockheed: With payments in Italy, Japan, and the Netherlands, the cash seemed to flow in only one direction. In June of this year, however, there were signs that it had, for years, been traveling the other way. The Special Prosecutor's office revealed that a citizen of Saudi Arabia, having received over the years more than $100 million from Lockheed for his influence in selling aircraft to the Saudis, had contributed $50,000 to Nixon's 1968 campaign; in May and November 1972, the Saudi citizen withdrew $200 million from his account in Bebe Rebozo's bank. Because of a "burglary" in Las Vegas, which was reported within a week of the start of the prosecutor's investigation, the Saudi lobbyist could produce no records of how that $200 million was spent. Or Grumman. On September 13, 1976, there was the former president of Grumman International testifying, under oath, that in 1972 a White House official had suggested that Grumman contribute $1 million to CREEP for the President's "assistance," on a forthcoming trip to Honolulu, in getting Japan to buy Grumman fighter planes. In April 1972, a Grumman official had visited the White House to discuss sales of fighter planes to Iran; a month later, on a trip to Iran, Nixon agreed for the first time to sell Iran virtually any weapon it wanted. Signs, anyway, of a rich foreign country that could afford to pay to influence an American decision now and then.

Looking further back, however, at the Patman hearings on secret foreign bank accounts, one finds, as early as 1968, premonitions of what I think must have happened in 1972. In 1968, well before Nixon's first inauguration, the Patman Committee already had found "kickbacks by Vietnamese importers to American exporters, involv-

ing a huge U.S. corporation. Again, Swiss bank accounts were used."
Assistant Attorney General Fred M. Vinson (who, in 1973, was the
attorney for Fred Larue in his tractations, over the $30,000 from a
foreign national, with Maurice Stans) testified, in 1968, as the Justice Department expert on these illicit foreign deals. But the scale,
then, was different, and the purpose was different. No one suggested, in 1968, that the Vietnamese kickbacks, through foreign
banks, went into American politics.

As, by 1972, I think they clearly did. Turning away from detail,
one is struck by the logic overall. It does not make sense, for example, that the President's fund-raisers would put by far the greatest
pressure of any political campaign in our history on so many sources,
individual and corporate, and *reject* a contribution from the most
logical of them all: the administration of South Vietnam, which had
the most to lose if the President's opponent (who had announced a
willingness to go, it must be remembered, to Hanoi on his knees for
peace) actually won. And although the President might have liked
to announce the war's end before any ordinary election, by the time
he sent Haig to undo Kissinger's late October accords, he knew he
did not need, in 1972, any peace to win. At the same time, Nixon
never seems to have felt any diminution of need for campaign contributions. In the fall of 1968, the South Vietnamese had only to dig
in their heels and wait, while the war cost Humphrey the election.
By the fall of 1972, if they wanted the support of the administration,
I think they had to pay.

And even the structure of the underlying proposition had occurred, minus only cash, in another context, at least once before: in
the secret bombing of Cambodia. The rationale for lying to the
American people, and to their elected officials, about the bombing
of Cambodia was, it was said at first, national security. But that
made no sense. Since the enemy knew, and certainly the Cambodian
people who were being bombed would know, Americans were the
only people it was being kept secret from. It was then that the entire
logic advanced a step, and the circle closed. Sihanouk, the administration said, had invited or acquiesced in the bombing of Cambodia.

In order that he could conceal this complicity from his own people, our administration had to keep it secret, too, from ours. It is the logical substructure that matters here. A pact can be arrived at, secretly and therefore deniably, between our leaders and theirs, which entails the killing of their people, in their own country, in their own ignorance of their leader's consent; and which entails the loss of our pilots' lives, in their country, without our knowledge of our leader's consent. That logic requires only the addition of money, money contributed by South Vietnamese officials to an American President, to explain why peace was not quite at hand in October 1972.

If one accepts, for a moment, the proposition that the awful secret that underlay the Nixon administration was money, from that source and for that reason, there is the question of what would have happened to the money, and how the former President could reach it now. John Wilson, the attorney for Haldeman and Ehrlichman, was the lawyer who, more than twenty years ago, won the major settlement which left the secrecy of Swiss bank accounts inviolable, even if—as in the case of the German investors in IG Farben, which became the American company General Aniline—the depositors in those accounts were likely to be former Nazis, who were precluded from access to their investments, under American law. At secret foreign bank accounts, the trail always ends. As for how Nixon could reach the money, however, there are several possibilities. There is, for instance, Rabbi Korff.

Rabbi Korff did not even enter the story until July 1973, when he took out a $5,000 ad in *The New York Times* in the name of the National Citizens Committee for Fairness to the President. A genuine friend of Nixon's since then, and truly committed to the former President's vindication, Rabbi Korff has been an unusual figure all along. Every few months, Korff holds a press conference to announce that the contributions he has been receiving from all over the country (for what has now become the United States Citizens'

Congress and the President Nixon Justice Fund) are great, but not sufficient to cover the former President's legal fees. Then, he journeys to San Clemente, to report on the former President's frame of mind. It stands to reason that, although there may be contributions every time the rabbi calls a news conference (among the largest of them are those of the DeWitt Wallaces of *Reader's Digest*, and strangely enough, those of Rabbi Korff himself, who is paid a salary by the committee, from which he contributes to the fund), citizens are not racing to send in their checks for the former President's defense. Then one remembers that the argument for those contributions— compassion, *legal fees*—precisely duplicates the cover story for payments to the Watergate burglars. It may be coincidental. It is just a cast of mind.

Whatever else is true, it is clear that Rabbi Korff has access to money, and both the opportunity and the explanation for conveying it to the former President. Korff's background has always been international, not to say swashbuckling. In the early forties, he was, he says, raising money to buy passports in Paraguay for Jewish inmates of Nazi camps and, by means of contacts in Switzerland, paying money to Himmler to get those prisoners out. There follows a period in which, Korff says, he spent a lot of time abroad, raising money for the Stern Gang and the Irgun. When one asks raising money from *whom*, the rabbi becomes vague and laughs. In the fifties and sixties, Korff actually had a congregation, a small one, and wrote a lot of speeches, he says, for Democratic congressmen. He now travels a lot abroad. And it proves, of course, nothing more than that the former President has got a loyal, well-traveled, fund-raising friend, whose declared source of funds—citizens sending in a dollar here, a dollar there—would not amount to much or make much sense. It has also been probable from the first that those "loans" from Robert Abplanalp and Bebe Rebozo were never loans in any normal sense. They were not meant to be paid back. Nor were they gifts. What seems clear if one pursues the records and this line of reasoning is that the money Nixon's friends have "loaned" him is in fact his own, which he cannot, for one reason and another, reach any other way.

But the story, the inference really, is not concerned with now—but with the fall of 1972, in Washington and South Vietnam. As for who would know, the South Vietnamese, of course; but they have their own foreign accounts, and no one would believe them anyway. As for who else—all those international money-raisers, Stans, Kalmbach, Connally, perhaps. And Haig. At about the time of the Nixon pardon, President Ford kept making decisions, and then reversing them, about whether or not former President Nixon would have access to his own presidential papers; in the end, Ford let only one set of the presidential papers leave the White House: the ones belonging to Alexander Haig.

As for Nixon himself, he would, I suppose, have managed to think that he made such a deal on patriotic grounds, in the interests of the free world. And it is not so bad to have been paid to do what one might have done out of conviction anyway. Except for this: that he was President of the United States. And that unlike Watergate, unlike Rebozo, or Hughes, or the CIA, or any previous administration in our history, such a bribe and the taking of it would have cost not just the American taxpayer's money but his sons. And if the South Vietnamese government was bribing an American President, with American money, to keep our investment and our boys there any longer than was necessary, it is not to be borne. And that's what I think they did. Like the underlying thesis of Moses and monotheism, the underlying proposition is what we have all, somehow, shared all along. It explains why all the many volumes produced by the inquiry, as Congressman Wiggins correctly pointed out, don't contain enough of a case to fill a single pamphlet. It explains why, in spite of Nixon's departure, nothing was resolved, or laid to rest. The impeachment inquiry did what it could, and the President was removed. But we were, I think, of legal and political necessity, at the tip of the wrong iceberg. The story that required the end of the Nixon presidency, I think, was not Watergate—or even "other high

Crimes and Misdemeanors." It was Treason and Bribery. I don't know what follows from it. I think it is the bottom line. It has brought a disorientation beyond reckoning. People died for it. We are going to have to live, I think, with that.

The Atlantic Monthly
December 1976

DECODING THE STARR REPORT

THE SIX-VOLUME Report by Kenneth W. Starr to the U.S. House of Representatives—which consists, so far, of the single-volume *Referral* and five volumes of *Appendices and Supplemental Materials*—is, in many ways, an utterly preposterous document: inaccurate, mindless, biased, disorganized, unprofessional, and corrupt. What it is textually is a voluminous work of demented pornography, with many fascinating characters and several largely hidden story lines. What it is politically is an attempt, through its own limitless preoccupation with sexual material, to set aside, even obliterate, the relatively dull requirements of real evidence and constitutional procedure.

Less obvious at first, and then altogether unmistakable, is the author's scorn for the House of Representatives. The power to prosecute an impeachment is the only important power that the Constitution grants solely to the House. Before the *Communication from the Office of the Independent Counsel, Kenneth W. Starr*, as the document is called, it was unthinkable that *any* official, of any branch of government, would presume to set forth, in a document submitted to the House, in the course of an impeachment inquiry, such conclusions as that the President "lied," or "attempted to obstruct justice," or any of the other judgments that the Report presumes to make on the very first page of its introduction—let alone include on its cover and as part of its title the name of its primary author. On the cover of this document the name of Henry J. Hyde, chairman of the House Judiciary Committee, does not appear. The words "United States House of Representatives" appear in letters about half the size of "Kenneth W. Starr."

From the moment Chairman Hyde permitted Mr. Starr thus to interpose his views between the committee and the evidence, and authorized the publication of these documents under the congressional seal, he set in motion an unprecedented process, in which the House is nearly powerless. On October 9, 1998, the chairman said he would permit his committee to call Mr. Starr, but that he saw "no need" to call, for example, Monica Lewinsky. Other members of the panel said they could rely, for the testimony of witnesses, on Mr. Starr's Report. Apart from the obvious implications of a proceeding in which the judge's major witness is the prosecutor—and other witnesses are neither cross-examined nor even called—this decision limits the power of the House to approving or disapproving the recommendations of the Independent Counsel. For the purposes of impeachment, the Independent Counsel has become the House.

There are signs that the document was never intended to be understood, or even read, by anyone. The absence of dates, tables of contents, index, chronology, context, accurate headings, and logic of any sort from the five supplementary volumes is almost the least of it. So are the distortions and misrepresentations in the Report itself of what the record actually shows. Documents published by the Government Printing Office are often a marvel of information and legibility, printed with great speed and under pressure. In the 7,793 pages that constitute just the *Appendices and Supplemental Materials*, however, there are embedded thousands of smaller pages (sometimes four, often six tiny pages, compressed within a single larger page) in type so minuscule that, quite apart from the time constraints on reporters and other citizens, visual constraints—the eyesight, for example, of aging congressmen—absolutely preclude the reading of vast portions of the text.

There are also countless redactions, blackings-out, excisions by the House Judiciary Committee, which add to the general disorder. The dates of birth of all but a few witnesses, for example, are blacked out—an attempt, presumably, to spare these witnesses (whose privacy is not just violated but mocked in these documents by the prosecutors' constant assurances that their testimony is "secret," and that "there are no unauthorized persons present") the embarrass-ment of having their ages widely known. Other deletions are inex-plicable. Names are blacked out in one place only to appear, in precisely the same context, in another. Relatively mild and perfectly obvious four-letter words are blacked out while other words, tradi-tionally regarded as stronger and more offensive, are left in. Variants of the word "shit," for example, are deleted, but Linda Tripp's re-mark to Monica Lewinsky "You never, ever realized whose dick you were sucking" is unedited.

There are printed invitations to parties, accompanied by the guest lists. The names of the hosts, on the invitations, are blacked out. These might be mere examples of work done innocently or in haste. It soon becomes clear, however, that a fundamental strategy of the authors is unintelligibility.

To submit a massive document in which it is literally impossible to find information by title, date, alphabetical or chronological se-quence, or context of any kind makes it difficult to check whether any particular conclusion is warranted—whether there is evidence for the opposite conclusion, or another conclusion altogether. As a series of anecdotes, of prurient gossip raised, for the first time, to the level of constitutional crisis, the story the Office of the Independent Counsel wants to tell is by now widely known. People seem to have made up their minds about it. Underneath that story, however, scat-tered in almost incomprehensible pieces throughout the text, are at least two other stories, which the authors go to considerable lengths to hide.

The setting is the White House—a peculiar, almost farcically disordered place of rumor, envy, spite, betrayal, birthday parties. Ev-eryone, from the President's secretary, Betty Currie, through the Uniformed Secret Service guards and the stewards in the Oval Of-fice pantry, seems to think nothing of accepting presents—ties, Go-diva chocolates, pocket handkerchiefs, body lotions, gift certificates for manicures and pedicures at Georgette Klinger—from Monica Lewinsky, a young woman who is regarded, almost universally and, as it turns out, with astonishing understatement, as a "stalker," a "hall surfer," a "cling on," and a "clutch." One of the pantry stewards, Bayani Nelvis, has dinners with Ms. Lewinsky, exchanges gifts and confidences with her, offers her the President's cigars, and, according to Ms. Lewinsky, calls her from a presidential vacation on Martha's Vineyard to invite her to come and share a house with him. Mr. Nelvis denies the invitation to stay with him on the Vineyard. On many other matters he is mum.

Another staff member, rumored to be a "graduate," or former intimate of the President's, "clomps" through the corridors wearing the President's shoes. Young people offend older staff members by spilling Coke on White House carpets and putting their feet up on White House chairs. The uniformed Secret Service guards at the White House feel free to spread scurrilous gossip—among themselves and to other people. On one occasion they tell Ms. Lewinsky, who is trying to enter the White House, that the President already has a female visitor in the Oval Office. Ms. Lewinsky flies into a rage—although she has not visited the President in weeks and was not invited this time. She berates Betty Currie for lying to her about the President's whereabouts. Ms. Currie scolds the guards for their indiscretion. The guards are miffed.

In the summer of 1995, Ms. Lewinsky, who frequently describes herself as "insecure," comes to the White House, as an unpaid intern. She repeatedly approaches the President and "introduces" herself. On November 15, 1995, Ms. Lewinsky says, she flashes her thong underwear at him, tells him she has a crush on him, and accompanies him to a secluded corridor. He asks if he may kiss her. Later that evening, when they meet again, she grabs his crotch and performs oral sex on him—an approach she tries to repeat at virtually every subsequent opportunity.

According to the testimony of Ms. Lewinsky—and she is not one to understate—there are, in all, nine incidents of these, as the Report calls them, "in-person" sexual encounters: three in 1995, four in 1996, and two in 1997. In January 1996, Ms. Lewinsky says, she and the President have phone sex. He does not call her for a week. Feeling "a little bit insecure about whether he had liked it or didn't like it" and wondering "if this was sort of developing into some kind of a longer-term relationship than what I thought it initially might have been," she goes to the Oval Office and asks him whether this is "just about sex," or whether he has some interest in trying to get to know her as a person. He assures her that he "cherishes" his time with her.

On February 19, 1996, the President tells Ms. Lewinsky that their physical relationship must end. He does not feel right about it. Their friendship, however, can continue. This is not an entirely unusual thing for one person to say to another. It is not often misunderstood. Ms. Lewinsky perseveres. Wherever the President is—in the Oval Office, at staff birthday parties, jogging, attending church, at fundraisers, departing on journeys and returning from them—Ms. Lewinsky contrives to "position" herself there. This does not go unremarked.

On April 5, 1996, the Friday before Easter, Ms. Lewinsky learns that she has been dismissed from her White House job and transferred—with a considerable rise in rank and salary—to the Pentagon. On that Sunday, which is Easter, she goes to the President to complain. He tells her that "after the election" he will be able to find her another White House job. Another young woman might have noticed, and been deterred by, the prospect of so long a separation. Not Ms. Lewinsky. She performs oral sex and departs. She renews her efforts, calling, writing, sending presents.

The President now wards off any private visits from her for nearly eleven months—from April 7, 1996, until February 28, 1997. Ms. Lewinsky hates her job at the Pentagon. She is bored by it. The job entails transcription. She has no typing skills and cannot spell. From her desk, by telephone, by email, and in person, she complains. She sends cards, ties, other presents, importuning letters. She harangues Ms. Currie with incessant calls. She wants to talk to the President, in person and by phone. She wants the White House job she feels she has been promised. The President and Ms. Currie say that they will try. Perhaps not surprisingly, there is no White House job for her. She still manages to position herself in the President's path. She keeps informed of his schedule through Betty Currie and the pantry steward Bayani Nelvis.

Finally, on February 28, 1997, she manages to visit the President again. He gives her a hatpin and Walt Whitman's *Leaves of Grass*. "I wanted to perform oral sex on him," Ms. Lewinsky testifies, "and so I did." On every prior occasion the President has insisted that Ms. Lewinsky stop before what she tends to call completion. On this day she persuades the President to let her continue. "It's important to me," she says. Afterward, Ms. Lewinsky finds—perhaps this was always her intention—semen on her dress. On March 29, 1997, according to Ms. Lewinsky, there is a similar event. The in-person sexual encounters are at an end.

On May 24, 1997, the President calls Ms. Lewinsky in. He says again that their affair, such as it is, is over. He tells her that she is "a great person" and that they will still be friends. He is determined to be good. Ms. Lewinsky attributes the breakup to the President's "wanting to do the right thing in God's eyes." Three days later, the Supreme Court announces its decision in the Paula Jones case. The Jones suit, which accuses him of sexual harassment, can proceed while he is still in office—without "distract[ing him] from his public duties." The decision is surely one of the worst in the Court's history. For now it is the law.

Ms. Lewinsky has never been reticent or soft-spoken. Now she becomes ever more implacable and wild. She phones and pages Ms. Currie at all hours, later even visits her at home. It would not be quite accurate to say that this is just a particularly intense love story. Ms. Lewinsky has too many other interests—shopping, M&M's, finding a good job—one that pays well, with a good title, and that will "intrigue" her—new men: an Australian, a "health nut," an employee of the Pentagon, a former lover, married, with whom she resumes an affair and whom she had blackmailed some years before, by threatening to disclose the affair to his wife if he did not see her again.

Meanwhile, Ms. Lewinsky has made friends with a third major character, Linda Tripp—a colleague, who has also been transferred, under murky circumstances, from the White House to the Pentagon. Ms. Tripp says that Ms. Lewinsky did not confide in her about the "affair" until late September or early October 1996. In January 1997, Ms. Tripp begins to advise Ms. Lewinsky about strategies for getting a new White House job and also for regaining the affection of the President. She edits Ms. Lewinsky's letters and helps her compose audiotapes to send to him. Within a month of this collaboration, Ms. Lewinsky manages to visit the President for the first time in a year, and this visit produces Mr. Starr's most famous piece of "evidence," the blue dress.

Sometime in May or June of 1997, Ms. Tripp begins (at Ms. Lewinsky's request, she claims) to keep a notebook of the history of Ms. Lewinsky's encounters with the President—in order, she says, to analyze them, and look for a "pattern." At approximately the same time, Ms. Lewinsky uses her computer at the Pentagon to create (at Ms. Tripp's suggestion, she says) a "matrix," or spreadsheet, detailing her meetings with the President. Ms. Tripp preserves her notebook. Ms. Lewinsky soon becomes as persistent with her new confidante—calling her at all hours, at home and at the office, leaving messages, interrupting meetings, visiting her at her desk several times a day—as she is with Ms. Currie or the President.

In November, Ms. Tripp testifies, she sees, for the second time, the dress in Ms. Lewinsky's closet, the dress Ms. Lewinsky wore during her visit to the President on February 28, 1997. Ms. Tripp is adamant in her insistence that the stain on the dress be preserved.

MS. TRIPP: Hey, listen, my cousin is a genetic whatchamacallit.... He said that [if a rape victim] has preserved a pinprick size of crusted semen 10 years from that time...they can match the DNA....

MS. LEWINSKY: So why can't I scratch that crap off and put it in a plastic bag?

MS. TRIPP: . . . [P]ack it in with your treasures. . . . It could be your only insurance policy down the road.

Tripp told the grand jury: "I wanted some way for there to be proof of what he was doing with Monica." Of course, by the time Ms. Tripp sees the dress, the President has not been "doing" anything with Monica—except trying to avoid her—for more than eight months.

In October 1997, Ms. Tripp, for whatever reason, begins to tape her phone conversations with Ms. Lewinsky. The prosecutors subsequently lead her through a vast amount of testimony, before the grand jury, about her own life and motives, as well as what she claims to know about Ms. Lewinsky. Fairly late in Ms. Tripp's testimony, a juror speaks up. The jury has a question. Nothing could be clearer than that the prosecutors do not want Ms. Tripp to answer it.

A JUROR: Why did you decide to document?

MR. EMMICK [associate independent counsel]: Can I interrupt, ma'am? I'm sorry. Just to clarify.

MR. SUSANIN [associate independent counsel]: So to clarify this grand juror's question—

A JUROR: Hold on. Can I get an answer to my question?

Apparently not.

MR. SUSANIN: Can I ask a question, ma'am. Just to clarify?

Forty confusing lines later, the juror tries again.

A JUROR: Ms. Tripp, why were you documenting?

THE WITNESS: Why was I documenting?

A JUROR: . . . documenting other than the notebook?

THE WITNESS: Oh, the notebook—well, maybe I should say different words so it doesn't sound contradictory at all because it wasn't. The notebook was something Monica asked me to do in my head to understand cause and effect of all the ups and downs of her relationship in intimate detail.

The jurors keep trying to find out why Ms. Tripp was constantly eliciting and making tapes of Ms. Lewinsky's confidences. None of Ms. Tripp's explanations of why she taped make any sense. To "arm myself with a record" so that she could testify about Monica Lewinsky, truthfully, under oath in the Jones case, without fear of being defamed, she says, by the President's lawyers or destroyed by others in the White House. She was "scared," she says many times, but her "integrity" required her to tell the truth. There was, however, no reason whatever, during the months when Ms. Tripp was taping, to imagine that she could possibly be subpoenaed in the Paula Jones case. All her testimony would have been inadmissable, as hearsay and on other grounds. It took a great deal of work, on Ms. Tripp's part and the Special Counsel's, to enable her to intrude herself in the case at all.

In March 1997, Michael Isikoff, a reporter from *Newsweek*, came to Ms. Tripp's desk in the Pentagon. He told her that Kathleen Willey claimed that the President had once subjected her to sexual harassment. Mr. Isikoff said Ms. Willey had given him Ms. Tripp's name as a confirming witness. Ms. Tripp told Mr. Isikoff she recalled the incident in question, but that Ms. Willey had actually solicited, welcomed, and subsequently boasted about the President's embrace. In August 1997, *Newsweek* published Mr. Isikoff's story—citing Ms. Tripp as a source. A lot has since been said—by Ms. Tripp and in the press—about the matter. What has gradually become clear is this: Ms. Tripp tried to persuade Mr. Isikoff to write not about Ms. Willey but about a former White House intern, "M," who was now working at the Pentagon. Ms. Tripp's testimony varies about when, and by what means, she conveyed Ms. Lewinsky's full name to Mr. Isikoff. She admits he knew it by October, the month when she began to tape.

And another chronology begins to emerge about Ms. Tripp. She describes herself to the grand jury as having once been a fairly "apolitical" member of the White House staff in the Bush administration, in the department of media affairs. (It was there, she says, that she first came to know Mr. Isikoff.) She stayed on until August 1994 in the Clinton White House. She believes that Hillary Clinton became "cold" to her—perhaps as a result, Ms. Tripp says, of a mistaken idea that Ms. Tripp had a romantic interest in the President —or that the President had a romantic interest in Ms. Tripp. Ms. Tripp was transferred to the office of White House Counsel Bernard W. Nussbaum, where she was, she says, as she had always been, "loyal" and "apolitical." She worked on what she called "sensitive matters," like "the appointment of the special prosecutor." Odd.

As early as 1993, however, Ms. Tripp had been so appalled, she says, by the Clinton White House that a friend, Tony Snow (a right-wing journalist and occasional stand-in for Rush Limbaugh), urged her to write a book. Mr. Snow offered to put her in touch with a literary agent, Lucianne Goldberg. Ms. Tripp declined. In the summer of 1996—perhaps coincidentally after Ms. Lewinsky's first months at the Pentagon—Ms. Tripp changed her mind. She took Mr. Snow up on his offer and met with Ms. Goldberg, who suggested a ghostwriter. Ms. Tripp ultimately abandoned the project. One character whom Ms. Tripp had intended to describe in her book, however, was none other than Kathleen Willey.

Ms. Tripp, it turns out, had known Kathleen Willey since 1993. As Ms. Tripp describes her, Ms. Willey was, at the time, an unpaid White House volunteer, infatuated with the President and determined to have an affair with him. According to Ms. Tripp, Ms.

Willey dressed provocatively, would "position" herself in the President's path, sent him notes, and contrived to bump into him. Ms. Tripp soon began to advise her on strategy and to help her edit cards and letters to the President. Ms. Tripp listened to Ms. Willey's confidences and received her frequent phone calls at home. In short, not an altogether unfamiliar story. As Ms. Tripp tells it, however, she harbors at least one trace of bitterness if not of envy. "I was annoyed," she says, because when Ms. Tripp left the White House, Ms. Willey was hired "essentially in my stead."

There is at least one other, rather hidden, element of Ms. Tripp's story. When she began to tape, Ms. Tripp tells the grand jurors in answer to a question, "I had never even thought about the Independent Counsel in my wildest dreams." This is a statement that the prosecutors—if not Ms. Tripp herself—had every obligation to amplify. Because Ms. Tripp had not only thought or dreamed of the Office of the Independent Counsel, she had appeared before it at least twice before—first under Robert Fiske, and then under Kenneth W. Starr.

According to an FBI report—whose very existence is not acknowledged anywhere in the Starr documents—Ms. Tripp appeared on April 12, 1994, at the Office of the Independent Counsel. Among her concerns was the death of Deputy White House Counsel Vincent Foster. She had suspicions about that death. One source of her suspicion, the FBI report says, was Mr. Foster's conduct when Ms. Tripp brought him what turned out to be his last lunch, a hamburger:

> He removed the onions from his hamburger, which struck Tripp as odd in retrospect. She couldn't understand why he would do that if he was planning to commit suicide. It did not make sense to her that he might be worried about his breath if that were the case. The agent adds: "Tripp does not know if Foster likes or dislikes onions."

Whatever her beliefs—or thoughts or dreams—the fact that neither Ms. Tripp in her testimony nor the prosecutors before the grand jury nor the Independent Counsel anywhere in his Report mentions these contacts at least three years previously between Ms. Tripp and the Office of the Independent Counsel suggests that the real reason Ms. Tripp was taping, from the first, was this: The Office of the Independent Counsel asked her to.

During the year or so—November 1996 to October 1997—when Ms. Lewinsky was still haranguing, plotting, and threatening, in her campaign to return to a White House job, Ms. Tripp had encouraged her to believe that this was a simple matter, and that failure to get such a job would appear to confirm her undeserved reputation as a stalker. Ms. Tripp professed to be outraged on Ms. Lewinsky's behalf that a job had not been found. Ms. Lewinsky became increasingly immoderate in her demands and her behavior. She had been "yelling," at the President, and at Ms. Currie. When she could not reach him on September 12, 1997, she had stood for an hour and a half at an entrance to the White House, "screaming."

On October 6, 1997, Ms. Tripp changed her advice to Ms. Lewinsky. She said that, according to "Kate," a friend of Ms. Tripp's at the National Security Council, Ms. Lewinsky would never work at the White House again, that she was, in fact, known and disliked there as a stalker, and that the best thing for her to do would be to get out of town. This had the not unpredictable effect of setting Ms. Lewinsky off on another frenzy of phone calls to the White House—this time, however, to arrange for a job in another city. Ms. Tripp suggested to Ms. Lewinsky that she ask for a job in New York. According to an FBI report, Ms. Tripp also advised Ms. Lewinsky "to find some way to ask for help from Vernon Jordan."

By this time, it seemed the White House was eager to get Ms. Lewinsky a job in New York, encouraging her not to be silent in any legal matter but merely to go away. In early November, Ms. Lewinsky was offered a job at the UN working for Ambassador Bill Richardson. Ms. Tripp found in this offer a new source of outrage. The offer came "too fast," "so they won't have to—so they will consider it settled." It had Ms. Lewinsky "railroaded," "backed into a corner" as to whether she wanted to take it or not. Ms. Lewinsky turned the job down. At this point, no matter what the President or Ms. Currie said or did, it became—for Ms. Tripp and then for Ms. Lewinsky— a fresh source of grievance and invective. Ms. Tripp encouraged Ms. Lewinsky to believe the White House did not appreciate how little trouble Ms. Lewinsky had been.

> MS. LEWINSKY: And I said [to the President], "You [expletive] tell me when I've been—when I've caused you trouble." I said, "You don't know trouble."

> MS. TRIPP: Man, he should be thanking his lucky stars.

> MS. LEWINSKY: No [expletive] shit.

> MS. TRIPP: That you're the farthest thing from trouble he's ever had. . . . I feel very strongly that he should be thanking his lucky stars, left, right, and center, that you are who you are. . . . Most people going through what you've gone through would have said hey, [expletive] you and the horse you rode in on and let me call the *National Enquirer*.

> MS. LEWINSKY: Yeah.

In December 1997, Ms. Tripp says, she became aware that in her home state of Maryland, surreptitiously taping phone conversations was illegal and that, far from being protected by this "insurance policy," this evidence of her truthfulness and integrity, she might actually go to jail. She contacted Ms. Goldberg, who began calling lawyers she knew, at the Chicago branch of Kirkland & Ellis, where Mr. Starr still worked at the time, sensing apparently no conflict of interest between his private practice and his work as Special Prosecutor. Ms. Goldberg also called lawyers at other firms, in Chicago,

New York, Washington, and Los Angeles, about making contact on Ms. Tripp's behalf with the Office of the Independent Counsel to obtain immunity for the illegal taping.

It is not clear why Ms. Tripp needed an intermediary to make contact with Mr. Starr's office, since—as we know, but the grand jury and readers of Mr. Starr's Report do not—Ms. Tripp had been in touch with the Independent Counsel for at least three years.

Ms. Tripp and the Independent Counsel's office claim that she came to them for the first time on Monday, January 12, 1998, the day before their agents and the FBI equipped her with a body wire for a last conversation with Ms. Lewinsky. To make such use of Ms. Tripp, the Independent Counsel needed authorization, on an "emergency basis," from Attorney General Janet Reno or the three-judge special division of the U.S. Court of Appeals. They needed a legal basis for drawing Monica Lewinsky into their investigation. This presented some difficulty: The Independent Counsel was explicitly barred from joining his investigation with the work of the attorneys for Paula Jones. If Ms. Tripp could elicit from Ms. Lewinsky some evidence of a conspiracy to break the law—some evidence, for example, that the President had authorized Vernon Jordan to find a job for Ms. Lewinsky as a bribe for her to commit perjury—Mr. Starr would have some sort of argument for the expansion of his jurisdiction. He could make Ms. Lewinsky herself an agent for the Independent Counsel's office. But the deadlines were tight. The President was due to testify in the Jones case on January 17, 1998. So Starr wired Ms. Tripp, two days earlier, before he had any authorization from the attorney general or the appellate court to do so. He had to hope that the evidence Ms. Tripp would elicit, and tape with her body wire, would override this procedural concern.

Here was the situation in the Independent Counsel's office by the time they came to Ms. Lewinsky. Mr. Starr had recruited lawyers with experience prosecuting organized crime. Since at least the days of Robert Kennedy, the custom in organized-crime cases has been to get the suspects, violate their rights, and if you cannot convict them of one crime then somehow indict them for another. From the day in 1994 when Judge Starr offered to write an amicus brief in the Paula Jones case—moreover, through the years when, as Special Counsel, he maintained his lucrative private practice at Kirkland & Ellis—it was clear that he was by no means remarkable for scruple and in no sense averse to conflicts of interest of the most glaring kind. Nothing could be more obvious than his emotional, ideological, even social and professional links to the old case of Paula Jones. He became Special Counsel in 1994. By the 1996 election, he must have been frustrated and humiliated. None of his expensive lines of inquiry had worked out—not the suicide of Vincent Foster, not Travelgate or Filegate, certainly not Whitewater. Susan McDougal, after more than a year in jail for contempt, was still of no use to him. Webster Hubbell, whom he had sent to jail but given a limited grant of immunity in exchange for his testimony, had not really helped him, either. Vernon Jordan, who found money and jobs for Hubbell, was thriving alongside the newly reelected President. The prosecutor had spent millions so far, and he had failed. He would obviously like to find the constellation—a crime committed on the President's behalf by a subordinate, preferably a bribe by Vernon Jordan—somewhere, before the expiration of the President's term. The love life of Monica Lewinsky seems an odd place to look for that configuration. Yet, with a little prosecutorial zeal and creativity, it might be found. Mr. Starr's documents have vestiges of an attempt to show that it is there.

Another case of the jurors pursuing a line of inquiry in spite of the best efforts of the prosecutors occurs near the end of the testimony of Monica Lewinsky. The jurors want to know about her first encounter with the prosecutors from the Office of the Independent Counsel, on January 16, 1998, when Linda Tripp lured her into the midst of the prosecutors and FBI agents, who would detain her for most of the day and night.

"Tell us about that day," a juror says, and then another juror inquires about the encounter between Ms. Lewinsky and all those men from the Office of the Special Prosecutor and the FBI.

"Maybe if I could ask, what areas do you want to get into?" Mr. Emmick asks. "Because there's—you know—many hours of activity." A few lines later:

A JUROR: We want to know about that day.

A JUROR: That day.

A JUROR: The first question.

A JUROR: Yes.

A JUROR: We really want to know about that day.

MR. EMMICK: All right.

The jurors are right to insist on a description of the day. That was the day, January 16, 1998—and the night—when the prosecutors came as close as they have so far to bringing the entire constitutional system down.

Ms. Lewinsky starts to tell about that day. Ms. Lewinsky and Ms. Tripp had arranged to meet at the food court of the Ritz-Carlton in the Pentagon City mall.

THE WITNESS: She was late. I saw her come down the escalator. And as I—as I walked toward her, she kind of motioned behind her and Agent [blank] and Agent [blank] presented themselves to me.... They told me ... that they wanted to talk to me and give me a chance, I think, to cooperate, maybe. I—to help myself. I told them I wasn't speaking to them without my attorney.

This is the turning point. This is the moment when the investigation begins to reveal itself as what it truly is. There is absolutely no doubt, none whatsoever, that the investigators—prosecutors and FBI agents alike—were obliged by law to stop right there, without another word, until Ms. Lewinsky brought in her attorney. Indeed, they were required, under Title 28 of the Code of Federal Regulations, to have contacted her attorney in the first place. They did nothing of the kind.

THE WITNESS: They told me...I should know I won't be given as much information and won't be able to help myself as much with my attorney there. So I agreed to go. I was so scared. (The witness begins crying.)

Two questions later, she turns to the lead attorney at this grand-jury hearing, Michael Emmick:

THE WITNESS: Can Karin [Immergut] do the questioning now? This is—can I ask you to step out?

MR. EMMICK: Sure. Okay. All right....

MS. IMMERGUT: Okay. Did you go to a room with them at the hotel?

A: Yes.

Q: And what did you do then? Did you ever tell them that you wanted to call your mother?

A: I told them I wanted to talk to my attorney.... And they told me—Mike [Emmick] came out and introduced himself to me and told me that—that Janet Reno had sanctioned Ken Starr to investigate my actions in the Paula Jones case, that they—that they knew I had signed a false affidavit, they had me on tape saying I had committed perjury, that they were going to—that I could go to jail for twenty-seven years, they were going to charge me with perjury and obstruction of justice and subornation of perjury and witness tampering and something else.

Q: And you're saying "they," at that point, who was talking to you about that stuff?

A: Mike Emmick and the two FBI guys.... And I just—I felt so bad.

This is an extraordinary scene. Monica Lewinsky, who has faced hour after hour, day after day of questioning about her most intimate experiences, has quietly drawn the line. She has asked the prosecutor, Michael Emmick, one of the participants in the events of "that day," to leave the room. It is a side of Monica Lewinsky that has not appeared before.

Q: I guess later, just to sort of finish up. I guess...was there a time then that you were—you just waited with the prosecutor until your mother came down?

A: No.

Q: Okay.

A: I mean, there was, but they—they told me they wanted me to cooperate. I asked them what cooperating meant, it entailed, and they told me...that they had had me on tape saying things from the lunch that I had had with Linda at the Ritz-Carlton...then they told me that I—that I'd have to agree to be debriefed and that I'd have to place calls or wear a wire to see—to call Betty and Mr. Jordan and possibly the President....

Q: And did you tell them that you didn't want to do that?

A: Yes. . . . Then I wanted to call my mom and they kept telling me . . . that I couldn't tell anybody about this, they didn't want anyone to find out and . . . that was the reason I couldn't call [her attorney] Mr. Carter, was because they were afraid that he might tell the person who took me to Mr. Carter.

The person who took her to her attorney, Francis Carter, was Vernon Jordan.

So obsessed are the prosecutors with the prospect of getting the President and Vernon Jordan, or rather the President *through* Vernon Jordan, that they fear that *any* attorney she might select would alert Mr. Jordan. They actually propose to Ms. Lewinsky that she call an attorney they have chosen.

A: They told me that I could call this number and get another criminal attorney, but I didn't want that and I didn't trust them. Then I just cried for a long time. . . . They just sat there and then . . . they kept saying there was this time constraint, there was a time constraint. I had to make a decision.

And then, Bruce Udolf [another prosecutor] came in at some point and then—then Jackie Bennett [yet another prosecutor] came in . . . and the room was crowded and he was saying to me, you know, you have to make a decision. I had wanted to call my mom, they weren't going to let me call my attorney, so I just—I wanted to call my mom and they . . . And they had told me before that I could leave whenever I wanted, but . . . I didn't really know. . . . I mean I thought if I left then that they were just going to arrest me.

As all the FBI agents and prosecutors from the Special Counsel's office gathered in that crowded room had every reason to know, they were in flagrant violation of Ms. Lewinsky's rights—and, not incidentally, their own oaths of office.

A: And so then they told me that I should know that they were planning to prosecute my mom for the things that I had said that she had done.

(The witness begins crying.)

A JUROR: So if I understand it, you first met the agents, Agents [blank] and [blank], at around 1:00 and it wasn't until about 11 p.m. that you had an opportunity to talk to a lawyer?

THE WITNESS: Yes.

Ms. Immergut now makes a small attempt to redeem the reputation of her colleagues:

Q: Although you were allowed to—the thing with Frank Carter was that they were afraid he would tell Vernon Jordan? Is that what they expressed to you?

A: Right. And I had—I had—I think that someone said that Frank was a civil attorney and so that he really couldn't help me anyway. So I asked him if at least I could call and ask him for a recommendation for a criminal attorney and they didn't think that was a good idea. . . .

A JUROR: Sounds as though they were actively discouraging you from talking to an attorney.

THE WITNESS: Yes.

Ms. Immergut tries again, with what is in no sense a question:

Q: Well, from Frank Carter.

A: From Frank Carter, who was my only attorney at that point.

MS. IMMERGUT: Right. Right.

THE WITNESS: So I could have called any other attorney but—

A JUROR: You didn't have another attorney.

THE WITNESS: I didn't have another attorney and this was my attorney for this case, so, I mean, this was—

A JUROR: And this is the attorney who had helped you with the affidavit.

THE WITNESS: Yes. And that—the affidavit—well, the affidavit wasn't even filed yet. It was Fed Ex'd out on that day.

This is an altogether remarkable revelation. For all the prosecutors' talk of "time constraint...time constraint" and pressure brought by a squad of no fewer than three prosecutors and two agents of the FBI on Ms. Lewinsky to "make a decision," the entire apparatus of the Independent Counsel's office, with prosecutors and FBI agents, its four-year, $40 million investigation, was now focused on this young woman—when her affidavit had not yet even been filed. It was Friday. The following Monday was Martin Luther King Day, a federal holiday. For all they knew, in spite of anything she had said to Ms. Tripp on any tape—and, as it turned out, she had lied to Ms. Tripp on several matters crucial to the case—Ms. Lewinsky might have changed her mind and filed a truthful affidavit. So at that point, Ms. Lewinsky, contrary to what the prosecutors were telling her and had told the U.S. attorney general and the court, had committed no crime. They had no right whatsoever to detain, let alone mislead her. They wanted her affidavit to arrive, and they wanted it to be false.

On Thursday, right after their taping, the Special Prosecutor's office had applied on an "emergency basis" to the attorney general, Janet Reno, and to the three-judge appellate court panel to extend the prosecutors' jurisdiction to the Jones case and to Ms. Lewinsky. All they had, at this point, was the suggestion—by Ms. Tripp, on Ms. Tripp's tapes—that Vernon Jordan might have asked Ms. Lewinsky to lie on her Paula Jones affidavit in exchange for a job. It is hard to see how, without deceiving Ms. Reno or the judges, the Special Prosecutor could justify his claim. Ms. Tripp, not the President, had come up with the idea of enlisting Mr. Jordan in the job hunt. Ms. Lewinsky had in fact signed her affidavit before she was offered a job (at Revlon) she found acceptable.

It is hard in any case to see how the possibility that someone will commit perjury can constitute an "emergency." The lie, after all, remains in the record. It will last and be detected in due course. A border crossing with drugs, or a conspiracy to murder might require emergency jurisdiction in that the evidence may vanish, or irreversible damage may be done. But it is the height of absurdity to claim an emergency in the loss of an opportunity to catch someone in a lie *that has not yet occurred*. What seems obvious is that the prosecutors were all too aware that the Tripp tapes really proved no crime. Their hope had to be that wiring Ms. Lewinsky, in conversation with Vernon Jordan and the President himself, might provide evidence of something else—a real obstruction of justice, say, or, better yet, evidence of some Whitewater- or Hubbell-related crime. Ms. Lewinsky refused to be wired.

A JUROR: During this time in the hotel with them, did you feel threatened?

THE WITNESS: Yes.

A JUROR: Did you feel that they had set a trap?

THE WITNESS: I—I—I did and I had—I didn't understand . . . why they had to trap me into coming there. . . . I mean this had all been a set-up and that's why I mean that was just

so frightening. It was so incredibly frightening.... They told
me if I partially cooperate, they'll talk to the judge....

A JUROR: So you didn't know what would happen if you left.

THE WITNESS: No.

It is all very well to say that Ms. Lewinsky is being overly dramatic; that she survived; that she did not collaborate in the prosecutors' efforts to make her, like Ms. Tripp, their agent; and that she
suffered no adverse consequences. But it is not true.

Quite apart from her eleven-hour ordeal, the interrogation was
not without adverse consequences for Ms. Lewinsky. That night,
when her mother, Marcia Lewis, arrived by train from New York,
one of the prosecutors took Ms. Lewis aside and conferred with her
alone. Later, in a phone call, made at Ms. Lewis's insistence, with Ms.
Lewinsky's father, in California, the prosecutor said that the matter
was "time sensitive." It may be that any family, under these conditions—in which the prosecutors made so clear their aversion to their
daughter's attorney—would have thought it wise to fire that attorney.
It may be that Ms. Lewinsky's parents thought things would go better
for their daughter with another lawyer. Certainly the prosecutors in
their time alone with Ms. Lewinsky's mother had ample opportunity
to tell her so. And, in fact, that night the Lewinskys decided to fire
Francis Carter and hired William Ginsburg—a California attorney
specializing in cases of medical malpractice. Whatever else might be
said about Mr. Ginsburg, he was not likely to strike fear into the
hearts of the prosecutors or to be in any way connected with Vernon
Jordan. He was not an expert in constitutional or criminal law, and
he did not move to have the case against Ms. Lewinsky thrown out
on grounds of prosecutorial abuses. If Ms. Lewinsky had had a constitutional lawyer, the case against her would have been thrown out.

Later, the Lewinskys may have thought that, to avoid further,
long and expensive litigation, they needed Beltway attorneys more
acceptable still to the forces arrayed against them. Plato Cacheris

and Jacob Stein, respected though they are, are also not without political affiliation. (Cacheris's most famous client, at the time of Watergate, was former attorney general John Mitchell. Stein had been
the attorney for Kenneth Parkinson, a Watergate defendant acquitted in the case before Judge Sirica.) Ms. Lewinsky would almost certainly have been better off with her original attorney, Francis Carter.

To return to the case. The President's deposition in the Jones case
was scheduled for the following day. Paula Jones' attorneys had
made it clear to Ms. Tripp that whatever information she had would
be useless to them after that date. Having failed to wire Ms. Lewinsky, Kenneth Starr is eager to supply the Jones attorneys with information to formulate questions for which the President will be
unprepared, and on which it is virtually impossible for the President, or any other person, to be entirely truthful, not just for the
obvious reasons—discretion, family, a reluctance to injure—but because such a line of inquiry never ends. The many people—journalists, government officials—who have expressed their belief that the
whole matter would have gone away if only the President had, from
the outset, "looked people in the eye and told the truth" seem not to
have considered where that sort of testimony would lead. Even in
Mr. Starr's documents, the counsel presses on and on, to elicit testimony about "masturbating," for example—which could have no
possible relevance in the case. There is the threat of perjury lurking
behind every such expression of the prosecutor's salacious appetite.
In fact, the volumes the Special Counsel has submitted to Congress
show precisely how detailed, ugly, preposterous, ultimately endless,
and unconscionable such questions are.

Since the chronology does not support Mr. Starr, the volumes
contain no chronology. Since so much of the "evidence" is irrelevant,
or contrived, or contradicted, or suspect in other ways, the Report
simply buries it in disorganization and sheer mass.

Taking but one example, there are the famous Linda Tripp tapes. Generally no date or context is given when they are cited in the communication. There are two separate lists of them, neither of which prefaces the transcripts. They give the following order: Tape 18, Tape 19, Tape 1, Tape 2, Tape 13, Tape 3, Tape 8, Tape 7, Tape 15, Tape 11, Tape 16, Tape 26, Tape 16, Tape 9, Tape 5, Tape 23, Tape 6, Tape 17, Tape 27, Tape 10, Tape 12, Tape 14, Tape 20, Tape 21, Tape 24, Tape 25, Tape 28.

It does not take a high level of acuity to see that there is something anomalous about this list. It could be just a result of the order of transcription that Tapes 1 and 2 follow 18 and 19, and so on.

Ms. Tripp testifies at length, however, that she had only one tape recorder and that she did not label tapes by date. As soon as each tape was full, or even before it was full, Ms. Tripp says, she put it in a Spode china bowl at some distance from her tape recorder; she was so anxious not to erase or alter anything that she used tapes one after another, never more than once, and often did not even risk turning a tape over to side B.

There seems no plausible explanation, then, for the fact that Tape 16 is said to hold the conversations of November 8, 11, 13, 14, and 16, while Tape 26 contains conversations of November 11. November 11 falls inescapably between November 8 and November 13. Ms. Tripp would have had to remove Tape 16 after she had recorded the conversations of November 8 and 11, used Tape 26 to record more conversations on November 11, and then put in Tape 16 again to record November 13, 14, and 16—not quite the process she describes.

An FBI report, moreover, states that the taping was sometimes affected by "Tripp's cats" having "activated the pause button." Riveting as some of the recorded conversations are, it seems hard to justify a great reliance on them.

In the 1960s, J. Edgar Hoover and his FBI clandestinely made tapes of Martin Luther King Jr. engaged in various sexual acts in hotel bedrooms. The Bureau sent copies of those tapes to several public officials and members of the press, and to Dr. King himself, in order to humiliate him and either drive him to suicide or hound him into retirement. Judge Starr and his staff, in their failure to make a legal case, have resorted in the end to the same strategy. One difference is that their target is the President. Another is that in the 1960s public officials and the press refused to disseminate such tapes. In the late 1990s the press welcomes, broadcasts, and dwells upon them. The House rushes to publish them, with the congressional imprimatur, and to use them as the basis for an impeachment inquiry.

Even in his worst excesses, Senator Joseph McCarthy made at least the claim of constitutional issues: the alleged infiltration and subversion of the American government by a foreign power. In the Nixonian crisis of Watergate, the issue was also constitutional: abuse of power by the President in his official capacity. In 1974 the House Judiciary Committee specifically rejected as an impeachable offense Nixon's cheating (and thereby lying under oath about it), in his private capacity, on his income taxes.

It is not often remarked that the Constitution protects not against the crimes of people against one another but against abuses by the state itself against its citizens. On January 16, 1998—and before and after—Kenneth Starr and his staff became precisely the governmental agents the Constitution guards against.

There is no question that the President was also very much at fault here: failures of judgment, failures of honor, failures of taste. It may be that each of us knows a Monica Lewinsky. Not every temperament finds it easy to escape from her. But Ms. Lewinsky, even if she turns out to have endearing qualities, is an extreme example. In his political life, the President has evidently found it easy to rebuff, even leave, people when he feels he needs to. Somehow, even when Ms. Lewinsky was at her worst—months after he had terminated any physical relations with her, when she would page Ms. Currie late into the night, with threats and abuse, when she would appear at the White House gate and "scream" until somebody (usually Ms.

Currie) came and brought her in—he could not seem to say, or enforce, a decisive no. He seemed to have the same difficulty with the special prosecutor and the grand jury. To have a White House, moreover, that cannot control its interns, pantry stewards, guards—cannot control even access to the President's person and his time—is a security risk and an administrative disaster. It seems, on the basis of these volumes, that the President is not only very nearly friendless but that there is something decidedly less than first-rate about the people with whom he surrounds himself. And, in spite of his intelligence, his interest in history, and concern with his "legacy," there is also something fundamentally wrong with his conception of what the presidency is.

The separation of powers, for example, requires the President to insist that the only court before which he will appear is the House in a matter of impeachment. Even the lowliest suspect in a criminal proceeding is not required to appear before a grand jury or submit to a sworn (let alone a videotaped) deposition. The President, as is so often remarked, is not above the law. In this case, he behaved as though he were below it. The very fact that he consented to testify diminished the powers of his office. Let the Independent Counsel come in waving stained dresses as he liked, he has no authority whatever to summon the President, let alone to take an example of his DNA. The House would look pretty silly deliberating over stains on dresses. In a proceeding of this constitutional order, the President cannot prevail with charm, semantics, or persuasion. To any court other than the House in an impeachment inquiry, he must say, as he should have said to Ms. Lewinsky, simply: No.

The grand jurors, in spite of the evident reluctance of the prosecutors, had been able to elicit testimony—to name but one example—from Linda Tripp which the House needs to examine. In reply to the crucial question of why she taped, she answers, at first, relatively calmly, because she was "afraid," because she needed "protection" against the enormous forces that were trying to "destroy her," to push her, in spite of her integrity, into a "felony" and a "perjury trap." A few questions more and she is talking about "the high level of drug use that was rampant in the White House when I was there," which may extend to the President himself, and testifying that there was a "list of forty bodies or something that were associated with the Clinton administration. At that time, I didn't know what that meant. I have since come to see such a list." Surely a list of forty bodies is something that—unlike the rest of the groundless and inadmissible trash he elicited elsewhere—would have been well within the jurisdiction of the Independent Counsel. The House needs to evaluate for itself the testimony of such a witness, along with the wisdom and good faith of an Independent Counsel who would reduce that testimony nearly to the size of a microdot, and not publish it earlier than page 4,277 of the fifth volume of his text.

The more closely one looks, then, at this huge mass of unsorted, often irrelevant and repellent matter, the clearer it becomes that the intent is to confuse, obscure, and intimidate. The facts the prosecutors were hoping to find—a bribe or other financial inducement to a witness to commit perjury, or at least to remain silent about some underlying crime—did not exist. In the case of Ms. Lewinsky, there was no obstruction of justice. In fact, there was no underlying crime. So they tried to create one. They thought they needed perjury from the President, so they set out to make sure he would commit it. They sent their agent Ms. Tripp to brief lawyers in a civil case with the sort of damaging information that would make it virtually impossible for the President to answer truthfully. Even with untruthful answers (which were peculiarly clumsy and inept), they had no crime—still less, a constitutional high crime or misdemeanor. So they just amassed their sludge and hurled it at the President, and hoped to prevail through embarrassment and disgust.

In one respect, the strategy seems to derive not just from Mr. Starr's staff of lawyers schooled in the prosecution of organized crime but also from Mr. Starr's own experience in the field of antitrust litigation. In the 1970s, it became common for huge corporations in antitrust cases simply to overwhelm the opposition with a huge amount of material, in the discovery phase of the trial, in hopes that the opposition could not find its case. The sheer mass of Mr.

Starr's volumes goes even further. It nearly conceals that he unleashed not just the legal mechanism entrusted to him but also a process that violates the ethical and legal norms of the society, on the basis of the—unconvincing, often even internally inconsistent—testimony of one embittered and compromised informant, and one unusually persistent, and demonstrably unreliable, woman of twenty-four.

Mr. Starr likes to dwell, with the press, on his reading of the Bible. There is in the Bible, after all, just one commandment that squarely meets the case as it now stands. It has to do with False Witness, and the false witness in question is not perjury. It is False Witness against Thy Neighbor, and these documents, this compendium of partially false and almost entirely scurrilous testimony, with its accompanying report, is a case of false witness so egregious as to set a standard for the millennium.

Vanity Fair
December 1998

ADDENDUM

On December 30, 1998, Charles Bakaly of the Office of the Independent Counsel wrote a letter to *Vanity Fair*, saying that "While we do not habitually correct published misinformation," he must dispute virtually every factual statement in my piece. On the very day the issue of *Vanity Fair* that contained Mr. Bakaly's letter was published —by apparent coincidence—Mr. Bakaly, having improperly "leaked" information to the press, left the OIC. Mr. Bakaly admitted the leak. He was subsequently found innocent of any legal wrongdoing in the matter. In spite of Mr. Bakaly's own admission that he *was* their source, the *Times* continued to protect his "anonymity." The following piece, in any event, was my answer to Mr. Bakaly's letter.

There can be no doubt that Mr. Bakaly and his colleagues at the Office of the Independent Counsel "do not habitually correct published misinformation." Their enterprise consists so precisely in generating misinformation, in such confusing and lurid volume—before the grand jury, the House Judiciary Committee, the courts, the attorney general, and the press— that by the time the truth emerges about any particular matter the news will simply have moved on. The strategy has so far served the Independent Counsel very well. As recently as this morning (February 10, 1999), *The New York Times* is still reporting, for example, that Linda Tripp "found her way to the Office of the Independent Counsel through a group of private lawyers," and that the Independent Counsel "first learned about the Lewinsky matter" on or about January 8, 1998— "four days before Linda R. Tripp contacted Mr. Starr's office." Ms. Tripp had testified that she contacted the OIC on January 12, 1998, and that her intermediary with Mr. Starr's office, as with Paula Jones's attorneys, was Lucianne Goldberg. Mr. Bakaly now repeats Ms. Tripp's claim that Ms. Goldberg was responsible for the (in his words) "decision to start taping" as well.

I don't know about Ms. Tripp's "decision to start taping," or what time Mr. Bakaly means by (in his other carefully chosen phrase) "at that time," but attempts to cast Ms. Goldberg as all-purpose motivator, intermediary, nexus, do not hold up. The fact, as I pointed out in my piece, was that, by January 1998, Ms. Tripp did not need intermediaries—Ms. Goldberg or any "group of private lawyers"—to contact the Office of the Independent Counsel, or to initiate taping for the OIC. By 1998, she had been Mr. Starr's witness, and before that Robert Fiske's, in various investigations, for almost four years.

Throughout the long volumes of the *Referral*, there is every evidence of a determination to conceal, and even falsify what the Office of the Independent Counsel actually knows about Linda Tripp. Nowhere in the *Referral*'s FBI reports, for example—which set forth, in considerable detail, both Ms. Tripp's own history and her intended testimony before the grand jury—is there any mention whatever of the fact that she has been interviewed at least once before, on April 12, 1994, on behalf of the Independent Counsel, by the FBI. In my piece, I mentioned the FBI's report of that April 12, 1994, interview—which I found, not in the Starr *Referral* but in documents that accompanied transcripts of the D'Amato hearings on Whitewater. Ms. Tripp was an enthusiastic witness. Her most sympathetic interlocutor was Lauch Faircloth, her fellow conspiracy theorist and one of two senators—the other was Jesse Helms—most directly responsible for the appointment of Kenneth Starr as Independent Counsel.

It is inconceivable that the FBI report of this interview is not in the files both of the FBI and of the OIC. In the whole Starr *Referral*, however, there is no mention of any such prior report, interview, or file. The almost inescapable inference is either that the *Referral*'s 1998 FBI reports were laundered to expunge any mention of the 1994 interview, or the FBI agents interviewing Ms. Tripp were instructed to omit any reference to it. An investigation of what became of these files, and why they were concealed from the grand jury, the House, and the Senate is surely overdue.

Similarly, when Ms. Tripp testified that, until January 12, 1998, she had "never even thought about the Independent Counsel in my wildest dreams," and that she needed Ms. Goldberg to contact the OIC, the grand jury was being actively misled. It was the obligation of the prosecutor immediately to disclose to the grand jury that this testimony, as he knew, if not from his own memory, then from his files, was false.

As for Ms. Tripp's tapes—which occupy literally thousands of pages of the *Referral*, but on which Mr. Bakaly now says the *Referral* "places no great reliance"—it is now clear that more than half of them exhibit doctoring (it is not clear

by whom), which the OIC chooses to characterize as "duplication." And it is quite untrue that any discrepancy in the sequence is, as Mr. Bakaly claims, "noted in an appendix to our
Referral." The pages that Mr. Bakaly cites are simply lists,
without any comment whatsoever on the sequence: They are
an *instance* of the lack of integrity, and not a notation of it. It
is, in any event, not the "tape," but the *conversation* that is out
of sequence: An earlier conversation appears between two
later ones—a metaphysical impossibility. The very extent of
the deception in defense of the tapes, together with the rapidity with which the OIC granted Ms. Tripp immunity for
them, make it clear whom Ms. Tripp was working for. Could
the prosecutors in a single evening really have reviewed the
contents of all those tapes, appraised their reliability, and
phrased questions for Ms. Tripp to pose during an interview
(at the Ritz-Carlton, with Ms. Lewinsky) the following day?
Surely only Ms. Tripp's prior work for the OIC can explain
the speed and degree to which they understood and trusted
her account, and the alacrity with which (without any legal
authority) they wired her.

There can really be no doubt, either, that on the night of
January 16, 1998, when the OIC was trying to coerce Monica
Lewinsky to cooperate in secret taping, the prosecutors were
aware—contrary to the statements in Mr. Bakaly's letter and
to sworn testimony, before the House Judiciary Committee,
by Kenneth Starr—that Ms. Tripp was going to meet Paula
Jones's attorneys that very night. In fact, as Ms. Tripp testified
before the grand jury, the terms of her agreement with Jones's
attorneys *required* her to brief them "before the President's deposition," which was, of course, the following day. Aside from
the certainty that Ms. Tripp, who was by this time incontest-
ably their agent, would have told them, the whole alleged basis
of her conversations with them was that *she was about to be a
witness in the Jones case.* Moreover (a fact concealed by the
prosecutors even in their representations to the court of Judge

Norma Holloway Johnson), throughout most of the hours on January 16, 1998, when prosecutors Jackie Bennettt, Michael Emmick, Bruce Udolf, and Stephen Binhak and FBI Special Agents Steven Irons, Patrick Fallon, and "other OIC attorneys and agents present at various times, mostly in an adjoining room" were detaining Ms. Lewinsky in one room of the Ritz-Carlton—one wonders how many prosecutors and FBI agents are required to detain an enemy spy, or a serial killer— Linda Tripp was waiting in another room of the same hotel. When Ms. Lewinsky declined to be wired, and it was clear the OIC would not be able to enlist her in one plan, Ms. Tripp needed to meet her deadline in setting up the President in another. Ms. Tripp left for her pivotal briefing of the Jones attorneys. Far from having "no inkling" where Ms. Tripp was going, the OIC sent one of their agents to drive her there.

The press, including the *Times*, has brought out some of the other extensive, manifestly illegal, contacts between the OIC and the Jones people, by way of partners in Mr. Starr's law firm and of Mr. Starr himself. There is at least one further clue, in the very basis of the interrogation of Ms. Lewinsky, to the degree of collaboration between the Jones attorneys and the OIC. In fact, the incident cannot even accurately be called an "interrogation." There is no evidence that the prosecutors and agents ever *asked* her anything. It was, rather, a protected exercise in threats, bullying, coercion, and intimidation, based not on inquiry but on what the prosecutors told Ms. Lewinsky they already knew. And the question is, How could they possibly have known it?

Ms. Lewinsky's affidavit had been signed, and mailed, but would not arrive until three days later at the court. Ms. Lewinsky, it must be remembered, had actually lied to Ms. Tripp—to the effect that she was taking Ms. Tripp's advice, and that she had not signed a false affidavit in the Jones case, and would not sign such an affidavit, until the President, through Vernon Jordan, had found her a satisfactory job. Ms.

Tripp, in other words, *did not know* that the false affidavit was already signed. How, then, did the prosecutors know—not just that it was false but that Ms. Lewinsky had signed it? The answer is this: Francis Carter, Ms. Lewinsky's attorney, had, five days earlier, informed the Jones attorneys, as a courtesy, of the contents of the affidavit. The Jones people told the OIC.

Finally, there is simply no question that, in this eleven-hour detention of Monica Lewinsky, OIC personnel were in flagrant violation of statutory and professional constraints on prosecutorial misconduct and of Ms. Lewinsky's constitutional rights. It is simply untrue that a federal court "summarily rejected" (Mr. Bakaly's phrase) any such claim, or that the court was ever presented a full and honest account of what occurred that night. The issue before Judge Johnson was whether to quash the OIC subpoenas not of Monica Lewinsky but of Francis Carter. Judge Johnson accepted the OIC accounts of what they actually did. Nonetheless, she wrote: "The Court expresses its concern that" the OIC "may have acted improperly." "This Court's supervisory power to control prosecutorial misconduct before grand juries," she also wrote, "is quite limited. However, the Court is extremely disturbed" that the prosecutors might have disrupted Ms. Lewinsky's relationship with her attorney, Mr. Carter. And that she would "consider referring this matter to the Department of Justice Office of Professional Responsibility for investigation."

After a blizzard of affidavits from the prosecutors and FBI agents that there had been no misconduct on their part (and without having received sworn testimony to the contrary, given, at risk of their immunity, by Ms. Lewinsky and her mother), Judge Johnson withdrew her threat of sanctions. None of the allegations was "summarily rejected." Subsequent testimony by Ms. Lewinsky and her mother made it absolutely clear that the prosecutors were in violation not just of the law but of Justice Department guidelines—by which the Office of the Independent Counsel is, in its authorizing statute, bound.

One has only to read the OIC's own affidavits, In Re Sealed Case, before Judge Johnson, about what they did on the night of January 16, 1998. One constitutional standard for such detentions is whether a "reasonable man" would have known that he was free to leave. There were more than seven men, some, according to their affidavits, alternately in the room and "standing in the doorway," while Ms. Lewinsky was alternately sobbing "hysterically" and staring "off into space." They point out that they gave her permission to go to the bathroom and shut the door. They say that Ms. Lewinsky's mother "thanked" them for giving Ms. Lewinsky "permission" (their word) to call her mother. They deceived her for hours with dire descriptions of what they said her legal situation was. Why did there need to be so many of them, if, as Ken Starr told the Judiciary Committee, they did not intend to "overbear"—another constitutional standard—"the will"? No reasonable person would have felt free to leave. Transcripts of the prosecutors' own affidavits are chilling. In time, this conduct of the OIC will enter history and the law as precisely the conduct, on the part of public officials, that the Constitution was designed to protect citizens against.

February 1999

A COURT OF NO APPEAL

IN JANUARY of this year, Simon & Schuster published my book *Gone: The Last Days of The New Yorker.* I had been at *The New Yorker* since 1963—with an absence of about fourteen months, during which I was Bosley Crowther's successor as the film critic of *The New York Times.* Though I had written for other publications, I thought I knew the magazine pretty well. *The New Yorker,* I wrote, is dead. I did not expect everyone to agree or to welcome my account of what happened to the magazine. Perhaps not surprisingly, the colleagues whom I had loved and admired through the years tended to share my views. Those of whom I thought less highly, and whom I portrayed less admiringly, did not.

Throughout the book, I referred to matters in the outside world, politics, travels, issues, assignments taken and not taken, discussions with William Shawn, the great editor, who, over that period of more than thirty years, naturally grew old, declined, and lost control of his magazine. A young editor whom I met in January said he thought I had treated *The New Yorker* as though it were the proverbial canary in a mineshaft. Its death meant something about the capacity of any living creative enterprise to survive within the culture. The thought had not crossed my mind. It has crossed my mind now.

On November 11, 1999, when my book was still in galleys, Charles McGrath, the editor of *The New York Times Book Review,* wrote to Simon & Schuster. Mr. McGrath had for many years been an editor at *The New Yorker.* I had described his tenure there in less than admiring terms. I had also raised questions about what seemed to me an inherent conflict of interest in his having assigned to himself, when he became editor of the *Book Review*, the review of another book in which he figured. "The other day," Mr. McGrath now wrote, "I received the galleys of Renata Adler's forthcoming book," and "as is my custom, I read through it prior to assigning it for review." He described as a "complete fabrication" an account of a lunch at which he had speculated to his cousin Laura ("who is not my cousin but, rather, my cousin-in-law") that he was, at that very moment, being designated successor to the editorship of the magazine. The lunch had, in fact, been described to me by several people. My account of it was harmless; it certainly had no legal implications. (Mr. McGrath's letter had ended with "cc:" to an attorney.) But I had also written that "no one, at least no writer in his right mind, wants to antagonize the *Book Review*." I thought, what the hell. I wasn't *at* the lunch. I had written, several times, about my distrust of journalism that relies, in quite this way, on "sources." So I replaced the passage with an account of a conversation in which Mr. McGrath spoke directly to me. I framed his letter, and hung it on my wall, as a little distillation of what I thought an editor of a major publication ought never to do.

The New York Times subsequently published no fewer than eight, arguably nine, pieces about my book. The first four (on January 12, January 16, February 6, and February 13, 2000) appeared in four sections: Arts, Sunday *Magazine*, Sunday Letters, and Sunday *Book Review*. They were unfriendly, but, apart from their sheer quantity, not particularly striking. The Arts piece, by Dinitia Smith, did mention Mr. McGrath's letter in approving terms ("The material to which he objected," Ms. Smith wrote, "was removed"), but added that Mr. McGrath said "he had decided to distance himself from reviews about current *New Yorker* books." What form that distancing would take, Ms. Smith did not say.

The next four pieces (April 3, April 5, April 6, and April 9, 2000) were dispersed among four more sections (Business/Media, Editorial, Op Ed, and Week in Review), treated as serious news, in other words, from Monday through Sunday of a solid week. It might have been, even as an episode of institutional carpet bombing, almost flattering. It seemed unlikely that the *Times* had ever devoted four,

let alone eight, polemical articles to a single book before. There is
perhaps an explanation and a story here for both waves of articles.
Let me begin with the second wave.

In mid-February, Jack Sirica, a reporter at *Newsday*, wrote a letter
to Simon & Schuster, calling attention to a sentence, at the end of a
passage on page 125 of my book, in which I wrote about having been
assigned, by Mr. Shawn, and deciding not to review, *To Set the Record Straight*, the autobiography (published in 1979, by Norton) of
Judge John J. Sirica, Jack Sirica's father. The sentence in question
said I had found that "contrary to his reputation as a hero, Sirica was
in fact a corrupt, incompetent, and dishonest figure, with a close
connection to Senator Joseph McCarthy and clear ties to organized
crime." Jack Sirica challenged me to produce "any evidence whatsoever" that his father was a "corrupt, incompetent, and dishonest figure" *or* "had clear ties to organized crime." He demanded that
Simon & Schuster "issue a public, written retraction" and "remove
the references" from all future editions of the book. He distributed
his letter widely to his colleagues in the press. A reporter from the
Associated Press called me and asked, in highly professional and
neutral terms, whether I planned to document my remarks in any
way. I said I did. The reporter asked when. I said soon. The reporter
asked where. I said in any place that seemed appropriate.

Some days later, I had a call from Felicity Barringer, a media correspondent of *The New York Times*. Ms. Barringer, I knew, is married to Philip Taubman, a member of the *Times* editorial board and
an assistant editor of the editorial page. From the outset the conversation had nothing of the tenor of an "interview." Ms. Barringer did
not even pretend to any interest in Sirica, only in "ethics in book
publishing." Would I give her my "sources"? "Come on. Yes or no.
Up or down?" Her deadline: forty-eight hours. No. Why would I
not disclose my evidence, if any, to her? Because, as the AP had reported, I was writing a piece of my own. Why wait? I was not waiting; I was writing.

Had I no concern meanwhile, she asked several times, about
what I had done to Judge Sirica's reputation? I said I didn't think

most people relied for their information about Judge Sirica on a sentence in a book about *The New Yorker*. In fact, none of the reviews, in the *Times* or elsewhere, had so much as mentioned the passage. Before Jack Sirica's letter, no one had apparently noticed it. "Well, that raises the old question, if a tree falls in the forest and no one is there to notice," Ms. Barringer said. A think piece, evidently.

If I did not wish to "disclose" my "sources" to her in an interview, Ms. Barringer said, "Why don't you post it on the Internet?" "You post a lot of your own pieces on the Internet, do you, Felicity?" It must be said that, although I was not, as far as I know, discourteous, I was not particularly deferential or awestruck, either. This was, it was true, the *Times*. It was also an unusually repetitive and mindless interrogation. The game, and its rituals, anyway, are fairly set. The reporter will write what she chooses—not infrequently regardless of what is said. It is one of the many reasons I have always preferred to work with documents, including depositions. They can be verified and checked. Ms. Barringer had a final question: Was my source G. Gordon Liddy? No.

The following Monday, April 3, Ms. Barringer's piece appeared on the front page of the Business section. On Wednesday, April 5, a piece, by Eleanor Randolph but unsigned (I had mentioned Ms. Randolph unfavorably in my book), appeared as an editorial. On Thursday, April 6, there was an op-ed piece, written by, of all people, John W. Dean. On Sunday, April 9, the *Times* published the last (at least so far) of these pieces in its Week in Review.

Ms. Barringer's article was, in its way, exemplary. In my "offhanded evisceration of various literati," she reported, not many people had noticed "Ms. Adler's drive-by assault on the late Judge Sirica." She deplored the lack of "any evidence" and managed to convey her conviction that none existed. Ms. Barringer's own "sources," on the other hand, were the following: Jack Sirica (whom she did not identify as a *Newsday* reporter); John F. Stacks, who co-wrote Judge Sirica's autobiography (and who said Sirica "didn't have the imagination to be anything but straight all his life"); "those who have read just about all books about the Watergate" and "those most steeped in Watergate lore" (whether these "those" were coextensive was not clear); two lawyers, who confirmed that "the dead cannot sue for libel"; an editor, who did not claim to know either me or anything about Sirica, who "explained" (not, for Ms. Barringer, "said"), in five paragraphs of a bizarre fantasy, what I must have said to my editor and he to me ("It is, 'Love me, love my book.' If that's what she wants to say... it's either do the book or don't do it"); and Bob Woodward, coauthor of *All the President's Men*, who "absolutely never heard, smelled, saw or found any suggestion" that Sirica had ever had "any connection whatever" to organized crime.

An impressive roster, in a way. I had once, as it happened, unfavorably reviewed, on the front page of *The New York Times Book Review* itself, a book by Mr. Woodward, but he was certainly the most impressive of Ms. Barringer's sources in this piece. Mr. Woodward could of course have crept into Judge Sirica's hospital room, and elicited from him on his deathbed the same sort of "nod" he claimed to have elicited from CIA Director William Casey on *his* deathbed, and then claimed, as he did with Casey, that to divulge even the time of this alleged hospital visit would jeopardize his "source." And when asked, as he was in an interview, what color pajamas the patient was wearing, he could, as he did in the instance of Casey, express a degree of outrage worthy of the threat such a question poses to the journalist's entire vocation. That is evidently not a kind of "sourcing" that raises questions for a media correspondent at the *Times*.

Ms. Barringer, in any case, did not conceal her views or quite limit her account to a single issue. "The attack on the basic honesty and decency of the judge," she wrote, "is of a piece with the whole work." Then came a memorable line. "What she writes and when she writes it, she said," Ms. Barringer actually wrote, with all the severity of the bureaucrat deep in a Politburo, "is for her to decide." Who else, I wondered, at least in our society, could possibly decide it? Her essential formulation, however, was this:

As it stands, Ms. Adler and Simon & Schuster, a unit of Viacom, are either cheaply smearing Judge Sirica—with legal impunity—or they have evidence. But neither the publisher nor the author shows any urgency about resolving the issue, either by retracting the accusation or establishing its accuracy.

Jack Sirica merely demanded "any evidence whatever." Ms. Barringer wanted evidence (to her standards, presumably, and Mr. Woodward's), with "urgency," and "establishing accuracy." Otherwise, in spite of that lamentable "legal impunity," a retraction. An interesting position, from a reporting, First Amendment, or even a censorship point of view. I will return to that, and even get to the evidence about Judge Sirica. But first a bit more about conditions in the mineshaft.

The editorial, two days later, entitled "A Question of Literary Ethics," ran immediately below a slightly shorter piece, "Justice in Bosnia." "In an irritable little book published late last year about The New Yorker," it began. Why the *Times* would address an entire editorial to a "little book," "irritable" or not, was not entirely clear. One might have thought that, almost thirty years after the Watergate and more than sixty years after some of the events in question, the country really does turn for its information about Judge Sirica to a passage in a book about *The New Yorker* magazine. "Since Judge Sirica is dead," the editorial again pointed out, "he is unable to sue for libel." True enough. "But that does not lift the ethical burden from Ms. Adler to support her charges with evidence that she says exists," but "that she and her editors at Simon & Schuster, for some unfathomable reason, omitted from her book." Then, a new standard, not just "evidence" but a cognate of "proof" crept in. "If Ms. Adler was referring to allegations about Judge Sirica's father . . . she will need to document that unproven contention and show how it relates to the judge himself."

It was interesting to learn what I needed to document and show. I found it difficult, however, to see in what sense my "burden" was (as Ms. Randolph, writing anonymously for the *Times*, put it) "ethical"—or how the passage in my book could have raised an issue of "ethics," "literary" or other. Professional issues, perhaps. Issues of fact, history, judgment. Ethics, no. I was either right or I wasn't, and I either had evidence or I hadn't. (The questions were, by no means, the same.) The *Times*, as it turned out, had not the slightest interest in Sirica or his history. No reporter for the *Times*, or as far as I know any other publication, made any effort to investigate the nature of the connection with Senator McCarthy—let alone the basis for an assertion of clear ties to organized crime. This lack of curiosity seemed to me extraordinary. The sole preoccupation was with a kind of meta-journalistic question—not what happened, but what were my sources and my obligations. As to what was, however, "for some unfathomable reason omitted," the *Times* had only to look at its own op-ed piece the following day.

That piece, entitled "A Source on Sirica?," consisted of John Dean's speculation about something the *Times* had reason to know not to be the case: that my "source" was Dean's old enemy, and current adversary in an embittered lawsuit, G. Gordon Liddy. What was remarkable, however, was less the content of the piece than the words with which the *Times* identified its author. The caption, in its entirety, read as follows:

> John W. Dean, an investment banker and the author of "Blind Ambition," was counsel to President Richard M. Nixon.

If this is the way Mr. Dean will enter history, then all the *Times* pieces in this peculiar episode have value.

That Sunday, April 9, there was the Week in Review section. A single sentence, in an "irritable little book published late last year," had now become part of the news, perhaps more accurately the meta-news, of that week. The word "evidence" was entirely abandoned, replaced by "proof." My book had "announced without proof"; "Ms. Adler told a *New York Times* reporter that she would publish proof when she pleased," and so on. I had, of course, said nothing of the kind. In repeating what had long been a *Times* characterization of Judge Sirica as "a scrupulously honest jurist," the piece surpassed even the op-ed page in the brevity of its identification of John Dean.

It described him simply as "former Nixon counsel." The laconic formulation was apparently designed to lend him credibility, in contrast to G. Gordon Liddy, "whom Judge Sirica sent to prison for his role in Watergate." Under other circumstances, this might have been simply a howler. (Dean, of course, was also sentenced to prison by Judge Sirica "for his role in Watergate." One might as readily characterize Liddy as a "former FBI agent and candidate for office in Milbrook, New York"). By now, however, these descriptions of Dean had gone beyond inadequacy. They relied upon and actively perpetuated the ignorance of readers. The *Times*, for some reason, was publishing disinformation.

I have always read the *Times*. In a day of perhaps more distinguished and exigent editing, I even worked for it. On the day Ms. Barringer's piece appeared, I wrote a letter objecting to certain demonstrable errors. I said I hoped Ms. Barringer had made a tape of our conversation, so that my claim of inaccuracies could be verified. No dice. No acknowledgment, even, of the question of a tape. On April 6, I received a phone call from the secretary of the deputy editor of the editorial page. "They have decided not to run your letter," she said, in a very cheery voice. They have? I said. Did they give any reason? "No. They just asked me to call and tell you they have decided not to run your letter." April 6 was the day they ran the op-ed piece by John Dean. On April 7, Jared Stern, of the *New York Post*, ran a piece quoting from my letter—which had been given to him by Blake Fleetwood, a friend of mine and for years a reporter for the *Times*. A spokesman for the *Times* told Stern, what was plainly untrue, that my letter was still "being considered for publication." That very afternoon, an editor called to ask whether I would like to submit another letter.

One of my adventures in this mineshaft had already been to learn that, as a matter of policy, the *Times* does not publish letters that question, or criticize in any way, the work of its reporters. Any claim of inaccuracy or unfairness must be made to the department of Corrections or the Editor's Note. In these departments, however, the reporter, in consultation with her editor, decides the issue—which,

I suppose, is why the Corrections in particular always seem to consist of rectifications of middle initials, photo captions, and remote dates in history. (In one recent week, the corrections column pointed out that the correct spelling of Secretary of State Madeleine Albright's "given name" is "Madeleine, not Madeline," and that the middle name of William D. Fugazy, "the chairman of the National Ethnic Coalition of Organizations," is "Denis," "not Dennis.") There *are*, as a rule, no genuine corrections. These departments are cosmetic, a pretense that the paper has any interest in whether what it has published is, in some important or for that matter unimportant way, false.

This, I would say, raises issues, fundamentally, of ethics. So does covering up conflicts of interest: unsigned editorials by writers mentioned unfavorably in books the editorials disparage; quotations, without any acknowledgment of conflict, from "sources" whose work, whose very methods, have been attacked by the person under discussion, in the pages of the *Times* itself. So does the concealment of undeniably relevant information: the fact that Jack Sirica was not just the son of Judge Sirica but a reporter at *Newsday*, a journalist, a colleague (imagine the *Times* coming to the defense, against a single passage, of the father of anyone who was not a fellow journalist); even the omission of virtually defining facts about John Dean. And finally, the bullying, the disproportion, in publishing eight disparaging pieces (seven in nonreviewing sections) about what was after all one little book. The *Times*, clearly, was cross about something. But there are ethical issues, I think, raised even by this sort of piling on.

To turn, then, at last, to Judge Sirica. More than twenty years ago, when I read Sirica's book, I noticed what seemed to me astonishing discrepancies and revelations. I did some research, gave the matter thought, and decided not to review the book. I was sure newspaper or magazine journalists would pick up these anomalies and write about them. By the time I published my book about *The New Yorker*, I assumed other journalists *had* found and written about them. It

turned out they had not—had, it seemed, no interest in these matters, apart from the recent questioning of my right to address them,
even now.

> Contrary to his reputation as a hero, Sirica was in fact a cor-
> rupt, incompetent, and dishonest figure, with a close connec-
> tion to Senator Joseph McCarthy and clear ties to organized
> crime.

There can scarcely be any question that this sentence is true. One
major source for almost every element of my characterization is Sirica's own story, as told in interviews and in his book. That Sirica had
a "close connection to Senator Joseph McCarthy" is not in dispute—although, as far as I know, I was the first reporter to call attention to it. Certainly no major piece, book, newspaper, or magazine
article—about Sirica, or the Watergate, or Senator McCarthy for
that matter—mentions the connection. Certainly not (until its recent reaction to Jack Sirica's reaction to my book) *The New York
Times*.

Sirica's own account of the connection is as follows. In 1952,

> While in Chicago, I ran into Senator Joe McCarthy. We had
> been friends for several years, double-dating once in a while
> and going to the racetrack together from time to time. I liked
> Joe a lot in those days....
>
> Then in 1953, Joe McCarthy offered me the job of chief
> counsel to his Senate subcommittee which was investigating
> Communist influence in government.
>
> I must say that I found the offer very attractive ... I wasn't
> especially excited by McCarthy's charges about Communist
> infiltration, but it seemed to me at the time to be an impor-
> tant matter that needed further examination. By the time Mc-
> Carthy made his offer, I had moved over to Hogan & Hartson
> and was finally earning a decent living. But I was still in-
> trigued by his proposal.

Lucy [Sirica's wife, whom he had married the year before, at the age of forty-seven] . . . was strongly opposed, feeling that since I was now a partner in a good firm, I would be foolish to leave. Joe stopped by our apartment one evening and I told him I felt I had better stay where I was. He agreed that it would be a mistake to leave a good firm like Hogan & Hartson. He told me that since I wasn't going to take the job, he was probably going to hire a young New York lawyer named Roy Cohn. . . . I would never have become a federal judge if I had taken that job with Joe McCarthy. I'm sure, looking back, that had I been single, I would have done so. Thank God for Lucy Camalier Sirica.

There is something almost stunningly preposterous about this story. Sirica devotes less than a page to it. The friendship between Sirica, by his own account an obscure, impoverished, unsuccessful lawyer who had, for the "several years" in question, not even managed to earn a living, and Senator Joseph R. McCarthy, one of the most powerful and feared senators in Washington, makes no sense. How did they meet? What views, interests, or other friends did they have in common? How did they come to double-date? McCarthy had made his first famous speech ("I have here in my hand a list of two hundred and five names known to the Secretary of State as being members of the Communist Party"), in February 9, 1950, to the Republican Women's Club in Wheeling, West Virginia. In the intervening years, he had attacked, as virtual or outright traitors, not just the Secretary of State, Dean Acheson, and General George C. Marshall, but countless others, at every level of public and private life. By 1953, the McCarthy Era (what Senator Margaret Chase Smith called the "Four Horsemen of Calumny: fear, ignorance, bigotry, and smear") was already at its height. Judge Sirica's position ("I wasn't especially excited by McCarthy's charges about Communist infiltration, but it seemed at the time to be an important matter that needed further examination") is not just inherently equivocal and inane. It is also irreconcilable with the intemperate, opinionated man Sirica and his admirers have always admitted him to be. Leaving aside his lack of professional qualifications, Sirica has entirely omitted from this account any ideological basis for McCarthy's offer of this job to him. Roy Cohn, after all, had credentials of a sort. His agenda, his methods, and his ideology were clear. In Sirica's account, nothing—neither the politics that produced the offer nor the social circumstance that fostered the friendship—is revealed.

The rest of his story, as he describes it, and as his legend would have it, turns out to make no sense either. Born in 1904, in Waterbury, Connecticut, Sirica is the impecunious, poorly educated, and for many years unsuccessful son of Ferdinand (Fred) Sirica, an Italian-American barber, who also seems to fail at everything. Between 1910 and 1918, for example, Ferdinand takes the family "on a sad sort of odyssey, from city to city," Dayton, Jacksonville, New Orleans, Jacksonville again.

> In each place the story was the same. My father would try to earn his living with one kind of business or another. Each time he would fail. In several cities he purchased small enterprises, only to discover that the income they produced was much less than had been promised by the seller.

In 1918, "uprooted again," they move to Washington, D.C.—where they are so poor they can hardly find a place to live. Somehow, in this "continuous uphill struggle against poverty," Sirica manages to attend two nonparochial private high schools, Emerson Preparatory, "for a year or so," and then Columbia Preparatory. In 1921 he enters George Washington University Law School, where, within a month, he finds himself out of his depth ("I couldn't begin to understand what the professors were talking about") and quits. The following year, he goes to a better law school, Georgetown University, but again, within a month, fails to understand his courses, and quits again. It is not clear why Sirica went to private schools, or what "small enterprises" his father "purchased" in all those cities, or how, having failed "each time," his father managed to purchase *any* enterprises, let alone "one kind of business or another" at all. Sirica does not account for any of these discrepancies.

He starts boxing professionally. "I was pretty good, or at least I thought so." As early as 1921, between his first law school and his second,

> I boxed almost every day with local professional welter-weights and middleweights. I had begun boxing at local clubs in exhibition bouts with the professionals. I thoroughly enjoyed my new life as an athlete and felt I had finally found something at which I could excel.

In 1922, however, his father has another contretemps:

> By this time, my father, in another of his attempts to better himself, had bought a small poolroom with two bowling alleys and a snack bar. He had spent all his savings on the business, and soon realized that he had sunk his money into a very rough place. He wasn't making any profit to speak of and didn't like the type of people who frequented the establishment. I used to help out in the evenings, racking up balls for the pool players and setting pins for the bowlers. But my father was again in despair. As he had so often before, he had trusted someone only to be deceived. We lived in rooms above the place. I remember Dad coming upstairs one night after closing. He poured himself a drink as the tears rolled down his face. He was again facing the fact that his hopes were being dashed.
>
> I guess my father wanted to hold on long enough to sell the place and recover his money. But things just got worse. One evening a particularly unpleasant group came in. Many of them had been drinking, even though this was during prohibition.
>
> I don't think my father owned the place quite a year. He knew that a lot of gamblers and bootleggers came in, but he

also knew that if he threw out all the undesirables, he'd be
without enough customers to make any money at all. Men
from the Government Printing Office, just down North Capitol Street, would come in from work, order a soft drink, and
then mix in a little hard liquor from the pints in their pockets.
The low point in that whole experience came one night when
the city police, aware of the kinds of people who visited the
establishment, made a search of the premises. Stashed in the
men's room, they found a small quantity of bootleg liquor, apparently left there by one of my father's customers. The police
took my dad to the police station and charged him with violation of the Volstead Act. He was not locked up, and the next
day, when he appeared in police court with his lawyer, he explained that the liquor must have belonged to a customer and
that he didn't even know it was there. No charges were filed,
but the incident embarrassed the whole family.

There is perhaps no need to parse this account too thoroughly.
How, having in the past, as we know, "failed each time," did he have
"savings" to spend "all of," or "money" to have "sunk" into such a
place? Why does Sirica find it necessary to point out that many of
this unpleasant group "had been drinking, although this was during
prohibition," when his father, just five lines before, had "poured
himself a drink" (without any comment from Sirica) in his "despair"
over having, "as he had so often before ... trusted someone only to be
deceived"? What was the deceit?

"He knew that a lot of bootleggers and gamblers came in"; also
"men from the Government Printing Office," who bought soft
drinks (from the snack bar, presumably) and then mixed in "a little
hard liquor from the pints in their pockets." It seems almost unfair
to go on. Even the elaborate formulation "one night ... the city police, *aware of the kinds of people who frequented the establishment*,
made a search of the premises." One can understand not wanting to
say *aware of the nature of the establishment*, but why put in a qualify-
ing phrase at all? Why not just: "One night the police raided the

premises"? Similarly, why a "*small* quantity of bootleg liquor, *apparently left there by one of my father's customers.*" All these clauses and qualifiers. The next day, when his father, not having been locked up, "appeared in police court with his lawyer" and "explained that the liquor must have belonged to a customer and that he didn't even know it was there," any reader of ordinary intelligence and understanding realizes that the object of the story is—as it was in the McCarthy story—not to tell but to conceal something. How, as the *Times* editorial put it, this incident "relates to the judge himself" is not hard to fathom. Sirica was living in his father's apartment above the poolroom, and he was employed "racking up balls for the pool players" and also as a bouncer there.

To go back, however, to the career trajectory of John J. Sirica as he tells it. In 1926, on his third try, Sirica did manage to complete and graduate from law school. By this time, "I was tempted by the idea of becoming a professional boxer," he writes, "since I felt more confident of my ability as a fighter than as a lawyer."

> On the morning the bar exam was to be given I had breakfast with Morris Cafritz. I had pretty well decided to skip the bar exam and head for Florida to see my father and mother....
>
> [Morris] knew that I was thinking about becoming a professional boxer. "Don't be foolish," he told me. "Even if you're not prepared, take the exam."

He has already described Mr. Cafritz as a "man who advised and encouraged me a great deal," while he was struggling through law school, and as "at the time becoming one of the most prominent and successful real-estate developers in Washington." It is true that Morris Cafritz went on to become immensely successful in real estate in Washington—and a highly respected citizen and generous benefactor of charities of every kind. At the time he was advising, encouraging, and having breakfast with Sirica, however, he was already very wealthy. Again, one wonders, what can have been the basis of this friendship between the poor and unpromising young law student and this highly influential figure. What Sirica does not mention is that Cafritz, too, at the time he "took a liking" to young Sirica, had an establishment involved with liquor and, like Sirica's father's, bowling. In his early twenties (according to Leslie Milk, in an article in the *Washington Magazine* of October 1996), Cafritz had borrowed $1,400 from his father and, a few years later, "bought a saloon."

> But not just any saloon: Cafritz' was across from the Washington Navy Yard.... Saloonkeeping was a rough business.... Cafritz was his own bouncer. He slept over the bar and kept a gun under his pillow to protect the profits. Cafritz soon moved from barkeeping into a safer game. By 1915, he was known as the bowling king of Washington.

All of this is a bit more raffish, and in some ways more appealing, than what Sirica describes. In the event, after his breakfast with Cafritz, Sirica, who has not even taken the bar review course, does take the bar exam, and goes on to visit his parents in Miami. While he is down there, he finds out, by telegram and to his surprise, that he has passed. He is unable to find work as a lawyer in Miami. He goes back to Washington, finds no legal work, goes back to his family in Miami. To earlier questions about his story is added another: Where, failing as he constantly does to find a job, does he get the money to keep traveling back and forth to Miami? And what was his family doing there?

One source of income, for Sirica, has always been, although he never quite acknowledges it, professional boxing. In Washington, as early as 1921, we know, he has been boxing "almost every day" with local professionals, and "at local clubs in exhibition bouts with the professionals." In 1926, in Miami, after "a local promoter needed someone to box in a semi-windup at Douglas Stadium," Sirica prepares for the fight not just by weeks of sparring but by "running every day at a golf course in Miami Beach"—under whose sponsorship he does not say. Perhaps, in those days, Miami Beach had a public golf course. Sirica's opponent, at Douglas Stadium, is "a six-foot-tall welterweight who was known for having fought one of the roughest bouts ever staged in Miami." ("Back in Washington, I had fought about thirty exhibitions…but nothing I ever did worried me as much as that oncoming fight.") Sirica beats him.

> The write-ups in the newspapers the next day were all good, even though they didn't spell my name correctly. I was on my way as a professional boxer.

His mother, he says, "heard about the fight," and objected. He had, of course, as he has already told us (and as his mother must have known), been fighting professionally for years. He would also organize and promote professional boxing matches. What he does not mention, does not perhaps remember or think important, is that professional boxing in this country was at the time, and had been since at least 1903, controlled by organized crime.

That professional boxers, and particularly *organizers* and *promoters* of professional boxing, had such ties was established, for example, in the Kefauver Hearings (U.S. Senate Special Committee to Investigate Organized Crime, May 1950 through August 1951). As the syndicated sportswriter Bob Kravitz recently put it:

> In the mid-fifties, a politician named Estes Kefauver chaired hearings on the sad state of the game, hoping to reform the sport and get it out of the hands of the Mob. When it was over, he realized the corruption was too deeply imbedded, too systemic.
>
> The only way to get rid of corruption in boxing is to get rid of boxing. At a meeting of Mob bosses and boxing managers in 1957, Mafia operative Binky Palermo worried about his boys losing their grip on it. Palermo had nothing to worry about.

As for the boxers themselves, in Washington, D.C., as it happens, *all* professional boxing was illegal—not just in 1921 when Sirica began but throughout the years he was boxing there—until 1934, when Congress finally legalized it in the District. Professional boxing in Washington, in other words, was a violation of the criminal statute. That Sirica knew this is beyond doubt. All the years he boxed professionally in the District before 1934 (including the years 1930 to 1934, when he was actually an assistant in the U.S. Attorney's office), he used, although he does not mention this either, fictitious names. It is, of course, possible to be a criminal without ties to organized crime—a pickpocket, say, or a burglar. Illegal boxing, however, requires payoffs, for the arena, the police, the referee, the promoters, and so on. You simply cannot do it freelance or on your own. It requires a syndicate—notoriously hostile to encroachments on its turf. So that's two sets of "clear ties to organized crime": through professional boxing—as an organizer, boxer, and promoter in various cities at a time when mob control of the sport was essentially complete—and for more than thirteen years in the District, boxing professionally when it was still illegal there.

Is that all? Well, no, it isn't. But it is all I said. It was not I, but the *Times* and its acolytes, who made a sensation of this. I wrote a little sentence, in a specific context, which is all I meant to write. The documentation for it is ample. Ms. Barringer, her "sources," and her colleagues could have found it, if her agenda had really been journalism: the gathering, that is, and publishing of firsthand information. Judge Sirica, as Ms. Barringer and the *Times* kept pointing out, is dead. But if he were alive and he sued for libel, as the *Times* in all its pieces seemed to suggest he might have done—imagine the preposterousness of a federal judge, even Judge Sirica, suing for libel—he would lose.

And that is not all. To resume his own story, in 1926, after being turned down by law firms everywhere, he does get a job as a "sort of messenger" at a criminal law office on Fifth Street. "It wasn't much, there was no regular pay, but it was a start." Meanwhile, he has made another early, implausible, and apparently lifelong friendship with a rich and powerful man, Morris Kronheim, a wonderfully interesting figure—and later, like Cafritz, an extraordinary citizen and a generous benefactor of every sort. Kronheim became, through several administrations, one of the most influential and beloved figures in Washington. In 1903, at the age of fifteen, Kronheim, whose father owned a tavern, started his own liquor store. By 1985, he had the largest wholesale liquor distributorship in Washington and one of the largest in the country.

During his three years at the Fifth Street criminal office, Sirica lost thirteen of fourteen felony cases assigned him by the court. The first case he was allowed to handle involved a "violation of the prohibition laws." He lost. In 1930, however, Sirica was appointed (on what professional basis is unclear) to the U.S. Attorney's office—whose major responsibilities, in those years, included prosecutions under the Volstead Act. Sirica says he got "valuable trial experience" as Assistant U.S. Attorney, but he mentions no specific prosecutions, certainly none of bootleggers, or of promoters of professional boxing. In fact, he devotes only a single sentence to the whole four years.

In December 1933, Prohibition was repealed. Within two weeks, Sirica resigned from the U.S. Attorney's office, "to start my own practice." The practice was not a success. He entered what he calls "my starvation period," from 1934 to 1949, *fifteen years*, when he says, "I really lived from hand to mouth," it "seemed the phone never rang," and "I nearly had to quit the law altogether." He lived in his parents' house in Washington, and "without that free lodging I would have gone under."

Sirica traveled, in those years, not just to Miami but to "New York for weekends," to visit Jack Dempsey, whom he met in 1934. He does not explain how he paid for these travels. He says he earned a fee by "successfully defending Walter Winchell against a defamation case." What? Walter Winchell? Who brought the case? He does not say. The case he means, at least according to his obituary in *The New York Times*, was brought by Eleanor (Cissy) Patterson, the Chicago publisher. But that didn't sound quite right. I looked it up. It turned out that Cissy Patterson was in fact the owner of the *Times-Herald*, which published Winchell's column. The lawsuit was part of a long feud between them. Cissy Patterson dropped the case. Sirica may have played some part in the defense; but Winchell's attorney of record was Morris Ernst.

According to Sirica, this period, "when I nearly had to quit the law altogether," lasted "essentially until 1949, when I joined the firm of Hogan & Hartson." He was not a success there either. On April 2, 1957 (again, it is unclear on what professional basis), he became a federal judge. By 1970, he had become the most reversed federal judge in Washington.

In 1971, on the basis of seniority, he became chief judge of the circuit. In June of 1972, he read about the Watergate break-in and assigned himself the first of the Watergate cases. He ultimately tried the cases of both the break-in and the cover-up, with the results we know. Or thought we knew.

But wait a minute. To return for just a moment to 1930, and Sirica's situation at the time of his improbable appointment to the U.S. Attorney's office. In 1930, Sirica writes.

> my parents had moved back to Washington from Florida. My dad was barbering again and his financial situation had improved somewhat. He had managed to buy a little house on Fourteenth Street, N.W., and I lived there during my years in the U.S. attorney's office.

The years of Fred Sirica's apparently constant business failures, and Sirica's own inability to find a job, had not been Depression years—only, beginning in 1920 throughout the country (three years earlier, in 1917, in Washington, D.C.), years of Prohibition. The 1930s, however, *were* Depression years—yet the "financial situation" of Sirica's father, "barbering again," had "improved somewhat," to the degree in fact that "he had managed to buy a little house on Fourteenth Street."

Not such a little house. According to the Washington City Directory, the house at 6217 Fourteenth Street, N.W., was large enough so that both John J. Sirica and his brother, Andrew, had apartments there. The place where his father was "barbering again" (called, according to the directory, the Empire Barbershop) at 523 Ninth Street, N.W., was not small either. It held fourteen chairs. The reason Fred Sirica and his wife traveled so often to Miami was that they spent part of their winters there. The Siricas were buying property in Miami. Hard to account for, in the heart of the Depression, even with fourteen chairs, on the proceeds of haircuts at 25 cents per customer.

According to William Emmons, Jr., the son of Fred Sirica's partner in the Empire Barbershop, the barbers were salesmen, selling liquor to customers who could afford it. Packages were stored in both the backroom and the basement. Fred Sirica himself handled the whiskey, splitting the proceeds with his partner, William E. Emmons, Sr. Sirica, living in his father's house and working in the U.S. Attorney's office, can hardly have been entirely unaware of his father's business. Ninth Street in the 1930s had five motion picture houses within a block and a half of the barbershop. The Gayety Theater was only three doors away. There was bookmaking in the back of the shoe store at 519 Ninth Street. The whole neighborhood, in other words, was not so far removed, in its look and its patronage, from the poolroom that had so seriously disillusioned the impecunious barber and his son the law student more than ten years before. Nowhere in his autobiography, *To Set the Record Straight*, does the author so much as mention the name of the barbershop or the address of the "little house" on Fourteenth Street. Both can be found under "Sirica, Fred" (and also under "Sirica, John J. atty" and "Emmons, William E.") in the city directory for at least the years 1930 to 1934. There were no embarrassing misunderstandings, as there had been at the time of the poolhall, at any police station. According to Emmons, the police of the First Precinct were paid off—and there was whatever protection was implied by a son who had become an assistant in the U.S. Attorney's office.

Even 1934, when one thinks about it, was not just the year when Prohibition ended, and Sirica quit the U.S. Attorney's office—and Congress at last legalized professional boxing in Washington. It was also a year *deep* in the Depression, a particularly odd time for a young lawyer to leave a government job and start his own practice. It was the year as well when Sirica says he met Dempsey, and when he tried to start and promote a boxing arena with a "local prizefighter," Goldie Ahearne. It goes by now almost without saying that Goldie Ahearne could not, any more than Sirica himself, legally have been a "local prizefighter" before 1934.

There are countless peculiarities in Sirica's story. His professions of patriotism, for example, coupled with his lack of military service, in any capacity whatever, in World War II. He was, after all, a bachelor. The whole war took place during what he called his "starvation period." The *Times*, in its unusually fulsome obituary of August 15, 1992, which described Sirica as "indisputably... a hero," "a great scholar" (and "by seemingly unanimous agreement, an honest man"), particularly stressed that he was "patriotic," "unabashedly patriotic," and added to its repeated characterizations of Sirica as "an authentic American hero" a military component.

> In World War II, he tried to get a Navy commission, but failed for physical reasons.... So, during much of the war, he toured the country with Mr. Dempsey on bond-selling drives.

The "for physical reasons," at least on the basis of *To Set the Record Straight*, seems unlikely, considering Sirica's account of his superb physical condition—and of course there are other capacities in which a bachelor, sitting idly in his office "waiting for the phone to ring," might serve in the military. In his book, Sirica never so much as mentions the possibility of military service. But the *Times*'s claim that "during much of the war, he toured the country with Mr. Dempsey on bond-selling drives" is beyond description. Here is the relevant passage from *To Set the Record Straight*:

> Jack and I had some great times together. In 1942, he was touring with the Cole Brothers Circus and wanted some company. I met the circus in North Carolina and spent three days with

Jack on the circus train. I'll never forget Jack charming the ladies....

In 1942, the Cole Brothers Circus was Clyde Beatty's circus, with no connection to war bonds or a war effort of any kind. In 1945, in other words *after* the war, it is true, when Dempsey went on a tour selling "savings bonds," Sirica went with him. "While thoroughly enjoying myself," Sirica writes, "I also felt I was doing something important for my country." Perhaps he was.

Among Sirica's unlikely, and in this book and his legend unmentioned, friends and correspondents is FBI Director J. Edgar Hoover. Why would a judge of Sirica's renown *not* have become friends with the FBI director? Because Sirica was not yet at all renowned. Hoover died in May 1972, a month before the break-in at the Watergate. His friendship with Sirica dates from the fifties—overlapping, for all one knows, with the friendship with Senator Joseph McCarthy—when Hoover, fighting the Communist menace, was still denying the very existence of organized crime. There must be a true story here somewhere, but so far no one has told or apparently even looked into it.

> Contrary to his reputation as a hero, Sirica was in fact a corrupt, incompetent, and dishonest figure, with a close connection to Senator Joseph McCarthy and clear ties to organized crime.

That is all I said or wanted to say about the subject. If a reader were to read this sentence, at least as quoted and discussed in the *Times*, to suggest that while Sirica was presiding over the Watergate cases he was taking payoffs from the mob, that is not a plausible reading. I was writing, after all, about Sirica's autobiography. "A close connection to Senator Joseph McCarthy"—in the phrase that directly precedes "clear ties to organized crime"—would necessarily have ended on May 2, 1957, when McCarthy died. Sirica had not yet even assumed his position on the bench. If I had meant that Sirica was taking such payments on the bench or at any other time, I would of course have said so.

But enough. I do not need and never did intend to investigate the story of John J. Sirica. At the time I read his book, I had already written extensively about Watergate. I had also worked, until the day of President Nixon's resignation, for the impeachment inquiry. It only became clear, from the book itself and then in retrospect, that the legend, the accumulation of clichés, received ideas, and bromides— the "scrupulously honest man," the "hero," who rises from humble beginnings to confront "the most powerful man on earth" and to find (if need be in disregard of the rules of evidence) "the truth for the American people"—had almost no basis in reality.

The legend of Sirica as a "scupulously honest man" and a "hero" rests, of course, on the Watergate trials. The conduct of those trials, criticized at the time, raises questions of all kinds. It is by no means clear, for example, why Judge Sirica assigned the cases to himself. There is evidence that, far from seeking to expedite the Watergate investigations, Sirica may have sought for several crucial months to delay them. In putting off the first trial until after the election, he says he was determined to have "a fair trial, not a quick one." Look at that phrase a moment. The fairness of his conduct in those trials has always been precisely the matter most in dispute. In October, on account of "back pain," he postponed the trials again, until January. It may also be that, in spite of the legend, Judge Sirica was less interested in getting at, as he put it, the "truth for the American people" than in some entirely other agenda—for example, in frustrating the investigation of the House Committee on Banking and Currency, the Patman Committee, which was the one investigative body that would have known where to look for the deeper truth about the Watergate—not the burglary or the cover-up but the sources of the cash. The Patman investigation concerned President Nixon so intensely that he sent then-Congressman Gerald Ford to persuade the committee Republicans to deny Patman the subpoena power. He sent Attorney General Richard Kleindienst, an old friend of Sirica's, to persuade the judge, in the name of "protecting the defendants' civil rights," to issue an unusually broad "gag order," forbidding anyone (government officers, witnesses, defendants, lawyers) from making statements about "any aspects of the case" to anyone, including congressional committees. The gag order, as even Sirica acknowledged, "strengthened the hand of the administration in stonewalling Patman." Patman protested, in a five-page letter, to Sirica. By the time Sirica agreed to modify his order, Congressman Ford had persuaded the Republicans. Subpoena power for Patman's Committee on Banking and Currency was denied.

A great deal has been made of what Sirica himself seems to consider the crucial break in the Watergate case: a letter from one of the convicted Watergate burglars, James McCord, alleging that perjury had been committed, that persons higher up than the original burglars were implicated, that "pressure" had been applied to the defendants to "plead guilty and remain silent." McCord himself was a mysterious figure, formerly CIA and formerly FBI, as well as former guard of John Mitchell's loquacious and frequently inebriated wife. On Friday, March 13, 1973, Judge Sirica read McCord's letter melodramatically in open court. Ever since, that reading has been regarded as a turning point in the entire case. This seems highly improbable for two reasons: McCord did not *know* (or at least did not divulge) anything either important or admissible in the case; and he had sent a copy of his letter to the *Los Angeles Times*, so that it would have become public in any event.

The accepted chronology of Sirica's life was always mystifying, and as a career pattern it is almost incomprehensible. It may even be that the real progression in Sirica's life was not as the legend would have it, but rather this: first, the man of Prohibition and illegal boxing, in the U.S. Attorney's office; then McCarthy's man and even J. Edgar Hoover's, with whatever politics that implies; then perhaps just the Republican Party's man, its emissary to Italian communities (mostly, in those days Democratic); then a federal judge, the worst on the Washington bench; then Nixon's man, an irascible figure who repeatedly expresses disdain for the rules of evidence; then, in his unprecedented use of "provisional sentencing" as a form of coercion, a vain sort of bully, who is concerned not "to sit like some nincompoop" while the defendants, under appropriate sentences, are "laughing at us"; then, a sort of obsessed prosecutor, who does not really discover any "truth"; and finally, in his vanity and posturing, a man, a "hero," for the press.

A judge, after all, is not meant to be a hero. The only judges in our times who could legitimately be described as heroes were Frank Johnson, Elbert Tuttle, John Minor Wisdom, and the other judges of the Fifth Circuit, who took genuine risks, and suffered for them, for justice in the South. And judges, under the Constitution, are not meant to ascertain, least of all to prosecute or to coerce by sentencing, the "truth," "for the American people," or even for the jury. They are to preside fairly, under the adversary system, over cases presented by lawyers for the plaintiffs and the defendants before them. Anything else, whether it is posturing for the media, or coercing defendants with outrageous "provisional sentences," or working on behalf of some party not before the court, undermines the system. Far from demonstrating that "no man is above the law," it suggests that the judge himself is above it. We do not, under the Constitution, have a system wherein judges are inquisitors. In any event, though there may be material for a real biography of Judge Sirica, there is also this inescapable and awkward truth: Even in the Watergate investigations, he made no important contribution, except to the lore.

For the moment, almost as a housekeeping matter, just two relatively minor instances of dishonesty, corruption, incompetence—instances where they seem to overlap. In the matter of *voir dire*: Judge Sirica, having promised, at the request of both prosecution and defense, to interview prospective jurors individually, and in chambers, did not do so. As a result, when one juror was reported, at a crucial moment in the trial, to have violated the sequestration rules and spoken at length by telephone with his wife, Sirica interviewed that juror to ascertain whether he had obtained information from the outside world, and perhaps communicated it to other jurors. It turned out that the juror had in fact obtained such information. It also turned out that the juror knew only Spanish, and neither spoke nor understood English. To cover for this error—the juror could understand neither the testimony about the burglary nor instructions in the law—Sirica dismissed the juror and simply *sealed* this embarrassing portion of the record. The incident involved incompetence, surely, followed by a substantial lapse of integrity.

More serious was his use of "provisional sentencing" and outright dishonesty in at least one instance of it. Having imposed "temporary sentences" of unprecedented severity on the five defendants who pleaded guilty, Sirica told them that their actual sentences might depend on their cooperation with subsequent investigations. This was, in itself, a highly improper use of provisional sentencing—widely criticized, as "extortion," "abuse of power," and "the torture rack," by two presidents of the American Bar Association and scholars ranging from Monroe Freedman to Philip Kurland. Provisional sentencing is a procedure to make sentences contingent on reports about the defendants' character, and not a device for judges to coerce testimony when the adversary system (which is, after all, the American system) has already run its course. Far from demonstrating the bromide that no man, not even the President, is above the law, Judge Sirica proceeded as though one man, the judge himself, were above it.

The outright falsification was as follows. On March 23, 1973, Judge Sirica said that the sentences for the five defendants who had pleaded guilty would depend on their cooperation in implicating people higher up.

> Other factors will of course be considered but I mention this one because it is one over which you have control and I mean each one of the five of you.

By 1975, the President had resigned. John Dean, John Mitchell, Bob Haldeman, and John Ehrlichman, government officials higher up than any of the first seven Watergate defendants, had all been tried, convicted, and sent to jail. In denying an appeal for reduction of sentence by a defendant who had not pleaded guilty, had not received a provisional sentence, and was not one of the original five, Sirica simply "quoted" the last sentence of his March 23, 1973, Memorandum of Opinion and Order, as follows:

> Other factors will, of course, be considered but I mention this one because it is one over which *you have control* and I mean each and every one of you.
>
> —397 F. Supp. pp. 949 and 963

There is no doubt that Judge Sirica altered this passage deliberately. About "you have control," he even notes "italics added." The key alteration, however, is from "I mean each one of the five of you" to "I mean each and every one of you." The latter would have included the defendant, G. Gordon Liddy, among those who had pleaded guilty and whose sentences were contingent on their "cooperation." Liddy was never one of them, and Liddy's sentence was never contingent on any cooperation. The falsification was crucial. It enabled Judge Sirica to keep Liddy in jail, in worse conditions and for a far longer term than any other Watergate defendant, including those far higher up in the administration—on the pretense that Liddy had not accepted an offer that Sirica never made to him. The D.C. jail to which Sirica sent him was ancient, dirty, overcrowded, rat-infested, with temperatures that reached 104 degrees. Liddy was for a long time the only white prisoner there. (The D.C. jail has since been closed.) On April 12, 1977, when President Jimmy Carter commuted Liddy's twenty-year sentence to eight "in the interests of justice," Judge Sirica complained to the press.

Why, then, was the *Times* so heavily committed to the received idea that Sirica was "an authentic hero," "by seemingly unanimous agreement an honest man," even "a great scholar," and so forth. Part of the reason is that the *Times* itself has said so, in its obituary—an accretion of myth, clichés, received ideas, and self-serving fables recounted by the subject himself, unusually fulsome even for obituaries. Partly because a relatively recent, complacent kind of sloth on the part of many reporters—sitting at a desk, phoning around, either repetitively badgering or, more commonly, passively receiving quotes from anonymous, self-interested, possibly lying, or even nonexistent sources—tends to welcome and to perpetuate every sort of conventional wisdom and cliché. Partly because the *Times* is committed most profoundly to a certain notion of itself. In the past, this commitment took a highly honorable form. The publisher and his family, one knew, were devoted, financially and in almost every other way, to the quality of the newspaper. Now, much of the paper is devoted to itself in quite another sense—as a bureaucracy, a complacent, unchallenged, in some ways totalitarian institution, convinced of its own infallibility.

As for what it was that made the *Times* so very cross about my sentence, nothing could be clearer than that it was not concern about Judge Sirica's reputation. The most distinguished First Amendment lawyer I know said that the *Times* did more damage to Sirica's reputation in three days than I could ever do. The reputation they were concerned with was, oddly, mine. Virtually every sentence in Ms. Barringer's piece gave that much away: "You could say this is a churlish, lowdown thing Renata Adler has done," for example, and "You could take the position that it says more about the writer than about what she's writing." There it is. These, and other examples of prose in this series of pieces—"smear," "cheaply smearing," "offhanded evisceration of various literati" (imagine, if you will, an offhanded evisceration), "veering from her literary prey," "cavalier," "even more irresponsible," elsewhere "despicable," "Iago," "lacking a conscience and a soul"—were not, whatever else they may have been, the prose of journalism.

I have friends who have said jokingly, and some not so jokingly, that they fear retaliation from the *Times*. As well they might. I am not entirely lacking in experience in the writing of polemical pieces. I have always found that it is not that easy. It requires some thought, and some familiarity with the material under review. On the other hand, honorable polemic, I would have thought, does not call in reinforcements, attacks rather than joins mob journalists. Here we find almost a parody—journalists not addressing underlying fact but interviewing *one another* about what they "heard" or "smelled." The *Times* editorial said that my "charges" had "startled some of the nation's best investigative journalists who had covered Watergate and found Judge Sirica to be a principled jurist." "Startled" them! The herd, advancing bravely not as single spies but in battalions, thinks the real world consists of received ideas they share with colleagues.

It is true I had criticized, sometimes directly, sometimes by implication, not just Mr. McGrath and the *Book Review* but the *Times*. I had written a book, *Reckless Disregard*, that was largely a criticism of the press. There may even have been implicit criticism, in pieces I wrote over the years. In recent articles, for example, in *Vanity Fair* and the *Los Angeles Times*, I had found, in writing about the Starr Report and its accompanying volumes, proof that Linda Tripp had not required, as the *Times* kept reporting, a set of "elves," under the direction of the literary agent Lucianne Goldberg, to make her way, surreptitiously and at the last minute, to the Special Prosecutor's office. She had, in fact, been working for that office for almost four years.

But that did not account for it either: the eight pieces, the alternately derisive and punitive tone, the pressure to recant. And the prose itself—there can be no clearer indication than this sort of writing that there is no news, no information, no substance there. I had written a sentence. Someone, offended, had asked me to document the sentence. I had said I would do so. Not much of a story, one would have thought. In the days when there was still a standard of reporting, and of editing, "those who have read just about all the books on Watergate" and "those most steeped in Watergate lore," whoever they might be, would have been utterly unacceptable, in the *Times*, as sources. If the reporter had any genuine interest in the matter, she would have "steeped" herself in "Watergate lore" and read the "books on Watergate" (beginning perhaps with Judge Sirica's book) herself. But no. Here's what it was. At one point, in answer—not, as Ms. Barringer would have it, to the question "Why wait?," to which I gave, repeatedly, the answer that I was not waiting at all—but to a repetition of yet another ad personam question, I said, "How can you be a working journalist and phrase a question as silly as that?"

This is not the way you are supposed to talk to the *Times*. I knew that. But here obviously was the core of the offense, and so seriously did Ms. Barringer take it that she attached it to the wrong question, and so seriously did the *Times* take it that the editorial was virtually based on this intimation on my part that a *Times* reporter could phrase a deeply silly question. "Even more irresponsible," the editorial went on, was a line, inaccurately quoted, in which I asked Ms. Barringer whether she worried "that much about reputation." "Of course we do," the editorial actually said. (Of *course*.) "And so should she."

I have always known, and even written, that the strongest, perhaps sole remaining taboo on freedom of expression, in this country, is any criticism of the press. But here I had not only questioned a received idea cherished by the *Times* but I had not been sufficiently deferential to this *Times* reporter—and the whole *Times* bureaucracy, instinctively, needed to *stamp out this disrespect*. It would, of course, have gone without saying, until the *Times*, through Ms. Barringer, cited it with indignation, that a writer does choose what to write and when to write it. Now the matter had come to this: If you do not accept some cliché, bromide, or myth of theirs, and are not sufficiently deferential to them, this is not just insubordination. It is a *breach of ethics*.

You must be admonished. You must be taught a lesson, so that other people may learn from it. Not only is your own reputation affected. You must, above all, recant. And this, this last issue—retraction—is where the question is inescapably, dangerously, altered. And why the whole series of attacks addresses something more serious than my little book. Look again at Ms. Barringer's formulation:

> As it stands, Ms. Adler and Simon & Schuster, a unit of Viacom, are either cheaply smearing Judge Sirica—with legal

impunity—or they have evidence. But neither the publisher nor the author shows any urgency about resolving the issue, either by retracting the accusation or establishing its accuracy.

This is nothing if not a coercive formulation, pressure not just on a writer but on her publisher, and even her publisher's owner, "Simon & Schuster, a unit of Viacom," to retract. Whenever—and I think this is true without exception—you find a publication, or a journalist, calling for a retraction or a recantation by, of all things, a single writer (and actual pressure on her publisher, "cheaply smearing"), you know what sort of realm you are in. It is a realm where received ideas are not just propagated but enforced—and it is an unmistakably totalitarian realm. What "issue," after all, could be "resolved" by a retraction? Nothing about Sirica, certainly. The only issue would be the power of *The New York Times*, in the person of Ms. Barringer and other writers, to coerce retractions. What this whole series amounted to was a show trial, with serial accusers, disinformation, designed to end, as show trials do, with recantations.

Well, it nearly worked. The *Times*, of course, is still drawing on trust and respect well earned some years ago. In the course of this recent episode, Joseph Lelyveld, the executive editor, told me as early as April 3 that he had no idea the *Times* had published so many disparaging pieces about my book. He would look out for this sort of thing. Later, he said he would, if it had been his call, have run my letter (revised, of course, to conform with *Times* policy), but he had no jurisdiction over the Letters column. I knew he had no jurisdiction over the editorial page or the op-ed pieces. (Either John Dean is inspired, and writes, submits his work, and is edited with extraordinary speed, or his piece was solicited right after I told Ms. Barringer, to her evident disappointment, that my source was not G. Gordon Liddy.) The editorial board, of which, as we know, Ms. Barringer's husband is a member, does have jurisdiction over both pages. Mr. Lelyveld is, however, in charge both of Corrections and the Editor's Note. On April 7, he sent me a fax. "I try to lean over backwards in matters of corrections and editor's notes," he wrote. He, and Ms. Barringer and her editor, had considered my note. "At this point the only solution I can see," he concluded, "is for us all to give the matter a rest." This was wonderful. The *Times* had attacked me eight times (only the last four of them had even the pretext of Judge Sirica), citing (perhaps this goes without saying) exclusively hostile "sources." These pieces had directly impugned my "ethics." They would not print a letter, an Editor's Note, or a Correction. In fairness he now felt that the only solution "for all of us" was to let the matter rest. Of course, the paper did not let it rest. Two days later, there was the news item in the Week in Review.

Other journalists—in solidarity and taking their cue from the trusted and venerated *Times*—checked in. Some were apparently under the impression that I had used the Sirica passage as a sort of headline, to "hype" my book. Why else, after all, would the *Times* have devoted so much space and so many pieces to it? Piece after piece, in one medium after another, accepted as fact John Dean's speculation that my source was Liddy. One spoke of my "trying to sell" my book with a libel that "shames all caring, responsible journalists." That sort of thing. A media reporter for the *Daily News* wrote, on the basis of the *Times* editorial, that my book had been "plagued by" a series of "forced retractions." In a novel use, by a media reporter, of the formula, she wrote, "Ms. Adler was unavailable for comment"—on the basis, perhaps, of having made no effort whatsoever to reach me. Perhaps the most surprising instance of this herd of indignant *Times*-inspired colleagues occurred on April 8, on CNN's *Capital Gang*. Mark Shields, not usually, I would have thought, so orthodox a member of the guild, said, "And now for 'The Outrage of the Week.'" I had "defamed," he said, Judge Sirica, who was (in the by now altogether obligatory mantra) a scrupulously honest hero. "Renata Adler owes the family John Sirica loved and the nation he served so well an immediate and public apology."

Owing the nation an immediate and public apology does seem a bit much. But the *Times*'s campaign began, I suppose, with that first letter from the editor who subsequently "said he had decided to distance himself." I should have left the galleys as they were. There followed the whole set of pieces, right through the almost laughably disingenuous characterization of John Dean. Disinformation. Show trial. Confession. Retraction. Not just yet. The *Times*, financially successful as it may be, is a powerful but, at this moment, not very healthy institution. The issue is not one book or even eight pieces. It is the state of the entire cultural mineshaft, with the archcensor, still in some ways the world's greatest newspaper, advocating the most explosive gases and the cutting off of air.

Harper's Magazine
August 2000

AFTERWORD

When I first wrote this piece, many journalists seemed to go more or less berserk. Without realizing it, they conceded that every word of my original sentence about Judge Sirica had been borne out. The ground, however, had shifted. The criticism now was that Sirica's dishonesty, incompetence, connections, and ties were not sufficiently grave, or sufficiently recent, or sufficiently "hot" to justify my having referred, however briefly, to them. There seemed no doubt, however, that if the *Times* itself had discovered any element of the story, especially the reference to Sirica's closeness to Senator Joseph McCarthy, it would have treated each element as a major scoop. Instead, the *Times* ran two more pieces, raising the total to ten, before my *Harper's* piece even hit the stands. One, by Alex Kuzscinsky, was the only one of the ten that could not have served as an example of execrable work in any sophomore journalism class. Another, by Martin Arnold, cited in my Introduction, assured readers that there was nothing in the *Harper's* piece; Martin deplored what was apparently his impression, that neither books nor magazines could meet the checking standards of newspapers like the *Times*. Ms. Barringer said, in an interview, that nothing I said about Judge Sirica could not be said equally about the heavyweight champion Joe Louis—which would be true, I suppose, if Joe Louis had ever fought, under fictional names, in districts where boxing was illegal, or if he had organized and promoted boxing, and served as Assistant U.S. Attorney in a district where his father ran an illegal liquor business, and so forth.

What seemed most to infuriate those journalists who reacted angrily was that I had based my passage mainly on evidence in Sirica's own book. I should, apparently, have claimed an "anonymous source." As it happens, I did have other sources, and other facts, which I would have thought Judge Sirica, or at least his co-author, John F. Stacks of *Time*, would have thought worthy of inclusion, and which the *Times* and its acolytes might have found with a modicum of research. In 1927, in Chicago, for example, John J. Sirica himself (not his father) was indicted, along with several co-conspirators, for fixing a prizefight and for income tax evasion. The indictments were sealed. The case never went to trial.

In his fine biography of Jack Dempsey, Roger Kahn writes that, in looking at a video of the second Dempsey-Tunney fight, with its famous "long count," "I am looking at a crooked referee." Perhaps. Perhaps not, or not just the referee. Kahn, like most other experts on boxing history, writes that Al Capone was very eager to back Dempsey in that fight but that Dempsey, man of honor that he was, firmly rebuffed him. Something seems amiss in the underlying logic of this story. Mob bosses approach fighters and (as in the Black Sox scandal, which also took place in Chicago) baseball players not to *win* matches but to lose them. Winning is what the fighters, or the players, want naturally to do, when they are not bribed to do otherwise. Dempsey, of course, did lose. The fight-fixing for which Sirica and others were named in the sealed indictment of 1927 was the Dempsey-Tunney fight. (No referee is mentioned in the sealed indictment.) My source for the information about Sirica's inclusion in the indictment (for fight-fixing and consequent tax evasion) was the

Criminal Investigation Division of the IRS—which published its own historical study for internal use.

In my *Harper's* piece, I confined myself to matters that virtually sprang off the page of Sirica's own autobiography, the book I chose not to review. It was not my intention to address anything more sensational than the literal meaning of a few words on page 125 of my own book. Suddenly, these heroic defenders of reputation (not the reputation, perhaps, of a single scientist, like Wen Ho Lee, in solitary and in shackles, on the basis largely of their institution's coverage) emerged, one after another, as though there were an honor roll: ten within the *Times* alone, to be followed by hundreds more. It was as though the press, self-important and self-righteous as it is, seems entirely unconscious of its own weight against any single, let alone dissenting, individual, or of its own role in the events it claims to cover. I thought this a more interesting and more important subject, than the details of Sirica's status. In view of the astonishing aftermath of the piece itself, however, just for the record, a bit more about what any genuine biography of Judge Sirica would include.

Though Sirica describes Dempsey, at least after 1934, as "my best friend," and although Dempsey, far more openly than Sirica, managed to avoid military service (after World War I, Dempsey was actually indicted and tried for draft evasion), there is, oddly, no mention of Sirica in the index of any Dempsey biography. Or for that matter, in the index of any biography of Senator Joseph McCarthy, or of Walter Winchell—at least two of whom, it may be remembered, had their own involvements with organized crime: Dempsey with Capone, and Winchell of course with Louis Lepke and Frank Costello.

By "organized crime," incidentally, I never for a moment meant the Sicilian Mafia. The interests in question were for the most part Jewish and even Irish. I did leave out one Italian connection: Al Capone. That connection was Neapolitan. Al Capone's father, Gabriel, had immigrated from Castellammare di Stabia, in the Bay of Naples, where he had learned his trade. Like Fred Sirica, who emigrated from San Valentino Torio (also in the Bay of Naples, a few kilometers from Castellammare di Stabia) Gabriel Capone was a barber. The two men were friends.

I leave aside any number of utterly incomprehensible omissions from Sirica's autobiography. Senator Hiram Bingham, of Connecticut, for example, is introduced to Sirica by "a cousin," who "happened to be active in local politics in Waterbury," so that Bingham will "endorse" Sirica for the job of Assistant U.S. Attorney. It is not surprising that we hear no more about the "cousin." Hiram Bingham, however, not only was one of the very few senators ever to incur a vote of censure by the full Senate (in 1929, for putting a lobbyist on the Senate payroll as his clerk). He also had been educated at Groton, Yale, Berkeley, and Harvard; served as lieutenant governor and then governor of Connecticut; written more than a dozen books, and, as a distinguished scholar and explorer, actually discovered the ruins of Machu Picchu. *That* Hiram Bingham.

Some readers seemed bewildered by what I could have meant, in the piece, by "totalitarian." They seemed to think that it meant "totalizing" or something. What I meant by a totalitarian reaction to a piece of writing was this: not debate (particularly not "the free, robust, and wide-open debate" envisioned by the First Amendment); not even invective, or mockery, or expressions of rage, scorn, indignation, disdain, or argument of any sort. But advocacy of *retraction, eradication, silencing*. Not "I disagree with what you say," but "I will attack to the death your right to say it, as well as the forum (book publisher, magazine) in which your work appears." Eradicate, in other words, not just a book or a piece but, if possible, the author and eliminate future outlets for this heresy. This view of what writing is, and the appropriate response to it, is nothing if not totalitarian.

Supposing, however, just supposing, what was not the case: that I had been mistaken. That Sirica had been brilliantly competent on the bench and in his conduct of the case, that he had never so much as heard of Senator Joseph McCarthy or of any form of organized crime, that his book and his life had been models of rectitude and forthrightness. What then? Nowhere, in any of the *Times* attacks, was there the slightest indication that my reputation did not rest entirely on this single sentence on page 125 of my sixth book. If they had misspelled Sirica's name, of course, or mine, they would have felt bound in fairness to run an Editor's Note or a Correction.

People forget things. Everyone forgets. I keep forgetting, for example, to mention that the Starr volumes are in their way a masterpiece that, quite apart from any prosecutorial or political matter, is full of fascinating incidents and characters. It ought to be published with type large enough to read.

2001

IRREPARABLE HARM

The Framers of the Federal Constitution...viewed the principle of the separation of powers as the absolutely central guarantee of a just Government....Without a secure structure of separated powers, our Bill of Rights would be worthless.... Frequently an issue of this sort will come before the Court clad, so to speak, in sheep's clothing.... But this wolf comes as a wolf.

> —Justice Antonin Scalia, dissent in
> *Morrison v. Olson*, June 29, 1988

When we make a difficult decision in many areas—and this was not the most difficult decision the Court has made.... My colleagues and I want to be the most trusted people in America....

> —Justice Anthony Kennedy, testimony before the
> House Appropriations Subcommittee, March 29, 2001

I.

NOT INFREQUENTLY, an event so radical that it alters everything appears for a time to have had no effect, or even not to have occurred. This is true in personal as in public life. A loss, a flood, a medical diagnosis, a rolling of tanks toward the statehouse—life goes on apparently as usual. Nothing is changed. It is particularly true of events that are irremediable. When there is nothing to be done, people go to work, eat their lunch, sleep, awaken to a vastly altered world, in ways that seem uncanny in their ordinariness. The decision of the Supreme Court in *Bush v. Gore*, in all three stages— accepting the case at all; reversing the judgment of the Florida State Supreme Court; above all, perhaps, granting a stay of the recount in Florida—gave rise to lots of comment. Outraged, gleeful, satisfied, resigned, the response seemed in almost every case to follow from the politics of the speaker. Republicans and "conservatives," for the most part, approved. Democrats and "liberals" did not. The decision seemed to close the subject. Normal life resumed. George W. Bush was president and that was that.

George W. Bush may become a distinguished president. As to the Court's "fundamental fairness" in the matter—its claim, as Justice Kennedy put it, on the people's "trust"—the issue seems settled in a single question: if Al Gore had been the petitioner, with the same set of facts and arguments brought by Bush, would the Court have decided as it did? A rhetorical question, surely. Not a single justice would have agreed to hear the case.

The major issue was never really who would become president, or even the immense damage that the Rehnquist Five have done to the integrity of the Court. Its moral, intellectual, and legal authority had already diminished over a long period of poorly reasoned opinions expressed in unseemly and unjudicial—often supercilious and even sneering—words. What remained was its power. The Supreme Court has made mistakes before: *Dred Scott, Plessy v. Ferguson, Korematsu,* and so on. What is unprecedented in *Bush v. Gore* is the exercise of power—specifically allocated by the Constitution to the states and to Congress, and specifically *not* to the federal judiciary—in the expression of a profound and absolute conflict of interest. The Rehnquist Five want the Court to become a self-selecting body. In their treatment of *Bush v. Gore*, they did what they could to achieve that result.

The decision, *per curiam*, unsigned, but apparently written by Justice Kennedy, with a separate concurrence by Justices Rehnquist,

Scalia, and Thomas, is a swamp. No matter where you look at it, you find something specious, mischaracterized, incoherent, internally inconsistent, false. Because it issues from the Supreme Court, however, legal scholars, lawyers, judges, congressmen, voters, and senators—above all, senators—are obliged to take it seriously. Its consequences are serious in ways that have nothing, or almost nothing, to do with the election of George W. Bush. He would have become president in any case. If the hand count had gone, as it would probably have gone, for Al Gore, the procedures established in our system would have yielded two slates of electors from the state of Florida: one for Gore, one (submitted by the Republican Florida legislature) for Bush. Congress would have had to choose. If Congress could not agree, the choice would revert to Florida to be made and certified by its executive, Governor Jeb Bush.

A disorderly process, certainly. It just happens that some of the processes in our democracy are disorderly. The votes in all of the counties in all of the fifty states, for example, are submitted and counted by widely varying means. In Florida, the Supreme Court found in this lack of uniformity a violation of the equal protection clause. Just this once, just in this case, just in this state, just on this day. The equal protection claim was specious anyway. Just who, if the counting had been permitted to continue, was being denied the equal protection of the law? A voter whose vote had already been tabulated by machine? But that voter might be a Bush voter or a Gore voter, and the votes being counted by hand, in every county, might be Bush votes or Gore votes. There might be disparate treatment, but there could be no systematic or intentional disparate treatment, favoring one candidate, or one voter, over another. The standard for counting votes, in Florida as in most other states, was "a clear indication of the intent of the voter." This was not something that needed to be "divined" or "discerned." A voter, even in chadless counties, who both checked and wrote in the name "Bush" or "Gore" on his ballot, had expressed his intent—in what was clearly a "legal vote." The machine would not count it. A manual recount would. The Supreme Court decision would disallow it.

In fact, both the decision and the concurrence express disdain for the legal standard, in Florida and in so many other states. Why, Justice O'Connor asked irritably during the oral arguments, could these voters not follow "clear instructions"? The concurrence actually devotes many lines to this sort of argument: "Florida law cannot reasonably be thought to require the counting of *improperly marked ballots*.... Each precinct ... provides *instructions on how properly to cast a vote*"—as though voting were some form of test, which those aspiring to vote might pass or fail. The concurrence derides voters who cast "ballots that are not *marked in the manner* that these voting instructions explicitly and prominently specify"—in contrast to the machines, which perform "precisely in the manner designed." (The machines performed, as it happened, poorly, and in some locations not at all.) Any other position, the concurrence goes on, in the diction that has become one of the Rehnquist Five's defining characteristics, "is of course absurd."

The difficulty remains: the standard for a "legal vote" is not an IQ test, or a test of classroom behavior that requires people to behave "properly" or to follow "instructions." (The "instructions" in some counties, anyway, told the voter to make sure to "cast a vote on every page." An unfortunate instruction: any voter who followed it would have produced an "overvote," which the machine would disallow.) The accusatory, punitive, even contemptuous dismissal of voters whom the Court apparently deems too stupid to be allowed to vote at all (echoes here of the "literacy test" that used to accompany the poll tax in the South) dismisses as well what is, in Florida and most other states, the law: the test is, inescapably, the "intent of the voter." It was according to this standard that the manual recount was proceeding when the Court brought it to a halt.

II.

The trouble with a swamp of a decision is that even to deal with it is to be drawn into it. The four dissents politely and eloquently demolished every element of both the decision and the concurrence, to the degree those elements could be articulated. Almost all subsequent commentary, whether in article or book form, demolished them in more detail. But always in ways that seem contingent. Some distinguished commentators have suggested that, if the Bush presidency turns out well, the decision will be vindicated. Or they have pointed out that when the Supreme Court has made mistakes before, it has with time corrected them. Or even that the real precedent for this judicial aberration was *Roe v. Wade*, when the Court made a decision that might, they felt, have been better left to Congress or the states. But all of them, I think, understate the gravity of what has happened, and its possible consequences for at least a generation.

To return for a moment to the decision—in particular, to Justice Scalia's concurrence (in itself unusual) in the Supreme Court's order, which abruptly halted the manual count by granting Bush's application for a stay. It is often forgotten that, in addition to Florida's state courts, lawyers for Bush had already brought their case before three *federal* courts (the U.S. District Courts of Orlando and Miami, and the U.S. Court of Appeals for the Eleventh Circuit Court in Atlanta), without success. A "stay" is a form of the ancient equitable remedy of injunction. Centuries ago, a petitioner might appeal directly to the king for a writ to "enjoin" his neighbor from doing something so drastic and destructive that it threatened the petitioner with "irreparable harm," damage, in other words, that could not subsequently be undone or compensated. The very basis of a petition for such a writ was an emergency.

A "stay"—and every application by petitioners Bush and Cheney in the federal courts to stop the manual recount was phrased in terms of "An Emergency Motion" or "An Emergency Application for a Stay"—is a drastic remedy. It is not to be granted unless the petitioner clearly establishes that he will suffer "irreparable injury" if the stay is denied; and that this threatened injury outweighs whatever damage the proposed injunction may cause the opposing party. He must also establish that granting a stay would not be adverse to the public interest.

In his concurrence, Justice Scalia did not trouble for a moment to consider whether the threatened injury to Bush if the counting continued outweighed the damage to Gore if it did not. Scalia went straight to "irreparable harm." If the manual count continued, he said, it "does in my view threaten irreparable harm to the petitioner, and to the country, by casting a cloud upon what he claims to be the legitimacy of his election."

Well, there it is. The irreparable harm of "casting a cloud." In the long and honorable tradition of injunctions and stays, this "irreparable injury" is a new one. Not just a cloud, but a cloud on "what he claims to be the legitimacy" of what he is claiming. By that standard, of course, every litigant in every case should be granted an injunction to halt the proceeding that offends him: the prosecutor casts a cloud on a claim of innocence; the civil plaintiff, a cloud on the defendant's claim that he has already paid him. And of course vice versa, the defendants casting clouds on plaintiffs and prosecutors. The whole adversary system consists of a casting of clouds.

Justice Scalia's choice of words seems derived, perhaps intentionally, from the laws of property: "cloud on title"—with, perhaps, an overtone of libel. As though a vote were a form of speech, unprotected by the First Amendment, and the counting of votes were, in some sense, defamatory and damaging to the candidate's reputation. But from tort claims to suits in antitrust, legal process virtually consists of this casting of clouds on claims of legitimacy. Perhaps all of them should be halted or enjoined.

Whatever "cloud" Scalia had in mind—and it seems to be emotional (anxiety perhaps, or the state of being miffed)—the "harm" to Bush could not possibly be "irreparable," since it was entirely within the power of the Court, or the manual count itself, to dispel it. If the count went for Bush, no cloud at all. If it went for Gore, the Court would have time to deem the results, if the Court so found, invalid. If the count went Gore's way, and the Court found no fault with it, the process would have gone just as the Constitution and our political tradition provided that it should, as though the Court had never entered the process—where it did not, in any event, belong.

Scalia's argument for the stay obviously did not "clearly establish" any, let alone all four, of the requirements for the remedy. His finding of "irreparable harm" was so obviously unserious that even the *per curiam* did not bother with it. Here is how, retroactively, the *per curiam* justified its halting of the count: "Given the Court's assessment that the recount process underway was probably being conducted in an unconstitutional manner, the Court stayed the order. "

"Given," "probably being conducted," "unconstitutional manner": this is not language on which to base an order for a stay. It is not language on which to base a decision of any kind. The word "probably" alone defeats the argument: the courts have always held that no stay will issue if the harm is "speculative." And the *per curiam* babbles vaguely on. The mandate of the Florida Supreme Court "is not well calculated to sustain the confidence that all citizens must have in the outcome of elections"; it "jeopardizes the legislative wish"; it "frustrates a legislative desire"; "a legislative wish...would counsel...against any construction that Congress might deem"— all these hypotheticals, wishes, frustrations, desires; what a "wish... would counsel...against," what Congress "might deem." The Court, when it speaks honorably, speaks in straight declaratory sentences. It speaks not of legislative wishes, but of commands; not of what Congress might deem, but of what it has said, enacted, or required.

Here is Scalia, waffling, with a little joke based on Alice: "Count first, and rule upon legality afterwards, is not a recipe for producing elections that have the public acceptance democratic stability requires." Recipe. The public acceptance democratic stability requires. Well calculated to sustain the confidence that all citizens must have in the outcome. All this is not just arguable, and certainly not before the Court. It is not the Court's business. As it happens, count (or take any action which the law does not specifically forbid) first, and rule upon legality afterwards, is precisely the basis of our free and entrepreneurial system. It is one of the reasons constitutional law requires the Court to consider only specific "cases and controversies" (in contrast to abstract, hypothetical, or contingent questions) and prohibits the Court from issuing what are called "advisory opinions." Halt the count, and rule upon legality beforehand, is presumably the "recipe" for producing the kind of elections (those "that have the public acceptance democratic stability requires") that Scalia has in mind.

But none of this, not a word or a concept, is the reasoning or the language of the law. And the vague, nattering—simultaneously brazen, timid, and evasive—quality of the decision culminates, of course, in this: "Our consideration is limited to the present circumstances, for the problem of equal protection in election processes generally presents many complexities."

Look at that sentence a minute. What can it possibly mean? It apparently *says* that, for some reason, the decision in *Bush v. Gore* is not to be regarded as precedent for any other. But if this were so, it would undermine, at one stroke, the whole basis of American and Anglo-Saxon law. That each case has precedential value, *must* have precedential value, is the bedrock of our system of justice. Otherwise each case can be decided ad hoc, at the caprice of judges—non-elected, federal judges with lifelong tenure. The Constitution and even the Magna Carta would be superseded, the justices would be kings.

It is, however, simply not in the power of the Court to determine that its decision has no precedential value. All decisions of the Court have such value, though it is hard to see how this particular travesty could serve as precedent for anything—or, for that matter, how it could be abandoned or overruled. But a special case, with no precedents and no future applications, is a case that, for ancient, profound, and lasting reasons, no court under our system is entitled to decide. No court has a right to say, This case is the law, crafted for one citizen, George W. Bush, and for him alone.

Linda Greenhouse, in *The New York Times* two days after the decision, got it just right. "Among the most baffling aspects of the opinion," she wrote, "was its simultaneous creation of a new equal protection right not to have ballots counted according to different standards and its disclaimer that this new constitutional principle would ever apply in another case." The "new constitutional principle" never could apply in another case, because it does not and could not exist. It would disallow every election in the country—in the history of the country. The Platonic ideal of a voting machine that the chief justice seems to envision, "precisely designed" to create uniform standards nationwide, does not exist either. If it did, the Court would have no power to impose it. Nor would Congress. The notion of machines, "precisely designed" and even of "uniform standards nationwide," raises the question of who, or what, designs, imposes, and oversees them. And the necessary centralization of power and order that this implies is precisely the way nations lose the power to vote.

In *Bush v. Gore*, the citation of "precedents" that are not precedents, particularly civil rights cases (*NAACP v. Alabama*, for example, or *Bouie v. City of Columbia*, a 1964 case involving black sit-in demonstrators: "What we would do in the present case," the concurrence says, "is *precisely parallel*") conveys the degree of disingenuousness and spite that has so frequently characterized Rehnquist's opinions. His tone in the majority has perhaps carried over from the years when he was most bitterly in dissent. Justice Ginsburg dealt with this sort of citation. The Florida Supreme Court, in its finding that "counting every legal vote" was the "overriding concern" of Florida's Election Code, "surely should not be bracketed with state high courts of the Jim Crow South." She dealt with the chief justice's other "casual citations" as well, pointing out how few and inapposite they were.

There is also, in the decision, an unusually high measure of hypocrisy, particularly in its affectation of helplessness: "None are more conscious of the vital limits on judicial authority than are the members of this Court.... However, it becomes our *unsought responsibility to resolve*...issues the judicial system has been *forced to confront*" and so forth. (In hearings before the House Appropriations Committee in March, Justice Kennedy, along with his remarks about "trust," actually pointed out, in defense of the *per curiam*, that it was not the justices who filed the suit.) Apart from outright misrepresentations of the law, there are several gratuitously insulting comparisons between Katherine Harris and the Florida Supreme Court ("The Florida Supreme Court, although it must defer to the Secretary's interpretations,...rejected her reasonable interpretation and embraced the peculiar one") and myriad inconsistencies. The decision, which has just said that the state court "must defer to the Secretary's interpretations," suddenly pretends that it confronts "a state court with the *power to assure uniformity*" in vote counts—a "power" that the Florida Supreme Court manifestly lacks.

And there are, at the core, some outright lies. Even the statement that seven justices of the court essentially agree, for example, and that "the only disagreement is as to the remedy," is false. The two justices whom the majority tries to embrace, Souter and Breyer, begin their dissents with clear statements that the Court should not have taken the case, that it was wrong to grant a stay, and that the decision itself is wrong. That puts rather a lot of weight on the "only." Souter and Breyer did try to salvage something from the debacle by giving the Florida Supreme Court another chance to meet even the most specious arguments of the *per curiam*. But the majority, with its own agenda, would not permit even this.

It is not enough to say that this is the most lawless decision in the history of the Court. People have said, Well, somebody had to decide what the outcome of the election was, one way or the other. But somebody *was* deciding (or rather had decided) it: the voters. If the outcome remained in doubt, Congress would decide, or remit the choice to the Executive of the state. Others have said that we were approaching chaos, a constitutional crisis, that only the Supreme Court, in its robes and its wisdom, could resolve. But there was no constitutional crisis, except the one of the Supreme Court's own creation. The events in Florida and the unfolding story were in fact a kind of political thriller. Voters were rather enjoying the suspense, when the Court, for its own reasons, jumped right in to stop the contest, so as to ensure that no one, ever, would find out the score.

What does it matter? The system has always been strong enough to withstand mistakes of every kind, poor policies and choices, corrupt administrations, bad judgments on the part of elected and electorate alike, bad laws, unjust verdicts, rigged elections, miscounted votes, and bad decisions by malign or misguided courts. In *Chapters of Erie*, still the best work of muckraking in our history, Charles F. Adams Jr. and Henry Adams devoted many chapters to the corruption of the courts. But there is something different about *Bush v. Gore*.

III.

It has now become clear that the recent case is only the latest and most extreme in a series of cases, *Morrison v. Olson, Clinton v. Jones*, and the initial remand to the Florida Supreme Court for "clarification." And it was Antonin Scalia, in his dissent in *Morrison v. Olson*, who gave us the clearest indication of what has happened here and what is really at stake. *Morrison v. Olson*, decided in 1988, was the case in which the Supreme Court overruled the Court of Appeals for the District of Columbia, and upheld, as constitutional, the Ethics in Government Act of 1978, which established the office of independent counsel. Justices Brennan, Blackmun, and Marshall were still members of that Court, but Scalia's was the sole dissent. His opinion was eloquent and well reasoned, and he alone was right. It was as though the justices, and everyone else who should have known better, were not paying attention.

Scalia pointed out that, under the act, the independent counsel, or special prosecutor, would have virtually unlimited power—scope, discretion, funds, staff, tenure. He quoted at length from a great speech by Justice Robert Jackson, delivered in 1940, when he was still attorney general, about the temptations and the duties of *any* prosecutor, his vast powers and immense discretion, and the dangers of abusing them—specifically, by not "discovering the commission of a crime and then looking for the man who has committed it," but "picking the man" and then "putting investigators to work, to pin some offense on him." Any prosecutor, Jackson said, "stands a fair chance of finding at least a technical violation of some act on the part of almost anyone," and then "the real crime becomes that of being unpopular with the predominant or governing group, being attached to the wrong political views, or being personally obnoxious."

Jackson's speech, and Scalia's opinion, contained a virtual blueprint of what the independent counsel's office, under Kenneth Starr, would become and do. But Scalia's main argument was that the Ethics in Government Act so seriously violated the constitutional separation of powers, which, for very good reasons, vests *all* the Executive power (including the power of prosecution) in the president, that it violated "the absolutely central guarantee of a just Government." "The purpose of the separation and equilibration of powers," Scalia said, "and of the unitary Executive in particular, was not merely to assure effective government but to preserve individual freedom." When the Court upholds as constitutional a law that creates a prosecutor outside the Executive, "this is not the government of laws that the Constitution established; it is not a government of laws at all." "That the Court could hold otherwise demonstrates the wisdom of our former constitutional system."

The warning was apt and it was prescient, but Scalia thought that the greatest danger wrought by this diminution of the Executive would come from the legislative branch. "The statute," he wrote, "is acrid with the smell of impeachment." Also, "this is an open invitation for Congress to experiment. The possibilities are endless, and the Court does not understand what the separation of powers, what 'ambition...countering ambition'...is all about, if it does not expect Congress to try them."

Congress, of course, did "try them," and the independent counsel himself set off the debacle of an impeachment process. But what I had not realized, what nobody so far as I know has pointed out, was a provision of the act that the majority in *Morrison* virtually relegates to a footnote. "Most importantly," Justice Rehnquist said, speaking for the Court, "the Act vests in the Special Division the power to choose who will serve as independent counsel and the power to define his or her jurisdiction." It is only Footnote Three that tells us what the newly created "Special Division" is to be. It "consists of three circuit court judges or justices appointed by the Chief Justice of the United States." The chief justice was, as he still is, Justice Rehnquist.

The wisdom of this arrangement is applauded in Footnote Thirteen: "Indeed, in light of judicial experience with prosecutors in criminal cases, it could be said that courts are especially well qualified to appoint prosecutors." If that doesn't give you a little chill, it may still shed light on the scene of the man in his Iolanthe-inspired robe presiding so affably in the Senate over a trial set in motion by a special prosecutor, whom he had selected and supervised.

Scalia's dissent in *Morrison* demolished the majority opinion delivered by Chief Justice Rehnquist. "The prospect is frightening," Scalia wrote, and there is nothing sarcastic, or insincere, in the tone of this opinion. "The fairness of a process must be adjudged on the basis of what it permits to happen." The appointment of "the mini-Executive that is the independent counsel," a prosecutor outside the Executive Branch, unelected and accountable to no one, destroyed "the equilibrium . . . the Founding Fathers envisioned when they established a Chief Executive accountable to the people." Above all, it destroyed the tension among the three branches, which limits the power of each and provides the "absolutely central guarantee of a just government." "That is what this suit is about. Power. The allocation of power . . . in such fashion as to preserve the equilibrium the Constitution sought to establish. Frequently an issue of this sort will come before the Court clad, so to speak, in sheep's clothing: the potential of the asserted principle to effect important change in the equilibrium of power is not immediately evident.... But this wolf comes as a wolf." The only thing that Scalia seemed less than prescient about was which branch was going to "experiment." The danger came not from the legislative but from the judiciary, not from Congress but from the Supreme Court.

In case after case since *Morrison*, the Court, with majorities that now include Scalia, has expressed its disdain for the other branches, for elective officials of every kind (now including, of course, state judges), for voters, for colleagues on the Court who are not members of the Rehnquist Five. The diction of those five has been marked by an overwhelming sense of their own superiority, while the quality of their reasoning and of their decisions has radically declined. In 1997, there was *Clinton v. Jones*, decided by a unanimous Court. It seemed for a time that even the best of the justices were asleep, or had lost contact with life in the outside world. The decision refused to stay the trial of Paula Jones's claims against President Clinton. The district judge had allowed discovery to go forward, but had concluded that an immediate trial, which "might hamper the President in conducting the duties of his office," could be postponed until the end of his term.

The Supreme Court held otherwise. While it might "consume some of the President's time and attention," a trial "appears to us highly unlikely to occupy any substantial amount of [his] time," or to impose an "unacceptable burden on [his] time and energy." There was also no "perceptible" or "serious" risk that a "trial might generate unrelated civil actions" that could "conceivably hamper the President" in the conduct of his office. Meanwhile Jones's "interest in bringing the case to trial" and the "timely vindication of her most fundamental rights" should not be subject to delay. "Delaying trial would increase the danger of prejudice resulting from the loss of evidence, including the inability of witnesses to recall specific facts, or the possible death of a party." Such a delay, because of the "unforeseeable loss of evidence" and so forth, would subject Jones to a "risk of irreparable harm."

So urgent was Jones's complaint that she did not file it until two days before the three-year deadline under the statute of limitations. Her claim at the time consisted of four parts: violation of her civil rights under state law; conspiracy to violate her civil rights under federal law; intentional infliction of emotional distress; and defamation. The Court's decision was certainly one of its least wise and prescient. What links it to *Bush v. Gore* (apart from considerable overlap among the authors of the briefs for Jones and Bush) is the question of a "stay" and "irreparable harm." The trial of Jones must not be stayed, even temporarily, because the delay may cause Jones irreparable harm. (The Supreme Court here seems out of touch even with the experience of ordinary citizens before the courts: there is *always* delay, with its attendant risks of loss of evidence, and so on.) But the manual count in the Florida counties *must*, permanently, be stayed, because of the risk of irreparable harm to—well, to George W. Bush. The combination of *Jones* and *Morrison* was nearly the destruction of the Executive.

IV.

And there we are. One risk that seems to have passed, until now, under the radar of some of the justices is that the extreme right has become adept at using politically correct buzzwords (words from civil rights cases, from feminism, from affirmative action, from multiculturalism, and so forth) to advance diametrically opposite agendas. With *Bush v. Gore*, the majority of the Court—in spite of the persuasiveness and the eloquence of the dissents, and the efforts of the dissenting justices to preserve somehow the continuity of the institution—has virtually parodied the history and the meaning of such words ("equal protection" is but one example) to become quite openly the most dangerous branch. It has simply taken over, almost casually seizing rights that belong to the state courts, Congress, the electorate, and defying anyone to do something about it.

And it is far from clear what can be done about it. Manual

counting of the votes is now, even as a matter of history, meaning-less. Many votes had already vanished by the time *The Miami Her-ald* started counting them; and more will surely change or disappear before *The New York Times* consortium is done. The election of Bush was never the real problem. The assertion of power—in a matter in which the Court is morally and constitutionally precluded from playing any part—is. The justices serve for life. They have now acted, in their judicial capacity, to promote their choice of a man who will select their colleagues and successors, who will also serve for life. The losses—of trust in the Court, of respect for the law, and of belief in the vote itself—are almost the least of it. The only citizens who can do anything about it are the president (who has already made clear his ideological preferences, and who is now also compromised and in their debt) and the members of the Senate. The line is drawn. Of course, surprises are always possible. But there can be no more lapses of attention, no more confirmations of ideological clones in ethnically mixed disguises, no more ideologues at all.

The difficulty, even the danger, is profound. It is embodied, after all, in that apparently harmless little shrug of a sentence about the decision being limited to the "present circumstances." If you once cede to the Court the power to decide elections, let alone even the power to halt counting of the votes, then you have ceded it every-thing. It is no use for the justices to claim that this case has no prec-edential value. The "just this once" promise is disingenuous on its face—especially in the "present circumstances." Every decision of the Court, under our system, becomes precedent; there is nothing to keep some future Court from responding in the same way, halting (on grounds of equal protection or whatever other specious grounds), in every county and in every state, a vote which displeases the major-ity of the Court. And there is no appeal.

This is by no means an unlikely consequence. What the Court says is the law *is* the law, until the Court itself says otherwise. The only leash on the Court, until now, was the Court's own history—its continuity as an institution that relies on precedent, reasoning, good faith, tradition, and its place among the three branches of gov-

ernment and within the federal system. It has now, with every affectation of helplessness, slipped that leash. There is no explanation
in *Bush v. Gore* that can fit within the function of the Supreme
Court, no rational explanation of this arbitrary exercise of power, in
the language that the Supreme Court has always used to explain
what it does. And all those affectations of helplessness—what it was
"compelled" or "forced" to do, those "unsought" responsibilities it
"could not abdicate"—were coupled with expressions of immense
self-satisfaction.

There seems, really, no question about it. This is a turning point.
Not because of its effect on this election or on the status of the
Court or on the people's trust. Least of all was it a simple matter of
choosing between two candidates in a close presidential election.
Almost all the books, articles, and commentaries about it have, in
one way or another, been useful—particularly *Bush v. Gore: The
Court Cases and the Commentary*, in that it includes so many of the
actual court decisions. Most critics speak of damage to the Court
itself; most supporters speak in terms of excusing little faults, in
view of what they seem to regard as a rescue of the system from
"chaos." Almost all speak as though there were some continuity between this decision and the entire history of the Court. But there is
no continuity. The legacy of this Court is disaster—which no façade
of collegiality, or relatively cuddly subsequent decisions, can conceal
or rectify.

One outcome of this case seems almost certain. Having once in-
tervened to effect the outcome of the electoral process (which it had
neither the authority, nor the competence, nor as it turned out even
the good faith to decide), the Court—under this Rehnquist or another, with the concurrence of this Kennedy and O'Connor or others—will try again, relying on (perhaps even "refining") the
ineradicable precedent of *Bush v. Gore*. As Scalia put it, in 1988, in
Morrison,

> Evidently the governing standard is to be what might be called the unfettered wisdom of a majority of this Court, revealed to an obedient people on a case-by-case basis. This is not only not the government of laws that the Constitution established; it is not a government of laws at all.

And,

> What if [the judges] are partisan, as judges have been known to be.... There is no remedy for that, not even a political one. Judges after all have life tenure.

And,

> The Court essentially says "trust us...." I think the Constitution gives ... the people more protection than that.

And finally,

> That the Court could possibly conclude otherwise demonstrates both the wisdom of our former constitutional system ... and the folly of the new system of standardless judicial allocation of powers we adopt today.

Scalia was writing, of course, only of the act that established the office of independent counsel. But he had at length quoted Jackson, for whom Rehnquist had clerked—and whose views Rehnquist has often managed, from the day of his confirmation hearings to this day, to misrepresent. Scalia's dissent even denounced, as an unconstitutional breach of the separation of powers, the special division that Rehnquist would head. The act which established the office of the special prosecutor, and which the Rehnquist Court upheld as constitutional, led to one disaster after another. Now it is the judiciary that has accepted the "invitation," under *Morrison*, to "experiment" with "possibilities."

The Court, even when it acts on a lawless basis, is beyond appeal. Our system provides for the lower courts no equivalent of civil disobedience, or jury nullification, or even the degree of freedom enjoyed by dissident prelates within the Church. It is not entirely inconceivable that even the lower federal courts will (in spite of Justice Kennedy's vague and unenforceable disclaimer) invoke *Bush v. Gore* to halt counts or otherwise intervene in elections. The damage is done, and cannot ever be quite undone. But it can be limited. If the Senate exercises, with the utmost care, its constitutional responsibility to advise and consent, *Bush v. Gore* really will with the passage of time have been just a radical aberration. If the Court succeeds, however, in having allocated to itself powers that belong to the states and to the other branches—and if the Senate's examination of any candidate for a federal court is in the least perfunctory—the tanks have really rolled. The Founding Fathers, who did after all vote by hand, will have left us a wonderful form of government, which we somehow permitted the Court to throw away.

The New Republic
July 30, 2001

ADDENDUM

Two months after this piece was published, there was the disaster of 9/11 and, in its aftermath, the passage of legislation which does not so much grant the Court even greater powers as fuse the powers of the three branches into a single power, the prosecutorial—of which Justice Scalia, quoting Justice Robert Jackson, once so eloquently warned. The Solicitor General of the United States, as it happens, is now Theodore Olson, the Olson of *Morrison v. Olson*, the case in which Scalia alone was right, in warning of the threat the establishment of the office of special prosecutor posed to the entire constitutional system. "The Court essentially says 'trust us,'" he wrote. "I think the Constitution gives...the people more protection than that." Much of what government has said, since the events of 9/11, has been a variant of "trust us."

The doctrine of preemption, in international affairs, amounts to a variant of injunction in drastic military form. The questions— whether the preempting nation will otherwise suffer irreparable injury; whether that injury outweighs whatever damage preemption itself might cause; and whether the preemption will not be adverse to the public interest—are much the same. There has, of course, been nothing inherently violent in the ancient equitable remedy of injunction. And a real injunction can issue only from a court, or other neutral tribunal. (In at least two cases now before the Supreme Court, the administration actually argues that the president, the military, even Intelligence "Interrogators" are, under recent law, just such "neutral" tribunals, which can be trusted like any other court; the cases reached the Court at about the same time photographs of the work of Interrogators came out of Abu Ghraib.)

In his dissent in *Morrison*, in 1988, Justice Scalia wrote, with some bitterness, of "the wisdom of our former constitutional system." In *Bush v. Gore*, decided four years ago, the balance of powers which sustains that system was radically undermined. Now, under vastly more critical circumstances, there is another national election. Whatever the outcome, and whether or not any court will intervene, the fusion of all powers in a single prosecutorial power, of unprecedented scope and almost limitless discretion, is sure to test the Court again. Whether we are already speaking of our "former constitutional system" will depend in great part on what that Court decides.

2004

THE PORCH OVERLOOKS NO SUCH THING

"THERE'S no complacency here. Never has been. Never will be."
(Arthur Sulzberger, Jr., publisher of *The New York Times*, July 14,
2003.) This is, in its way, a classic utterance. For one thing it begins
with a perfect example of the self-refuting sentence. In its underlying idiocy and limitless self-regard it also manages to embody, and
project through time, a virtual definition of the word "complacency." Sulzberger had assembled the *Times* staff to announce the
appointment of a new executive editor, Bill Keller, a popular choice.
The staff, however, was preoccupied with something else. Howell
Raines, Keller's predecessor, had appeared on *The Charlie Rose Show*
a few nights before, and expressed several views critical of the paper.
He had described the *Times* as "an irreplaceable national institution." He had even said (somewhat more debatably) that "the great
advantage" the *Times* has "over any other news organization in the
world" is "brain power." Raines had claimed, however, that the
Times had become a "culture of lethargy and complacency."

Well. It is hard to know what members of the *Times* staff can
have expected from a former boss whom they had savagely attacked
in every conceivable forum—from a "town meeting" in which he
had to listen to insults both personal and professional and even to
abase himself with the sort of confession reminiscent of a Maoist
party cell (with the added ignominy of having a toy moose placed in
his lap) through a campaign of venomous emails, posted all over the
Internet. Maureen Dowd was partly right in comparing this spectacle to *Lord of the Flies*—with this difference: the *Times*, in recent
years, has lost any awareness of the relation between the one and the

many, of the real moral questions raised by piling on and ganging up. The behavior of those assembled was characteristic in some ways of an institution whose chief principle of action has become increasingly this: it will not permit itself to be criticized, contradicted or even questioned, in public. The *Lord of the Flies* aspect, the fact that the critic in this case was a former boss, whom it had very recently humiliated and deposed, was incidental. As the *Times*'s powers have grown (through the attrition of other newspapers), its sense of the vulnerability of the individual in the face of those institutional powers has vanished. In fact, it feels victimized.

At the same time, its one inviolable belief has become simply this, not a politics, right or left, but an ideology: the *Times*, as an institution, believes what has been published in its pages. To defend this belief it will go very far. The search, the grail, the motivating principle for individual reporters has become, not the uninflected reporting of news, but something by now almost entirely unrelated: the winning of a Pulitzer Prize. In the interim, some other prize will do. But once won, the Pulitzer turns into both a shield and a weapon— a shield in defense of otherwise indefensible pieces by Pulitzer Prize winning reporters, a weapon in the struggle for advancement within the hierarchy of the *Times*. The paper still has some very fine editors and reporters, with highly honorable concerns. But a five-year moratorium on the awarding of Pulitzer Prizes to journalists at powerful publications might be the greatest service to journalism the Pulitzer Committee could now perform.

In any event, Howell Raines had said on *The Charlie Rose Show* that the *Times* was complacent. Sulzberger's words were intended— and perhaps somewhere perceived—as a rebuttal to this remark. In recent years, executive editors of the *Times* have tended to find the paper much improved during their tenure. At a retreat in Tarrytown, New York, in September 2000, Joseph Lelyveld had expressed to eighty newsroom editors, and a few colleagues from other publications, his belief that the *Times* had become "the best *New York Times* ever—the best written, most consistent, and ambitious newspaper *Times* readers have ever had." In July, in the course of the infamous

Charlie Rose Show, Howell Raines said, "The newspapers that we have produced over the past twenty months are the best in the history of the *Times*."

Whether or not these were expressions of complacency, they would have been unthinkable for the predecessors of these men—for the executive editors, Turner Catledge, say, or A. M. Rosenthal, who said he only wanted to be remembered as the editor who "kept the paper straight." Rosenthal did keep the paper straight, in a time that now seems unimaginably remote—with a first-rate staff and the discreet support of the *Times*'s publisher in those years, Sulzberger's father. In any event, the current Sulzberger's words on the subject of complacency, or non-complacency, marked the culmination of what has become the saga of *The New York Times* and Jayson Blair.

The saga began on April 26, 2003, when the *Times* published a piece which a 27-year-old staff reporter, Jayson Blair, had essentially cribbed from an article published eight days earlier in the *San Antonio Express-News*. The original article had been written by Macarena Hernandez, a former intern (and colleague of Blair's) at the *Times*; it consisted mainly of an interview with Juanita Anguiano, the single mother of an only son, Specialist Edward J. Anguiano, of Los Fresnos, Texas, the last American soldier still missing at that time in Iraq. Normally, as Jayson Blair had every reason to know, calling attention to errors in the *Times*, provided that they are absolutely trivial (misspellings of first or last names, mistaken middle initials, misidentifications of who is standing on the left and who on the right in photographs), may result in a Correction. Calling attention to major or substantial errors will have no result at all. The *Times*, committed to an image of infallibility on every important factual matter, will neither acknowledge them nor respond in any way.

In this instance, however, Robert Rivard, the editor of the San Antonio paper, had an exchange of emails with the editors of the *Times*

—who said they would "look into the matter." Rivard asked them to "acknowledge publicly" that the *Times* had wrongfully appropriated Ms. Hernandez's work. Perhaps aware of how such an allegation would normally be treated, Mr. Rivard took the trouble of sending copies of his email to others. So the saga began *publicly* on April 30, 2003—when both the Associated Press and Howard Kurtz of the *Washington Post* ran the story. Had the *Times* not been "caught," in this public way by rival publications, the paper would surely have done nothing and acknowledged nothing. In fact, it *did* nothing, until after the AP and *Washington Post* stories appeared. The next day, May 1, 2003, Jayson Blair resigned. On May 2, the *Times* reported his resignation, and added an Editors' Note to the effect that the paper had begun "an internal review" of the piece in question, that it regretted the "breach of journalistic standards," and that it planned an "apology" to the "family" that was the subject of the piece.

The apology, if any, seemed misdirected. If it was owed to anyone, one would have thought, it was to Ms. Hernandez, whose piece had been cribbed. The Anguiano family had been in no way harmed by Jayson Blair's piece; they were not even aware that it existed. On April 28, 2003, two days after the *Times*'s publication of the piece, the Department of Defense announced that Sgt. Anguiano was dead. On April 30 and May 1, however, the *Times* apparently found it necessary to phone his mother, to confirm in time for its report of May 2, that she "did not recall Mr. Blair's having visited her home in Los Fresnos, Texas." ("No, no, no, he didn't come," she said, according to the *Times*.) Everyone makes mistakes. Perhaps the reporter had called without reading the casualty lists released each day by the DOD. The *Times* account seemed an act of journalism run more seriously amok than anything contemplated by Jayson Blair. In any event, with the *Times* report, on May 2, 2003, of Mr. Blair's resignation, and the reason for it, the matter should have rested. A minor reporter had made a mistake, and a miscalculation. Other reporters, more famous and highly regarded than Blair, had made mistakes with more serious consequences, not just for individuals but in matters of national importance. With one exception, the *Times* had paid no attention to the problems raised by any of them. (The exception was its coverage, in 1999 and 2000, of Wen Ho Lee.) The *Times* should simply have dropped, for its insignificance, the matter of Jayson Blair.

But no. On Sunday, May 11, with four pieces, beginning on Page One, and totaling approximately 15,000 words, the *Times* let loose. The first piece (7,165 words) was a narrative, which cast Jayson Blair as a sometimes charming, basically calculating villain, whose intent was not (as any reader of ordinary intelligence might have thought) to publish a lot of pieces and get ahead, but to deceive and victimize his too credulous, forgiving—and even understaffed—employer. The narrative, by five reporters (one a fine lawyer, Adam Liptak) and two research assistants, relied on "more than 150 interviews," as well as expense accounts and phone records, to conclude that Jayson Blair, in 600 pieces written over a period of four years, had "flouted long-followed rules" at the *Times* in "a pathological pattern of misrepresentation, fabricating and deceiving." By turns accusatory, sanctimonious, sympathetic, self-exonerating ("the deceit of one *Times* reporter does not impugn the work of 375 others"), the article quoted outsiders, deans of journalism schools for example, to support the *Times*'s view of Blair's career, its importance and his motives.

"There has never been *a systematic effort to lie and cheat* ... comparable" to Blair's, said one. "It is difficult to catch someone who is *deliberately trying to deceive you*," said another. Lying. Riddled with lies. Journalistic fraud. Systematic fraud. A cause of "pain" and "hurt." This last was mystifying. Not one of Blair's pieces, mostly soft, human-interest news of the sort which the *Times* has increasingly favored, seemed harmful either in intent or in effect—at least for their subjects. On the contrary. One couple whom Blair had interviewed by phone, the parents of a Marine scout then stationed in Iraq, were so "delighted" with his piece that they wrote a letter, which the *Times* published. Another, a wounded soldier whom Blair also interviewed by phone, was so taken with a sentence Blair ascribed to him that he apparently could not quite bring himself to relinquish it: "he could not be sure," he told the *Times*, "whether he had uttered" the sentence—which the *Times* had, in fact, chosen, on April 19, 2003, as its "Quotation of the Day." The story, like many of Blair's stories—like many stories of far greater importance published routinely by the *Times*, among other newspapers—was largely false.

Stories published under deadline pressures, in an effort to cover the world on a daily basis, are bound to contain quantities of misinformation. The difficulty is to sustain, within the news itself, a continuous process of correction. (This is why the *Times* Corrections column, with its restriction to silly and often repetitive minutiae, creates a disingenuous impression of care for accuracy while it undercuts the fundamental integrity of the paper. A newspaper that insists on infallibility in large matters, while pointing out, as the *Times* does in correcting Jayson Blair, "The sister of Corporal Gardner is named Cara not Kara," is a less trustworthy source of news than a paper without a Corrections column of any sort.) But the subjects of these pieces did not care. The normal reader did not care. In fact, not even the most fanatically press-obsessed reader could much care about the endlessly detailed re-reporting of what had been from the outset trivial stories.

The narrative piece did contain, near the end, one nearly perfect anecdote, the capstone of its accusations, in a claim that Mr. Blair had in fact been assigned to something important, "one of the biggest stories to come from the war."

> After the Hunt Valley article in late March, Mr. Blair pulled details out of thin air in his coverage of one of the biggest stories to come from the war, the capture and rescue of Pfc. Jessica D. Lynch.... Mr. Blair wrote that Private Lynch's father, Gregory Lynch Sr., "choked up as he stood on his porch here

overlooking the tobacco fields and cattle pastures." The porch overlooks no such thing.

"Pulling details out of thin air," the *Times* seemed to forget was, from the very first day, the essence precisely of the story of Pfc. Jessica D. Lynch—at every stage of the military's coup in promoting through an obliging press a fiction, a highly implausible, unusually effective piece of propaganda, as "one of the biggest stories to come from the war." The *Times* went straight to the heart of the matter. Huffy, in a wonderfully schoolmarmish way, "The porch overlooks no such thing" could be one of the great lines in press criticism, if not in journalism itself. Though "Correcting the Record" was the title of the narrative (7,165 words)—as it was of the next of the four Jayson Blair pieces—of May 2, 2003, the *Times* never disclosed what the porch *does* overlook.

The second piece, the "accounting" (6,591 words), divided each of several flawed articles by Blair into (capitalized) categories of flaw: DENIED REPORTS; FACTUAL ERRORS; WHEREABOUTS; PLAGIARISM; FABRICATIONS; and OTHER ISSUES. As an intellectual matter, it was clear that there was something wrong with this list. Readers who noticed that "WHEREABOUTS" did not, in any obvious way, belong in a list of transgressions had to realize that the "dateline"—the place the reporter claims to be filing his story from—had become, in this case, an obsession, a subject of limitless horror and indignation for the *Times*. The investigators may have been too scandalized to name it with precision. Readers, who have long been aware that most journalists, particularly famous journalists, do a lot of their interviews by phone, probably pay little attention to even the most exotic datelines. If Lally Weymouth of *Newsweek* is reporting on an exclusive interview with Pervez Musharraf of Pakistan, it is important that she has in fact spoken directly with him in Karachi. If John F. Burns, of the *Times*, is reporting on his treatment by agents in Baghdad, it is crucial that he is in fact there and not filing on the basis of a call from a bedside phone at the Plaza in New York. But these are distinguished reporters, and their actual location, at the time of reporting, is part of the essence of their work. A "dateline" in itself is meaningless.

It is true that Jayson Blair's having almost never traveled to the place reflected in the dateline of his pieces seemed an extreme case. Perhaps he hated travel, had become phobic about it. Perhaps, since the *Times* narrative said he had (among other "personal problems") a cocaine habit, he wanted to stay near his dealer. Most likely, though, on the basis of the versatility and frequency of his pieces (sometimes, though the *Times* narrative does not mention this, two and even three bylined pieces in a single day), Blair was staying near home in order to write. Travel takes time. Blair, having been hired, promoted and given the status of full-time reporter under Lelyveld, and thrived under Raines, could only sustain his pace by making economies of time and energy: no travel, some appropriation of other people's work, some embellishment of stories, some fabrication. Grounds for dismissal, certainly—once Blair had made the cardinal mistake of stealing from a publication whose power to expose the theft was greater than the *Times*'s power to conceal it. Just to illustrate, however, the level of corrections the *Times* found it worth the huge expenditure of its own space and energy to make:

> February 10, 2003, FACTUAL ERRORS—"Ms. Adams did not suffer from back pain; she said she suffered from shoulder and neck pain."... OTHER ISSUES—"Mr. Ballenger said he discussed the fact that his son, James IV, had dropped out of college on the condition that it not be published, and that he was upset to see it in the paper."

This last point rests on two fairly odd assumptions: first, that a man who has "discussed" with a reporter a "fact . . . on the condition that it not be published" can, in most cases, expect the reporter to see to it that it is not published; and second, that when a Mr. Ballenger, having been "upset" to see a fact he regarded as private published in the paper on February 3, 2003, finds it published again in the same paper on May 11, something of value has been achieved.

The third *Times* piece that Sunday, May 11, 2003, carried the headline: "Editors' Note." It was brief, and remarkable mainly for the nature of its apology. Among those who deserved an apology, the *Times* included "all conscientious journalists whose professional trust has been betrayed by this episode." In its two long pieces, the narrative and the account, The *Times* had apparently been under the delusion (1) that by making corrections to already trivial stories it was conveying useful information, and (2) that it was engaged in some act of self-criticism, or even self-examination, in enumerating the errors of one small, unimportant reporter on its staff. What was beyond explanation was the need to apologize to a whole profession for an "episode" which can have caused no conceivable harm to any conscientious journalist, anywhere.

The sentence, however, brought inescapably to mind another "episode"—for which the *Times* has never offered an apology to anyone, least of all to its genuine victim, Dr. Wen Ho Lee. A series of pieces in the *Times*, between March 6, 1999, and September 26, 2000, played a major part in sending an innocent man to prison, and keeping him there, for nine months, in solitary confinement, often in shackles—until a federal judge, appointed by President Ronald Reagan, apologized to him on behalf of the United States government and ordered his release. If the *Times* had spent a fraction of the space, energy and zeal which it devoted to its "investigation" of the errors of Jayson Blair on a genuine investigation of its own factual and ethical transgressions in covering the case of Wen Ho Lee, it would have made a valuable contribution, even marked a turning point in the history of journalism, particularly its own.

Instead, on September 26, 2000, the *Times* published an Editors' Note, "a public accounting" (1,663 words), and, two days later, an editorial "Overview" (1,725 words), in which it appraised its own coverage of the case of Wen Ho Lee and found it good—"careful reporting that included extensive cross-checking and vetting of multiple sources," of which the paper remained "proud." On a single day, March 24, 1999, the paper had carried on its front page a story that Dr. Lee had once hired as a laboratory assistant a Chinese citizen "already under investigation as a spy." The FBI was looking for this suspect, to question him. "And the research assistant has disappeared."

A reporter who had actually traveled that day from Washington to Los Alamos saw the *Times* exclusive story and despaired. Then the reporter asked somebody at the lab whether he knew anything about the missing man. Certainly. It turned out the research assistant was a graduate student, an intern, who had returned to his regular studies at Penn State; he could easily be reached on the university's website or by phone. Neither the *Times* reporter nor anyone else from the *Times* (or the FBI apparently) had troubled to try so direct a route. Too busy with extensive cross-checking and multiple vetting of sources.

In retrospect, and in the context of the Jayson Blair pieces, the coverage of Wen Ho Lee looks worse than ever, based on profound, unacknowledged, continued and truly damaging errors—which the *Times* to this day insists were not errors at all. The paper was not just the instrument of other powerful institutions against the individual; it had become a driving force in the prosecution and vested its reputation there. This is not the role envisioned in the First Amendment for the press. No apology, then, to the few "conscientious journalists" (the late Lars-Erik Nelson of the *New York Daily News* chief among them) who virtually dismantled the *Times*'s case against Dr. Lee— or to the many, perhaps somewhat less conscientious journalists who trusted the *Times*'s story and took it up, or to readers who were and perhaps remain misled by it. And, far from an apology, in all subsequent *Times* pieces about the matter, continued attacks on Dr. Lee.

A newspaper, surely, cannot be said to have a subconscious and yet, in raising this curious question of apology, the *Times* called attention to what is really an unlikely nexus, not just between the "episodes" of Blair and Lee—each an unprecedented "investigation" by the *Times* of what has appeared in its pages—but in issues they raise: responsibility in the exercise of power; the identity and reliability of sources; politically correct "diversity" as defined by category (racial, ethnic, gender, sexual preference) so as virtually to exclude individuality, and thereby paradoxically assure uniformity; pack journalism; vendetta journalism; coerced agreement; the enforcement of received ideas; fear, widespread and justified, of the *Times*; and the issue of genuine openness to correction and journalism in good faith.

Not inconsistent with these considerations was the fourth document of May 11, 2003, the briefest of all (31 words). It too bore the headline Editors' Note. "Readers with information about other articles by Jayson Blair that may be false wholly or in part," it said, "are asked to e-mail the *Times*: retrace@nytimes.com." The *Times*'s appetite for hounding had reached the Internet. Having leveled virtually the entire arsenal of the paper at a man whom its own narrative had already described as "troubled," it now invited the whole world to join it in this hunt. Blair turns out after all to have been a fairly sturdy fellow, who read the *Times* "culture" very well. For all the lectures he was apparently subjected to, for all the talk of "disciplinary" action, "short leashes," "reprimands" (in much of the narrative, the *Times* sounds for all the world like a cross between the Curia and a particularly dull reformatory or boarding school), Blair showed that, while he had little respect for the system, he was all right with individuals. When he praised, as he often did, some other writer's work, he had the good sense for instance, uncommon even in professional writers, to single out "something far down in the story," as one of the *Times*'s really fine reporters said, "so you'd know he read it." On the other hand, at least one editor gave the right warnings, at the right time: the place to address problems with Blair's reporting was internally, and the way to resolve those problems would be to stop publishing his work.

The address on the web inviting further complaints about Blair ran in the *Times* for several days. After a while, there was some pretense that the invitation extended to complaints about any and all *Times* reporters, but this was clearly untrue. One of the finest, most beloved and respected editors at the *Times*, in the years of its greatest reliability, distinction, and aspiration toward objectivity and fairness, told me that he had never, in any publication, been quoted accurately. Since then I have met no one with experience of being quoted who has not made the same observation. A complaint of misquotation or any other error to a web address at the *Times* called *retrace*, everyone agrees, would be as futile as, say, a letter to the Book Review pointing out a complete and deliberate misrepresentation of a nonfiction book.

Retrace did, however, produce one, innocent casualty. Blair had clearly incurred, at the *Times*, a lot of envy. So, apparently, had a Pulitzer Prize winning reporter, Rick Bragg. A "reader" now apparently questioned whether Mr. Bragg had really done the reporting for a bylined piece about oystermen in Apalachicola, Florida. From the subsequent public expressions of outrage by *Times* reporters it was not hard to guess who the "reader" was, or were. Mr. Bragg had, in fact, made extensive use of the notes of a stringer, a young man named J. Wes Yoder, who greatly admired Mr. Bragg's work, and who had asked to work for him, in order to learn from him. Terrible. What a scandal. One would hardly know from the ensuing outcry that the practice is so widespread it is an assumed and honored part of the journalistic tradition. Stringers, legmen, a form of apprenticeship since before the days of the green eyeshade. In the Jayson Blair turmoil at the *Times*, however, Mr. Bragg was suspended for two weeks. Then Mr. Bragg did the unpardonable: he spoke the truth, in public. He said not only that stringers were not uncommon but also that he had always considered it a point of honor actually to go to the place mentioned in the by-now-sacred dateline, in time to claim it honorably for his piece. Well. The hounding began. Such a barrage of furious, self-righteous email posted by *Times* reporters. We might have been in the realm of dateline—or perhaps whereabouts—fraud again. Everyone knew, or rather everyone who paid any attention to the matter knew, that racing somewhere for a single day just to claim the authority of a dateline is a common practice even among the most admired journalists writing about the most serious, contentious subjects. Astonishment and dismay, however, expressed on many blogs. Much later, word from the *Times*'s current executive editor Bill Keller that if such an "outrage" had even been suspected, Mr. Bragg would have been out "in a heartbeat."

By then, Mr. Bragg had quit. He will be working with Jessica Lynch, to help write the story, presumably—since the Lynch family has always been (in contrast with all those who claim to speak for them) honest—the true story of Jessica Lynch. NBC has decided meanwhile to produce a special television program in time for the November sweeps. Jessica Lynch has withdrawn her cooperation. No matter. NBC has decided the story was always anyway an "action/ adventure" story, already largely in the public domain. "Frankly," NBC's Entertainment president Jeff Zucker said, Private Lynch had only "a minor role." The military will help with the program. And the real hero will be one Mohammed Odeh al-Rehaief—the Iraqi lawyer who, in early versions of the story, witnessed Private Lynch being "slapped," and therefore walked six miles, back and forth, several times, to inform the American military and draw a map of the hospital where she was. You may have wondered what happened to that Iraqi lawyer. Apart from this work for NBC (which will shoot the film from "his perspective"), and a large contract for a book, he has a job with a lobbying firm in Washington. In any case, the hounding of Mr. Bragg, who holds a Pulitzer Prize, was not without risk for the pack. The Pulitzer might lose some of its magic properties for them as well.

What will come of all this? I used to think one needed *The New York Times*, and perhaps one does, but not this *Times*. A reader has neither the time, nor the inclination, nor the resources to approach his newspaper with sufficient skepticism to doubt every single element of every story; to look in vain to the corrections column and find a correction of middle initials; and then to scour the earth for some good faith source of factual information. When there were many newspapers, with conflicting political positions, there was at least some equivalent of what is, in the law, the adversary system, and the idea that through this conflict some sort of truth is sorted out. Such conflicts may exist today among magazines, which also have the time, in the absence of daily deadlines, for genuine research and even for thought. But if a reader has reason, as he clearly does, to distrust his newspaper—not its Jayson Blairs, but its whole conception of what is important, what is true, what part genuine self-doubt as opposed to searching for scapegoats and examining other people's datelines plays in the process of finding out and reporting what is true—then the news itself will cease to matter to him. The paper will continue for a while, in its self-regard based on the values and achievements of another time. But that's it. In the absence of a basis for trust, the news itself becomes unascertainable, even ceases to exist—or is reduced, as is now almost the case, to contending strategies of public relations.

Then one remembers something Senator Daniel Patrick Moynihan used to quote from Michael Polanyi: People change their minds. Institutions can change as well. On May 11, 2003, Sulzberger was interviewed by *The Wall Street Journal*. Echoing the by now famous remarks quoted in his own paper earlier in the day, to the effect that there would be no searching the newsroom for "scapegoats" ("The person who did this is Jayson Blair. Let's not begin to demonize our executives—either the desk editors or the executive editor or, dare I say, the publisher"), he said, "This is not a Howell problem, this is not an Arthur Sulzberger problem—this was a bad man doing bad things."

> Mr. Sulzberger said that there is little anyone could have done to prevent Mr. Blair, who had worked at the *Times* nearly four years, from putting false information in the paper.
>
> "Do we have a system to uncover venality? No, we don't. And you know something, I guess I am not unhappy with that. I don't want us to become a police state where you suspect every employee of ripping off the company."

Whatever is meant by "scapegoat," "demonize," "venality," "police state," and even "ripping off the company," this is an odd formulation of the problem. Venality? Ripping off the company? Institutions change, but this is not the language of a change for the better in a newspaper. What is needed is the return of someone who would want to be remembered for having kept the paper straight.

The American Spectator
October 2003

RENATA ADLER was born in Milan and raised in Connecticut. She received a B.A. from Bryn Mawr, an M.A. from Harvard, a D.d'E.S. from the Sorbonne, a J.D. from Yale Law School, and an honorary LL.D. from Georgetown. Adler became a staff writer at *The New Yorker* in 1963 and, except for a year as the chief film critic of *The New York Times*, remained at *The New Yorker* for the next four decades. Her books include *A Year in the Dark* (1969); *Toward a Radical Middle* (1970); *Reckless Disregard: Westmoreland v. CBS et al., Sharon v. Time* (1986); *Canaries in the Mineshaft* (2001); *Gone: The Last Days of* The New Yorker (1999); *Irreparable Harm: The U.S. Supreme Court and the Decision That Made George W. Bush President* (2004); and the novels *Speedboat* (1976, Ernest Hemingway Award for Best First Novel) and *Pitch Dark* (1983).

MICHAEL WOLFF, currently a contributing editor at *Vanity Fair* and a columnist for *The Guardian, USA Today,* and British *GQ,* is one of the most prominent journalists and pundits in the nation. He has written numerous best-selling books, including *The Man Who Owns the News: Inside the Secret World of Rupert Murdoch, Burn Rate,* and *Autumn of the Moguls.* He appears often on the lecture circuit and is a frequent guest on network and cable news shows.